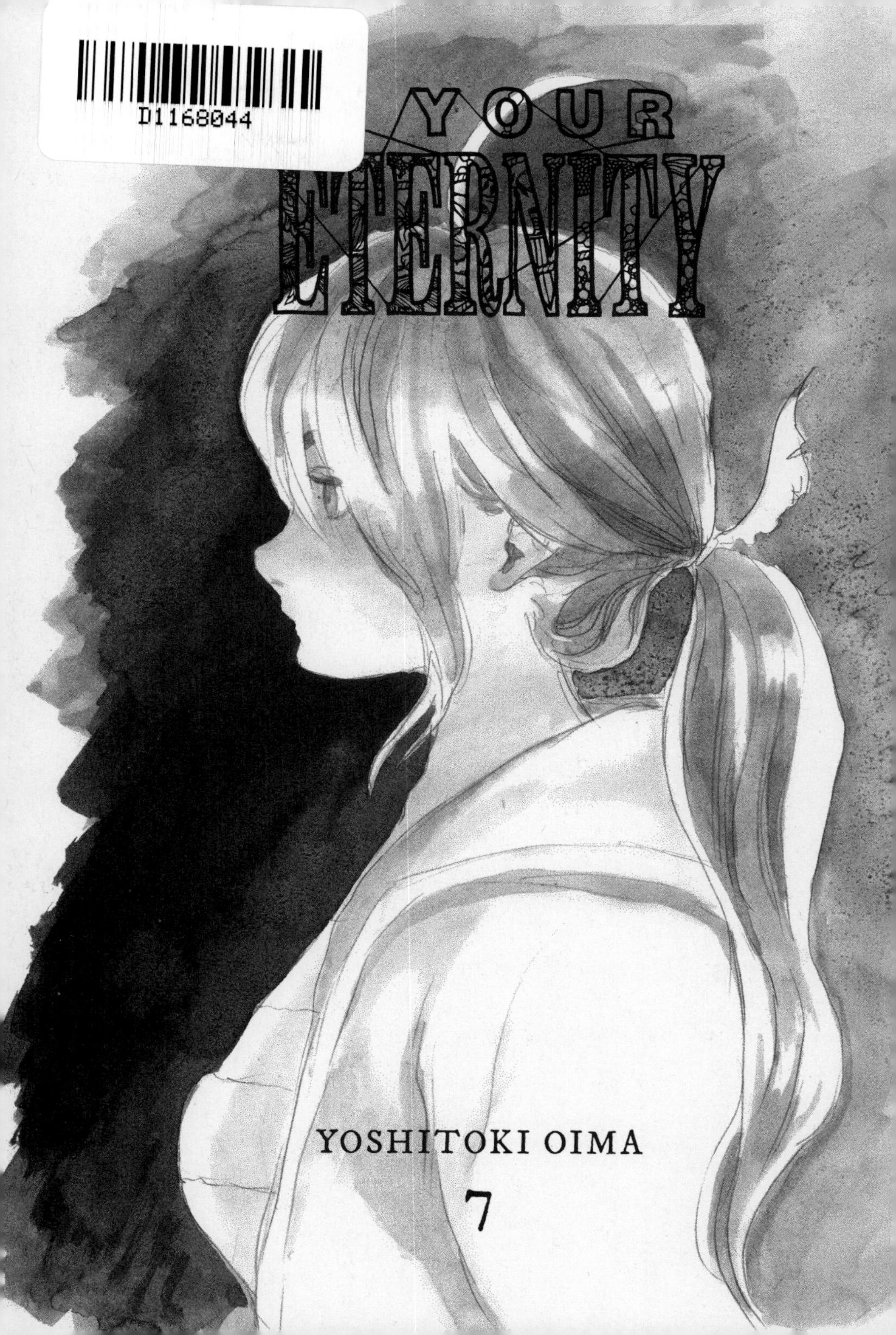
YOUR
ETERNITY
YOSHITOKI OIMA
7

CONTENTS

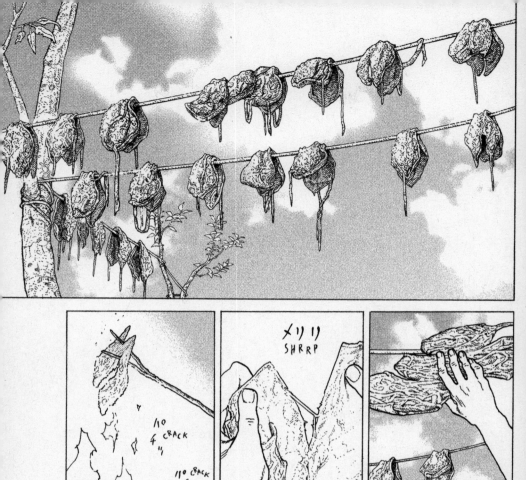

メリリ
SHRRP

パ
ク
CRACK

パ
ク
CRACK

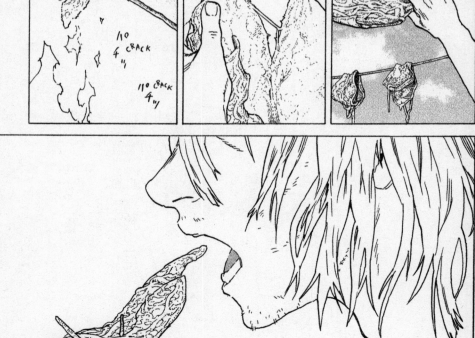

#55 Days of Boredom

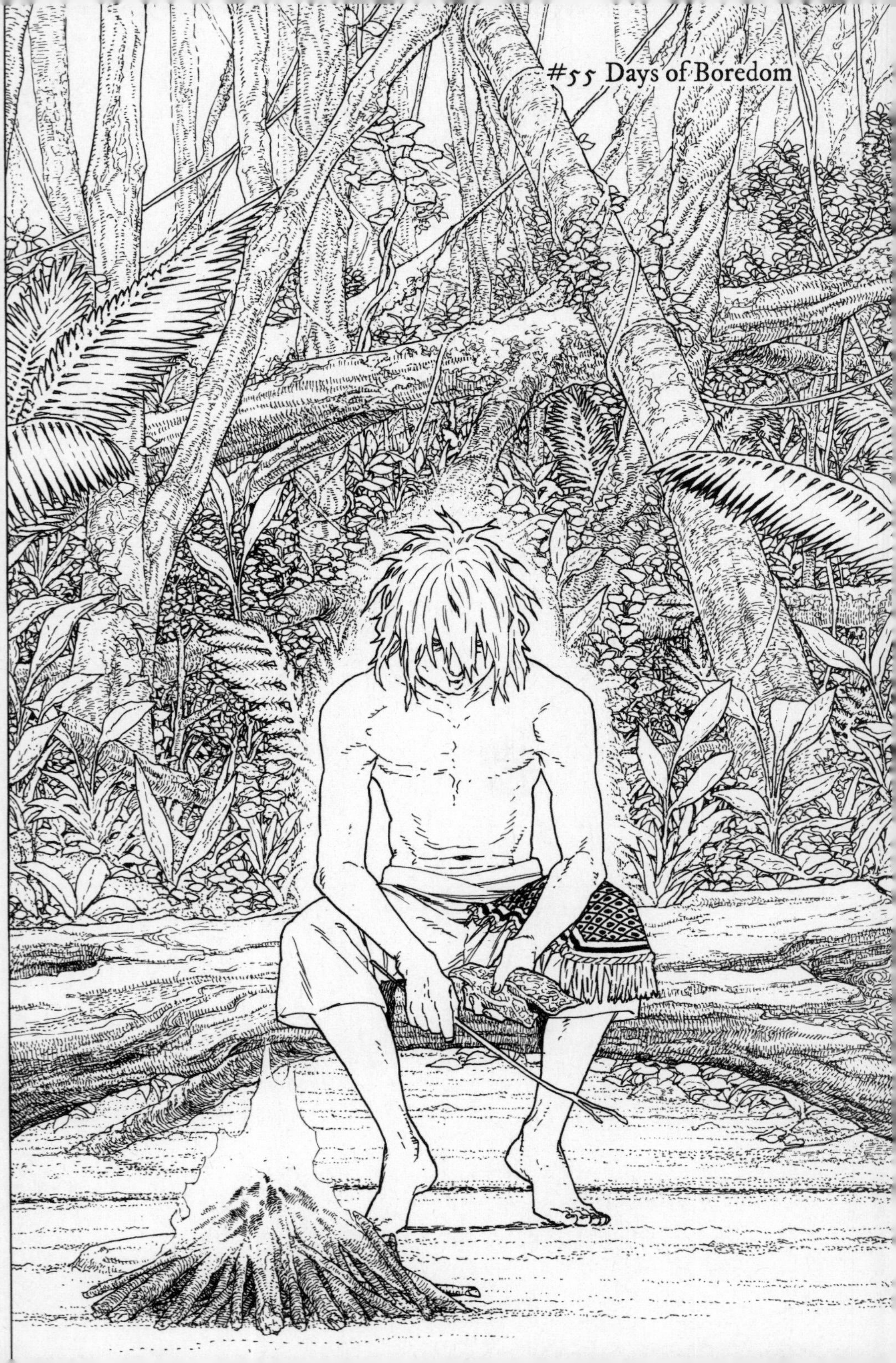

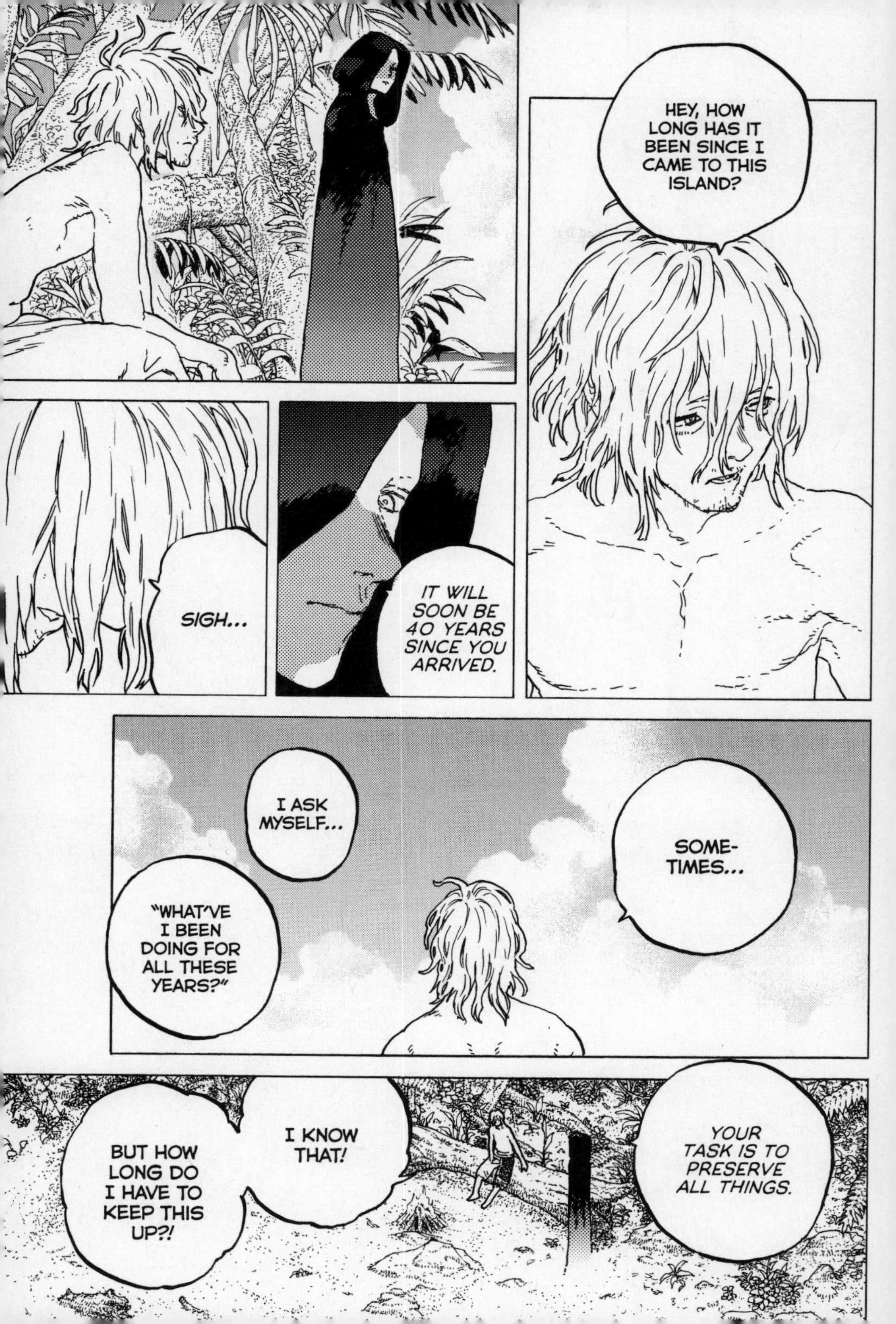
HEY, HOW LONG HAS IT BEEN SINCE I CAME TO THIS ISLAND?
IT WILL SOON BE 40 YEARS SINCE YOU ARRIVED.
SIGH...
SOME-TIMES...
I ASK MYSELF...
"WHAT'VE I BEEN DOING FOR ALL THESE YEARS?"
YOUR TASK IS TO PRESERVE ALL THINGS.
I KNOW THAT!
BUT HOW LONG DO I HAVE TO KEEP THIS UP?!

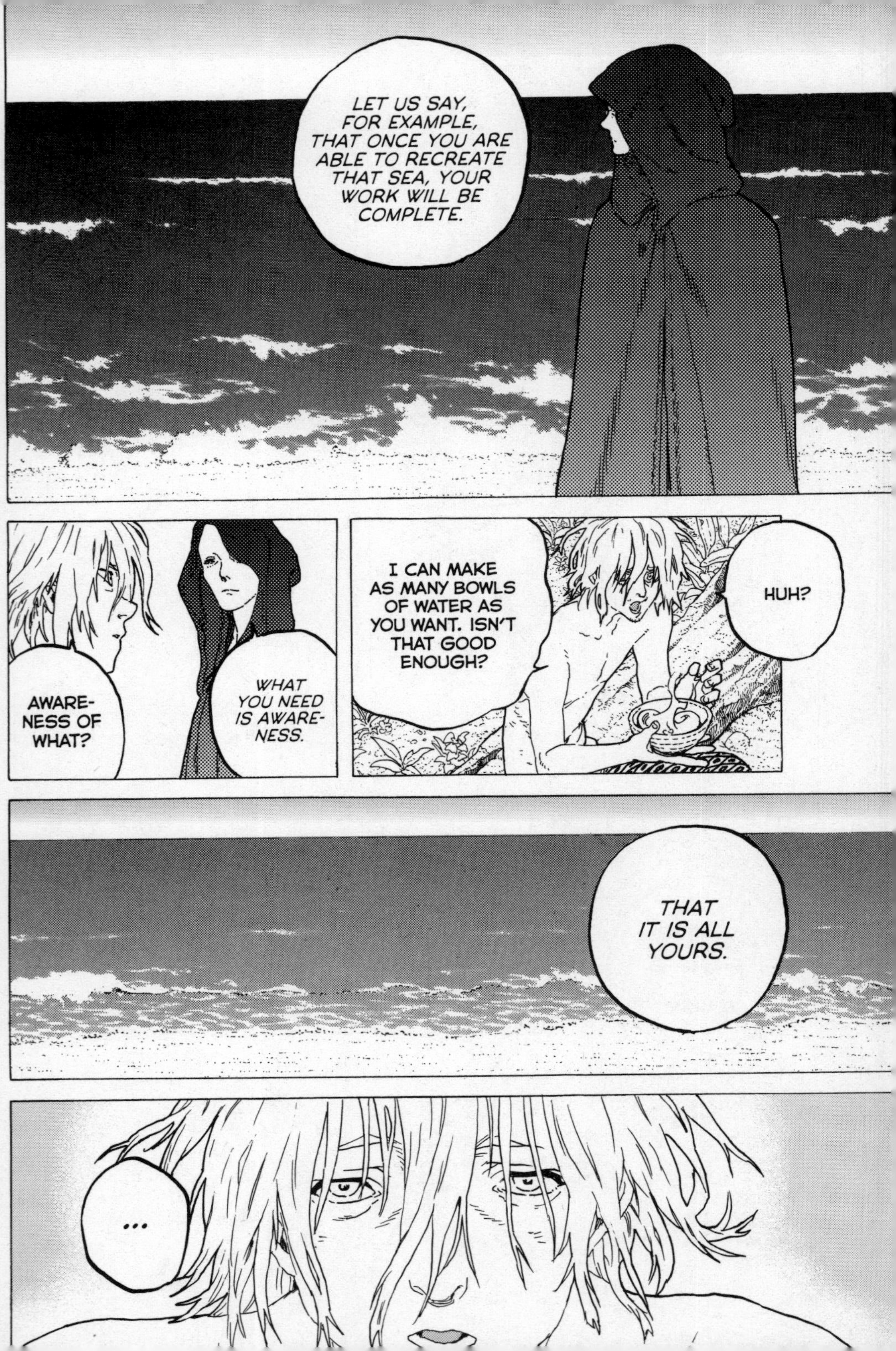
LET US SAY, FOR EXAMPLE, THAT ONCE YOU ARE ABLE TO RECREATE THAT SEA, YOUR WORK WILL BE COMPLETE.
HUH?
I CAN MAKE AS MANY BOWLS OF WATER AS YOU WANT. ISN'T THAT GOOD ENOUGH?
WHAT YOU NEED IS AWARENESS.
AWARENESS OF WHAT?
THAT IT IS ALL YOURS.
...

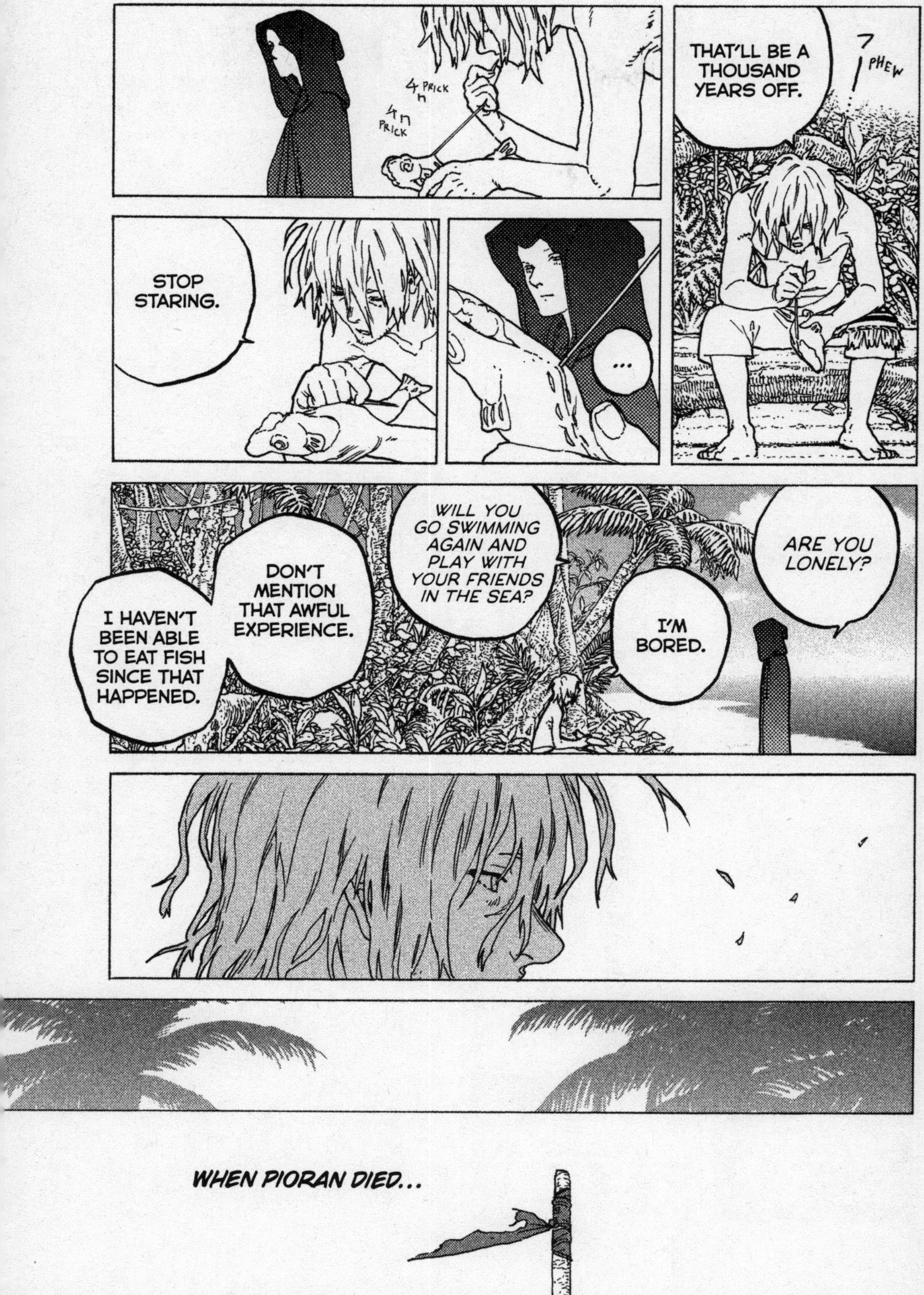
THAT'LL BE A THOUSAND YEARS OFF.
PHEW
PRICK
PRICK
...
STOP STARING.
ARE YOU LONELY?
I'M BORED.
WILL YOU GO SWIMMING AGAIN AND PLAY WITH YOUR FRIENDS IN THE SEA?
DON'T MENTION THAT AWFUL EXPERIENCE.
I HAVEN'T BEEN ABLE TO EAT FISH SINCE THAT HAPPENED.
WHEN PIORAN DIED...

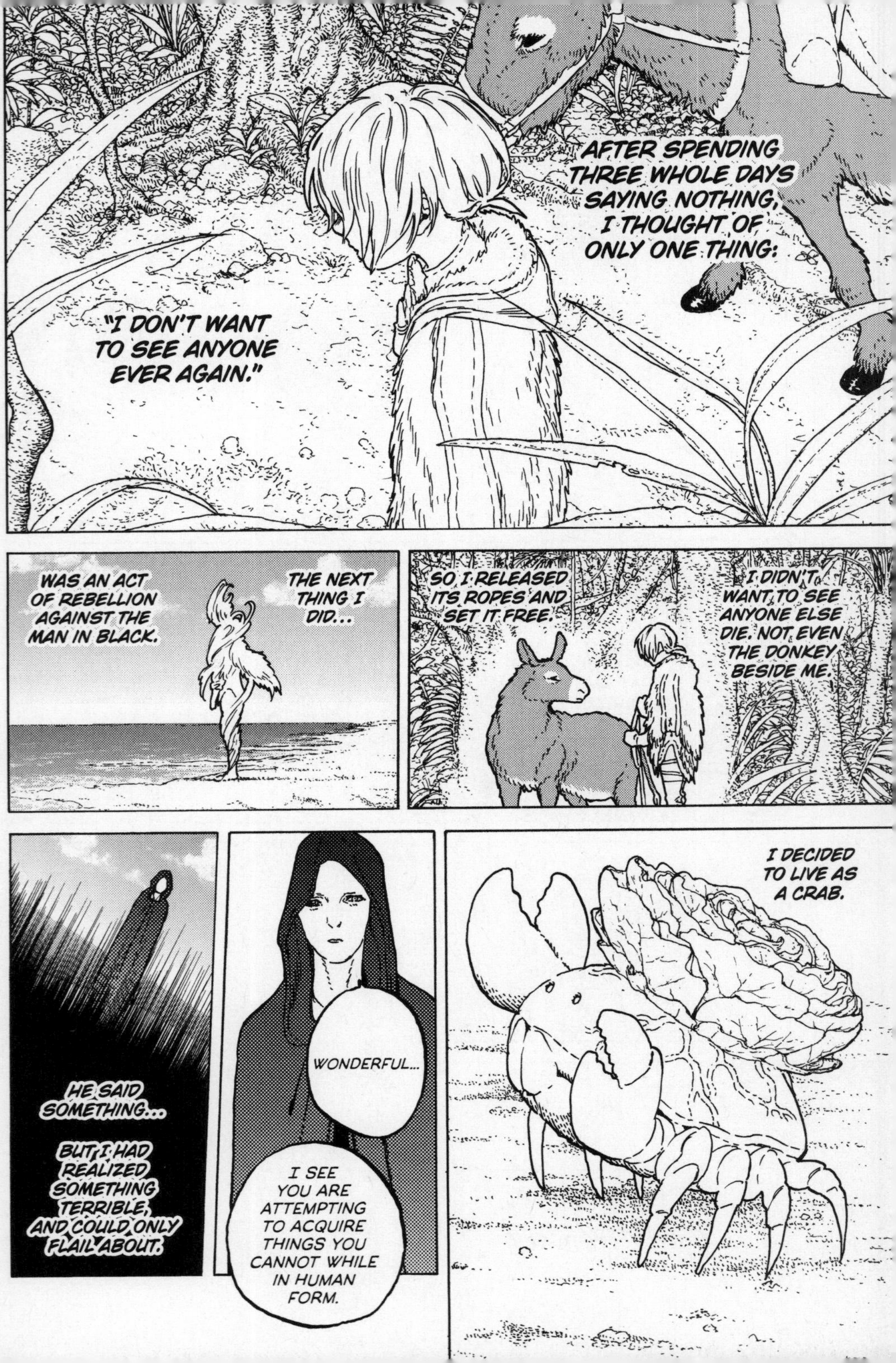
AFTER SPENDING THREE WHOLE DAYS SAYING NOTHING, I THOUGHT OF ONLY ONE THING:
"I DON'T WANT TO SEE ANYONE EVER AGAIN."
I DIDN'T WANT TO SEE ANYONE ELSE DIE. NOT EVEN THE DONKEY BESIDE ME.
SO I RELEASED ITS ROPES AND SET IT FREE.
THE NEXT THING I DID...
WAS AN ACT OF REBELLION AGAINST THE MAN IN BLACK.
I DECIDED TO LIVE AS A CRAB.
WONDERFUL...
I SEE YOU ARE ATTEMPTING TO ACQUIRE THINGS YOU CANNOT WHILE IN HUMAN FORM.
HE SAID SOMETHING...
BUT I HAD REALIZED SOMETHING TERRIBLE, AND COULD ONLY FLAIL ABOUT.

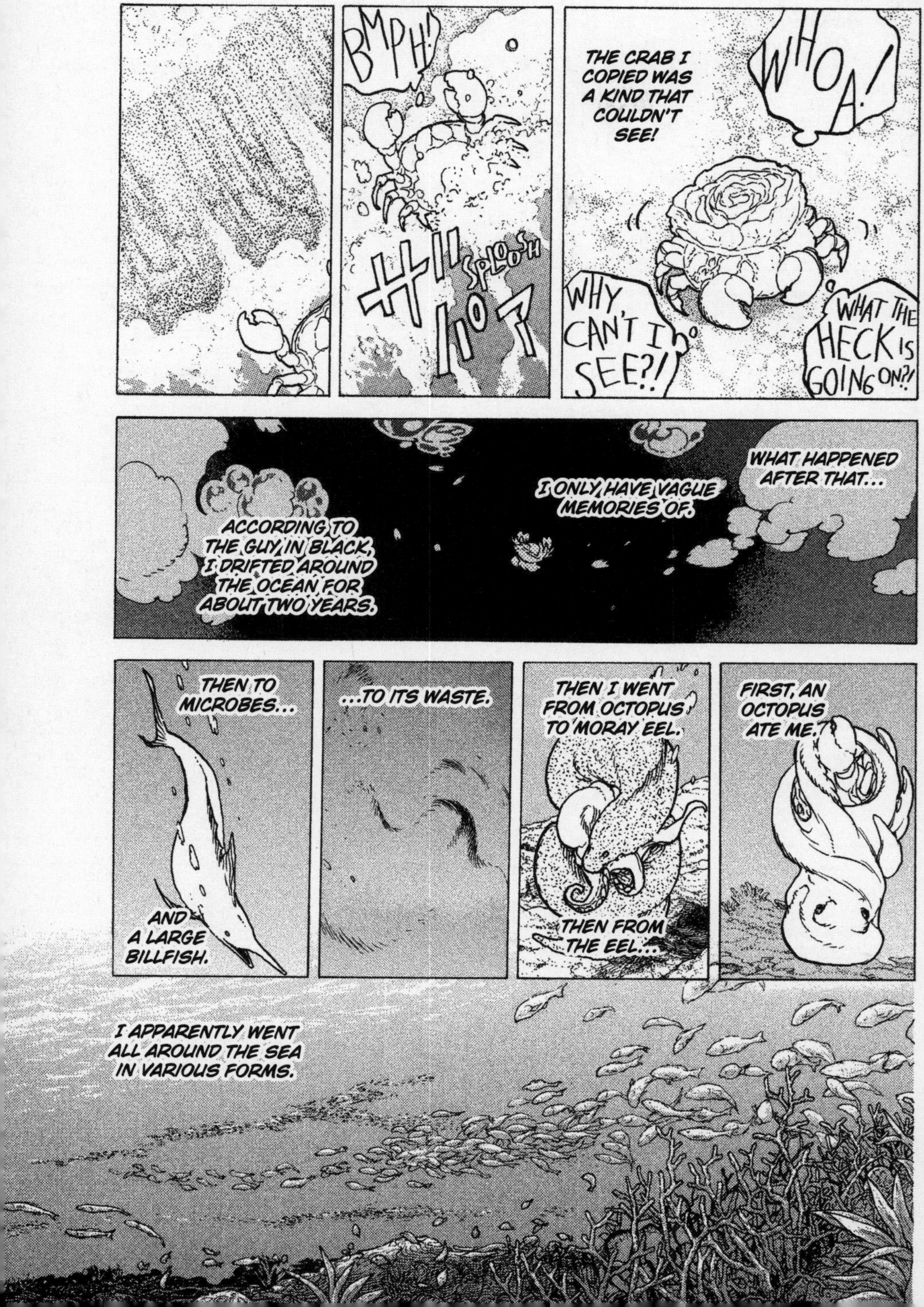
WHOA!
THE CRAB I COPIED WAS A KIND THAT COULDN'T SEE!
WHAT THE HECK IS GOING ON?!
WHY, CAN'T I SEE?!
BMPH!
SPLOOSH
WHAT HAPPENED AFTER THAT...
I ONLY HAVE VAGUE MEMORIES OF.
ACCORDING TO THE GUY IN BLACK, I DRIFTED AROUND THE OCEAN FOR ABOUT TWO YEARS.
FIRST, AN OCTOPUS ATE ME.
THEN I WENT FROM OCTOPUS TO MORAY EEL.
THEN FROM THE EEL...
...TO ITS WASTE.
THEN TO MICROBES...
AND A LARGE BILLFISH.
I APPARENTLY WENT ALL AROUND THE SEA IN VARIOUS FORMS.

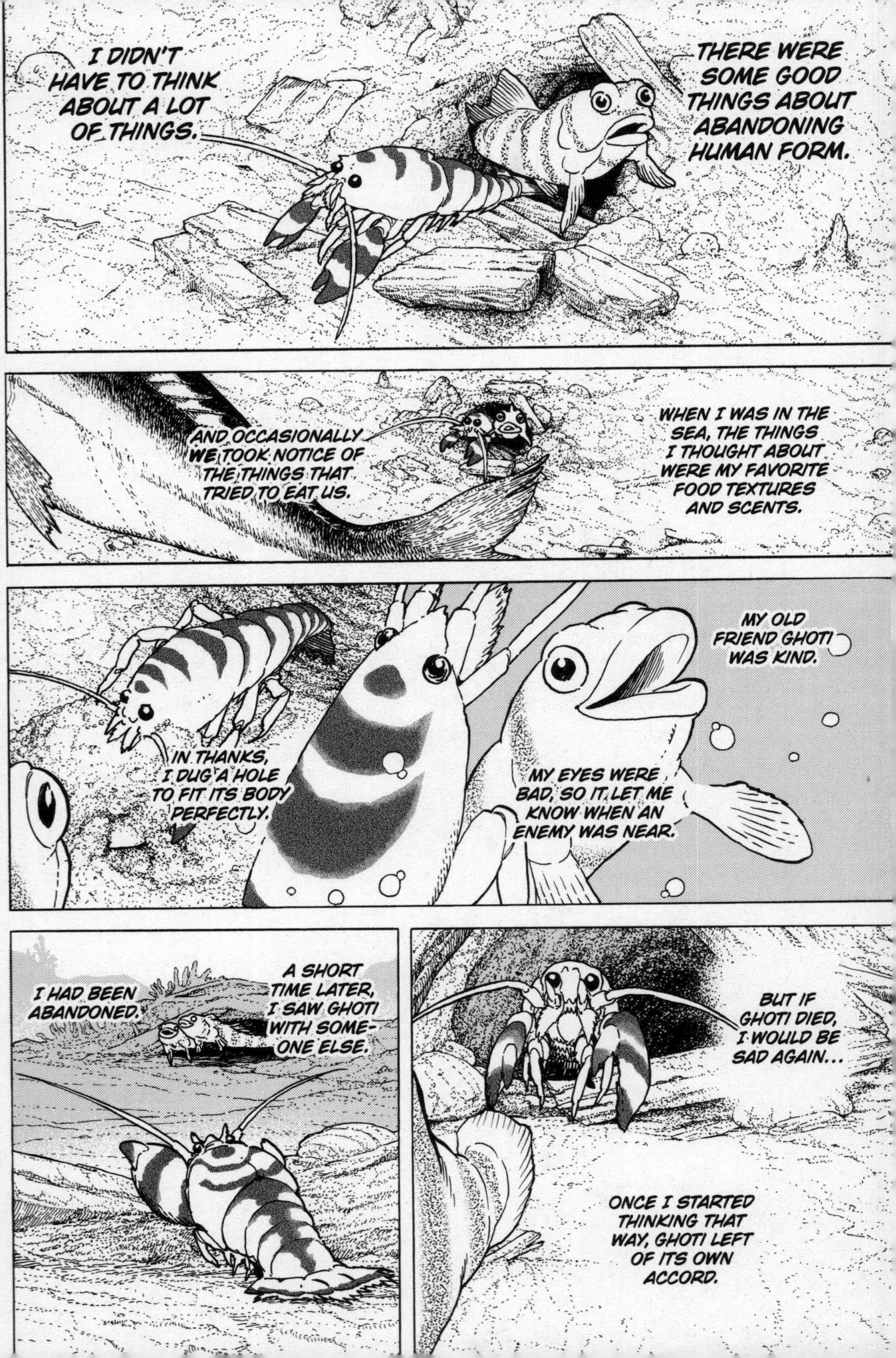
THERE WERE SOME GOOD THINGS ABOUT ABANDONING HUMAN FORM.
I DIDN'T HAVE TO THINK ABOUT A LOT OF THINGS.
WHEN I WAS IN THE SEA, THE THINGS I THOUGHT ABOUT WERE MY FAVORITE FOOD TEXTURES AND SCENTS.
AND OCCASIONALLY WE TOOK NOTICE OF THE THINGS THAT TRIED TO EAT US.
MY OLD FRIEND GHOTI WAS KIND.
MY EYES WERE BAD, SO IT LET ME KNOW WHEN AN ENEMY WAS NEAR.
IN THANKS, I DUG A HOLE TO FIT ITS BODY PERFECTLY.
BUT IF GHOTI DIED, I WOULD BE SAD AGAIN...
ONCE I STARTED THINKING THAT WAY, GHOTI LEFT OF ITS OWN ACCORD.
A SHORT TIME LATER, I SAW GHOTI WITH SOME-ONE ELSE.
I HAD BEEN ABANDONED.

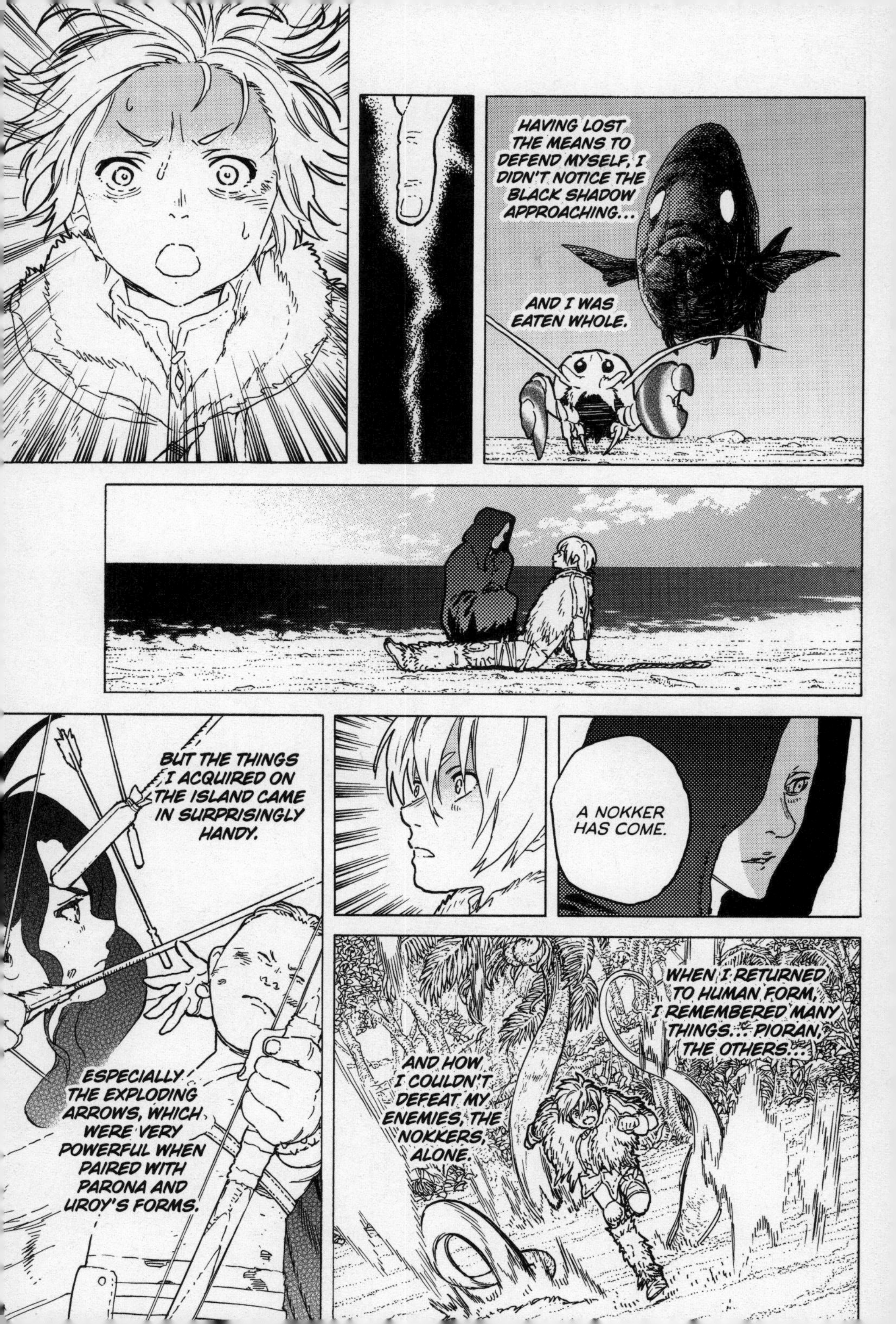
HAVING LOST THE MEANS TO DEFEND MYSELF, I DIDN'T NOTICE THE BLACK SHADOW APPROACHING...
AND I WAS EATEN WHOLE.
A NOKKER HAS COME.
WHEN I RETURNED TO HUMAN FORM, I REMEMBERED MANY THINGS... PIORAN, THE OTHERS...
AND HOW I COULDN'T DEFEAT MY ENEMIES, THE NOKKERS, ALONE.
BUT THE THINGS I ACQUIRED ON THE ISLAND CAME IN SURPRISINGLY HANDY.
ESPECIALLY THE EXPLODING ARROWS, WHICH WERE VERY POWERFUL WHEN PAIRED WITH PARONA AND UROY'S FORMS.

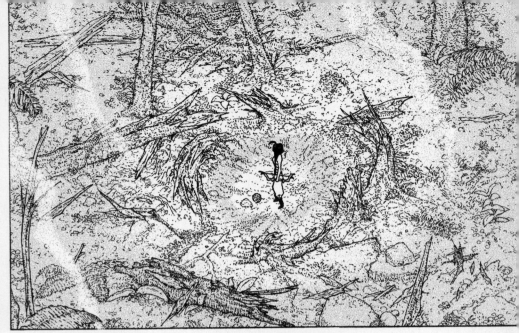

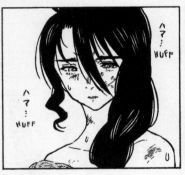

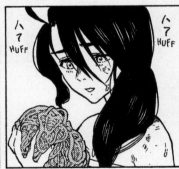

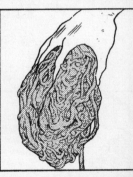

ハア
HUFF
ハア
HUFF
ハア…
HUFF
ハア…
HUFF
OCCASIONALLY, I'D GET SAD ALL OF A SUDDEN.
I THINK IT'S WHAT YOU'D CALL "GUILT."
I HATED MYSELF FOR LIVING ON, USING THE DEATHS OF OTHERS.
BUT I HATE THE THOUGHT OF LOSING THEM IN MEMORY, TOO.

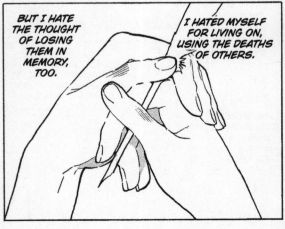

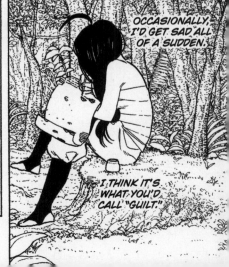

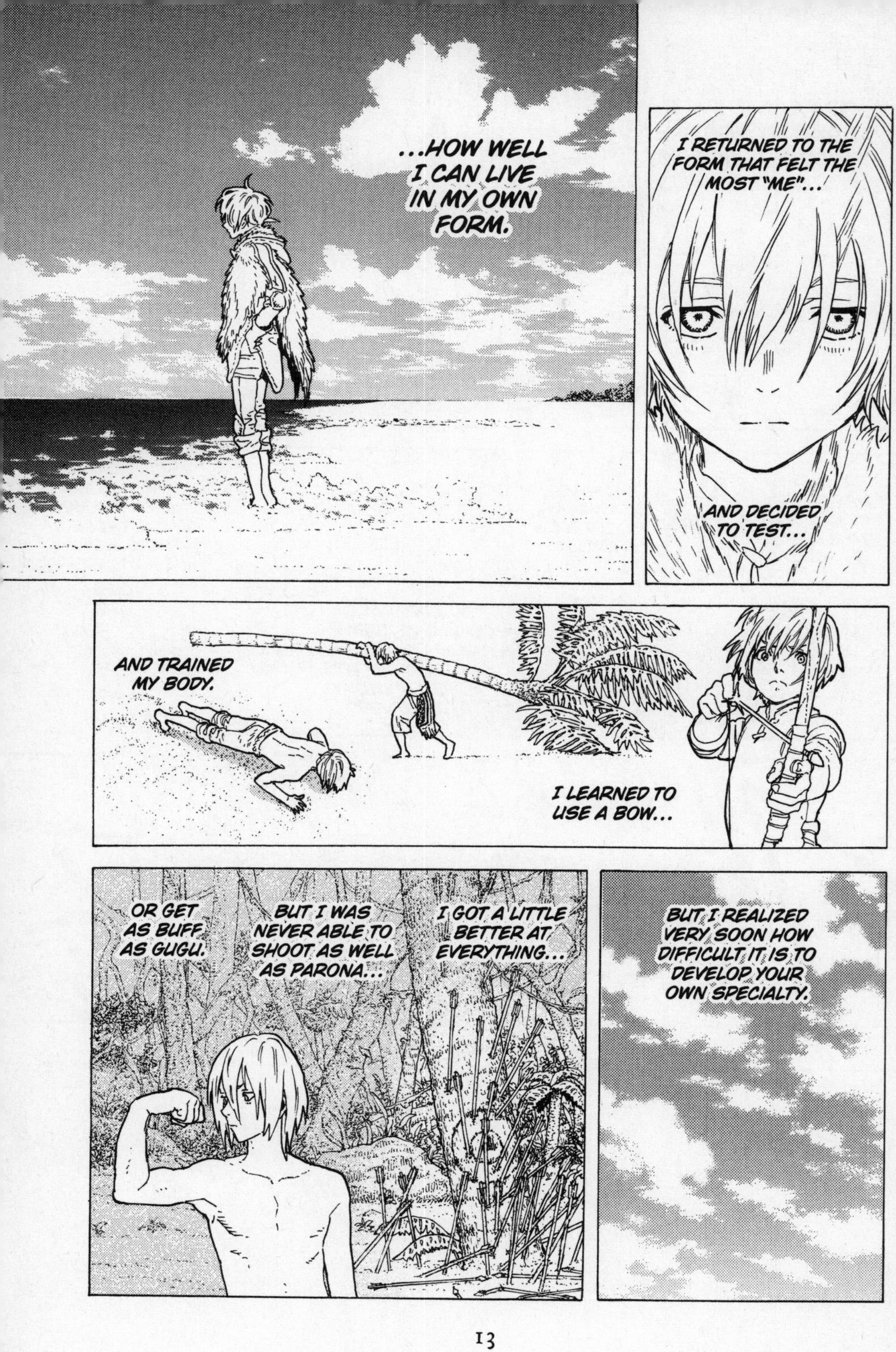
I RETURNED TO THE FORM THAT FELT THE MOST "ME"...
AND DECIDED TO TEST...
...HOW WELL I CAN LIVE IN MY OWN FORM.
I LEARNED TO USE A BOW...
AND TRAINED MY BODY.
BUT I REALIZED VERY SOON HOW DIFFICULT IT IS TO DEVELOP YOUR OWN SPECIALTY.
I GOT A LITTLE BETTER AT EVERYTHING...
BUT I WAS NEVER ABLE TO SHOOT AS WELL AS PARONA...
OR GET AS BUFF AS GUGU.

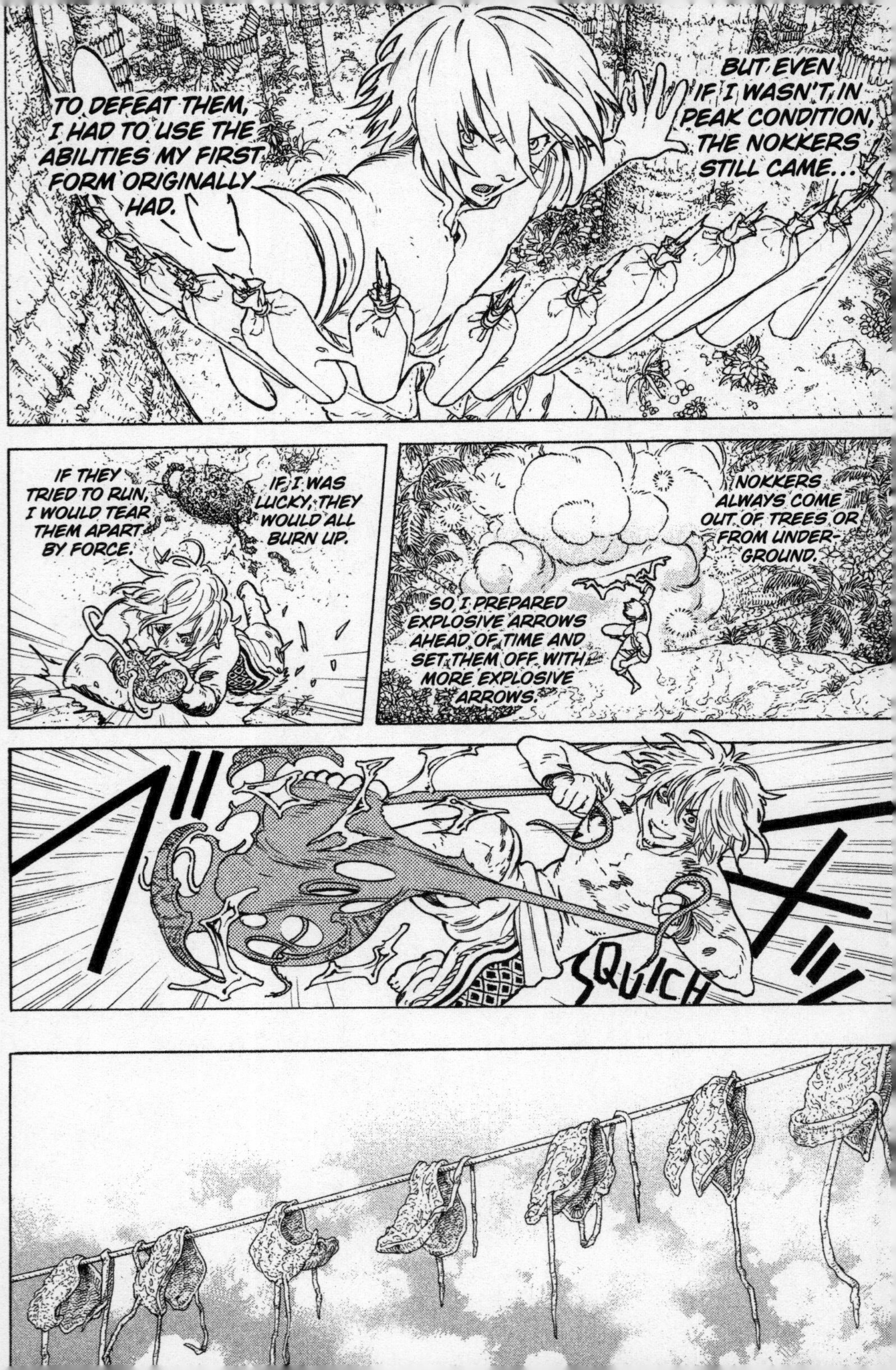
BUT EVEN IF I WASN'T IN PEAK CONDITION, THE NOKKERS STILL CAME...
TO DEFEAT THEM, I HAD TO USE THE ABILITIES MY FIRST FORM ORIGINALLY HAD.
NOKKERS ALWAYS COME OUT OF TREES OR FROM UNDER-GROUND.
SO, I PREPARED EXPLOSIVE ARROWS AHEAD OF TIME AND SET THEM OFF WITH MORE EXPLOSIVE ARROWS.
IF I WAS LUCKY, THEY WOULD ALL BURN UP.
IF THEY TRIED TO RUN, I WOULD TEAR THEM APART BY FORCE.
SQUICH

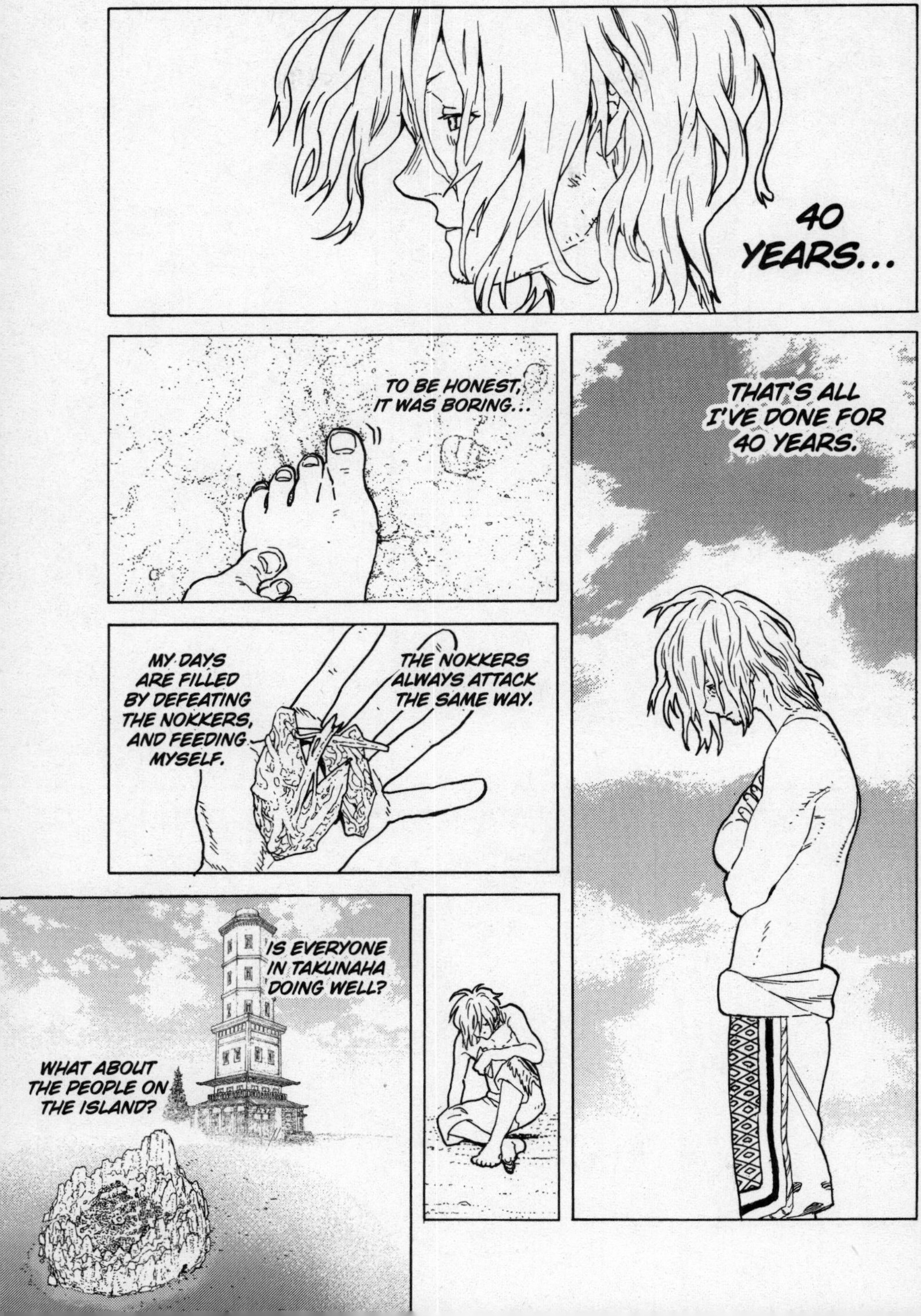
40 YEARS...
THAT'S ALL I'VE DONE FOR 40 YEARS.
TO BE HONEST, IT WAS BORING...
THE NOKKERS ALWAYS ATTACK THE SAME WAY.
MY DAYS ARE FILLED BY DEFEATING THE NOKKERS, AND FEEDING MYSELF.
IS EVERYONE IN TAKUNAHA DOING WELL?
WHAT ABOUT THE PEOPLE ON THE ISLAND?

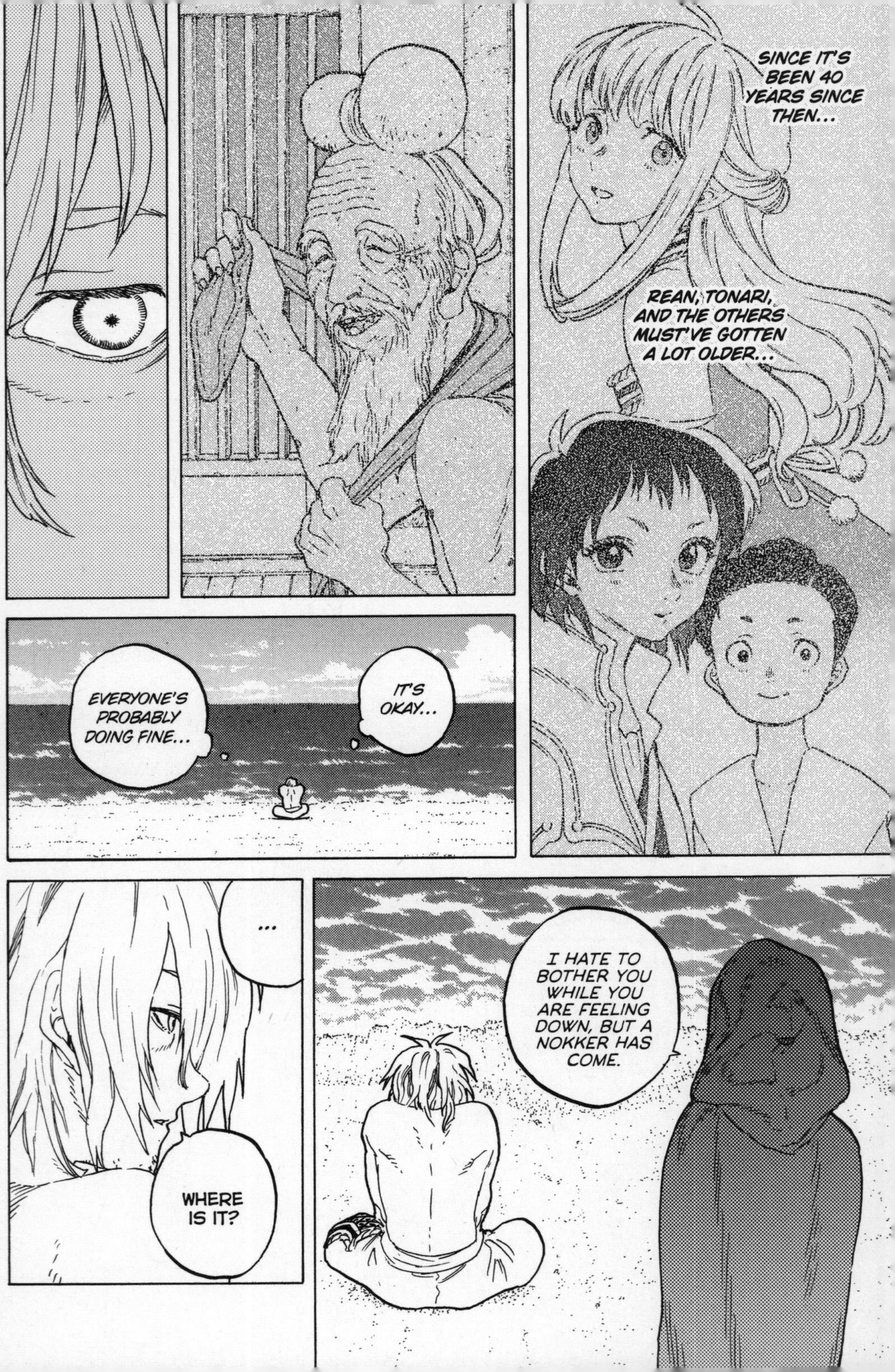
SINCE IT'S BEEN 40 YEARS SINCE THEN...
REAN, TONARI, AND THE OTHERS MUST'VE GOTTEN A LOT OLDER...
IT'S OKAY...
EVERYONE'S PROBABLY DOING FINE...
I HATE TO BOTHER YOU WHILE YOU ARE FEELING DOWN, BUT A NOKKER HAS COME.
...
WHERE IS IT?

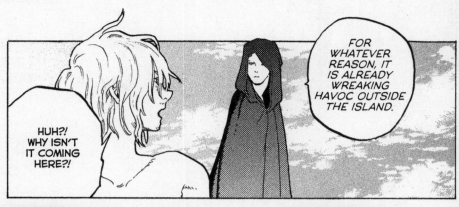

FOR WHATEVER REASON, IT IS ALREADY WREAKING HAVOC OUTSIDE THE ISLAND.
HUH?! WHY ISN'T IT COMING HERE?!
MAYBE THEY HAVE GIVEN UP ON YOU.
WHAT DO YOU MEAN?
MAYBE THEY ARE LAYING THE GROUNDWORK FOR A FUTURE ATTACK, OR PERHAPS THEY WISH TO LURE YOU OFF THE ISLAND. THERE ARE MANY POSSIBILITIES.
IS IT ATTACKING PEOPLE?
NOD

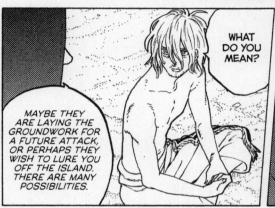

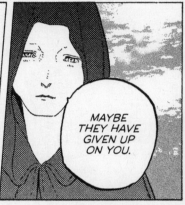

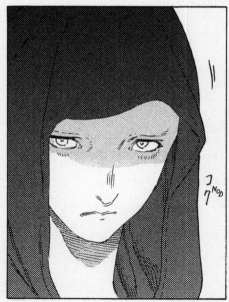

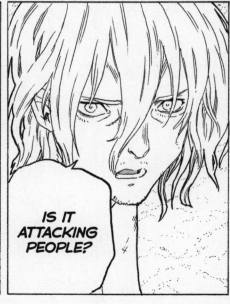

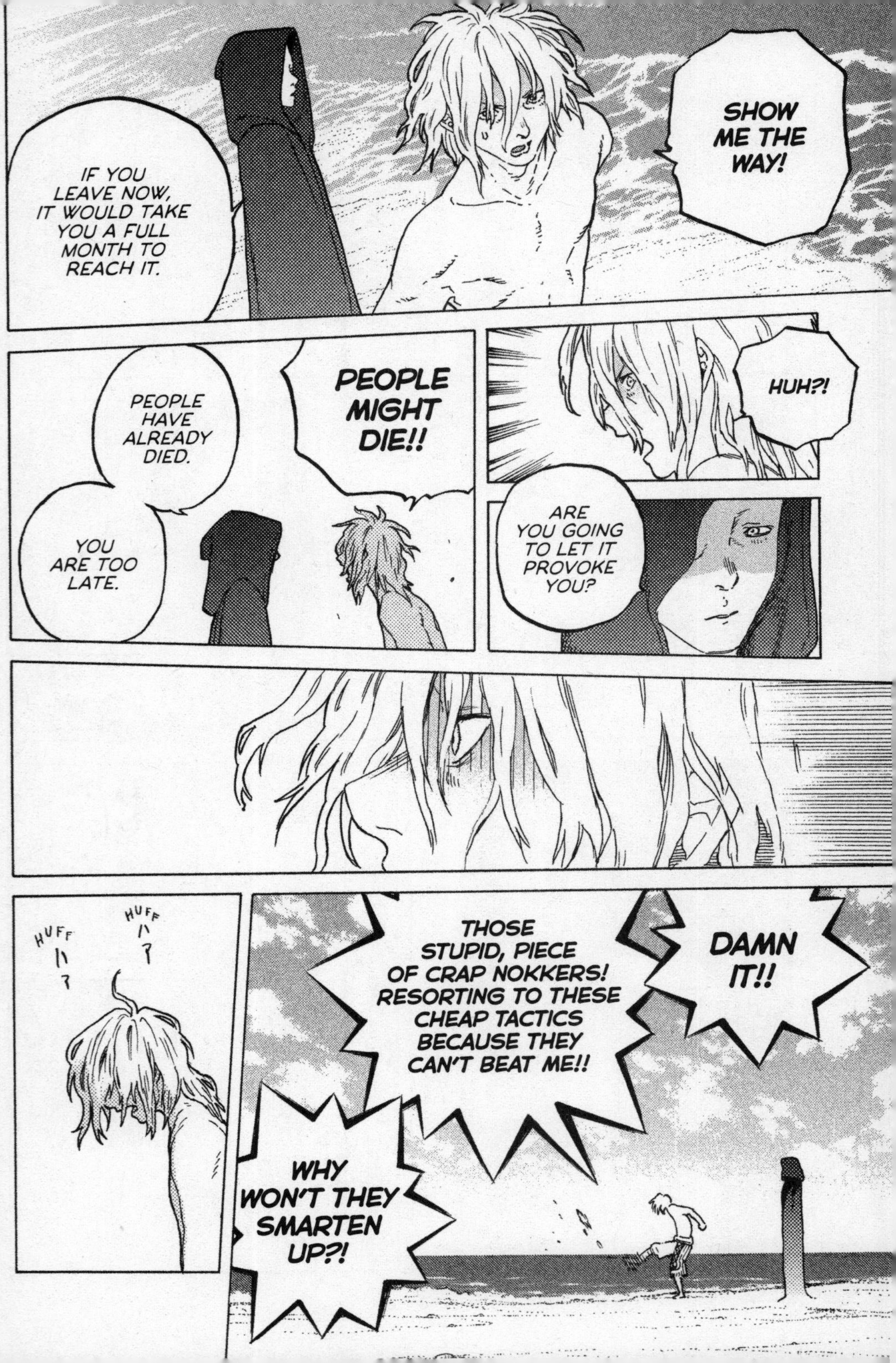
SHOW ME THE WAY!
IF YOU LEAVE NOW, IT WOULD TAKE YOU A FULL MONTH TO REACH IT.
HUH?!
ARE YOU GOING TO LET IT PROVOKE YOU?
PEOPLE MIGHT DIE!!
PEOPLE HAVE ALREADY DIED.
YOU ARE TOO LATE.
DAMN IT!!
THOSE STUPID, PIECE OF CRAP NOKKERS! RESORTING TO THESE CHEAP TACTICS BECAUSE THEY CAN'T BEAT ME!!
WHY WON'T THEY SMARTEN UP?!
HUFF ハァ
HUFF ハァ

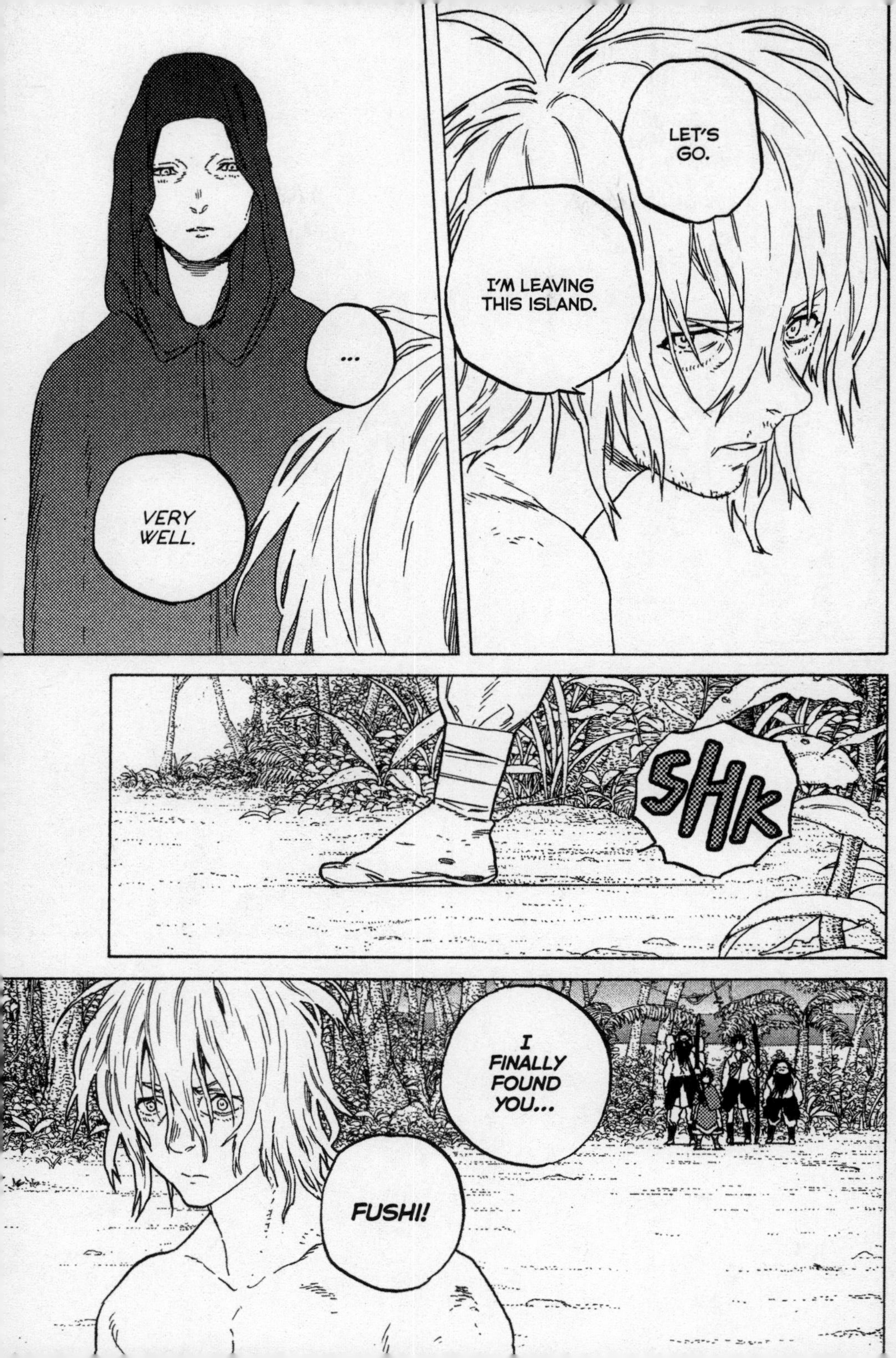
LET'S GO.
I'M LEAVING THIS ISLAND.
...
VERY WELL.
SHK
I FINALLY FOUND YOU...
FUSHI!

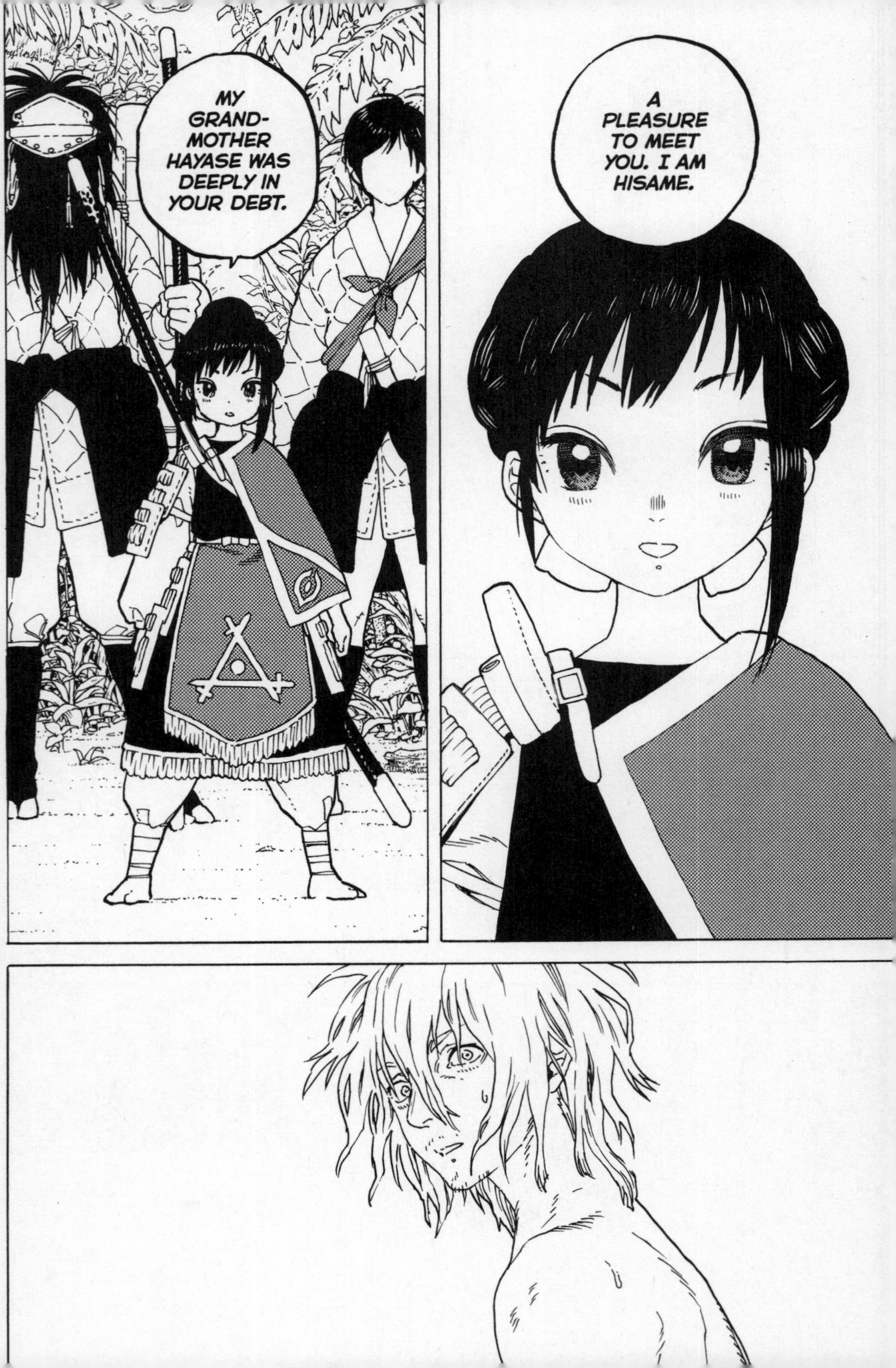
A PLEASURE TO MEET YOU. I AM HISAME.
MY GRAND-MOTHER HAYASE WAS DEEPLY IN YOUR DEBT.

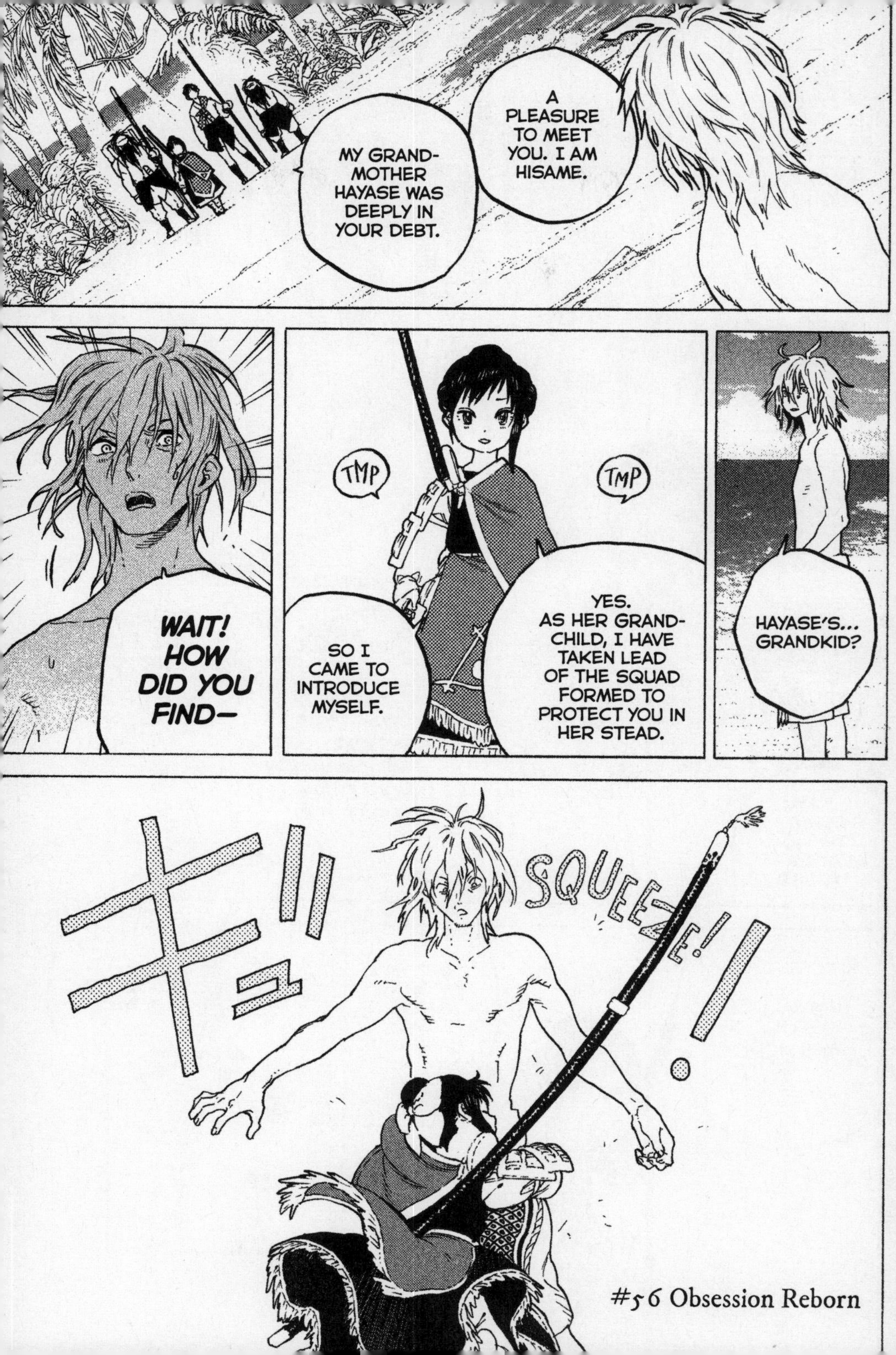

A PLEASURE TO MEET YOU. I AM HISAME.
MY GRANDMOTHER HAYASE WAS DEEPLY IN YOUR DEBT.
HAYASE'S... GRANDKID?
TMP
TMP
YES. AS HER GRANDCHILD, I HAVE TAKEN LEAD OF THE SQUAD FORMED TO PROTECT YOU IN HER STEAD.
SO I CAME TO INTRODUCE MYSELF.
WAIT! HOW DID YOU FIND—
ギュ!
SQUEEZE!

#56 Obsession Reborn

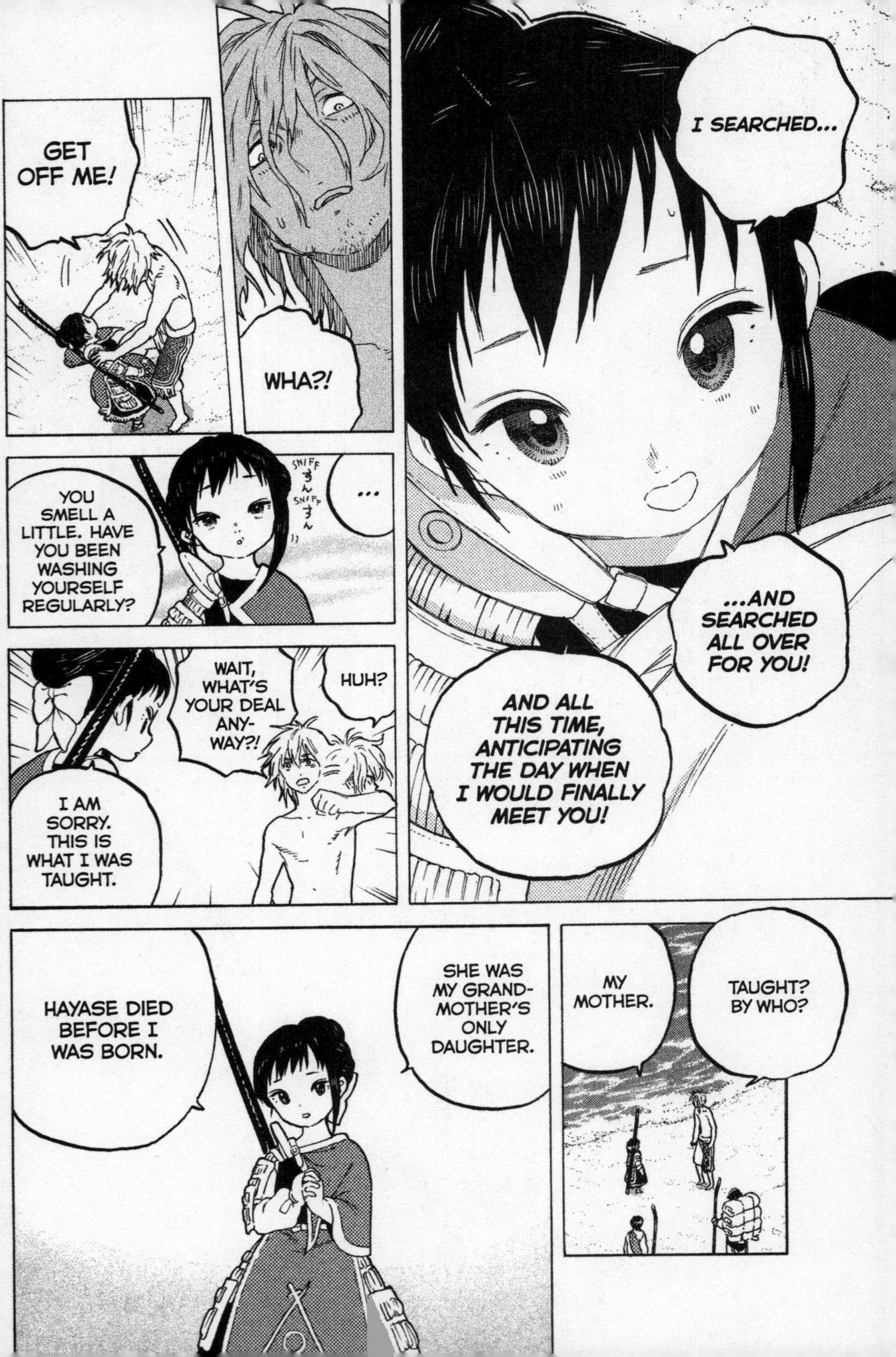
I SEARCHED...
...AND SEARCHED ALL OVER FOR YOU!
AND ALL THIS TIME, ANTICIPATING THE DAY WHEN I WOULD FINALLY MEET YOU!
WHA?!
GET OFF ME!
...
SNIFF すん SNIFF すん
YOU SMELL A LITTLE. HAVE YOU BEEN WASHING YOURSELF REGULARLY?
HUH?
WAIT, WHAT'S YOUR DEAL ANY-WAY?!
I AM SORRY. THIS IS WHAT I WAS TAUGHT.
TAUGHT? BY WHO?
MY MOTHER.
SHE WAS MY GRAND-MOTHER'S ONLY DAUGHTER.
HAYASE DIED BEFORE I WAS BORN.

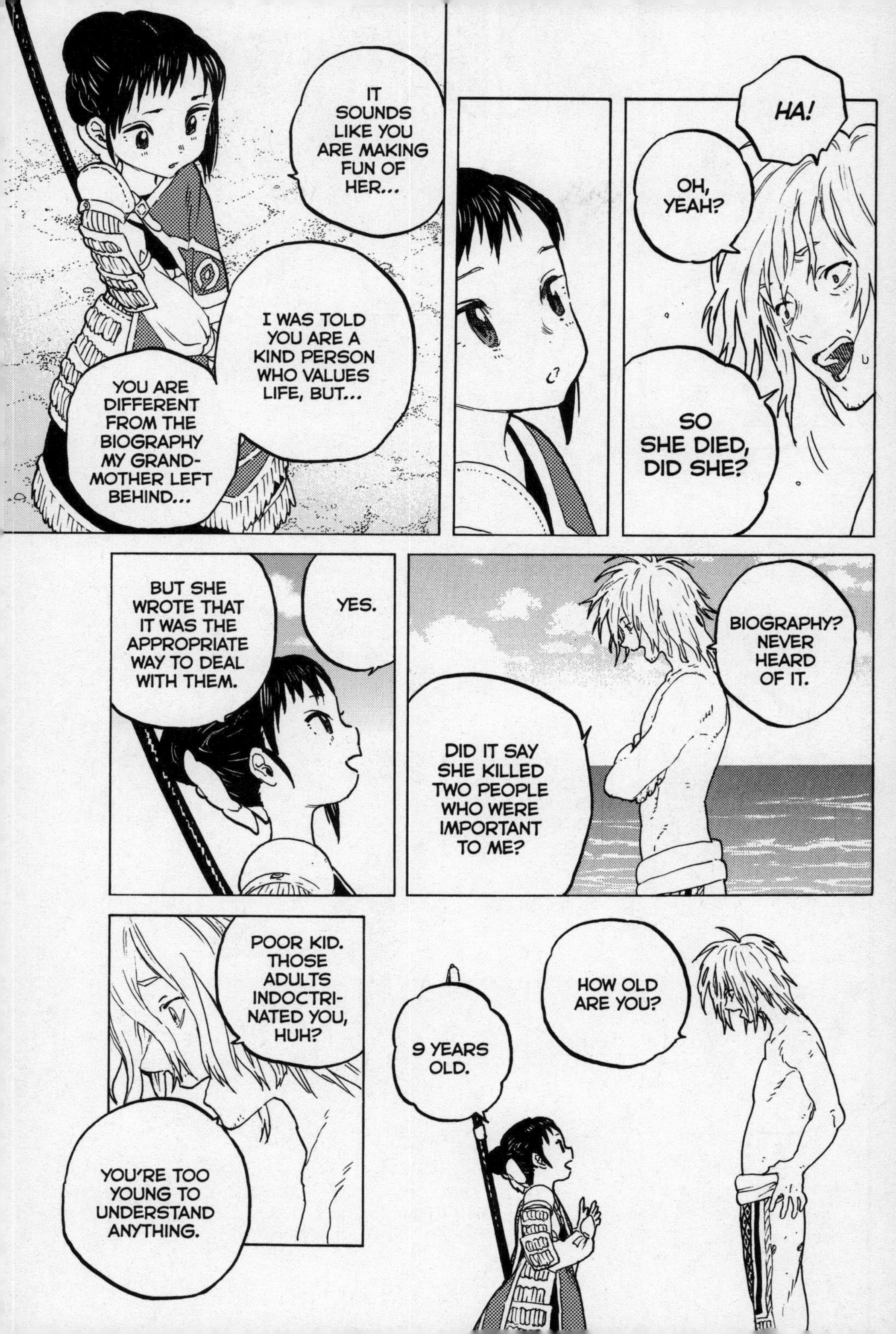
HA!
OH, YEAH?
SO SHE DIED, DID SHE?
IT SOUNDS LIKE YOU ARE MAKING FUN OF HER...
I WAS TOLD YOU ARE A KIND PERSON WHO VALUES LIFE, BUT...
YOU ARE DIFFERENT FROM THE BIOGRAPHY MY GRAND-MOTHER LEFT BEHIND...
BIOGRAPHY? NEVER HEARD OF IT.
DID IT SAY SHE KILLED TWO PEOPLE WHO WERE IMPORTANT TO ME?
YES.
BUT SHE WROTE THAT IT WAS THE APPROPRIATE WAY TO DEAL WITH THEM.
HOW OLD ARE YOU?
9 YEARS OLD.
POOR KID. THOSE ADULTS INDOCTRI-NATED YOU, HUH?
YOU'RE TOO YOUNG TO UNDERSTAND ANYTHING.

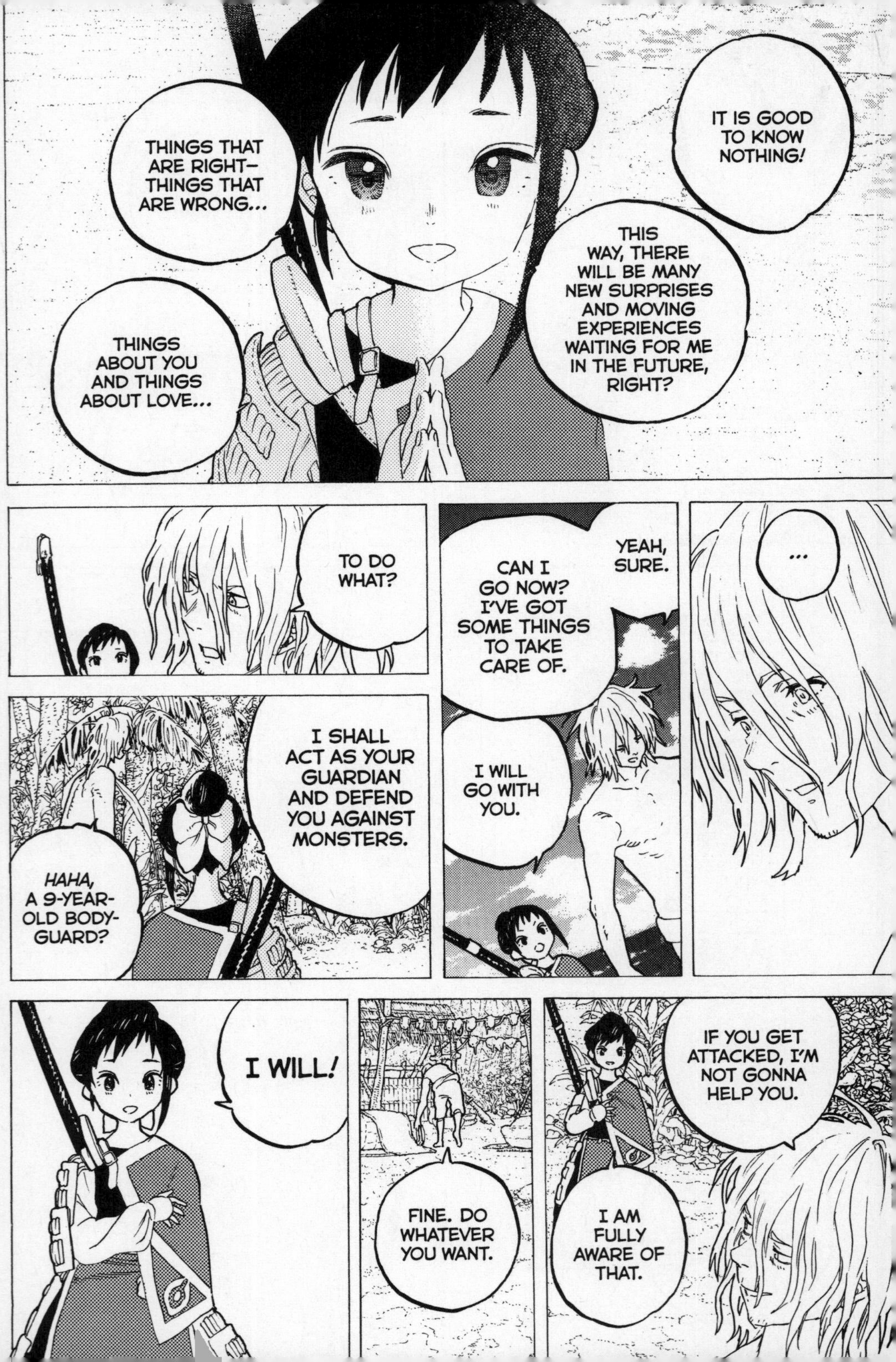
IT IS GOOD TO KNOW NOTHING!
THINGS THAT ARE RIGHT— THINGS THAT ARE WRONG...
THIS WAY, THERE WILL BE MANY NEW SURPRISES AND MOVING EXPERIENCES WAITING FOR ME IN THE FUTURE, RIGHT?
THINGS ABOUT YOU AND THINGS ABOUT LOVE...
...
YEAH, SURE.
CAN I GO NOW? I'VE GOT SOME THINGS TO TAKE CARE OF.
I WILL GO WITH YOU.
TO DO WHAT?
I SHALL ACT AS YOUR GUARDIAN AND DEFEND YOU AGAINST MONSTERS.
HAHA, A 9-YEAR-OLD BODY-GUARD?
IF YOU GET ATTACKED, I'M NOT GONNA HELP YOU.
I AM FULLY AWARE OF THAT.
FINE. DO WHATEVER YOU WANT.
I WILL!

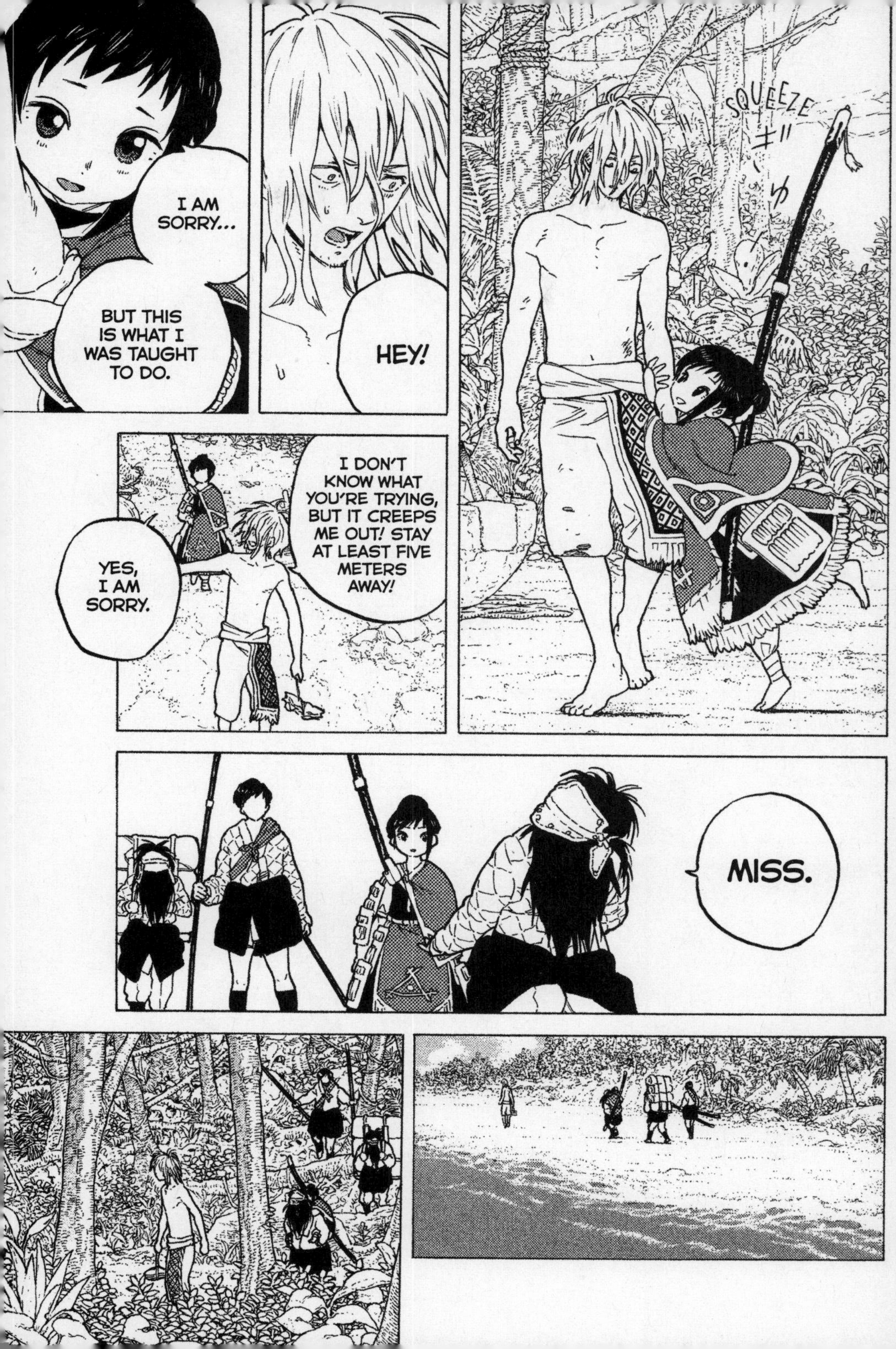
SQUEEZE
HEY!
I AM SORRY...
BUT THIS IS WHAT I WAS TAUGHT TO DO.
I DON'T KNOW WHAT YOU'RE TRYING, BUT IT CREEPS ME OUT! STAY AT LEAST FIVE METERS AWAY!
YES, I AM SORRY.
MISS.

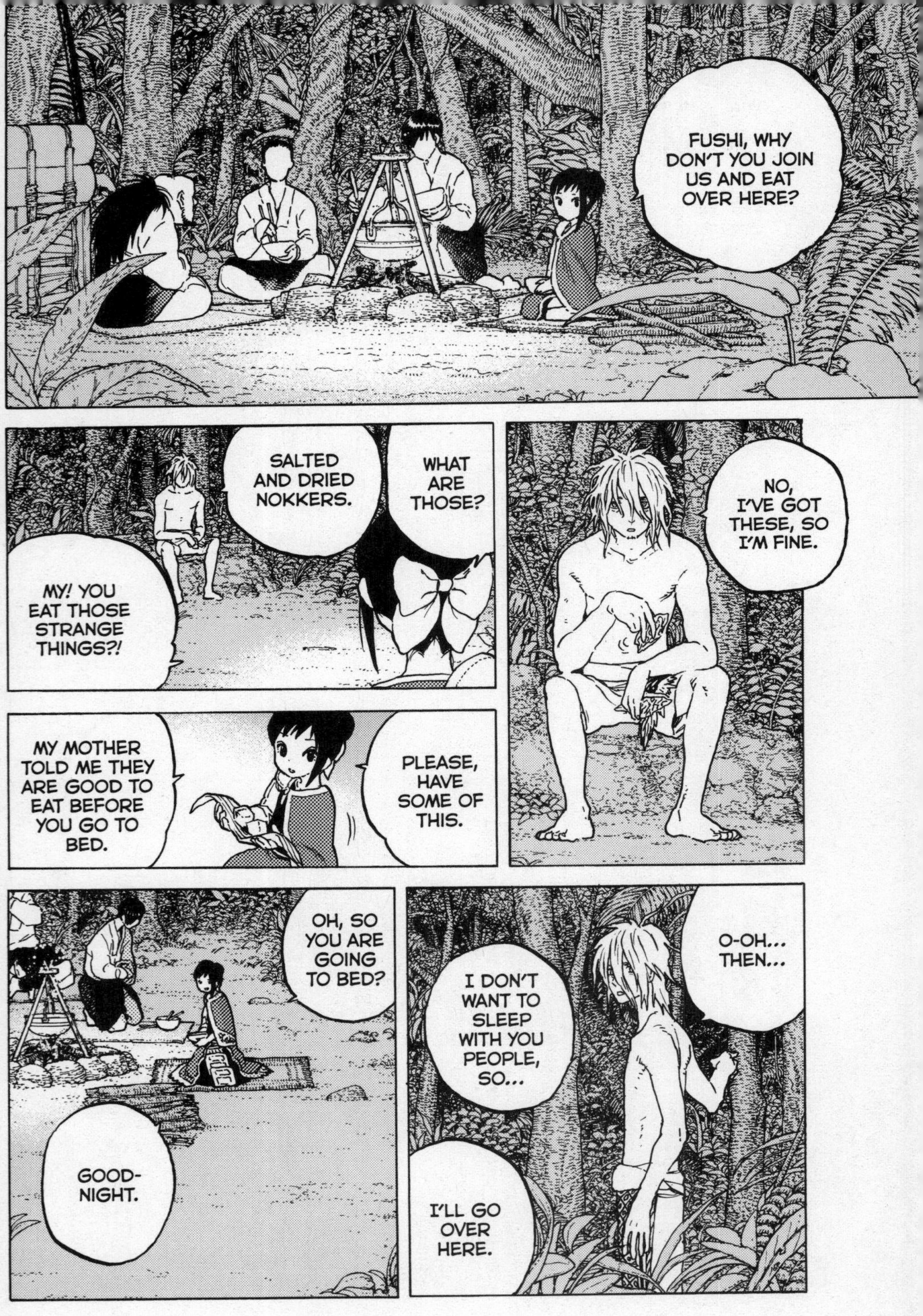
FUSHI, WHY DON'T YOU JOIN US AND EAT OVER HERE?
NO, I'VE GOT THESE, SO I'M FINE.
WHAT ARE THOSE?
SALTED AND DRIED NOKKERS.
MY! YOU EAT THOSE STRANGE THINGS?!
PLEASE, HAVE SOME OF THIS.
MY MOTHER TOLD ME THEY ARE GOOD TO EAT BEFORE YOU GO TO BED.
O-OH... THEN...
I DON'T WANT TO SLEEP WITH YOU PEOPLE, SO...
I'LL GO OVER HERE.
OH, SO YOU ARE GOING TO BED?
GOOD-NIGHT.

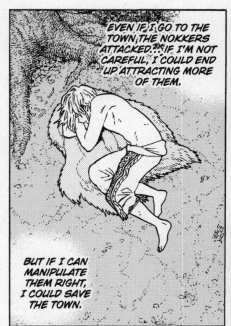

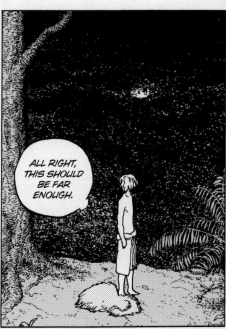

ALL RIGHT, THIS SHOULD BE FAR ENOUGH.
EVEN IF I GO TO THE TOWN THE NOKKERS ATTACKED... IF I'M NOT CAREFUL, I COULD END UP ATTRACTING MORE OF THEM.
BUT IF I CAN MANIPULATE THEM RIGHT, I COULD SAVE THE TOWN.
HISAME...
SHE'S WEIRD, BUT EVEN THOUGH SHE'S HAYASE'S GRANDCHILD, SHE DOESN'T SEEM DANGEROUS...

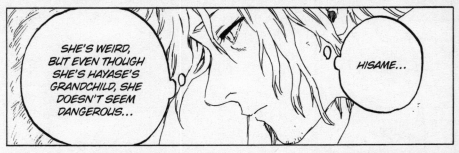

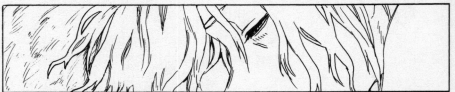

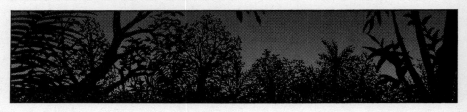

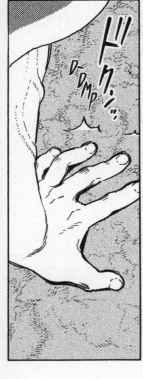

ドドン...
D-DMP...

...

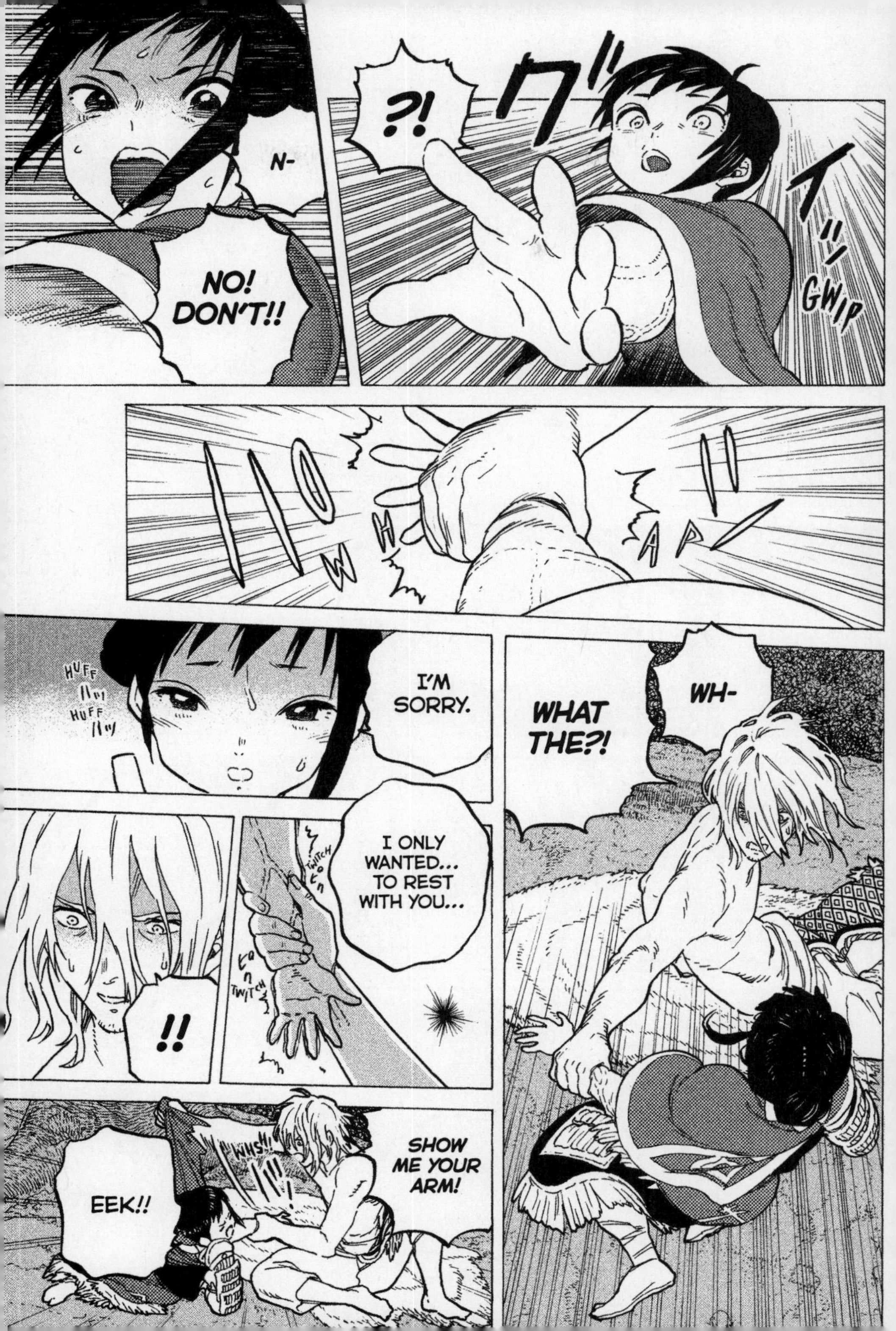
?!
GWIP
N-
NO! DON'T!!
WHAP
WH-
WHAT THE?!
HUFF HUFF
I'M SORRY.
I ONLY WANTED... TO REST WITH YOU...
TWITCH
TWITCH
!!
SHOW ME YOUR ARM!
WHSH!
EEK!!

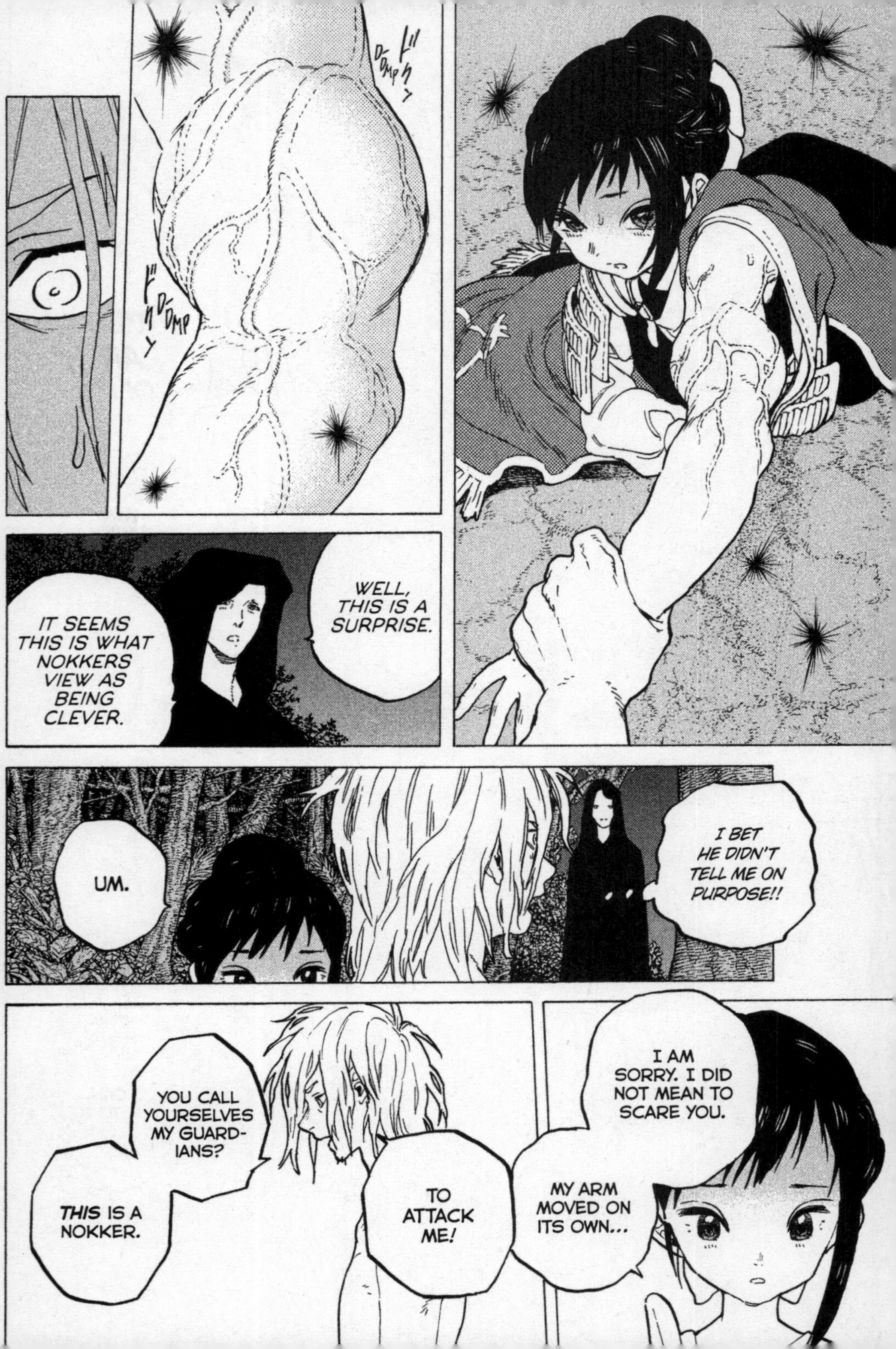
D-DMP
D-DMP
WELL, THIS IS A SURPRISE.
IT SEEMS THIS IS WHAT NOKKERS VIEW AS BEING CLEVER.
I BET HE DIDN'T TELL ME ON PURPOSE!!
UM.
I AM SORRY. I DID NOT MEAN TO SCARE YOU.
MY ARM MOVED ON ITS OWN...
TO ATTACK ME!
YOU CALL YOURSELVES MY GUARDIANS?
THIS IS A NOKKER.

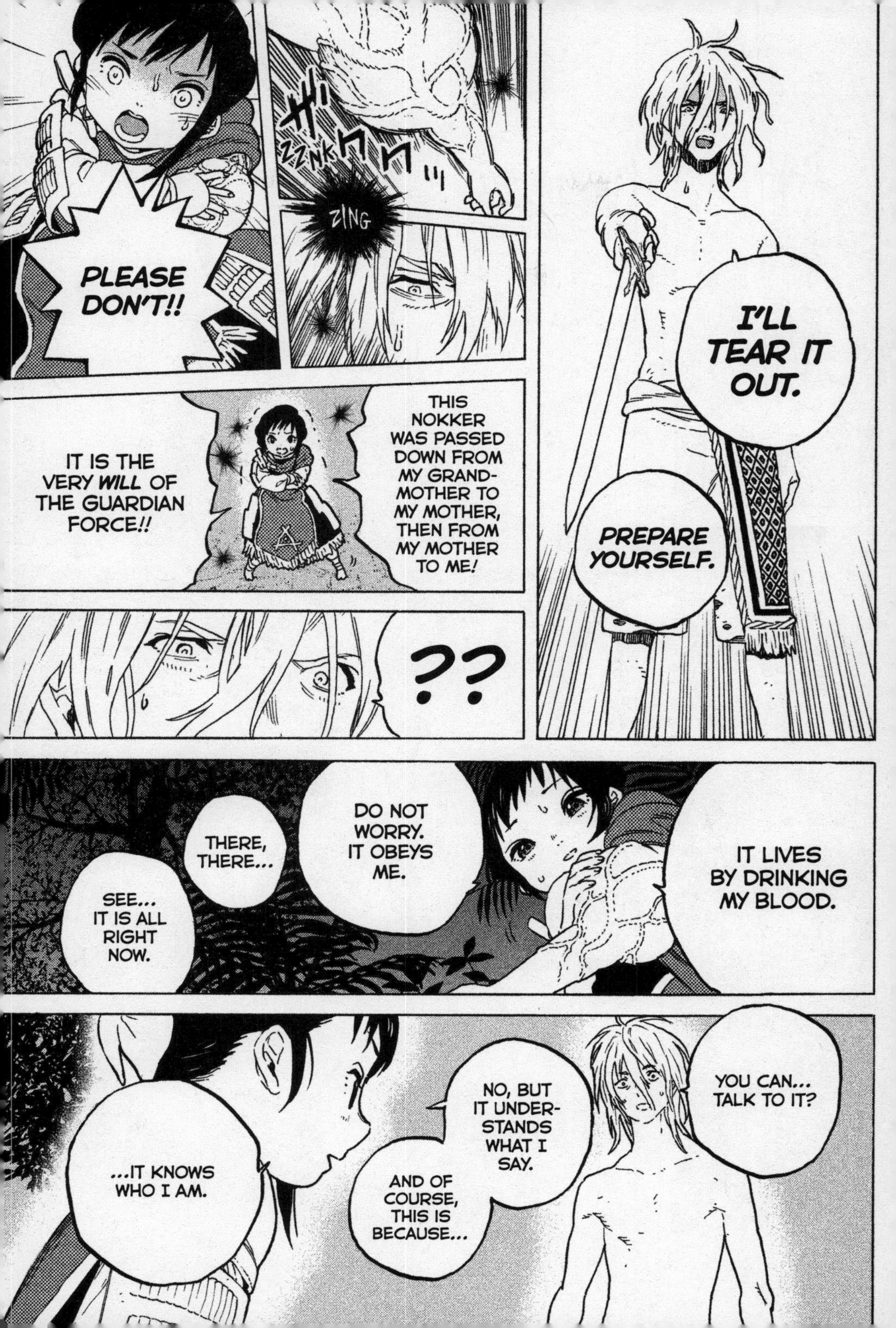
I'LL TEAR IT OUT.
PREPARE YOURSELF.
ZING
PLEASE DON'T!!
THIS NOKKER WAS PASSED DOWN FROM MY GRAND-MOTHER TO MY MOTHER, THEN FROM MY MOTHER TO ME!
IT IS THE VERY *WILL* OF THE GUARDIAN FORCE!!
??
IT LIVES BY DRINKING MY BLOOD.
DO NOT WORRY. IT OBEYS ME.
THERE, THERE...
SEE... IT IS ALL RIGHT NOW.
YOU CAN... TALK TO IT?
NO, BUT IT UNDER-STANDS WHAT I SAY.
AND OF COURSE, THIS IS BECAUSE...
...IT KNOWS WHO I AM.

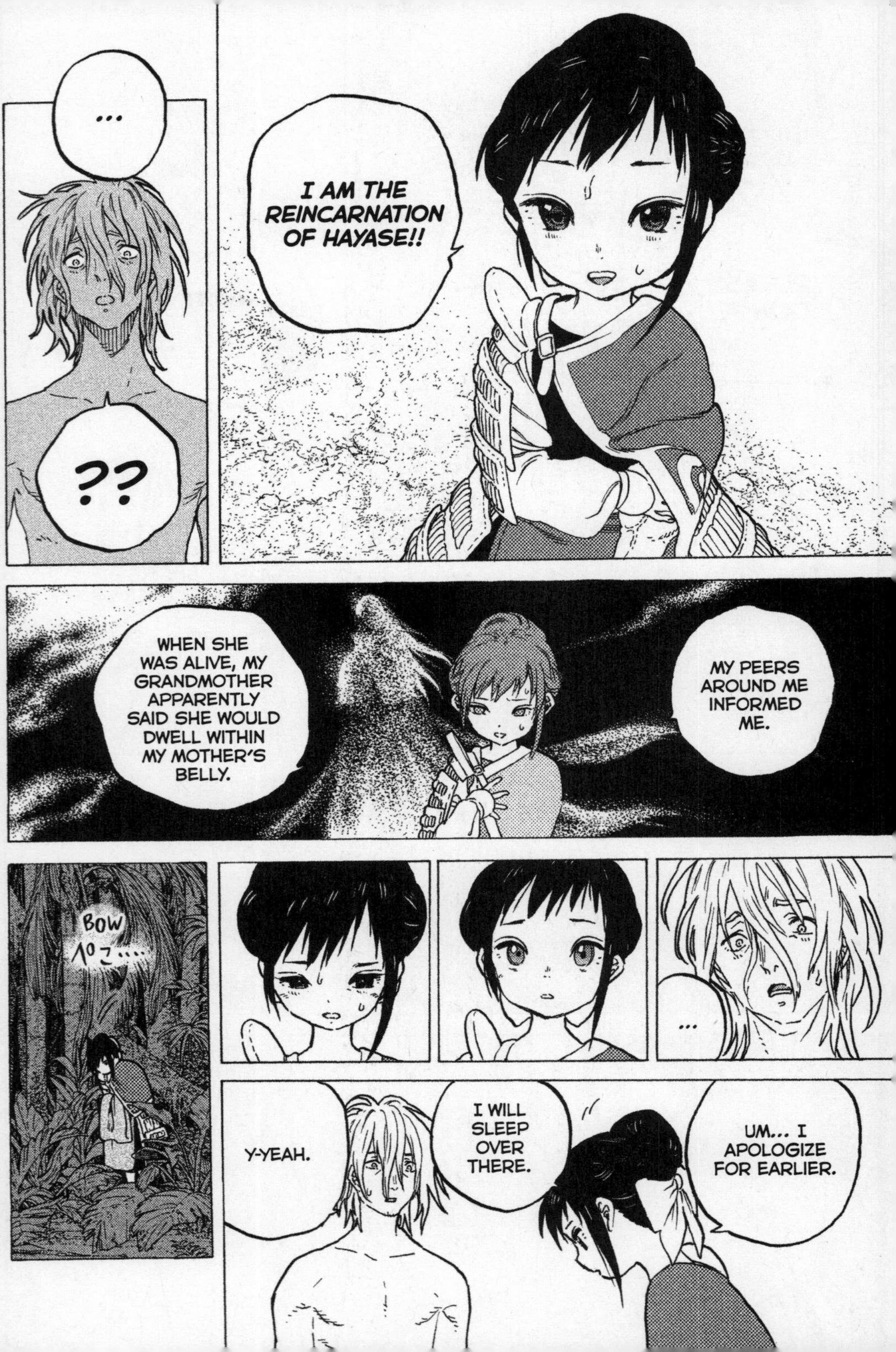
I AM THE REINCARNATION OF HAYASE!!
...
??
MY PEERS AROUND ME INFORMED ME.
WHEN SHE WAS ALIVE, MY GRANDMOTHER APPARENTLY SAID SHE WOULD DWELL WITHIN MY MOTHER'S BELLY.
...
UM... I APOLOGIZE FOR EARLIER.
I WILL SLEEP OVER THERE.
Y-YEAH.
BOW
ぺこ....

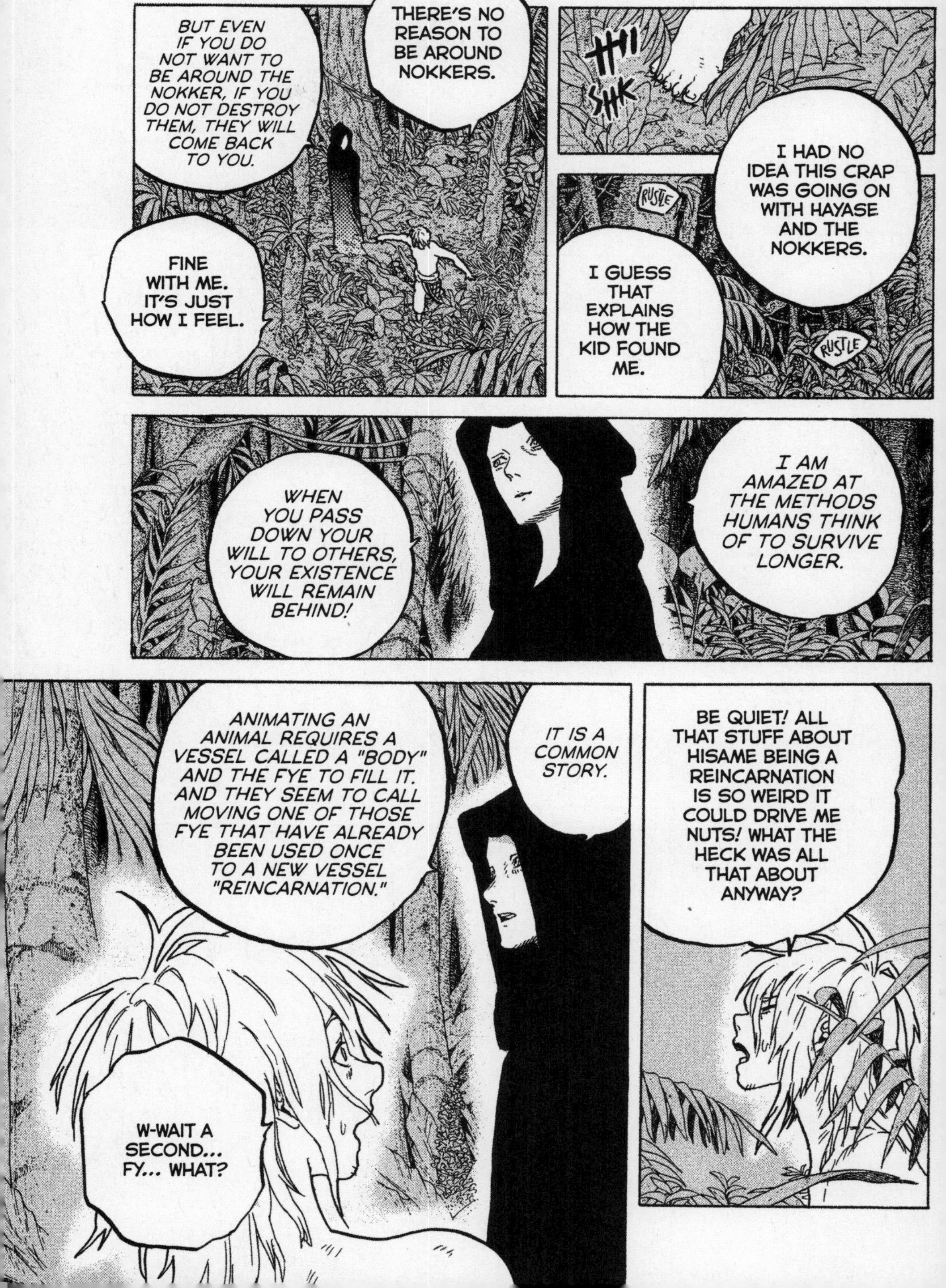
SHK
RUSTLE
I HAD NO IDEA THIS CRAP WAS GOING ON WITH HAYASE AND THE NOKKERS.
I GUESS THAT EXPLAINS HOW THE KID FOUND ME.
RUSTLE
THERE'S NO REASON TO BE AROUND NOKKERS.
BUT EVEN IF YOU DO NOT WANT TO BE AROUND THE NOKKER, IF YOU DO NOT DESTROY THEM, THEY WILL COME BACK TO YOU.
FINE WITH ME. IT'S JUST HOW I FEEL.
I AM AMAZED AT THE METHODS HUMANS THINK OF TO SURVIVE LONGER.
WHEN YOU PASS DOWN YOUR WILL TO OTHERS, YOUR EXISTENCE WILL REMAIN BEHIND!
BE QUIET! ALL THAT STUFF ABOUT HISAME BEING A REINCARNATION IS SO WEIRD IT COULD DRIVE ME NUTS! WHAT THE HECK WAS ALL THAT ABOUT ANYWAY?
IT IS A COMMON STORY.
ANIMATING AN ANIMAL REQUIRES A VESSEL CALLED A "BODY" AND THE FYE TO FILL IT. AND THEY SEEM TO CALL MOVING ONE OF THOSE FYE THAT HAVE ALREADY BEEN USED ONCE TO A NEW VESSEL "REINCARNATION."
W-WAIT A SECOND... FY... WHAT?

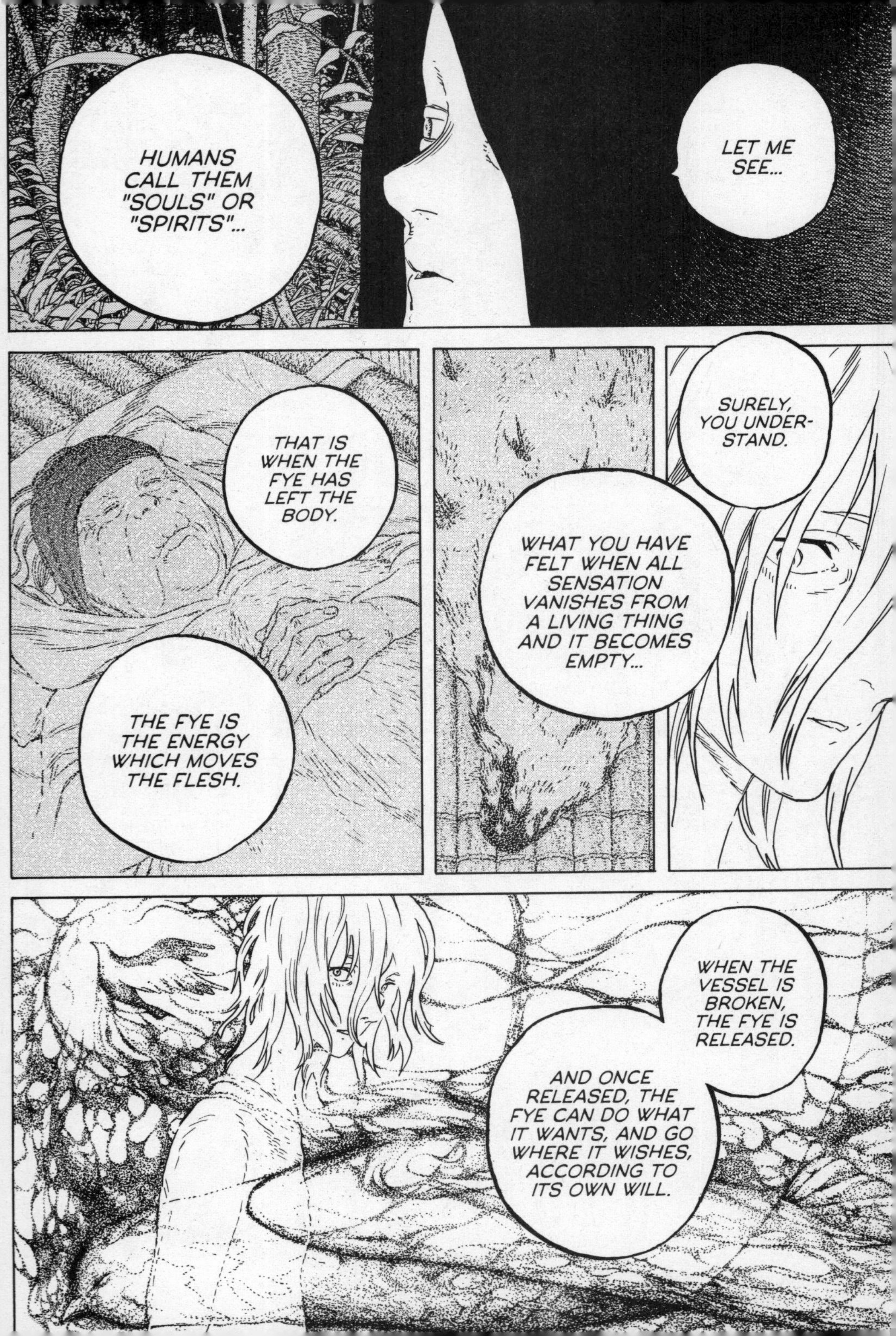
LET ME SEE...
HUMANS CALL THEM "SOULS" OR "SPIRITS"...
SURELY, YOU UNDERSTAND.
WHAT YOU HAVE FELT WHEN ALL SENSATION VANISHES FROM A LIVING THING AND IT BECOMES EMPTY...
THAT IS WHEN THE FYE HAS LEFT THE BODY.
THE FYE IS THE ENERGY WHICH MOVES THE FLESH.
WHEN THE VESSEL IS BROKEN, THE FYE IS RELEASED.
AND ONCE RELEASED, THE FYE CAN DO WHAT IT WANTS, AND GO WHERE IT WISHES, ACCORDING TO ITS OWN WILL.

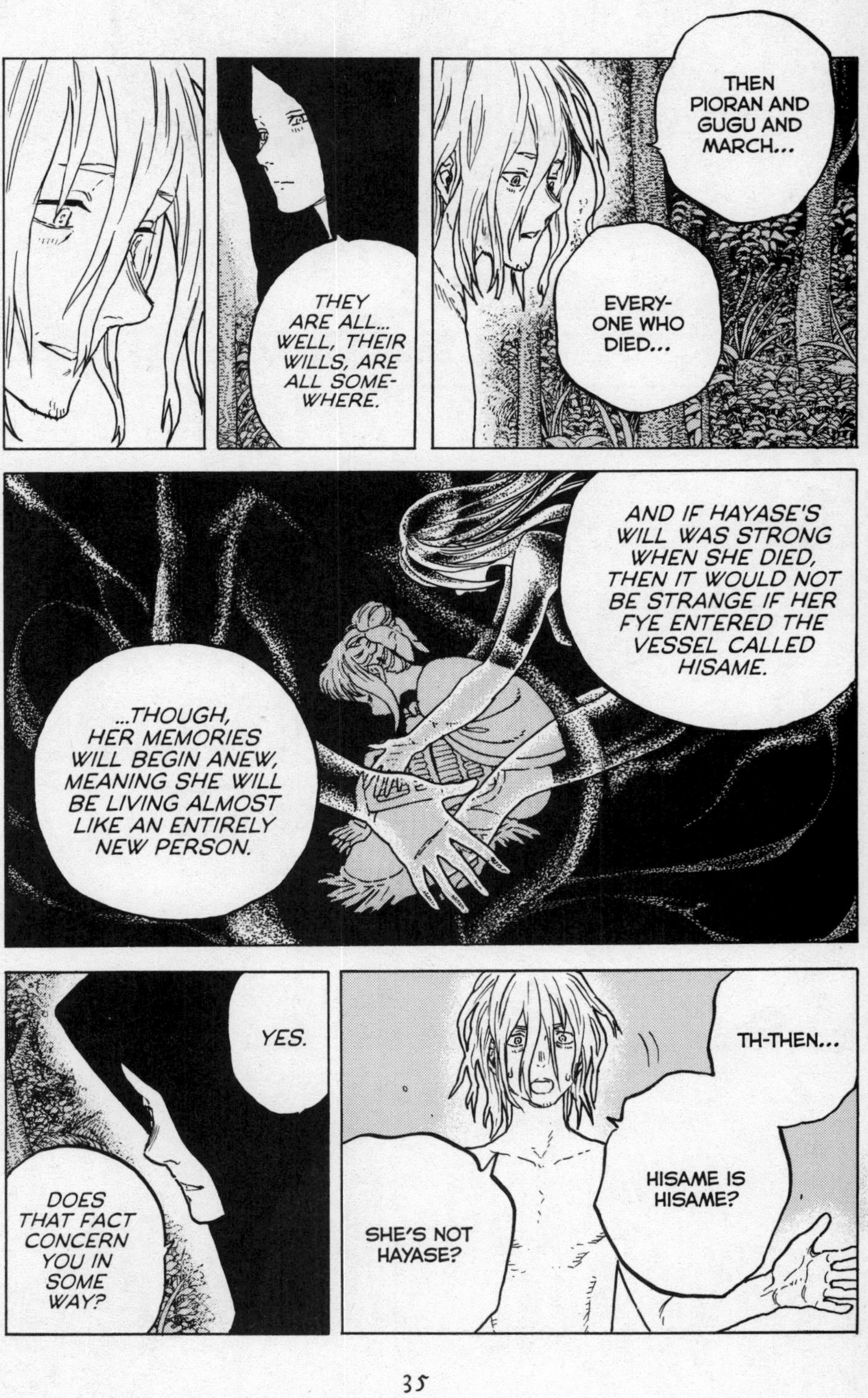
THEN PIORAN AND GUGU AND MARCH...
EVERY-ONE WHO DIED...
THEY ARE ALL... WELL, THEIR WILLS, ARE ALL SOME-WHERE.
AND IF HAYASE'S WILL WAS STRONG WHEN SHE DIED, THEN IT WOULD NOT BE STRANGE IF HER FYE ENTERED THE VESSEL CALLED HISAME.
...THOUGH, HER MEMORIES WILL BEGIN ANEW, MEANING SHE WILL BE LIVING ALMOST LIKE AN ENTIRELY NEW PERSON.
TH-THEN...
HISAME IS HISAME?
SHE'S NOT HAYASE?
YES.
DOES THAT FACT CONCERN YOU IN SOME WAY?

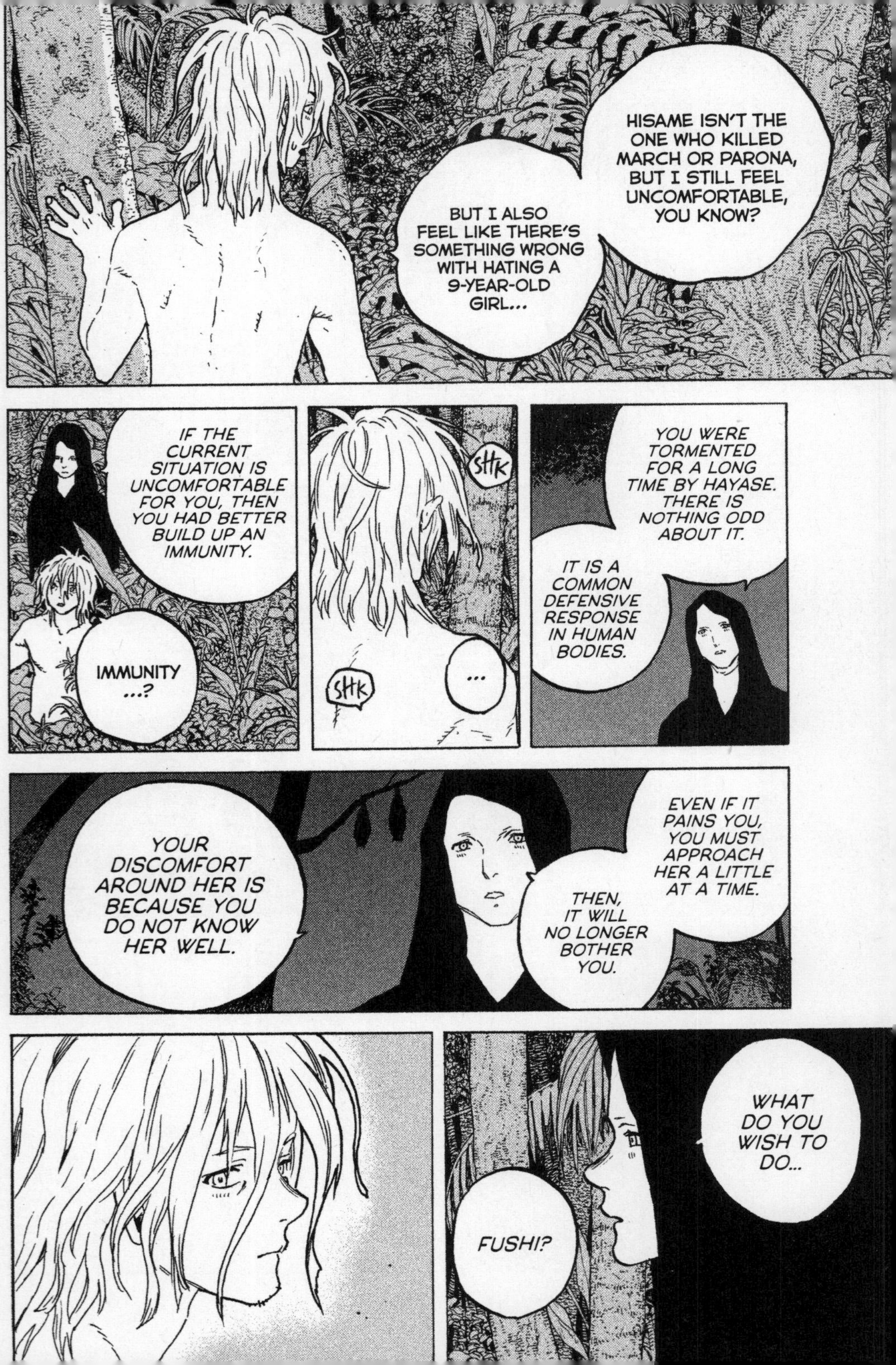
HISAME ISN'T THE ONE WHO KILLED MARCH OR PARONA, BUT I STILL FEEL UNCOMFORTABLE, YOU KNOW?
BUT I ALSO FEEL LIKE THERE'S SOMETHING WRONG WITH HATING A 9-YEAR-OLD GIRL...
YOU WERE TORMENTED FOR A LONG TIME BY HAYASE. THERE IS NOTHING ODD ABOUT IT.
IT IS A COMMON DEFENSIVE RESPONSE IN HUMAN BODIES.
SHK
...
SHK
IF THE CURRENT SITUATION IS UNCOMFORTABLE FOR YOU, THEN YOU HAD BETTER BUILD UP AN IMMUNITY.
IMMUNITY ...?
EVEN IF IT PAINS YOU, YOU MUST APPROACH HER A LITTLE AT A TIME.
THEN, IT WILL NO LONGER BOTHER YOU.
YOUR DISCOMFORT AROUND HER IS BECAUSE YOU DO NOT KNOW HER WELL.
WHAT DO YOU WISH TO DO...
FUSHI?

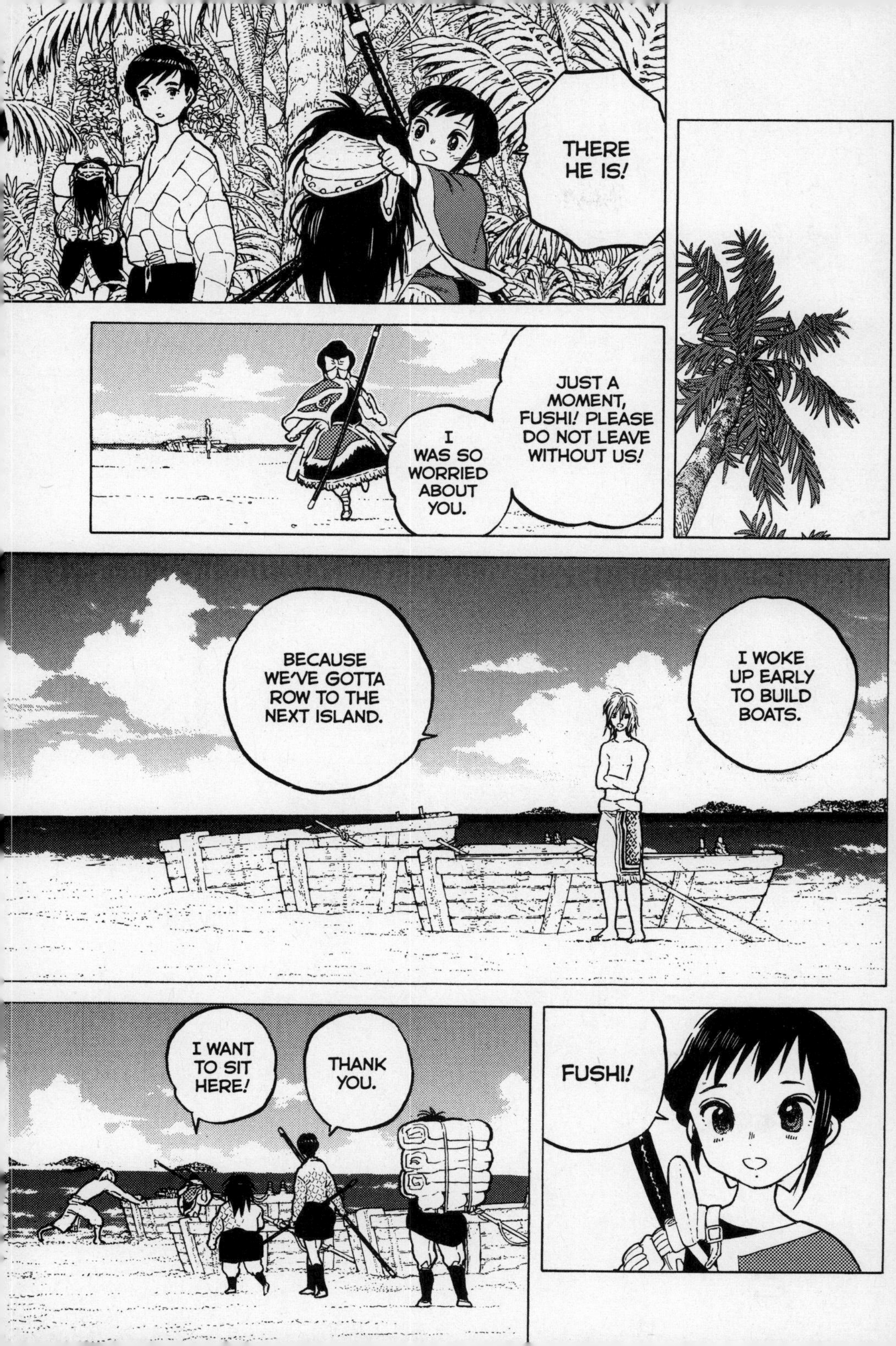
THERE HE IS!
JUST A MOMENT, FUSHI! PLEASE DO NOT LEAVE WITHOUT US!
I WAS SO WORRIED ABOUT YOU.
I WOKE UP EARLY TO BUILD BOATS.
BECAUSE WE'VE GOTTA ROW TO THE NEXT ISLAND.
FUSHI!
THANK YOU.
I WANT TO SIT HERE!

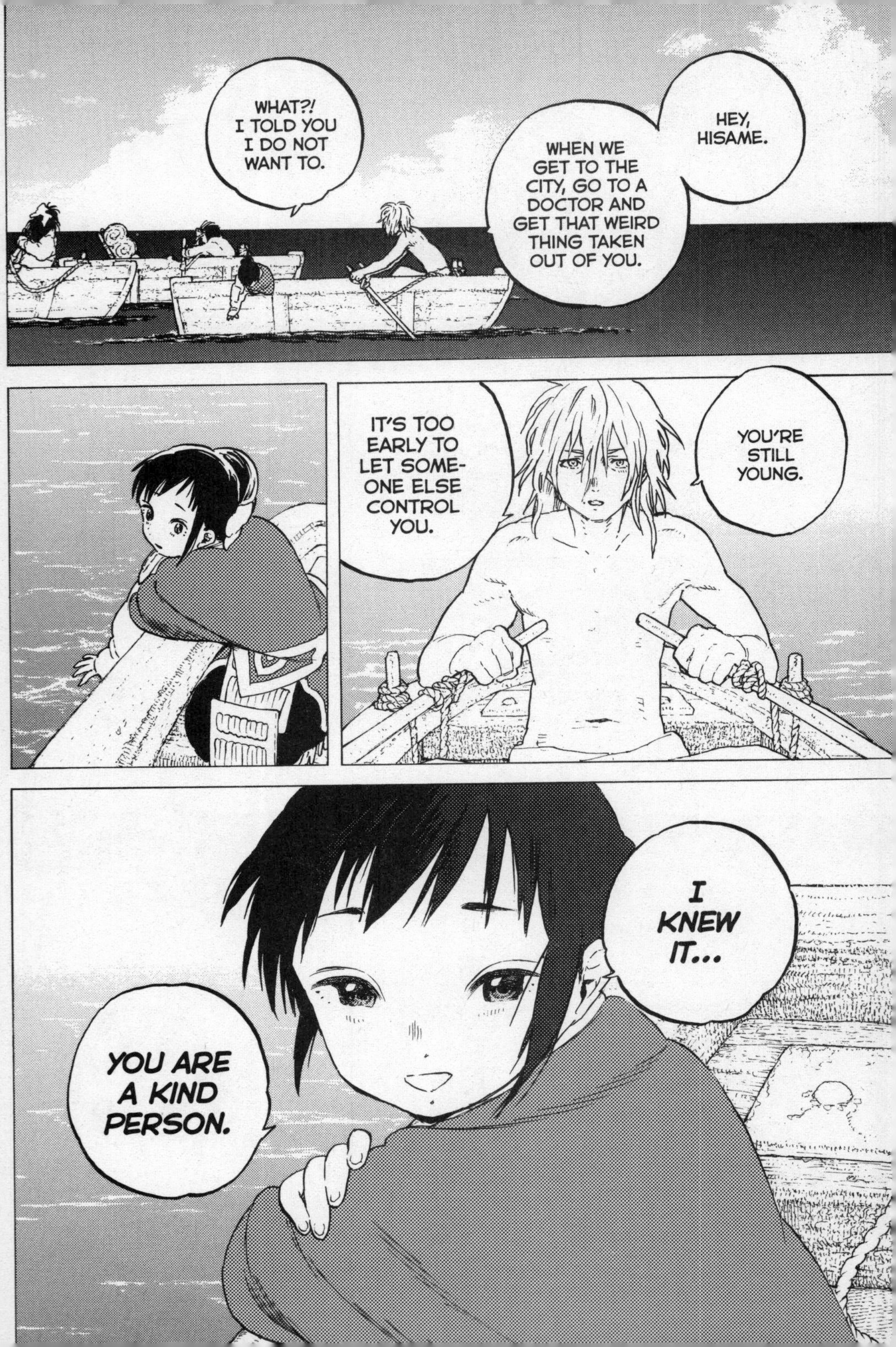
HEY, HISAME.
WHEN WE GET TO THE CITY, GO TO A DOCTOR AND GET THAT WEIRD THING TAKEN OUT OF YOU.
WHAT?! I TOLD YOU I DO NOT WANT TO.
YOU'RE STILL YOUNG.
IT'S TOO EARLY TO LET SOME-ONE ELSE CONTROL YOU.
I KNEW IT...
YOU ARE A KIND PERSON.

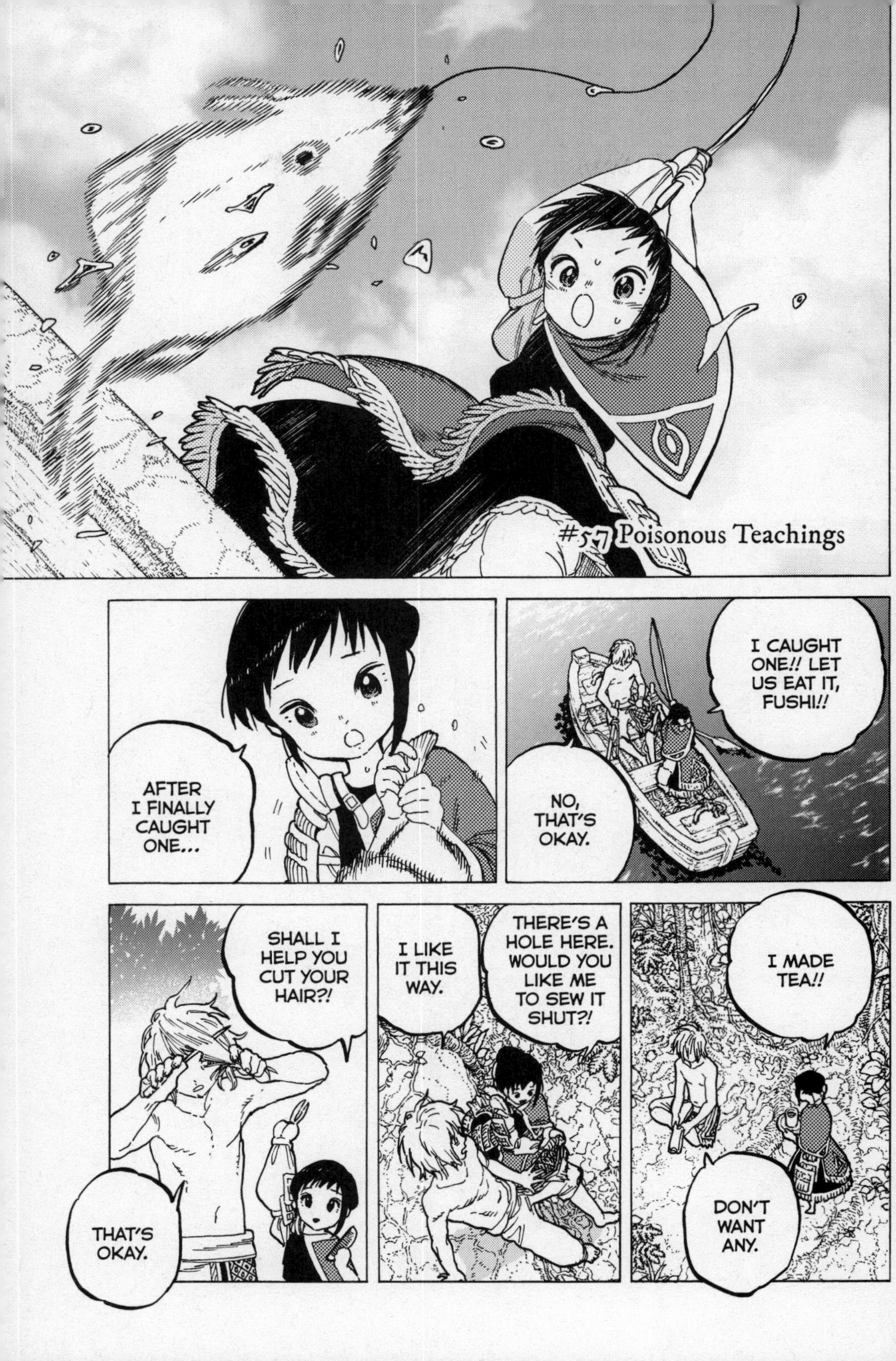
#57 Poisonous Teachings
I CAUGHT ONE!! LET US EAT IT, FUSHI!!
NO, THAT'S OKAY.
AFTER I FINALLY CAUGHT ONE...
I MADE TEA!!
DON'T WANT ANY.
THERE'S A HOLE HERE. WOULD YOU LIKE ME TO SEW IT SHUT?!
I LIKE IT THIS WAY.
SHALL I HELP YOU CUT YOUR HAIR?!
THAT'S OKAY.

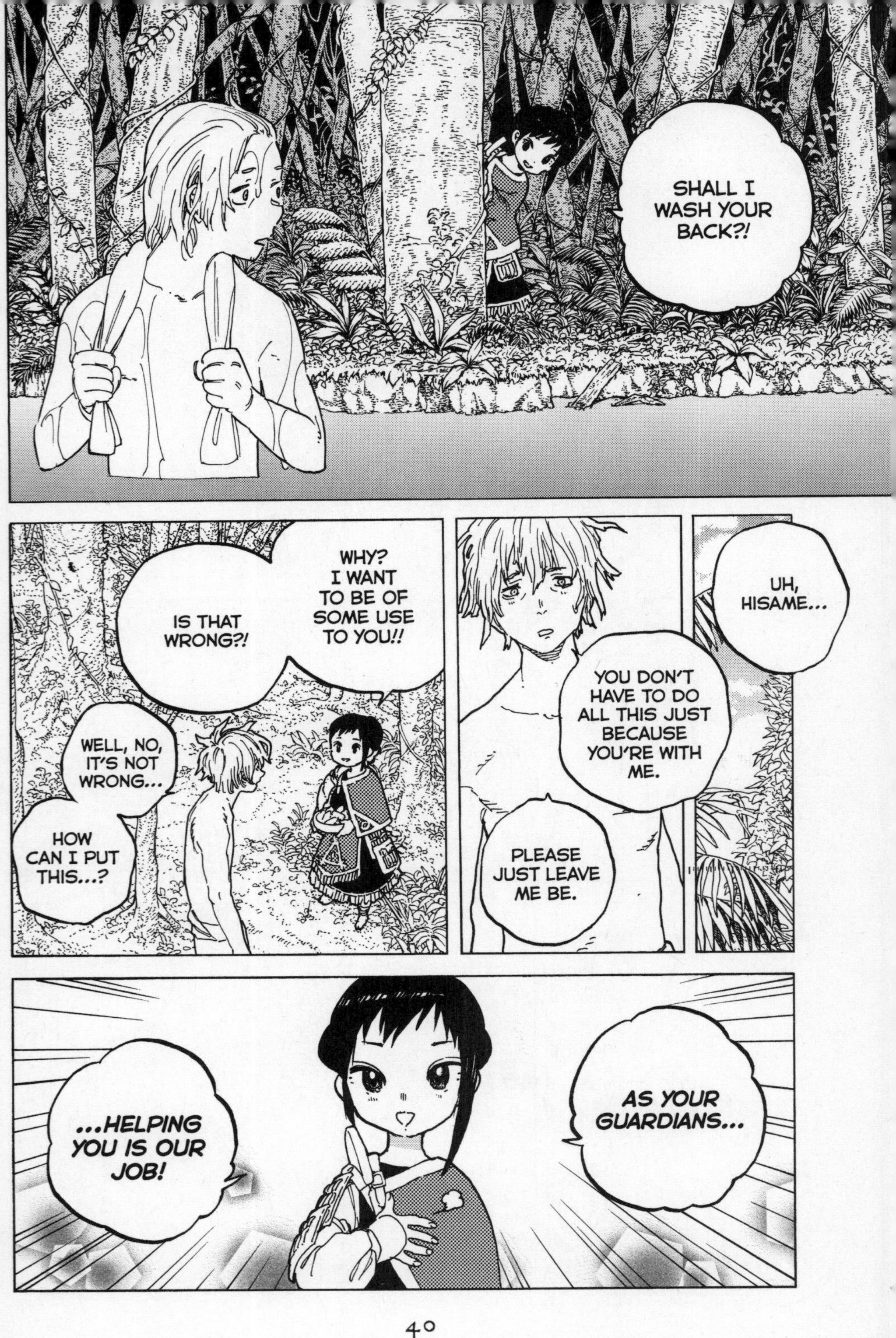
SHALL I WASH YOUR BACK?!
UH, HISAME...
YOU DON'T HAVE TO DO ALL THIS JUST BECAUSE YOU'RE WITH ME.
PLEASE JUST LEAVE ME BE.
WHY? I WANT TO BE OF SOME USE TO YOU!!
IS THAT WRONG?!
WELL, NO, IT'S NOT WRONG...
HOW CAN I PUT THIS...?
AS YOUR GUARDIANS...
...HELPING YOU IS OUR JOB!

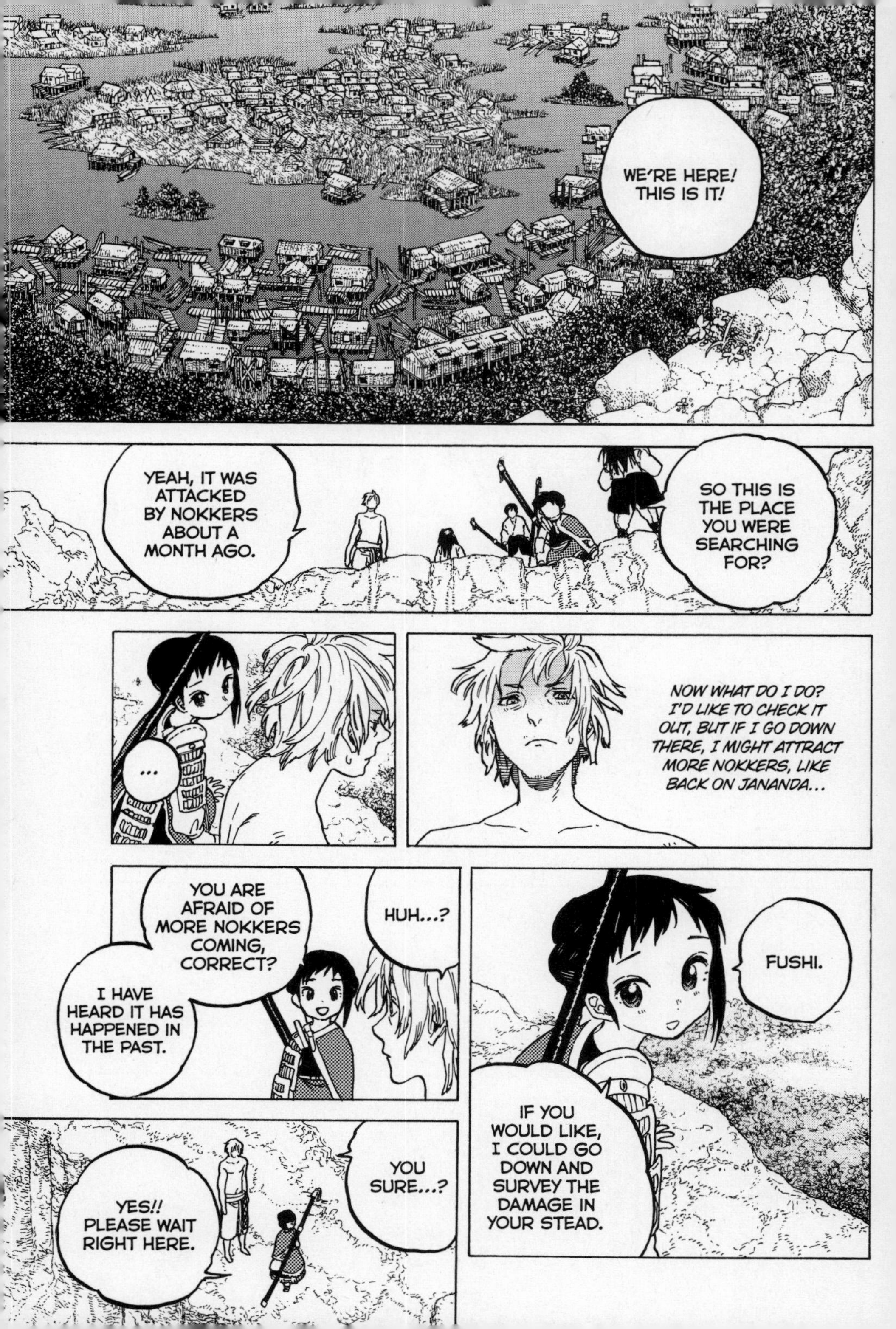
WE'RE HERE! THIS IS IT!
SO THIS IS THE PLACE YOU WERE SEARCHING FOR?
YEAH, IT WAS ATTACKED BY NOKKERS ABOUT A MONTH AGO.
NOW WHAT DO I DO? I'D LIKE TO CHECK IT OUT, BUT IF I GO DOWN THERE, I MIGHT ATTRACT MORE NOKKERS, LIKE BACK ON JANANDA...
...
FUSHI.
IF YOU WOULD LIKE, I COULD GO DOWN AND SURVEY THE DAMAGE IN YOUR STEAD.
HUH...?
YOU ARE AFRAID OF MORE NOKKERS COMING, CORRECT?
I HAVE HEARD IT HAS HAPPENED IN THE PAST.
YOU SURE...?
YES!! PLEASE WAIT RIGHT HERE.

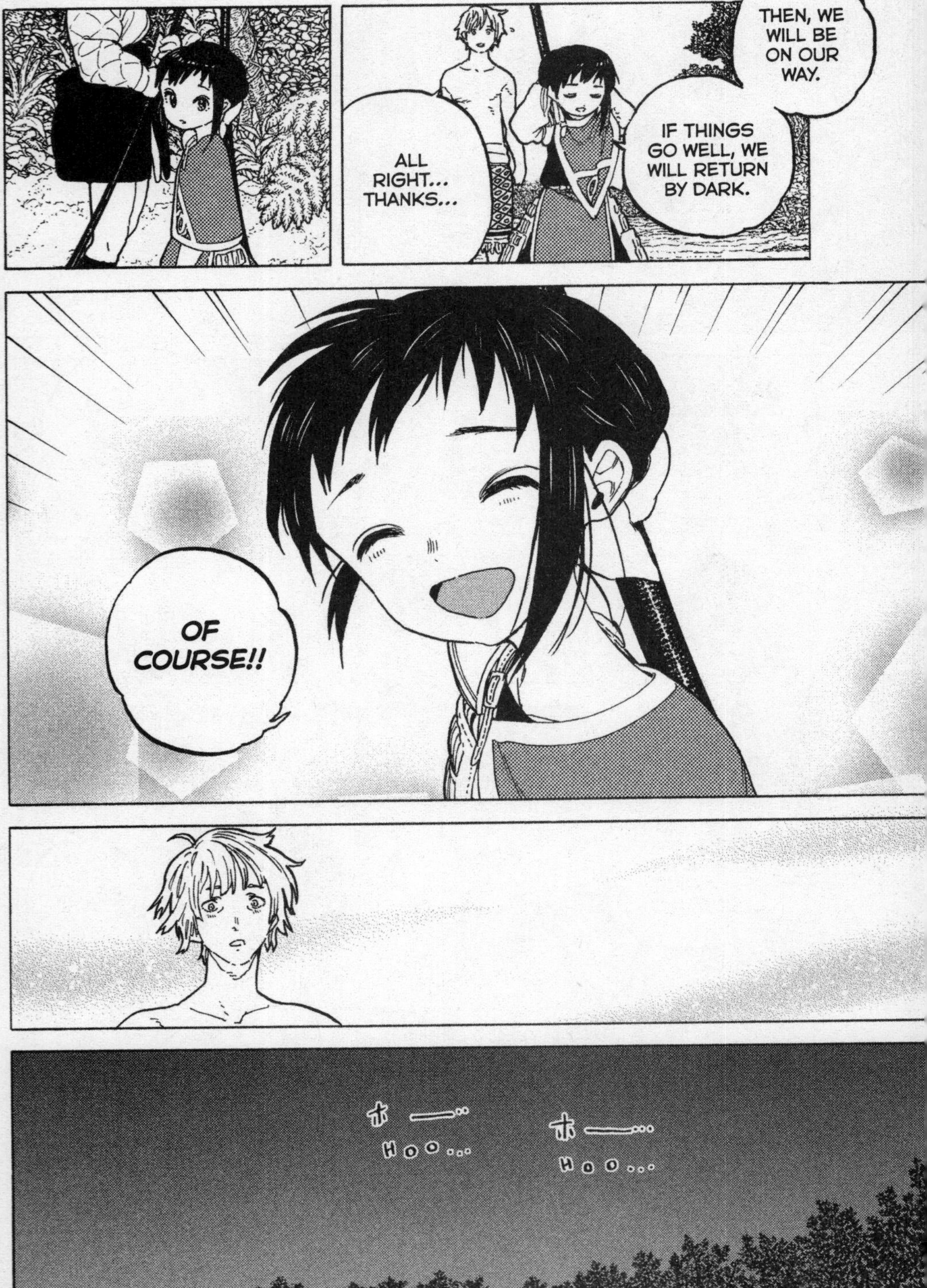
THEN, WE WILL BE ON OUR WAY.
IF THINGS GO WELL, WE WILL RETURN BY DARK.
ALL RIGHT... THANKS...
OF COURSE!!
ホー…
HOO...
ホー…
HOO...

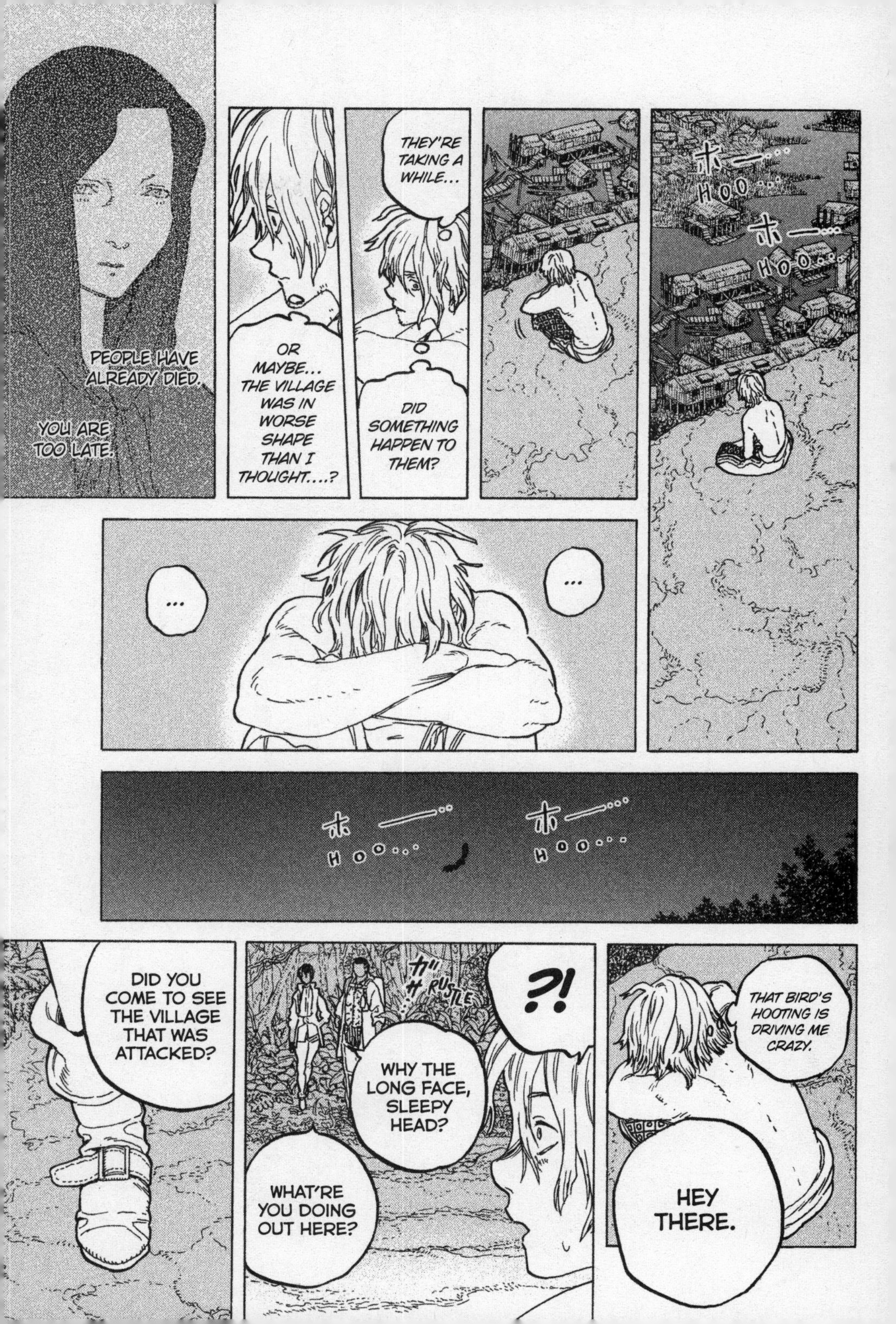
ホー…
HOO…
ホー…
HOO…
THEY'RE TAKING A WHILE…
DID SOMETHING HAPPEN TO THEM?
OR MAYBE… THE VILLAGE WAS IN WORSE SHAPE THAN I THOUGHT….?
PEOPLE HAVE ALREADY DIED.
YOU ARE TOO LATE.
…
…
ホー…
HOO…
ホー…
HOO…
THAT BIRD'S HOOTING IS DRIVING ME CRAZY.
HEY THERE.
?!
RUSTLE
WHY THE LONG FACE, SLEEPY HEAD?
WHAT'RE YOU DOING OUT HERE?
DID YOU COME TO SEE THE VILLAGE THAT WAS ATTACKED?

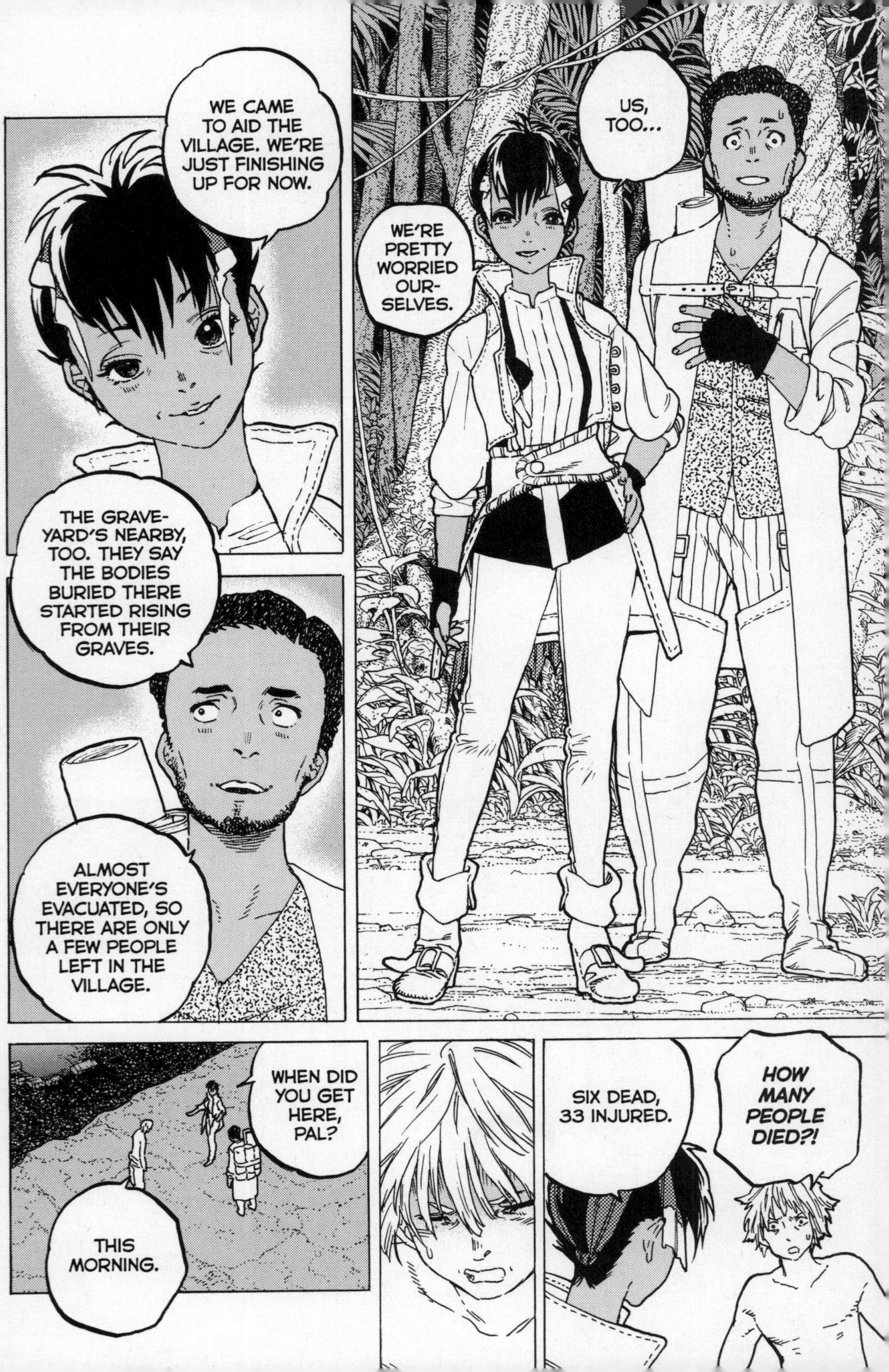
US, TOO...
WE'RE PRETTY WORRIED OUR-SELVES.
WE CAME TO AID THE VILLAGE. WE'RE JUST FINISHING UP FOR NOW.
THE GRAVE-YARD'S NEARBY, TOO. THEY SAY THE BODIES BURIED THERE STARTED RISING FROM THEIR GRAVES.
ALMOST EVERYONE'S EVACUATED, SO THERE ARE ONLY A FEW PEOPLE LEFT IN THE VILLAGE.
HOW MANY PEOPLE DIED?!
SIX DEAD, 33 INJURED.
WHEN DID YOU GET HERE, PAL?
THIS MORNING.

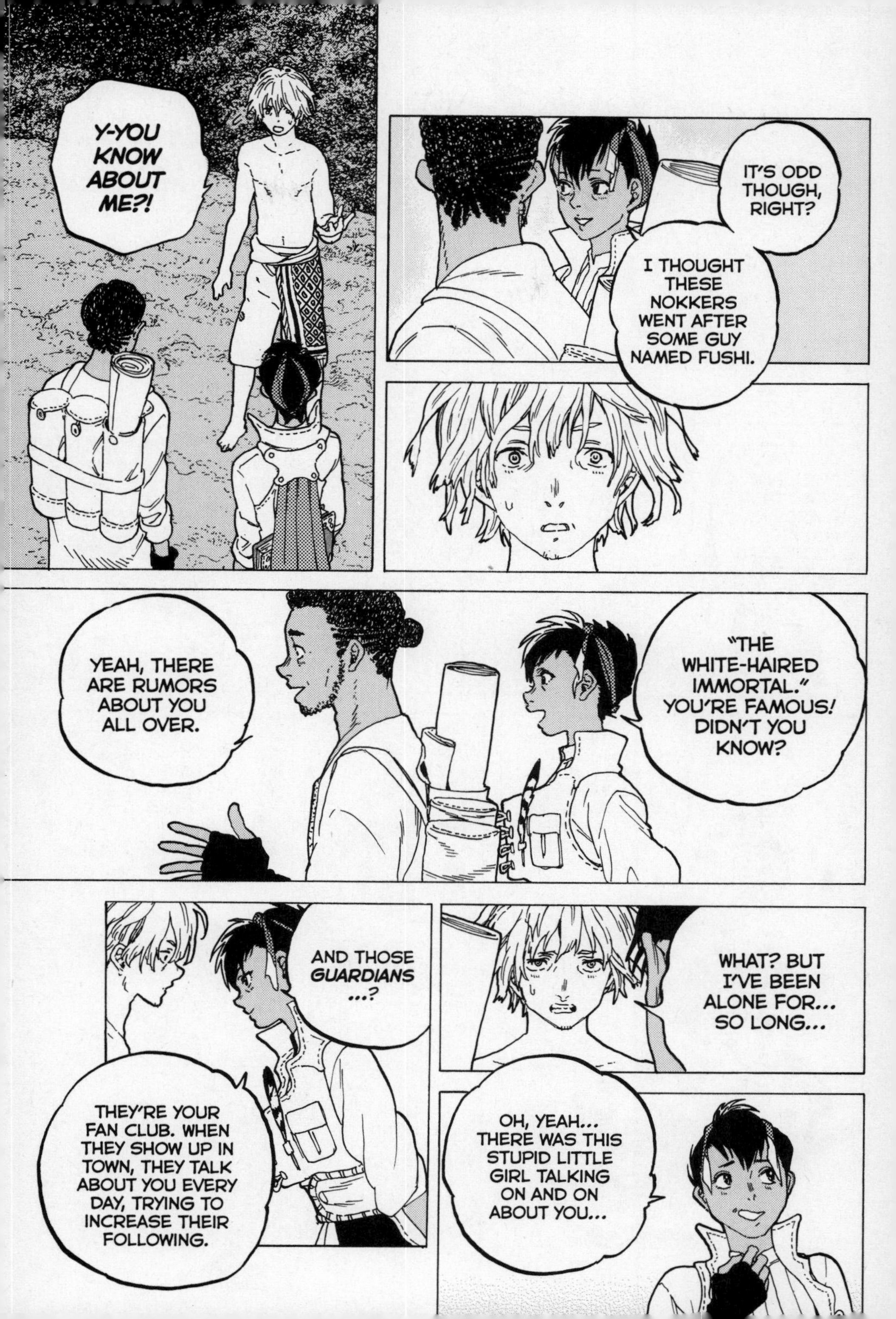
IT'S ODD THOUGH, RIGHT?
I THOUGHT THESE NOKKERS WENT AFTER SOME GUY NAMED FUSHI.
Y-YOU KNOW ABOUT ME?!
"THE WHITE-HAIRED IMMORTAL." YOU'RE FAMOUS! DIDN'T YOU KNOW?
YEAH, THERE ARE RUMORS ABOUT YOU ALL OVER.
WHAT? BUT I'VE BEEN ALONE FOR... SO LONG...
OH, YEAH... THERE WAS THIS STUPID LITTLE GIRL TALKING ON AND ON ABOUT YOU...
AND THOSE *GUARDIANS*...?
THEY'RE YOUR FAN CLUB. WHEN THEY SHOW UP IN TOWN, THEY TALK ABOUT YOU EVERY DAY, TRYING TO INCREASE THEIR FOLLOWING.

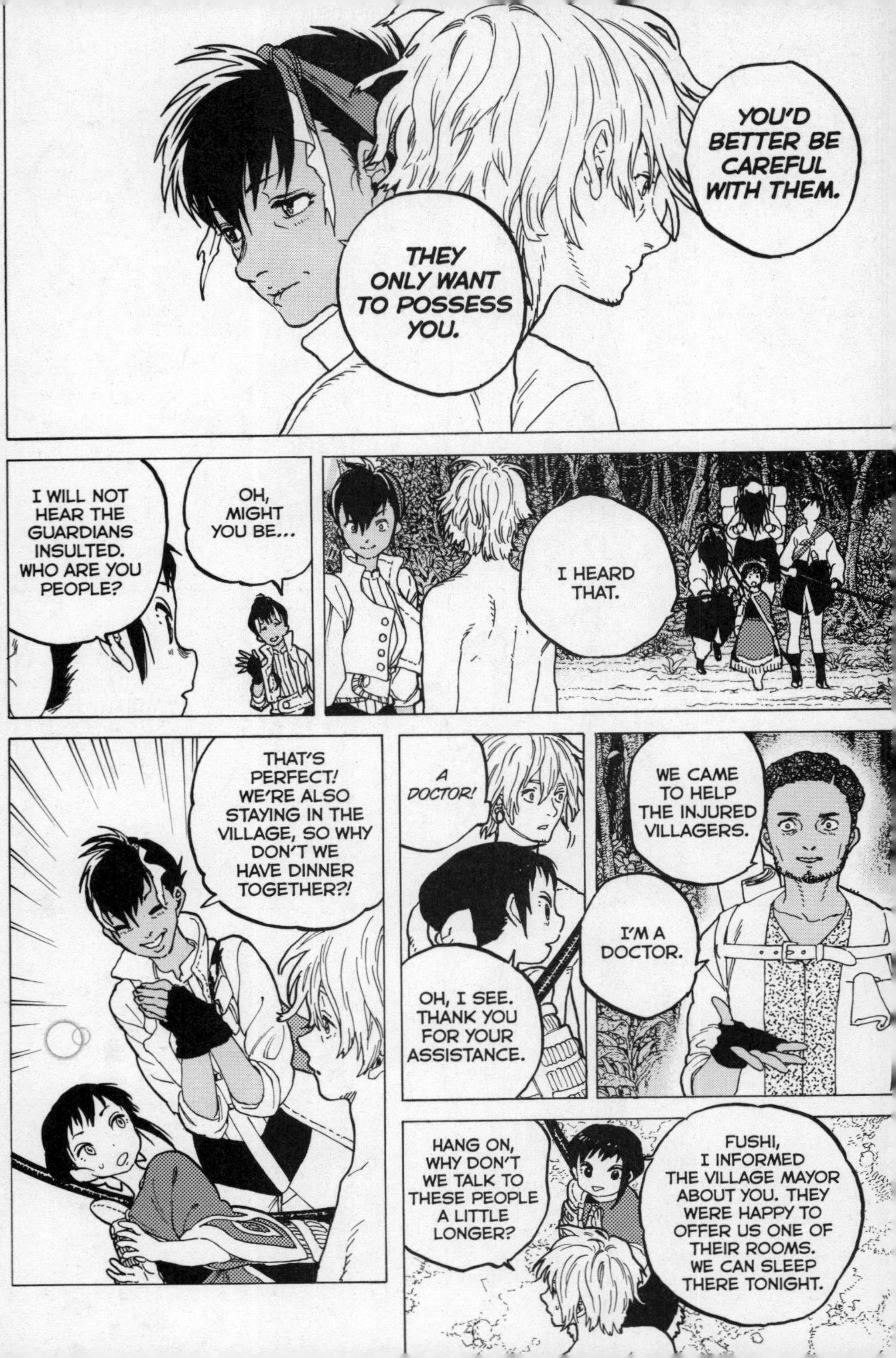
YOU'D BETTER BE CAREFUL WITH THEM.
THEY ONLY WANT TO POSSESS YOU.
I HEARD THAT.
OH, MIGHT YOU BE...
I WILL NOT HEAR THE GUARDIANS INSULTED. WHO ARE YOU PEOPLE?
WE CAME TO HELP THE INJURED VILLAGERS.
I'M A DOCTOR.
A DOCTOR!
OH, I SEE. THANK YOU FOR YOUR ASSISTANCE.
FUSHI, I INFORMED THE VILLAGE MAYOR ABOUT YOU. THEY WERE HAPPY TO OFFER US ONE OF THEIR ROOMS. WE CAN SLEEP THERE TONIGHT.
HANG ON, WHY DON'T WE TALK TO THESE PEOPLE A LITTLE LONGER?
THAT'S PERFECT! WE'RE ALSO STAYING IN THE VILLAGE, SO WHY DON'T WE HAVE DINNER TOGETHER?!

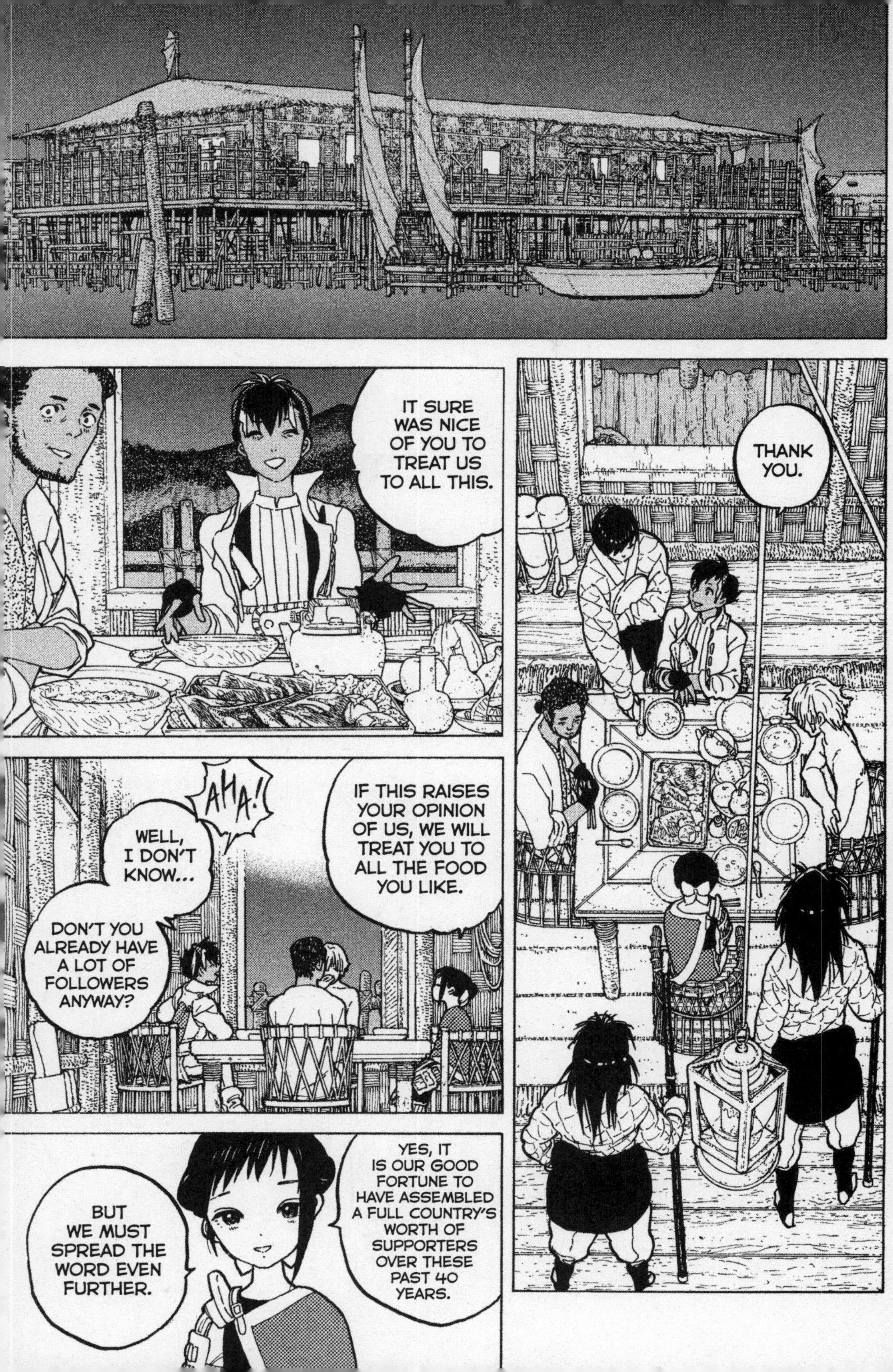
THANK YOU.
IT SURE WAS NICE OF YOU TO TREAT US TO ALL THIS.
IF THIS RAISES YOUR OPINION OF US, WE WILL TREAT YOU TO ALL THE FOOD YOU LIKE.
AHA!
WELL, I DON'T KNOW...
DON'T YOU ALREADY HAVE A LOT OF FOLLOWERS ANYWAY?
YES, IT IS OUR GOOD FORTUNE TO HAVE ASSEMBLED A FULL COUNTRY'S WORTH OF SUPPORTERS OVER THESE PAST 40 YEARS.
BUT WE MUST SPREAD THE WORD EVEN FURTHER.

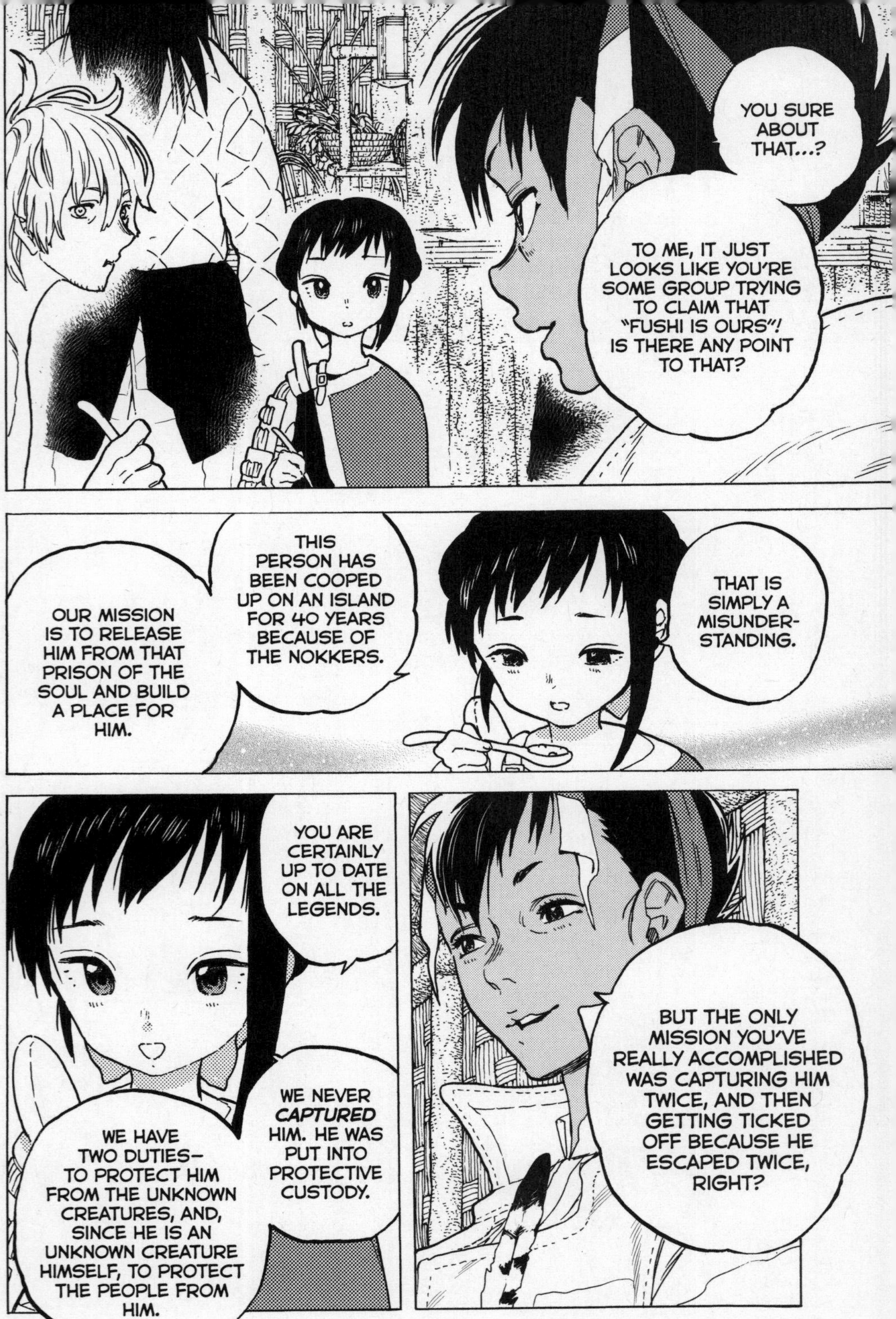
YOU SURE ABOUT THAT...?
TO ME, IT JUST LOOKS LIKE YOU'RE SOME GROUP TRYING TO CLAIM THAT "FUSHI IS OURS"! IS THERE ANY POINT TO THAT?
THAT IS SIMPLY A MISUNDER-STANDING.
THIS PERSON HAS BEEN COOPED UP ON AN ISLAND FOR 40 YEARS BECAUSE OF THE NOKKERS.
OUR MISSION IS TO RELEASE HIM FROM THAT PRISON OF THE SOUL AND BUILD A PLACE FOR HIM.
BUT THE ONLY MISSION YOU'VE REALLY ACCOMPLISHED WAS CAPTURING HIM TWICE, AND THEN GETTING TICKED OFF BECAUSE HE ESCAPED TWICE, RIGHT?
YOU ARE CERTAINLY UP TO DATE ON ALL THE LEGENDS.
WE NEVER *CAPTURED* HIM. HE WAS PUT INTO PROTECTIVE CUSTODY.
WE HAVE TWO DUTIES— TO PROTECT HIM FROM THE UNKNOWN CREATURES, AND, SINCE HE IS AN UNKNOWN CREATURE HIMSELF, TO PROTECT THE PEOPLE FROM HIM.

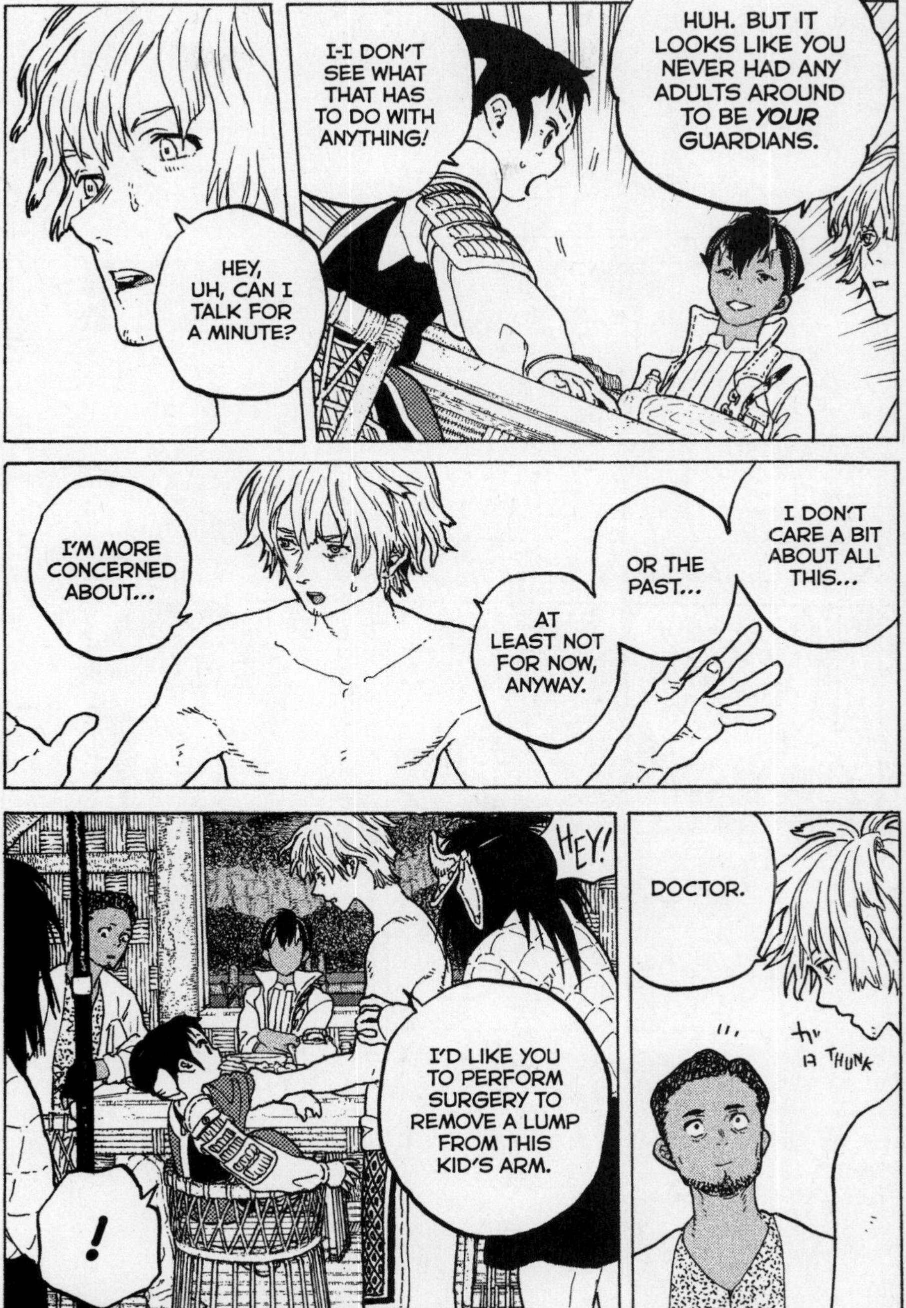
HUH. BUT IT LOOKS LIKE YOU NEVER HAD ANY ADULTS AROUND TO BE *YOUR* GUARDIANS.
I-I DON'T SEE WHAT THAT HAS TO DO WITH ANYTHING!
HEY, UH, CAN I TALK FOR A MINUTE?
I DON'T CARE A BIT ABOUT ALL THIS...
OR THE PAST...
AT LEAST NOT FOR NOW, ANYWAY.
I'M MORE CONCERNED ABOUT...
DOCTOR.
THUNK
HEY!
I'D LIKE YOU TO PERFORM SURGERY TO REMOVE A LUMP FROM THIS KID'S ARM.
!

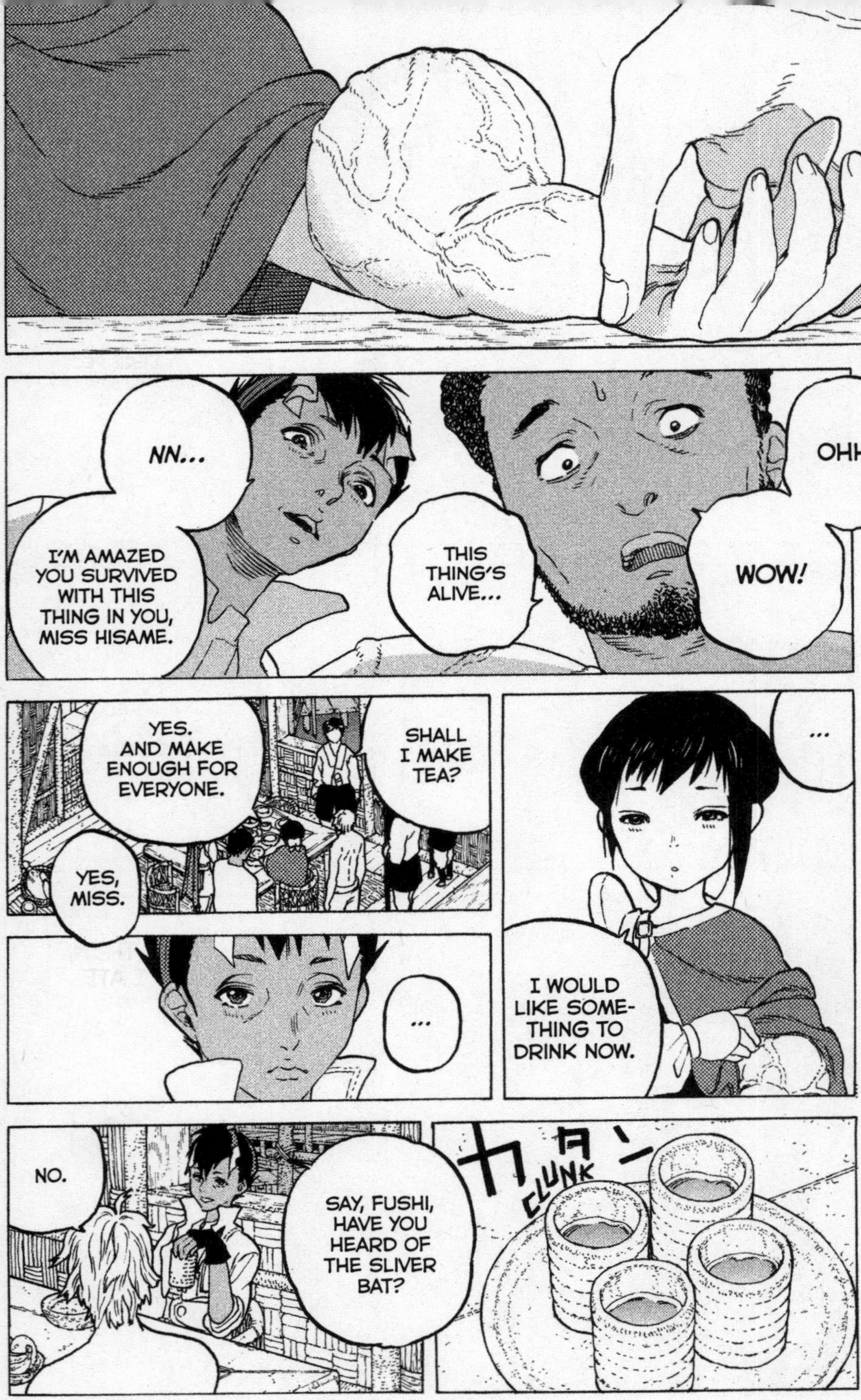
OHH!
WOW!
THIS THING'S ALIVE...
NN...
I'M AMAZED YOU SURVIVED WITH THIS THING IN YOU, MISS HISAME.
...
I WOULD LIKE SOME-THING TO DRINK NOW.
SHALL I MAKE TEA?
YES. AND MAKE ENOUGH FOR EVERYONE.
YES, MISS.
...
カタン
CLUNK
SAY, FUSHI, HAVE YOU HEARD OF THE SLIVER BAT?
NO.

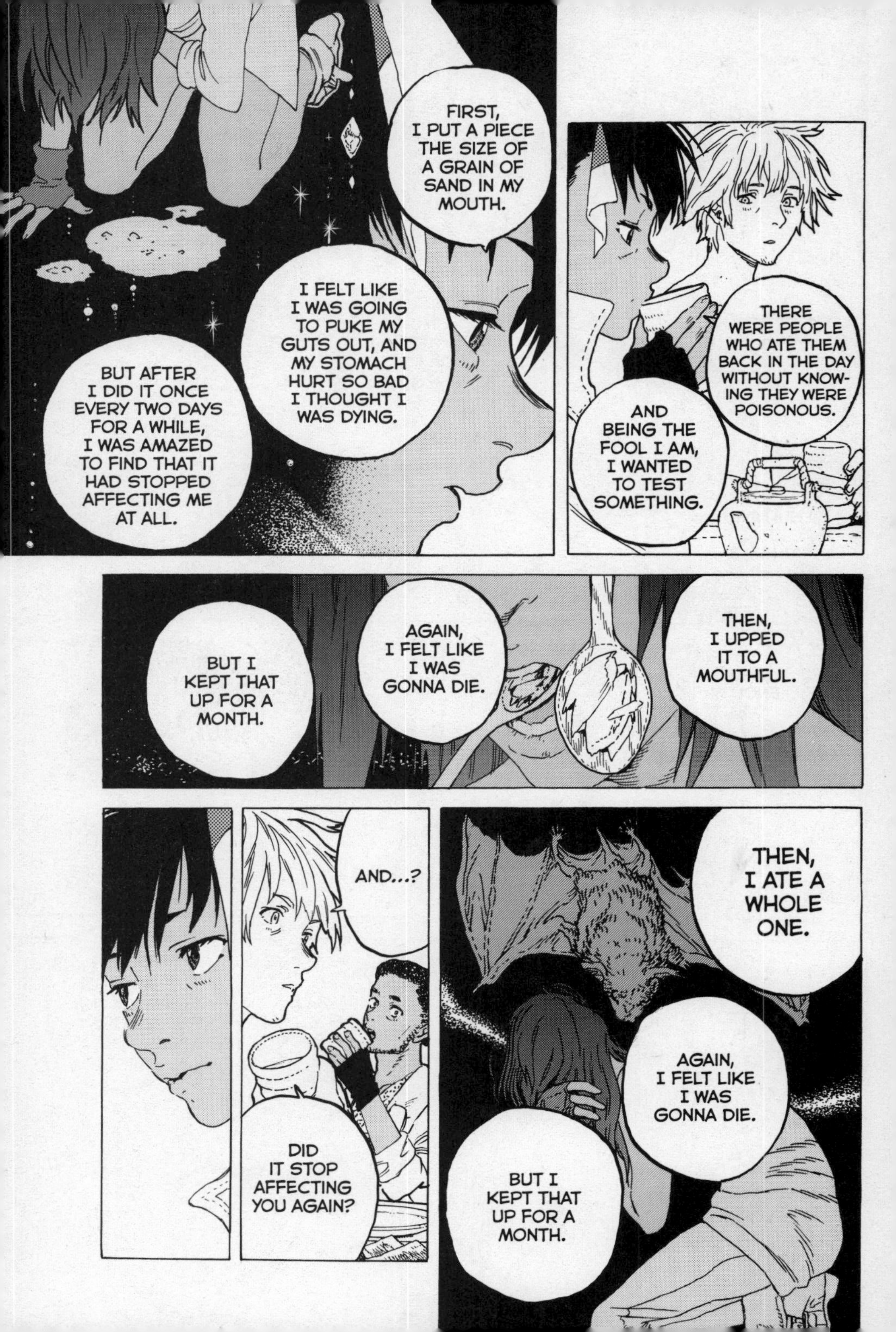
THERE WERE PEOPLE WHO ATE THEM BACK IN THE DAY WITHOUT KNOW-ING THEY WERE POISONOUS.
AND BEING THE FOOL I AM, I WANTED TO TEST SOMETHING.
FIRST, I PUT A PIECE THE SIZE OF A GRAIN OF SAND IN MY MOUTH.
I FELT LIKE I WAS GOING TO PUKE MY GUTS OUT, AND MY STOMACH HURT SO BAD I THOUGHT I WAS DYING.
BUT AFTER I DID IT ONCE EVERY TWO DAYS FOR A WHILE, I WAS AMAZED TO FIND THAT IT HAD STOPPED AFFECTING ME AT ALL.
THEN, I UPPED IT TO A MOUTHFUL.
AGAIN, I FELT LIKE I WAS GONNA DIE.
BUT I KEPT THAT UP FOR A MONTH.
THEN, I ATE A WHOLE ONE.
AGAIN, I FELT LIKE I WAS GONNA DIE.
BUT I KEPT THAT UP FOR A MONTH.
AND...?
DID IT STOP AFFECTING YOU AGAIN?

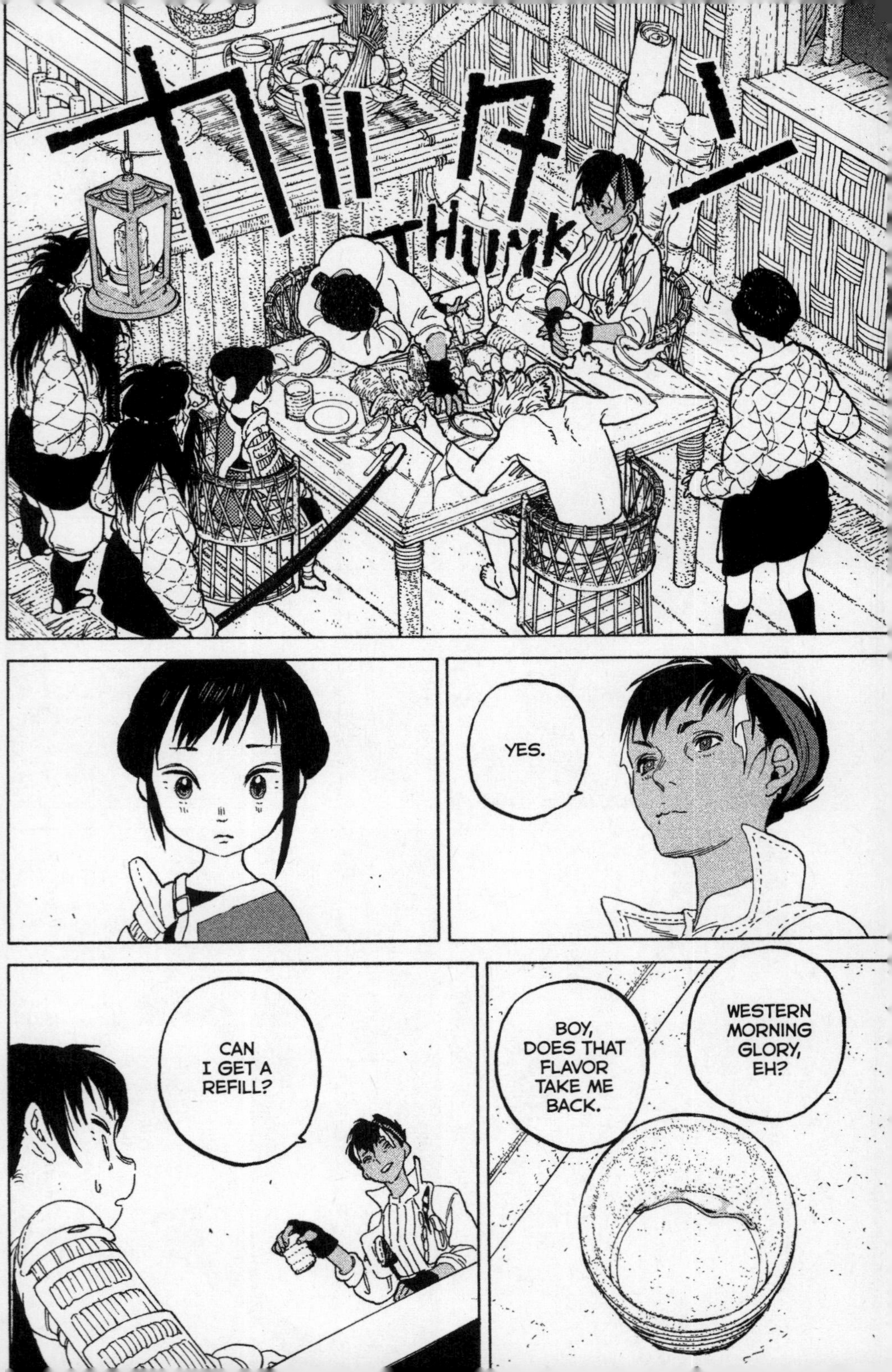
THUNK
YES.
WESTERN MORNING GLORY, EH?
BOY, DOES THAT FLAVOR TAKE ME BACK.
CAN I GET A REFILL?

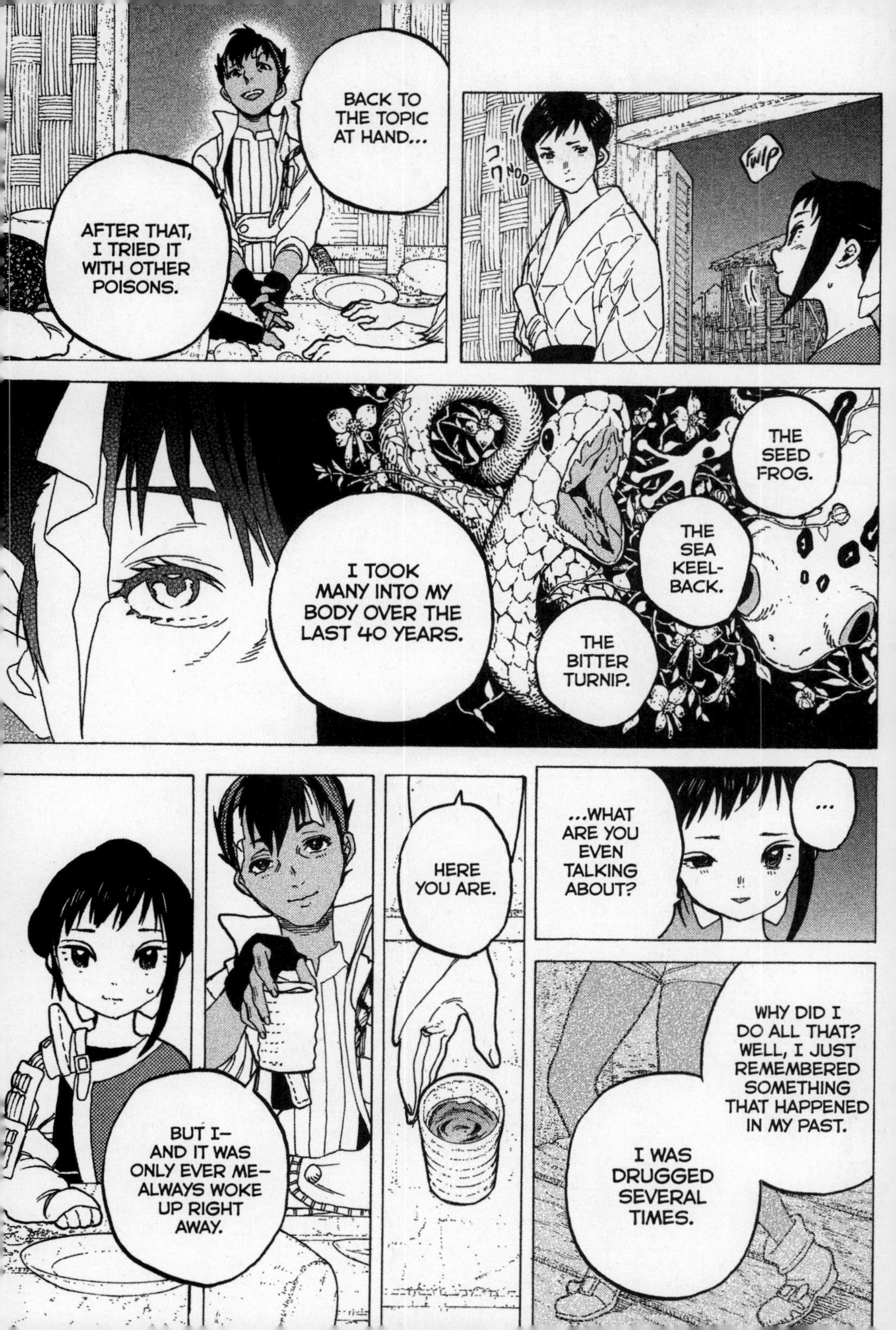
FWIP
NOD
BACK TO THE TOPIC AT HAND...
AFTER THAT, I TRIED IT WITH OTHER POISONS.
THE SEED FROG.
THE SEA KEEL-BACK.
THE BITTER TURNIP.
I TOOK MANY INTO MY BODY OVER THE LAST 40 YEARS.
...
...WHAT ARE YOU EVEN TALKING ABOUT?
WHY DID I DO ALL THAT? WELL, I JUST REMEMBERED SOMETHING THAT HAPPENED IN MY PAST.
I WAS DRUGGED SEVERAL TIMES.
HERE YOU ARE.
BUT I— AND IT WAS ONLY EVER ME— ALWAYS WOKE UP RIGHT AWAY.

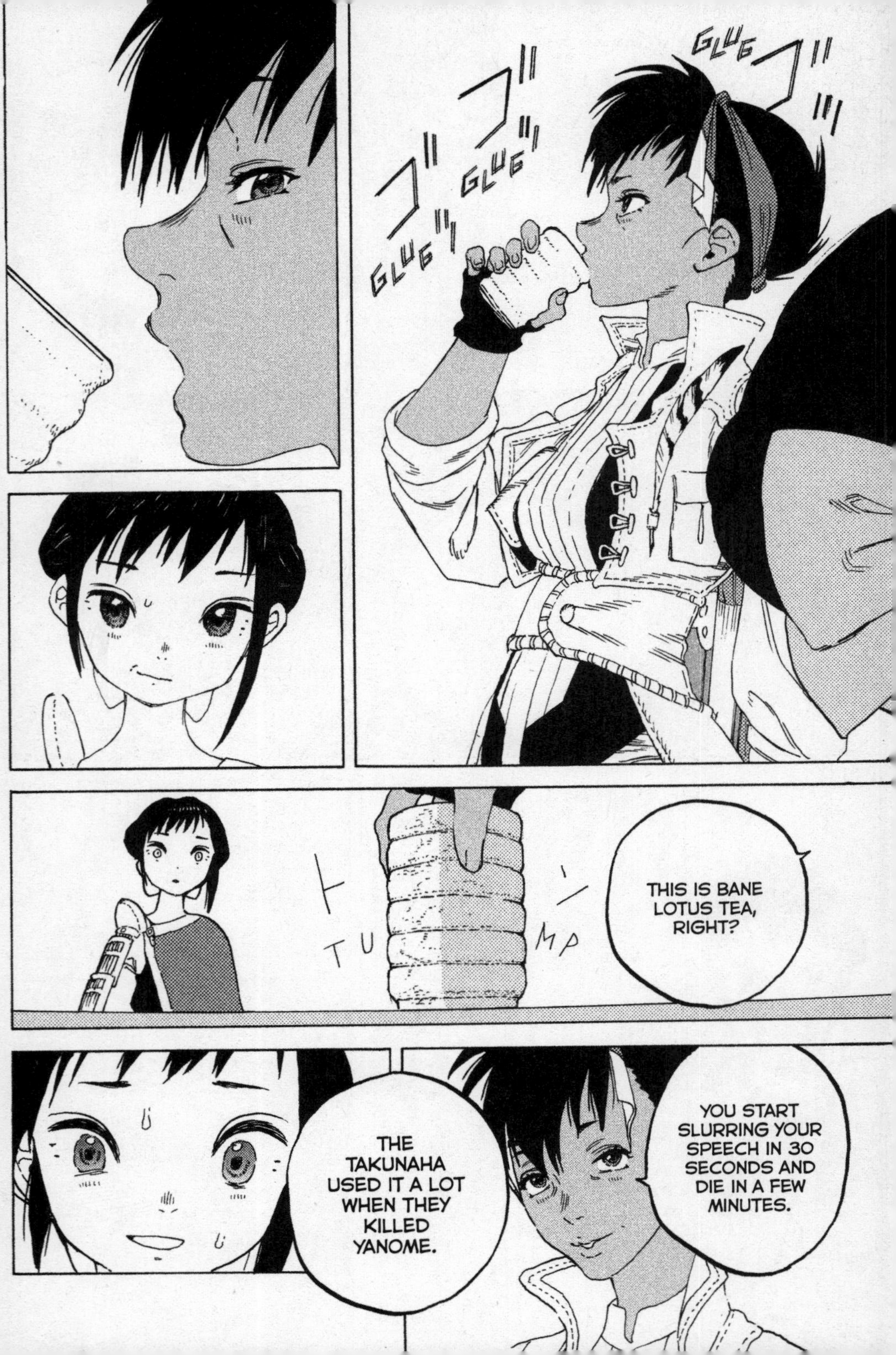
GLUG
GLUG
GLUG
TUMP
THIS IS BANE LOTUS TEA, RIGHT?
YOU START SLURRING YOUR SPEECH IN 30 SECONDS AND DIE IN A FEW MINUTES.
THE TAKUNAHA USED IT A LOT WHEN THEY KILLED YANOME.

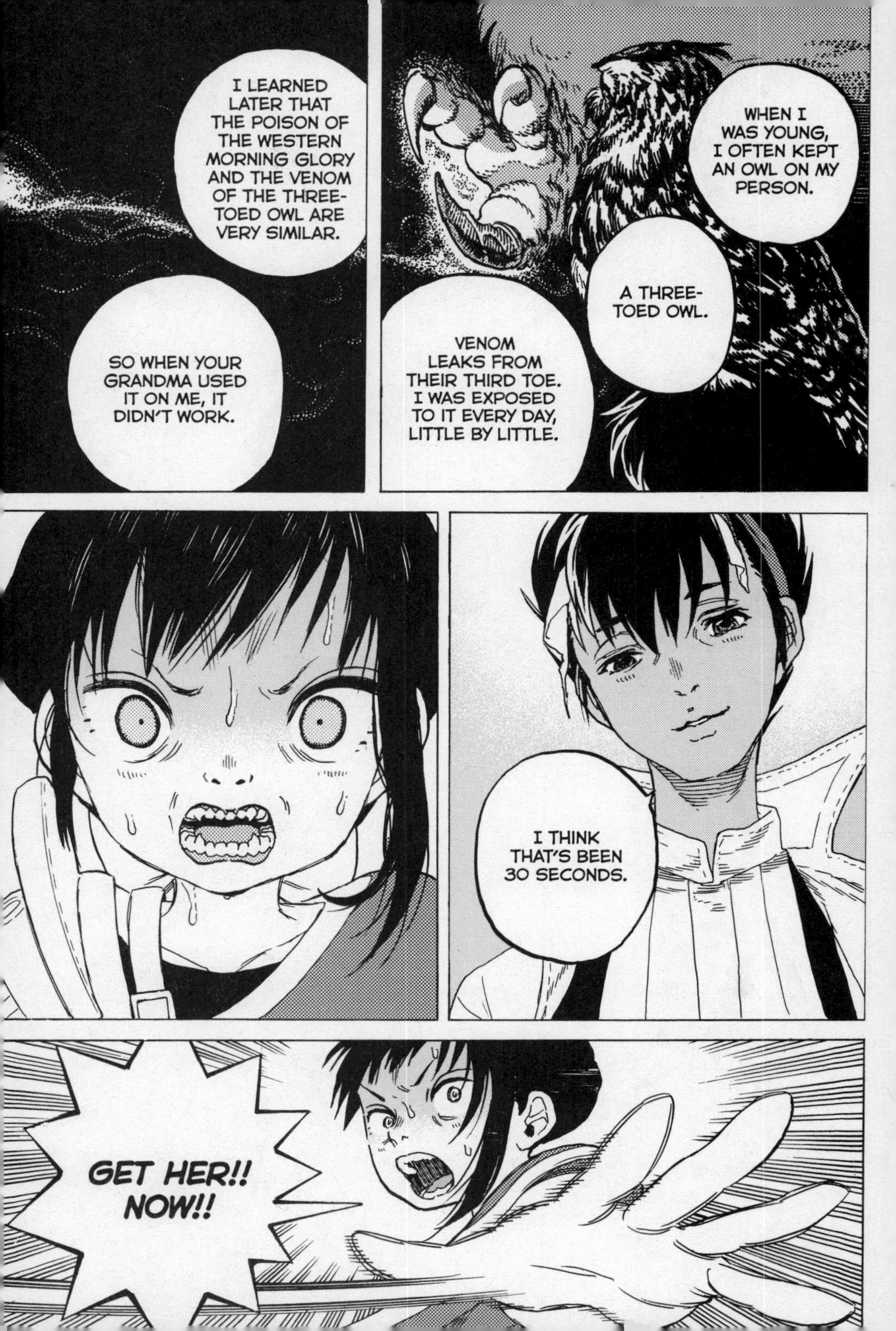
WHEN I WAS YOUNG, I OFTEN KEPT AN OWL ON MY PERSON.
A THREE-TOED OWL.
VENOM LEAKS FROM THEIR THIRD TOE. I WAS EXPOSED TO IT EVERY DAY, LITTLE BY LITTLE.
I LEARNED LATER THAT THE POISON OF THE WESTERN MORNING GLORY AND THE VENOM OF THE THREE-TOED OWL ARE VERY SIMILAR.
SO WHEN YOUR GRANDMA USED IT ON ME, IT DIDN'T WORK.
I THINK THAT'S BEEN 30 SECONDS.
GET HER!! NOW!!

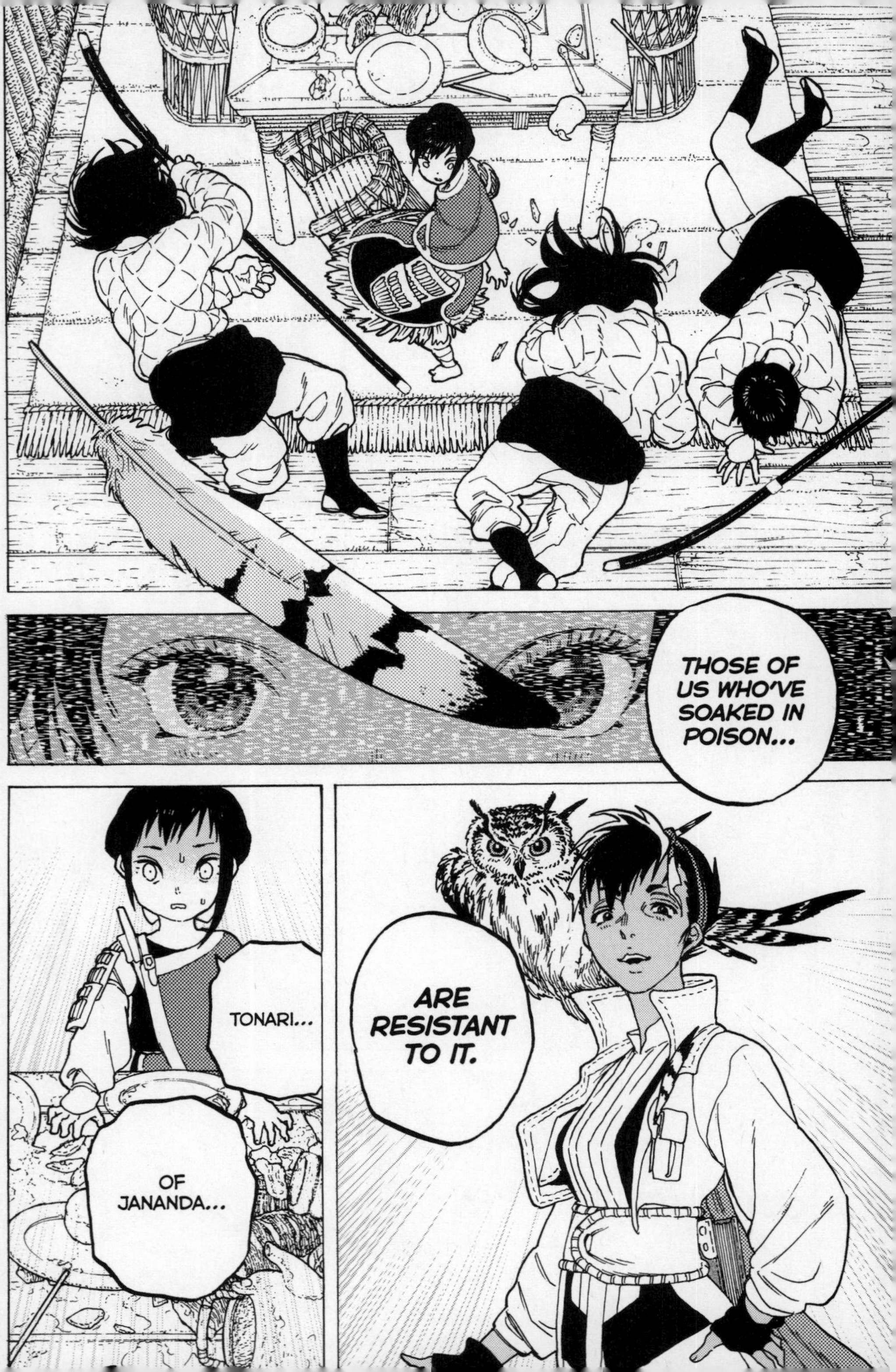
THOSE OF US WHO'VE SOAKED IN POISON...
ARE RESISTANT TO IT.
TONARI...
OF JANANDA...

#58 The Left Hand of Vengeance

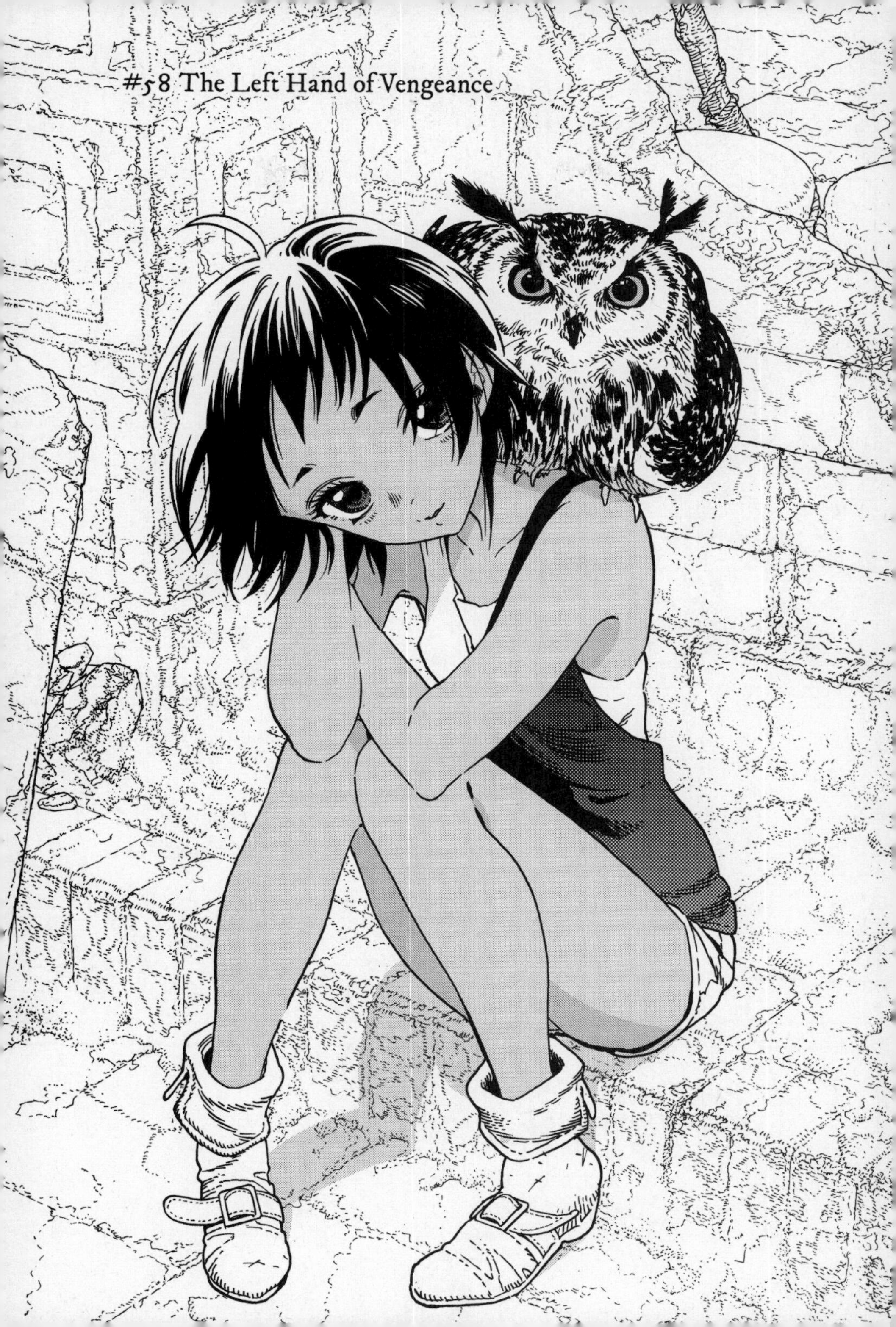

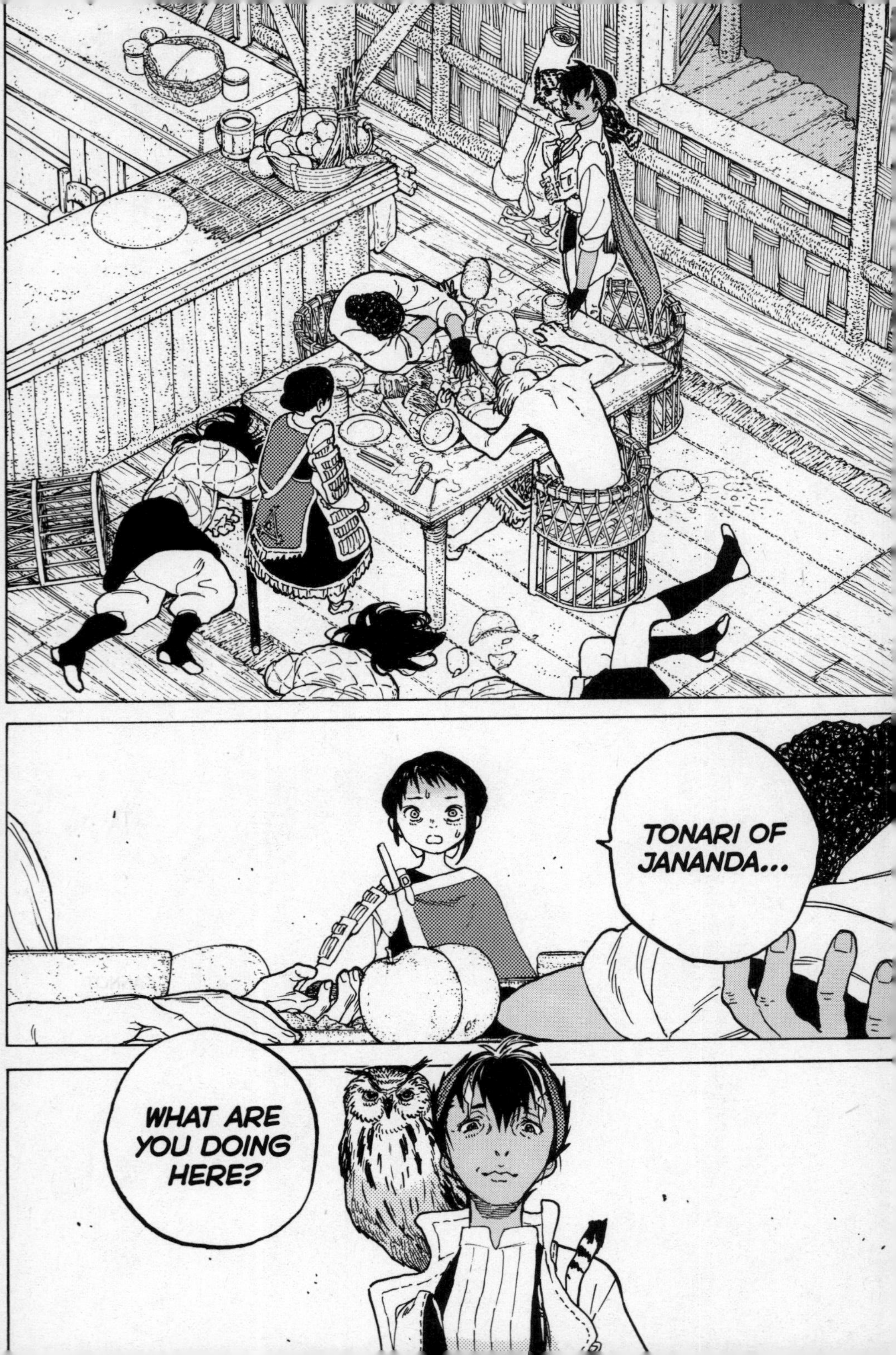
TONARI OF JANANDA...
WHAT ARE YOU DOING HERE?

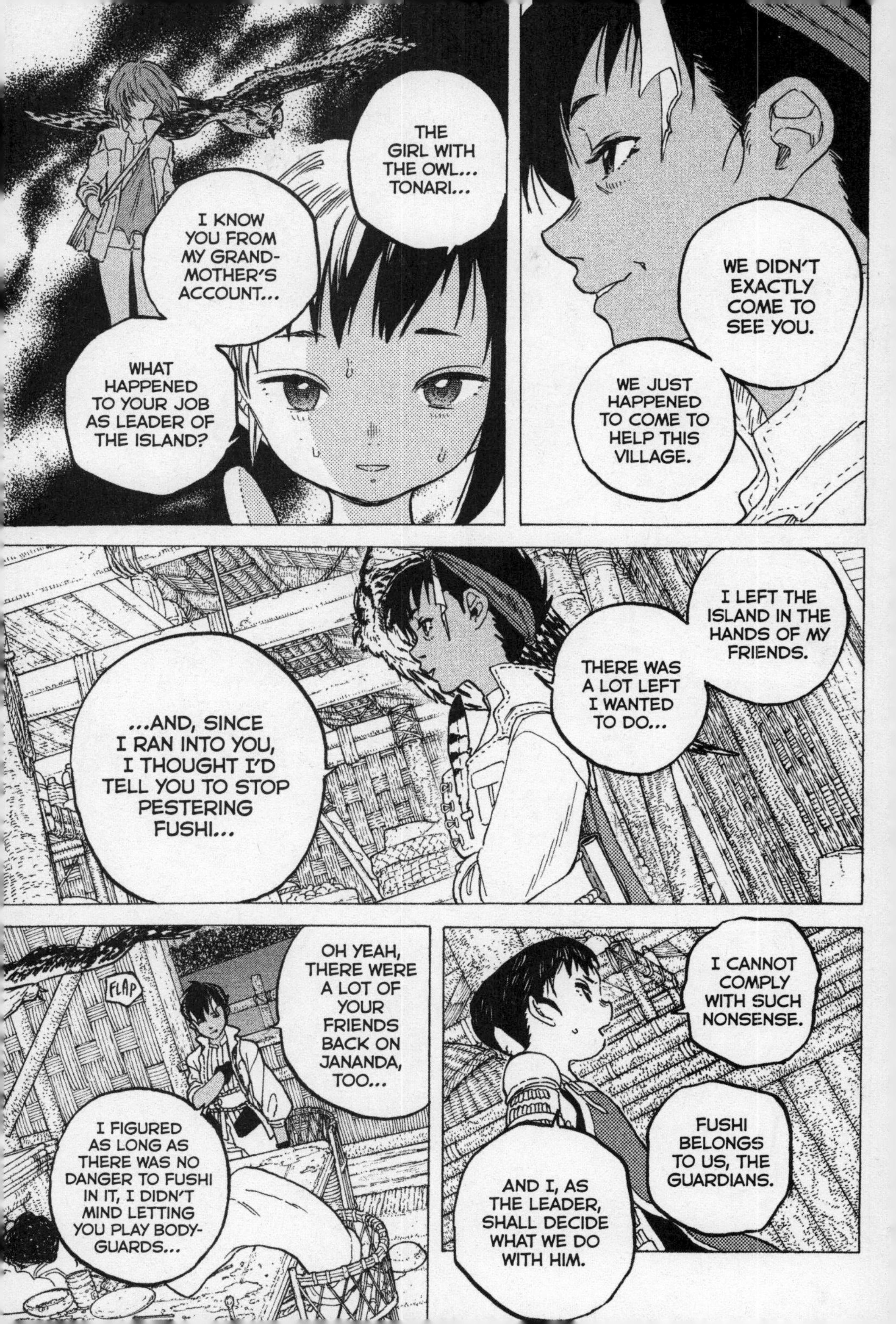
WE DIDN'T EXACTLY COME TO SEE YOU.
WE JUST HAPPENED TO COME TO HELP THIS VILLAGE.
THE GIRL WITH THE OWL... TONARI...
I KNOW YOU FROM MY GRAND-MOTHER'S ACCOUNT...
WHAT HAPPENED TO YOUR JOB AS LEADER OF THE ISLAND?
I LEFT THE ISLAND IN THE HANDS OF MY FRIENDS.
THERE WAS A LOT LEFT I WANTED TO DO...
...AND, SINCE I RAN INTO YOU, I THOUGHT I'D TELL YOU TO STOP PESTERING FUSHI...
I CANNOT COMPLY WITH SUCH NONSENSE.
FUSHI BELONGS TO US, THE GUARDIANS.
AND I, AS THE LEADER, SHALL DECIDE WHAT WE DO WITH HIM.
FLAP
OH YEAH, THERE WERE A LOT OF YOUR FRIENDS BACK ON JANANDA, TOO...
I FIGURED AS LONG AS THERE WAS NO DANGER TO FUSHI IN IT, I DIDN'T MIND LETTING YOU PLAY BODY-GUARDS...

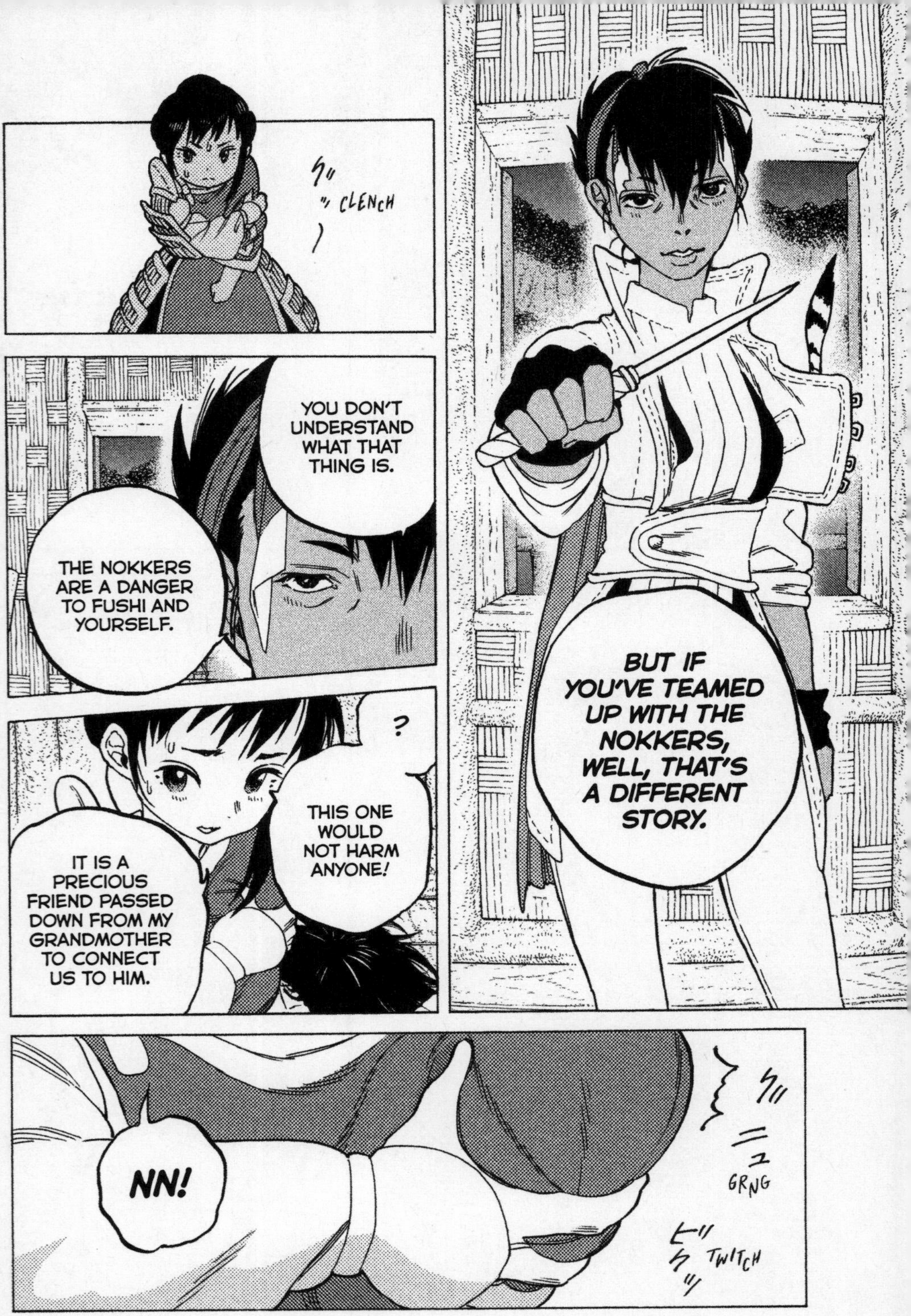
BUT IF YOU'VE TEAMED UP WITH THE NOKKERS, WELL, THAT'S A DIFFERENT STORY.
CLENCH
YOU DON'T UNDERSTAND WHAT THAT THING IS.
THE NOKKERS ARE A DANGER TO FUSHI AND YOURSELF.
?
THIS ONE WOULD NOT HARM ANYONE!
IT IS A PRECIOUS FRIEND PASSED DOWN FROM MY GRANDMOTHER TO CONNECT US TO HIM.
GRNG
TWITCH
NN!

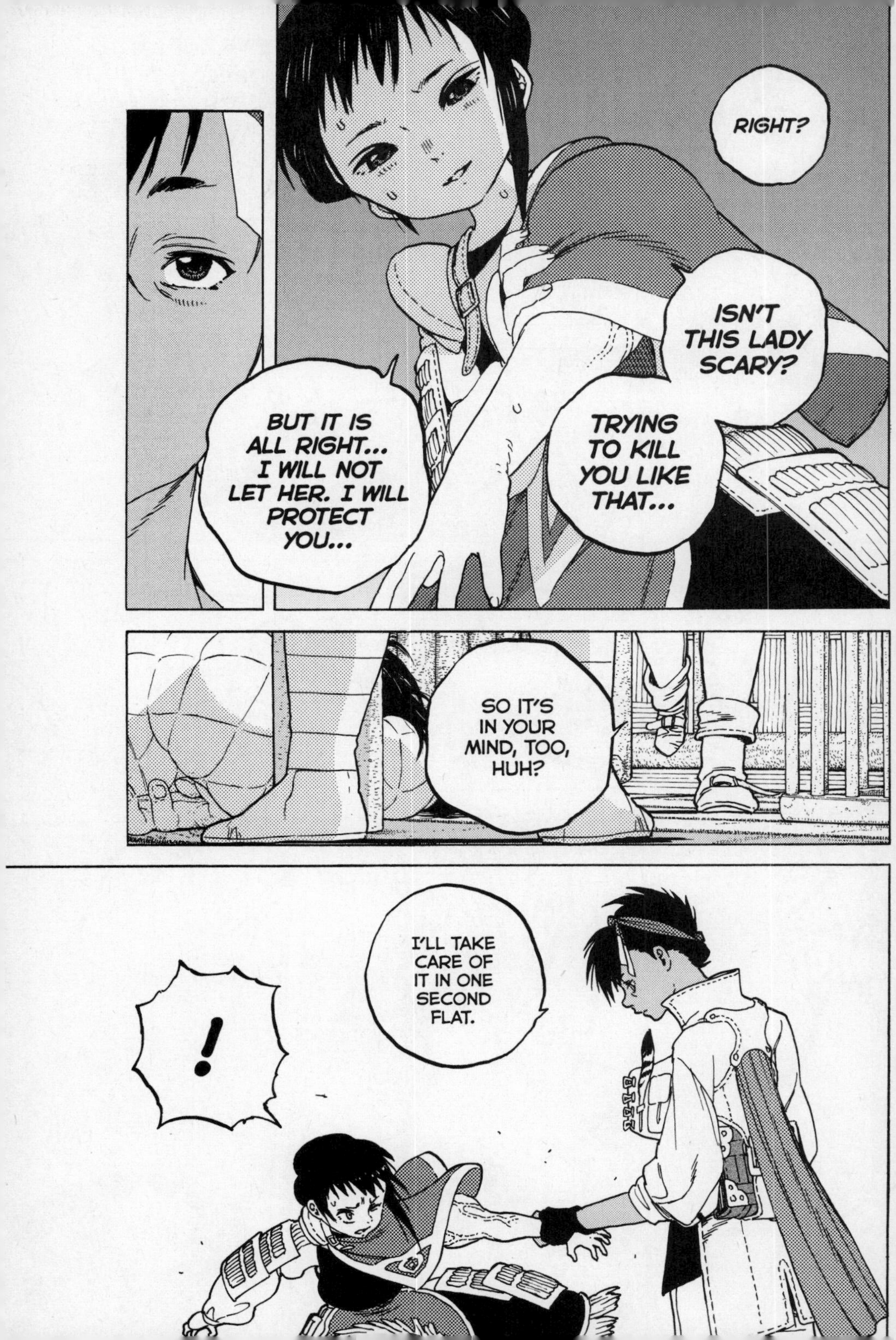
RIGHT?
ISN'T THIS LADY SCARY?
TRYING TO KILL YOU LIKE THAT...
BUT IT IS ALL RIGHT... I WILL NOT LET HER. I WILL PROTECT YOU...
SO IT'S IN YOUR MIND, TOO, HUH?
I'LL TAKE CARE OF IT IN ONE SECOND FLAT.
!

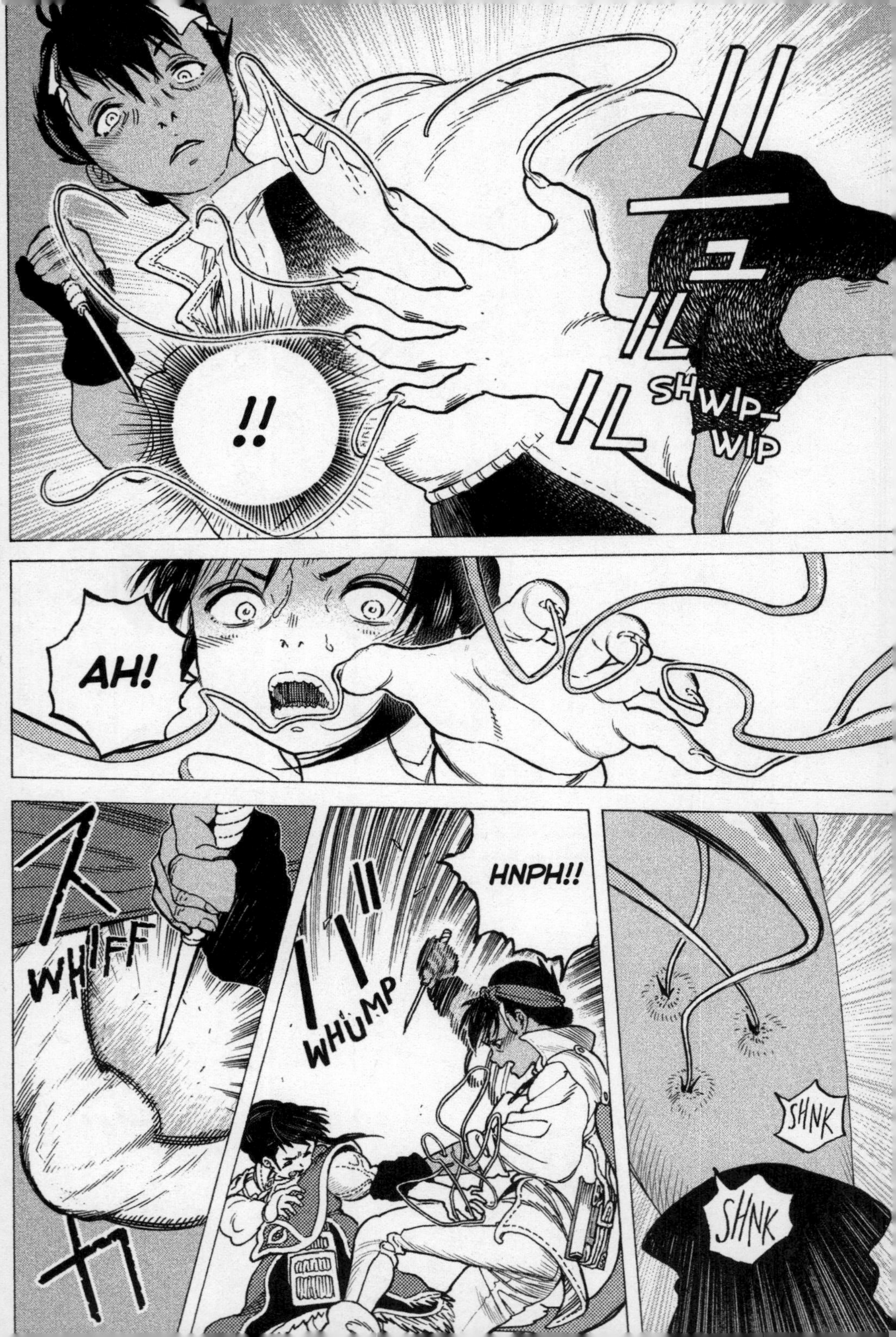
SHWIP-WIP
!!
AH!
SHNK
SHNK
HNPH!!
WHUMP
WHIFF

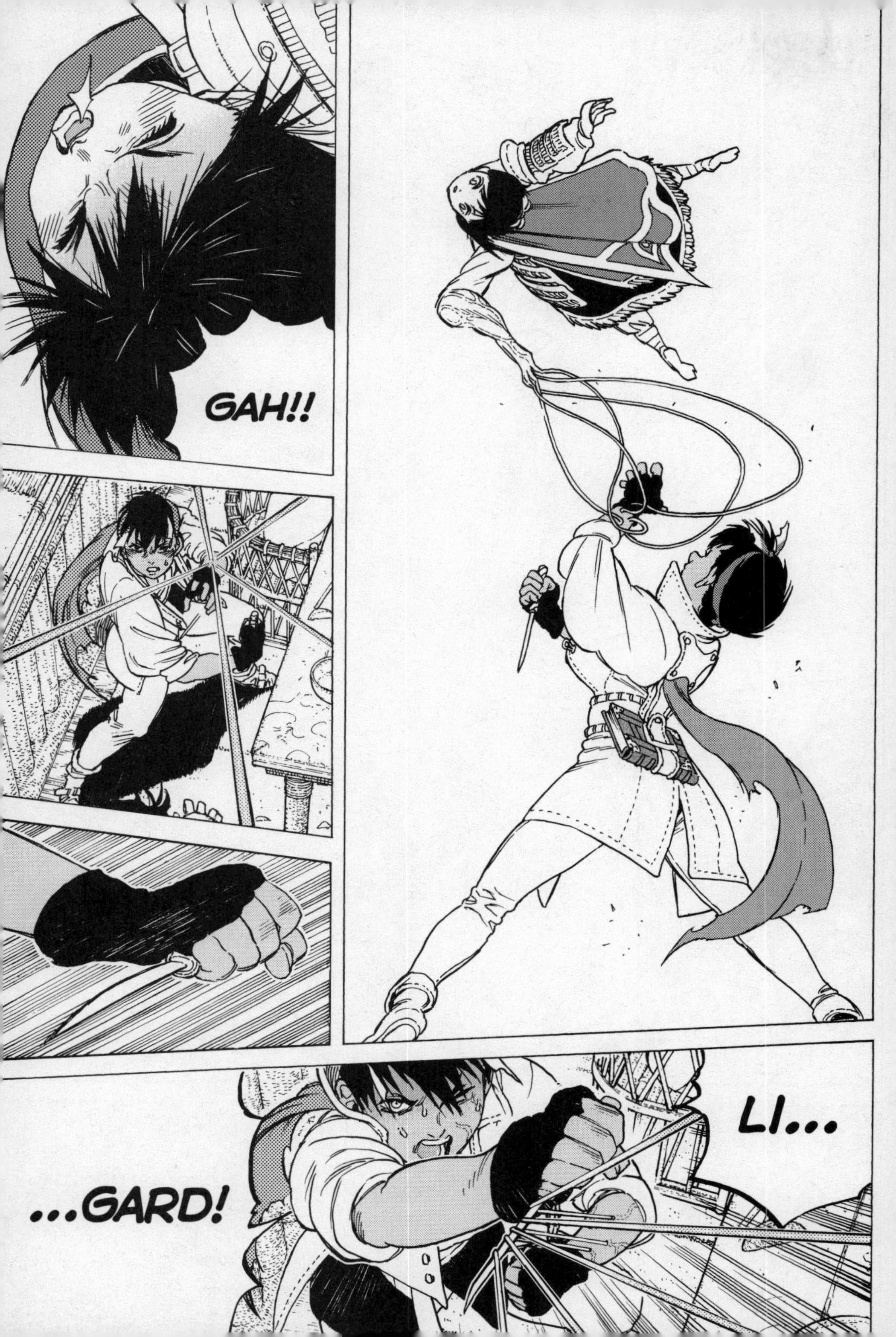
GAH!!
LI...
...GARD!

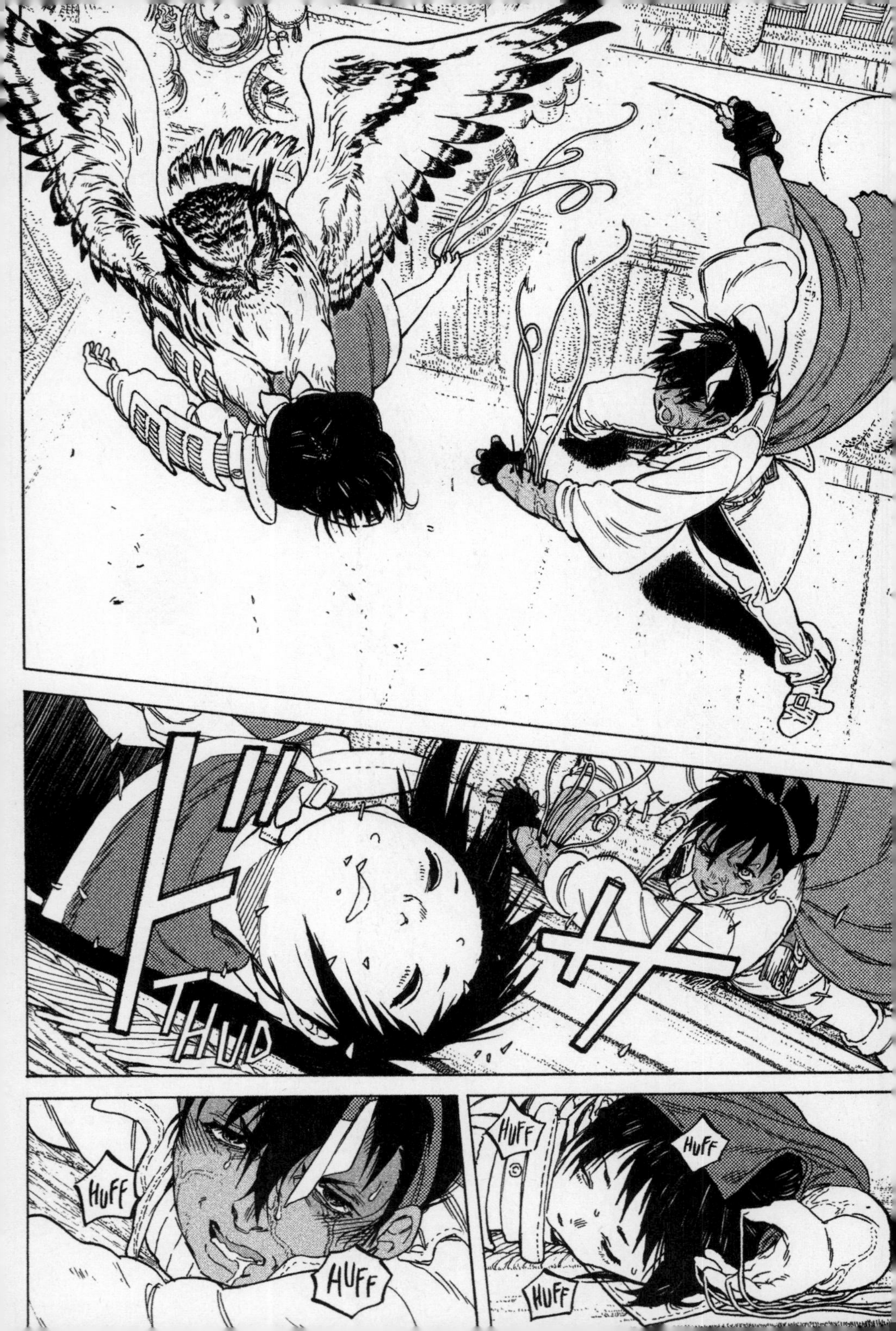
THUD
HUFF
HUFF
HUFF
HUFF
HUFF

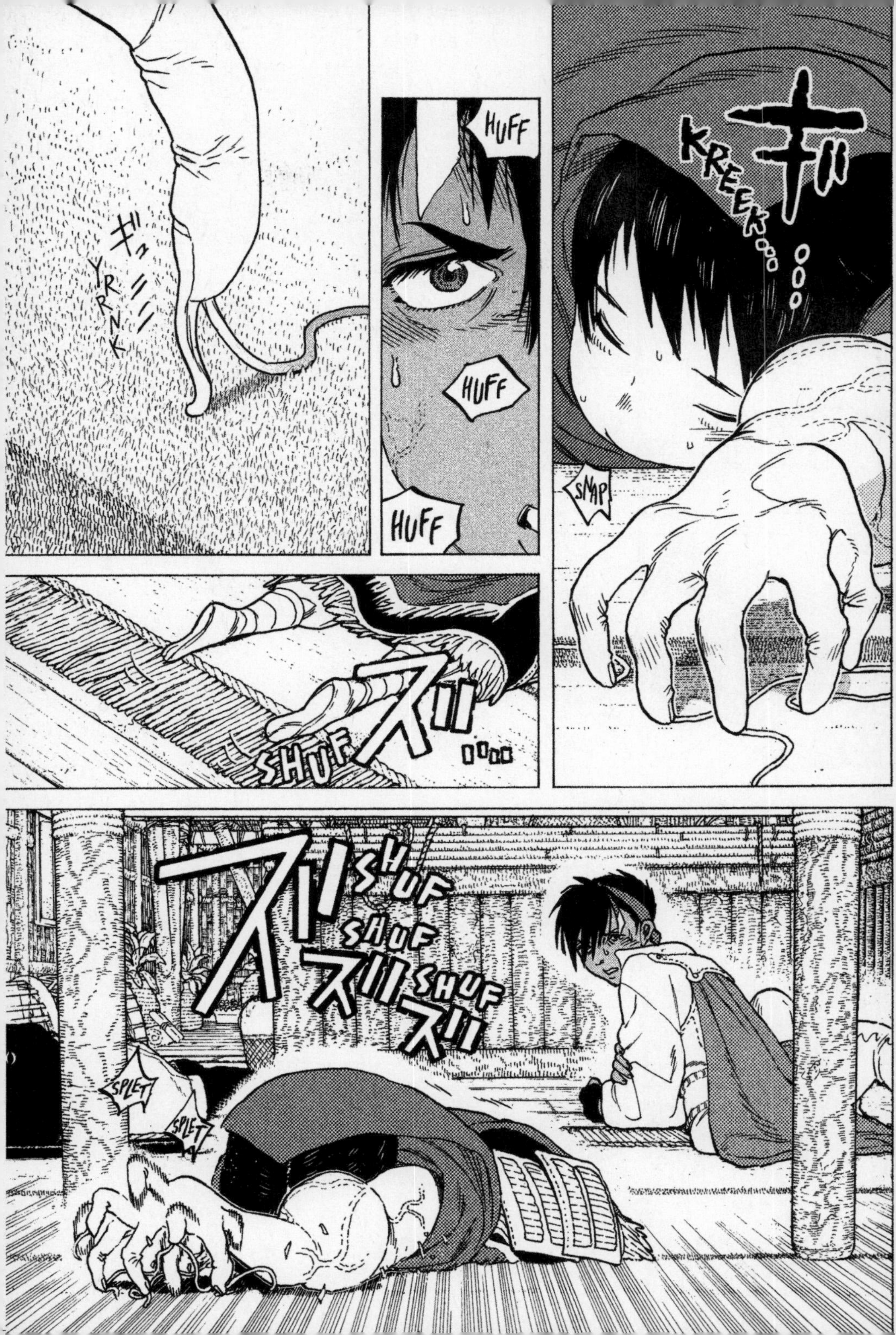

KREEK...
SNAP
HUFF
HUFF
HUFF
YRRNK
SHUF
SHUF
SHUF
SHUF
SPLET
SPLET

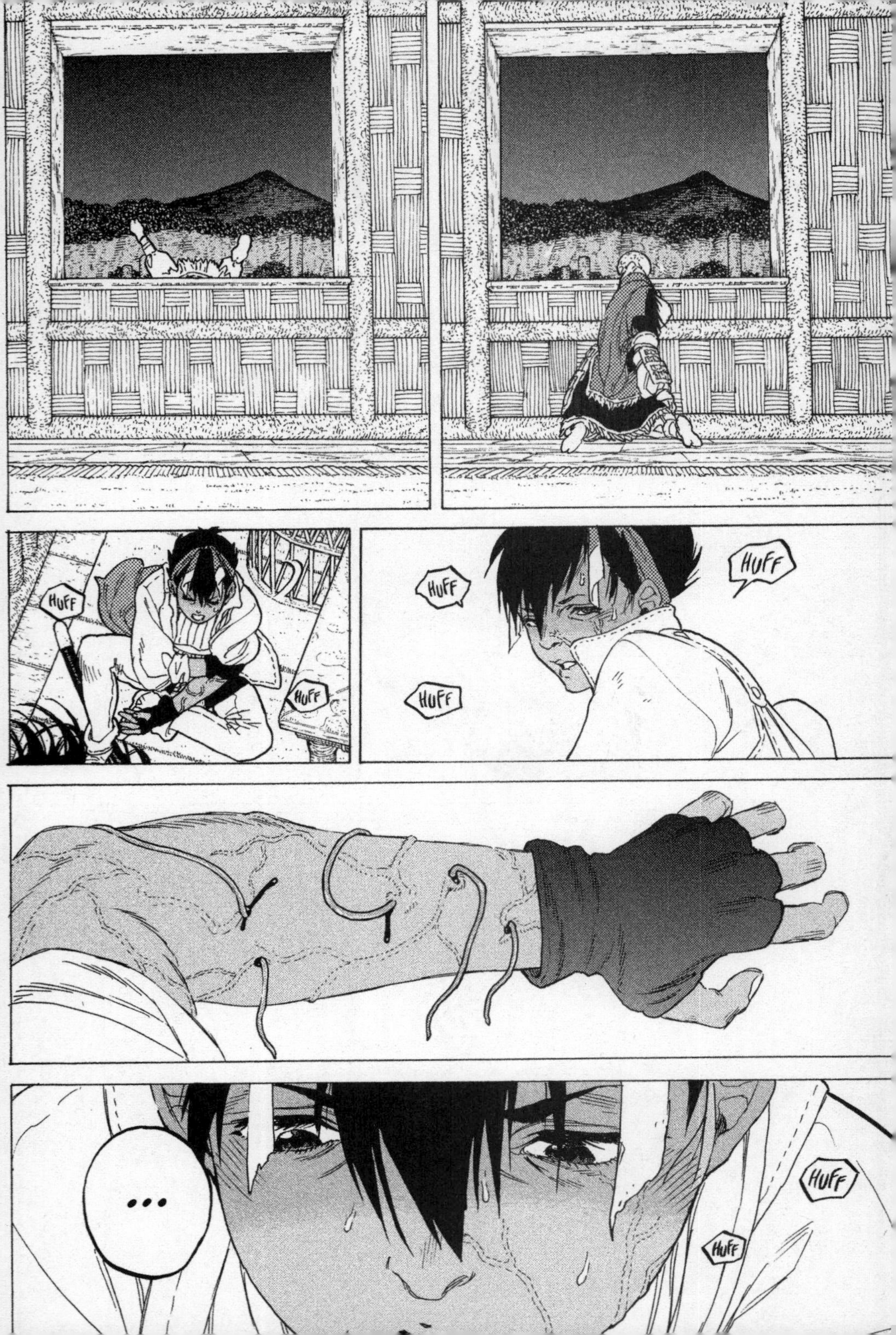
HUFF
HUFF
HUFF
HUFF
HUFF
HUFF
HUFF
...

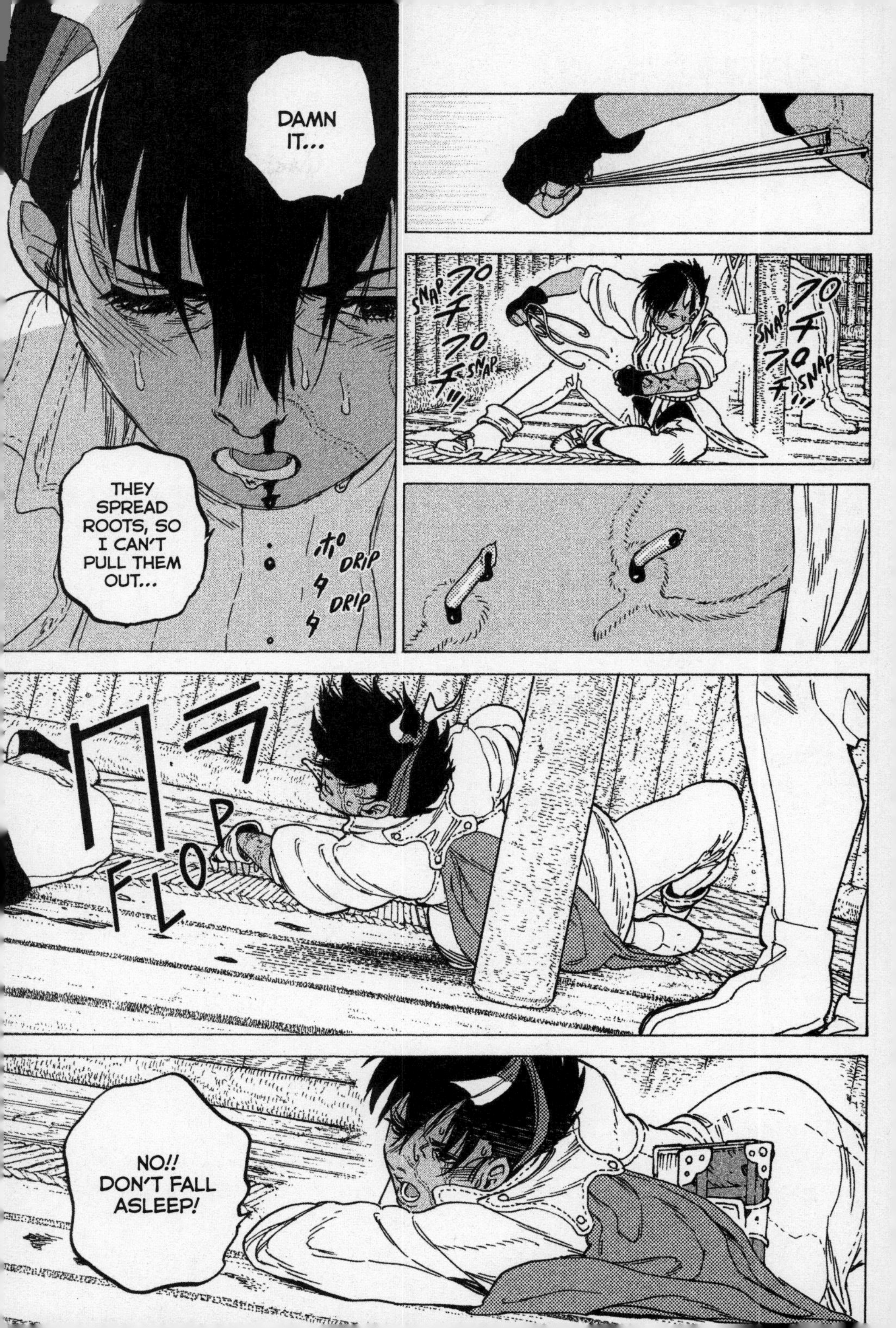
SNAP
SNAP
SNAP
SNAP
DAMN IT...
THEY SPREAD ROOTS, SO I CAN'T PULL THEM OUT...
DRIP
DRIP
FLOP
NO!! DON'T FALL ASLEEP!

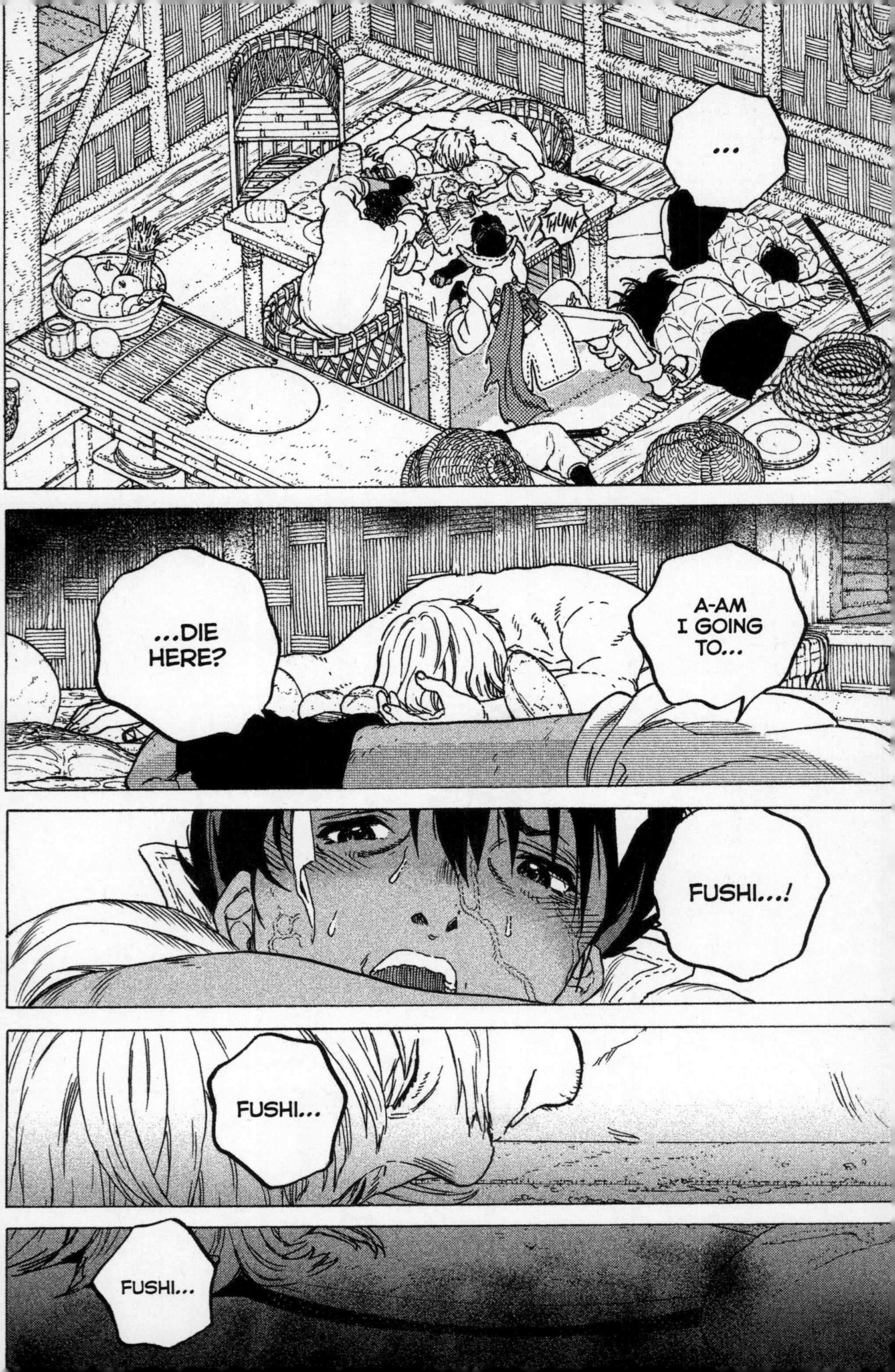
...
THUNK
A-AM I GOING TO...
...DIE HERE?
FUSHI...!
FUSHI...
FUSHI...

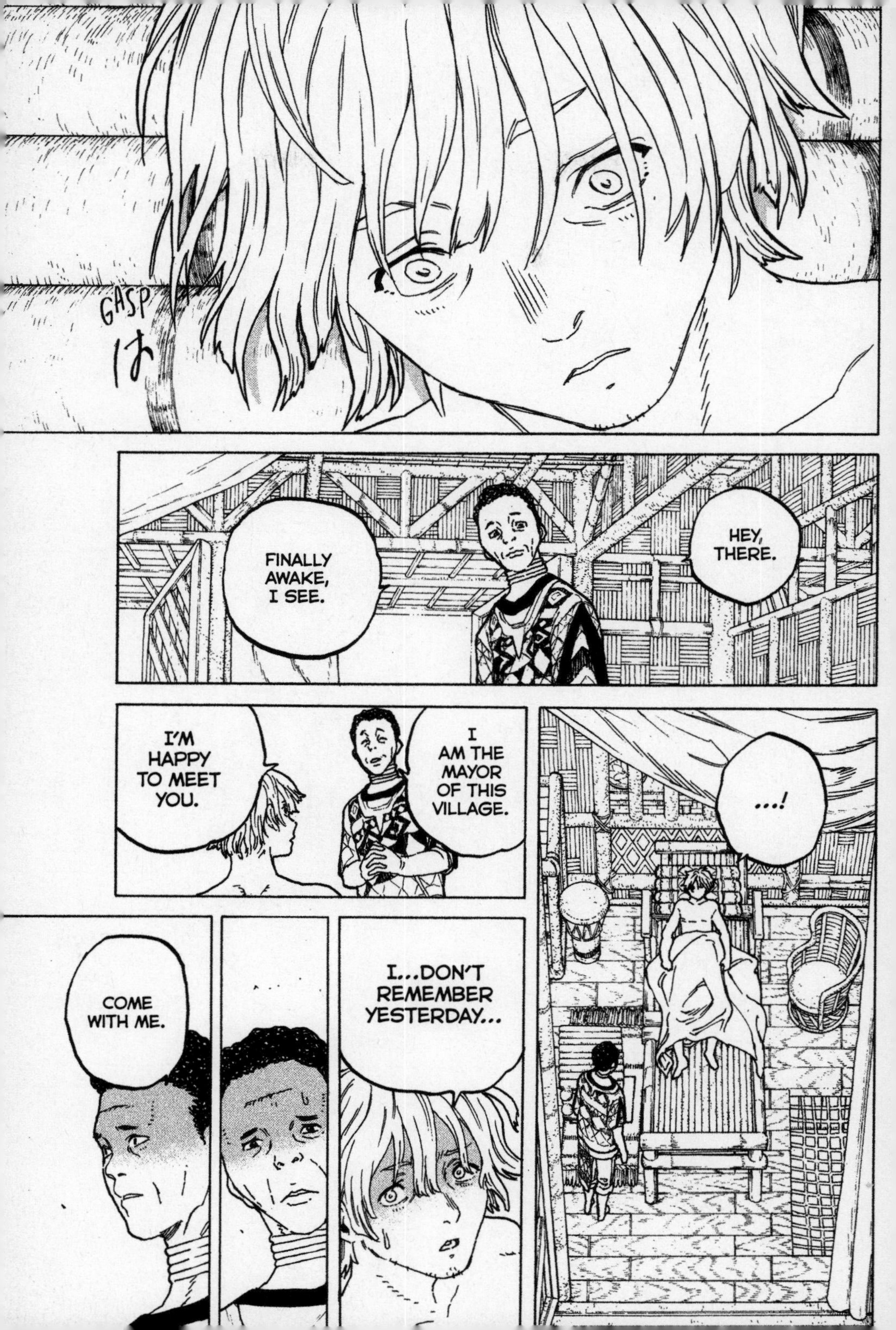
GASP
は
HEY, THERE.
FINALLY AWAKE, I SEE.
...!
I AM THE MAYOR OF THIS VILLAGE.
I'M HAPPY TO MEET YOU.
I...DON'T REMEMBER YESTERDAY...
...
COME WITH ME.

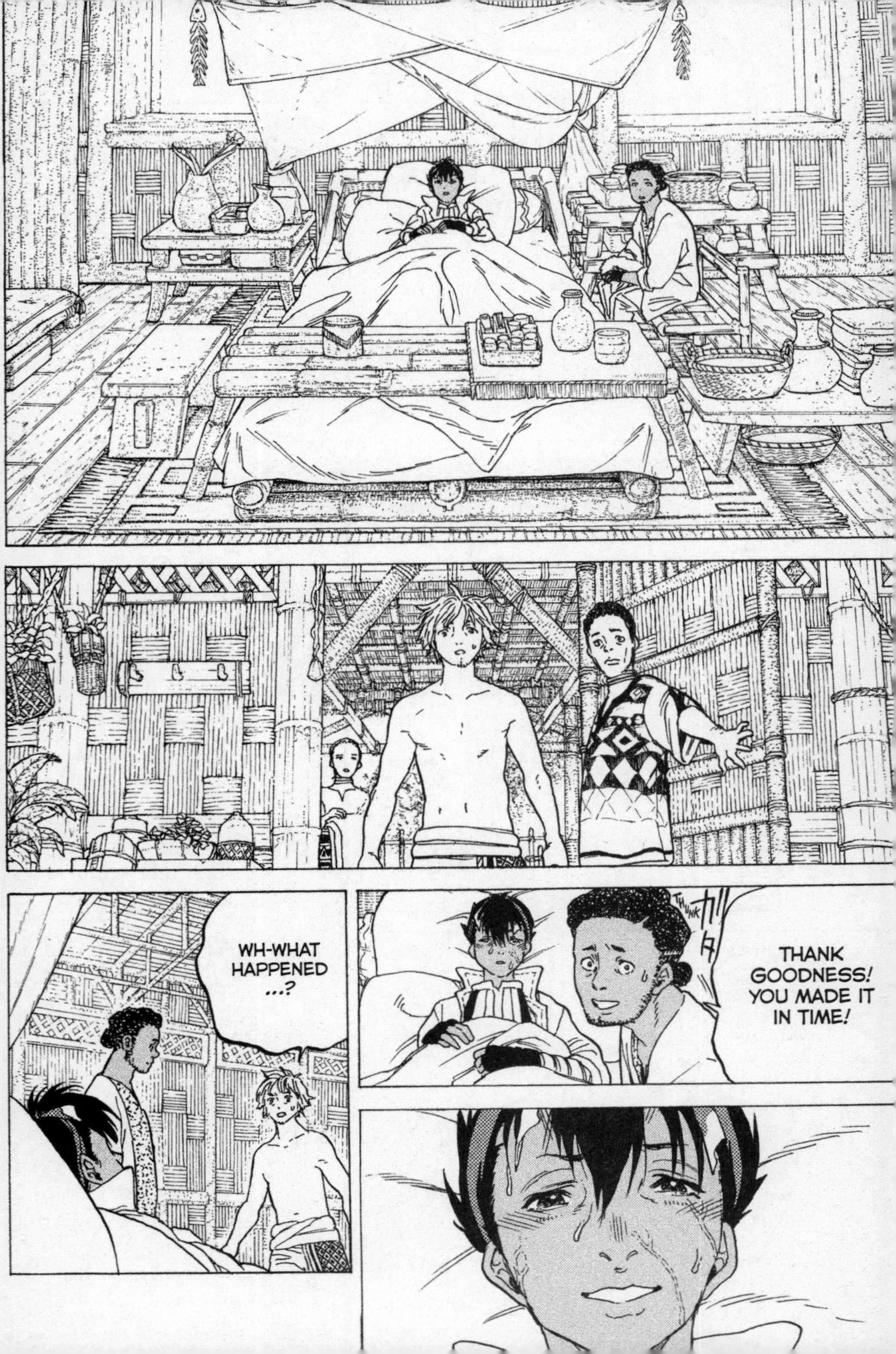
THUNK
THANK GOODNESS! YOU MADE IT IN TIME!
WH-WHAT HAPPENED ...?

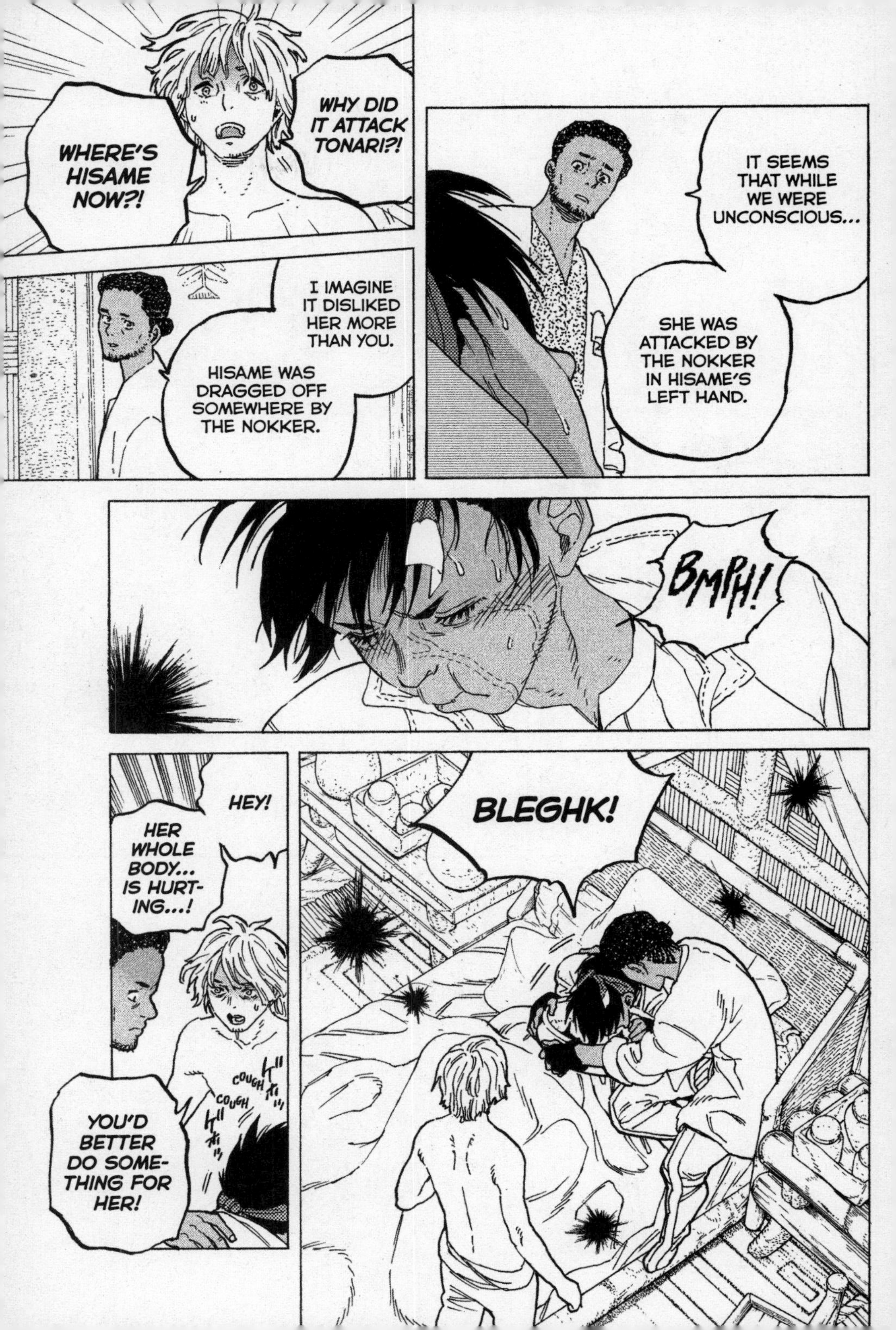
WHY DID IT ATTACK TONARI?!
WHERE'S HISAME NOW?!
IT SEEMS THAT WHILE WE WERE UNCONSCIOUS...
SHE WAS ATTACKED BY THE NOKKER IN HISAME'S LEFT HAND.
I IMAGINE IT DISLIKED HER MORE THAN YOU.
HISAME WAS DRAGGED OFF SOMEWHERE BY THE NOKKER.
BMPH!
BLEGHK!
HEY!
HER WHOLE BODY... IS HURT-ING...!
COUGH
COUGH
YOU'D BETTER DO SOME-THING FOR HER!

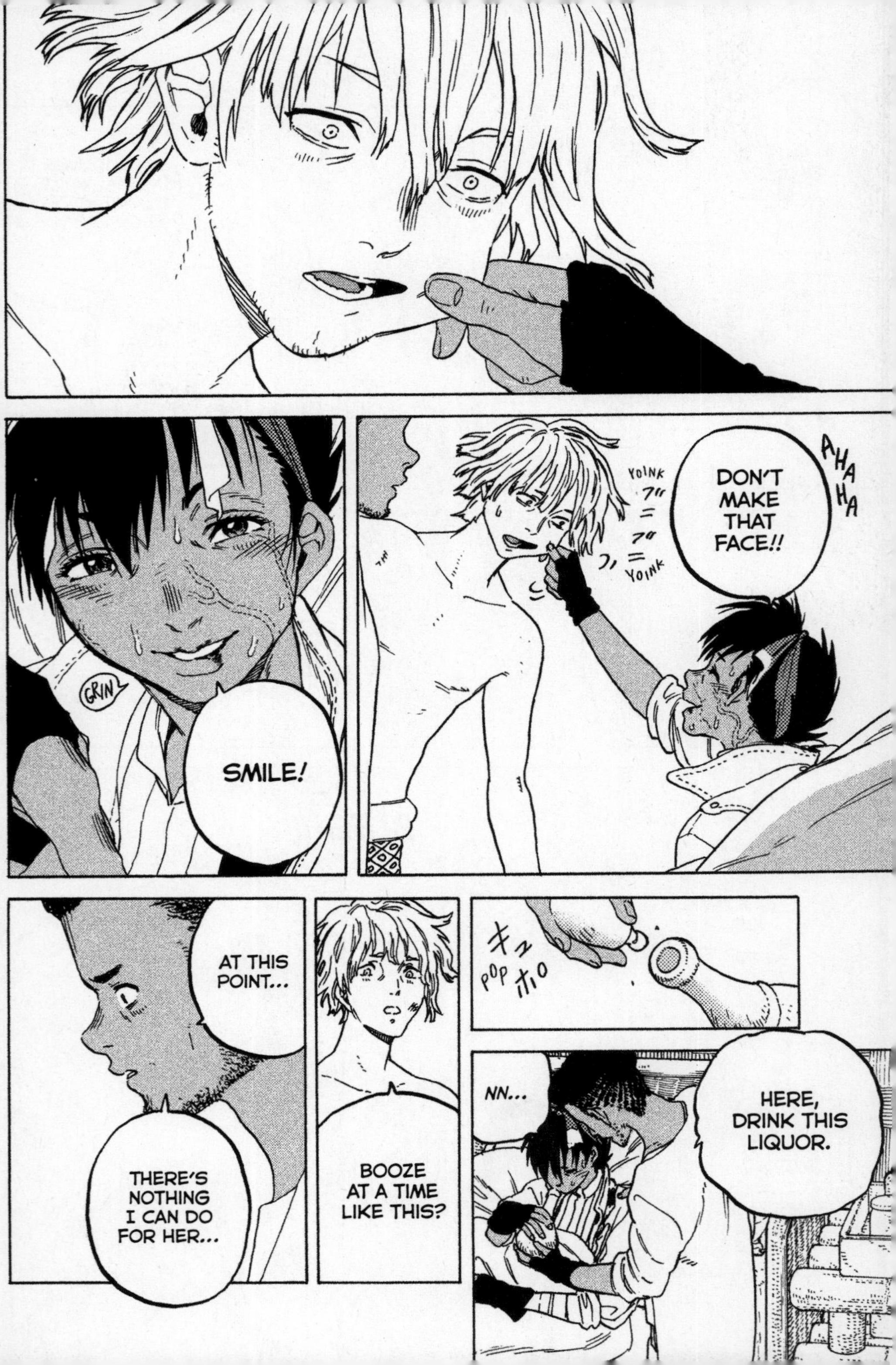
AHAHA
DON'T MAKE THAT FACE!!
YOINK
YOINK
GRIN
SMILE!
POP
HERE, DRINK THIS LIQUOR.
NN...
BOOZE AT A TIME LIKE THIS?
AT THIS POINT...
THERE'S NOTHING I CAN DO FOR HER...

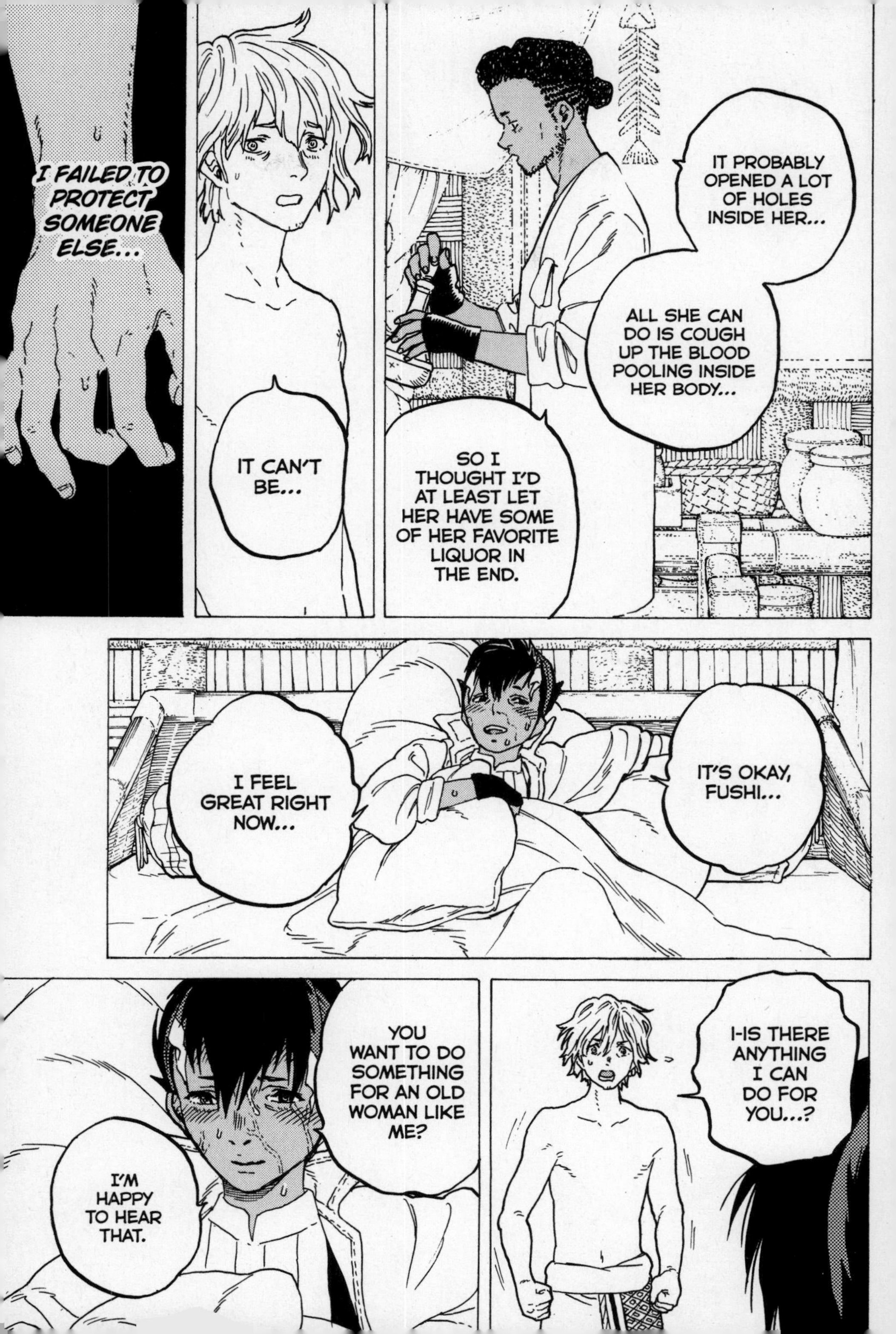
IT PROBABLY OPENED A LOT OF HOLES INSIDE HER...
ALL SHE CAN DO IS COUGH UP THE BLOOD POOLING INSIDE HER BODY...
SO I THOUGHT I'D AT LEAST LET HER HAVE SOME OF HER FAVORITE LIQUOR IN THE END.
IT CAN'T BE...
I FAILED TO PROTECT SOMEONE ELSE...
IT'S OKAY, FUSHI...
I FEEL GREAT RIGHT NOW...
I-IS THERE ANYTHING I CAN DO FOR YOU...?
YOU WANT TO DO SOMETHING FOR AN OLD WOMAN LIKE ME?
I'M HAPPY TO HEAR THAT.

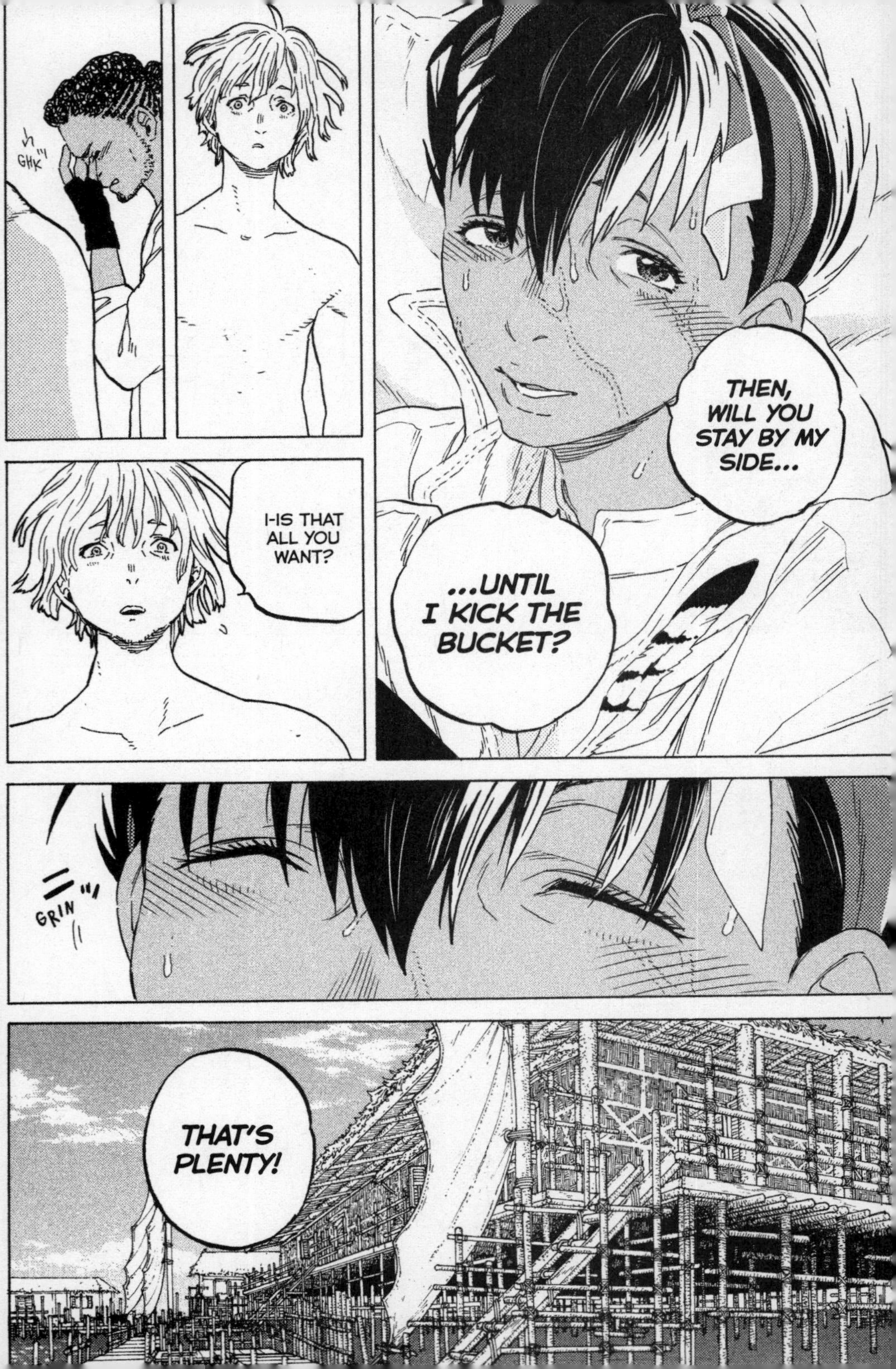
THEN, WILL YOU STAY BY MY SIDE...
...UNTIL I KICK THE BUCKET?
GHK
I-IS THAT ALL YOU WANT?
GRIN
THAT'S PLENTY!

TO YOUR ETERNITY

フシの無人島日記

Fushi's Notes from the Desert Island

Things I Still Can't Make:

Big Boats   Big Trees   Big Rocks
Whole Houses
Water   Fire
Nokker Cores

I don't remember the rest.

#59 Beating Will

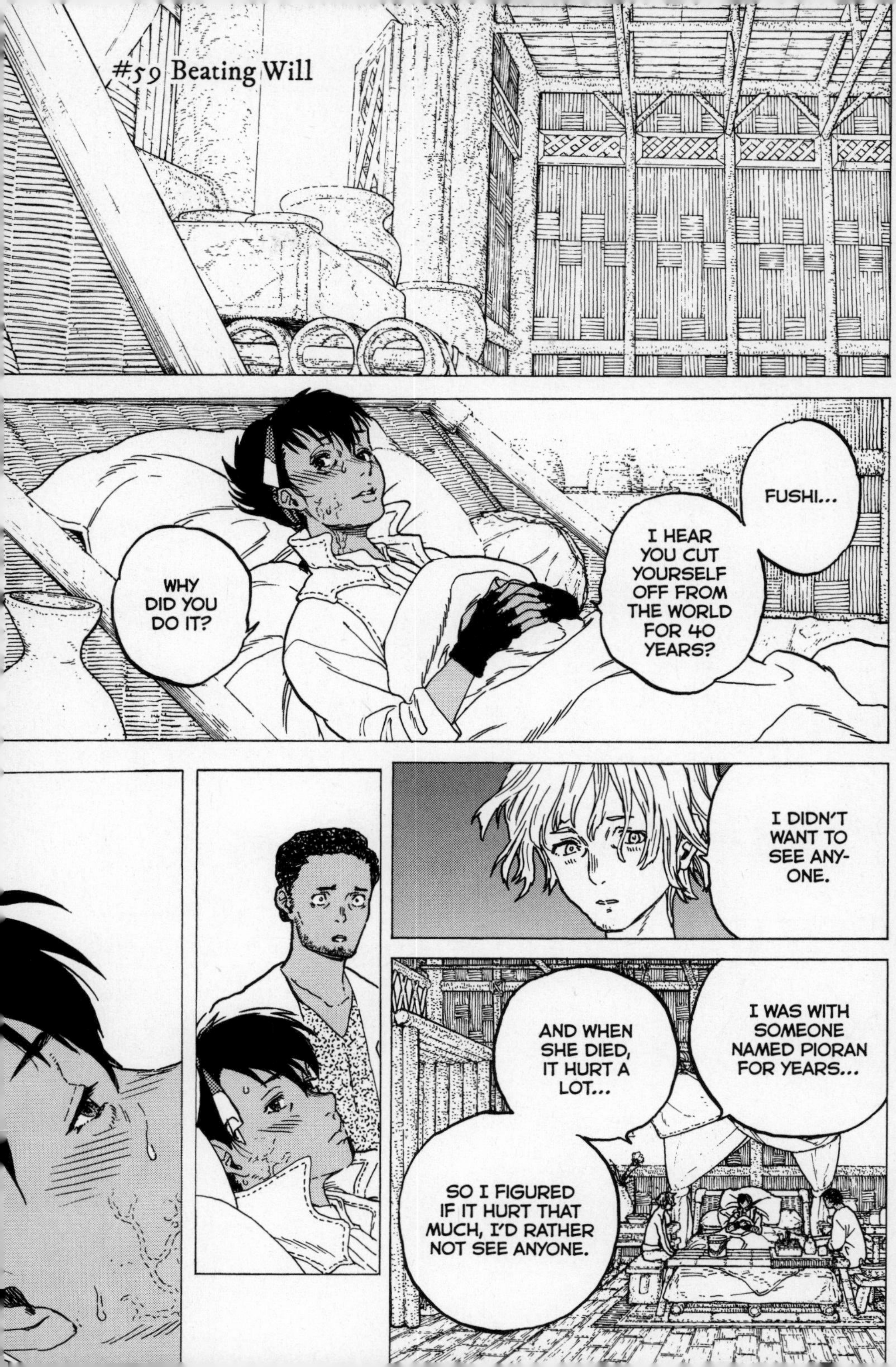
FUSHI...
I HEAR YOU CUT YOURSELF OFF FROM THE WORLD FOR 40 YEARS?
WHY DID YOU DO IT?
I DIDN'T WANT TO SEE ANY-ONE.
I WAS WITH SOMEONE NAMED PIORAN FOR YEARS...
AND WHEN SHE DIED, IT HURT A LOT...
SO I FIGURED IF IT HURT THAT MUCH, I'D RATHER NOT SEE ANYONE.

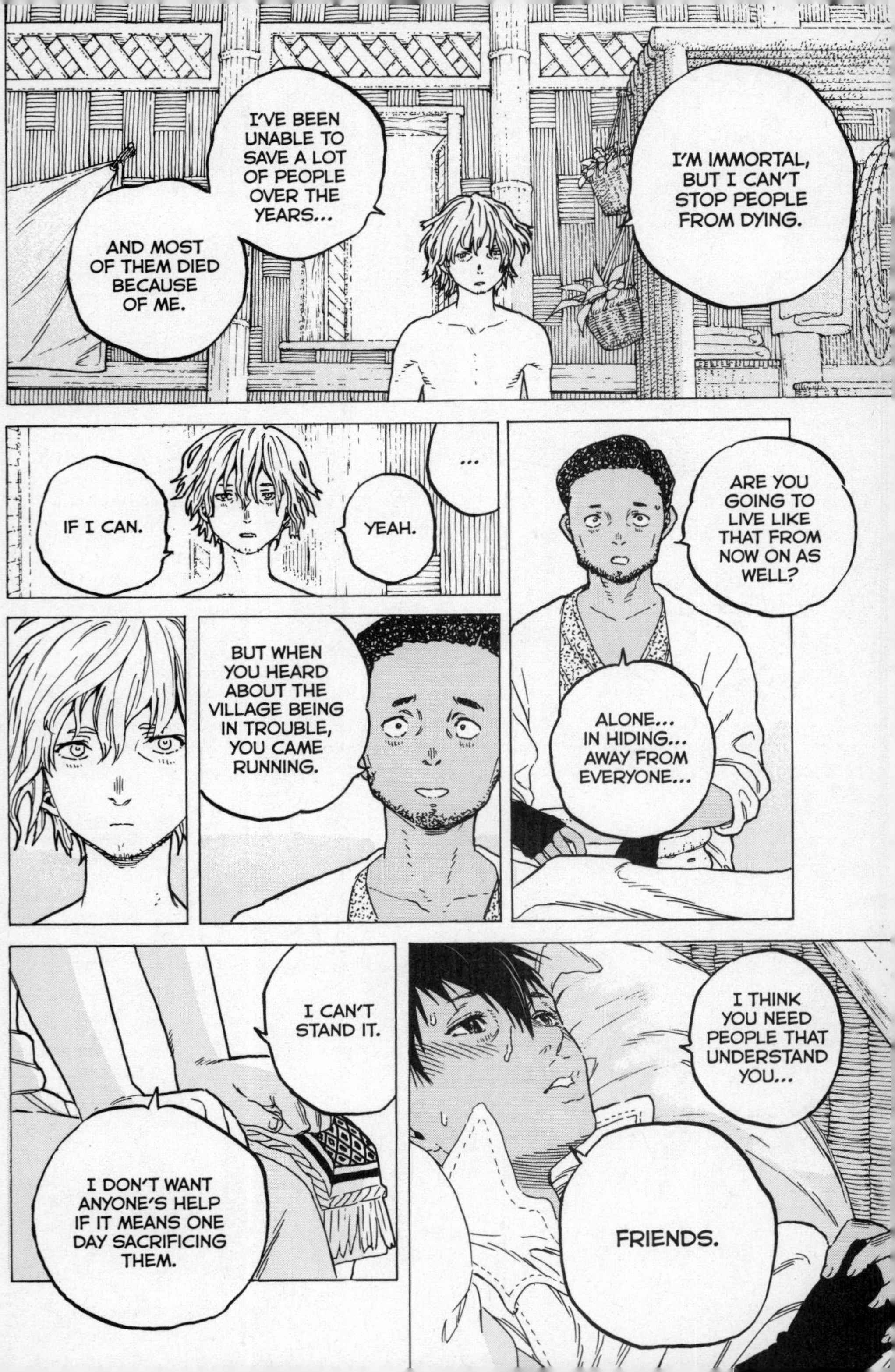
I'M IMMORTAL, BUT I CAN'T STOP PEOPLE FROM DYING.
I'VE BEEN UNABLE TO SAVE A LOT OF PEOPLE OVER THE YEARS...
AND MOST OF THEM DIED BECAUSE OF ME.
ARE YOU GOING TO LIVE LIKE THAT FROM NOW ON AS WELL?
ALONE... IN HIDING... AWAY FROM EVERYONE...
...
YEAH.
IF I CAN.
BUT WHEN YOU HEARD ABOUT THE VILLAGE BEING IN TROUBLE, YOU CAME RUNNING.
I THINK YOU NEED PEOPLE THAT UNDERSTAND YOU...
FRIENDS.
I CAN'T STAND IT.
I DON'T WANT ANYONE'S HELP IF IT MEANS ONE DAY SACRIFICING THEM.

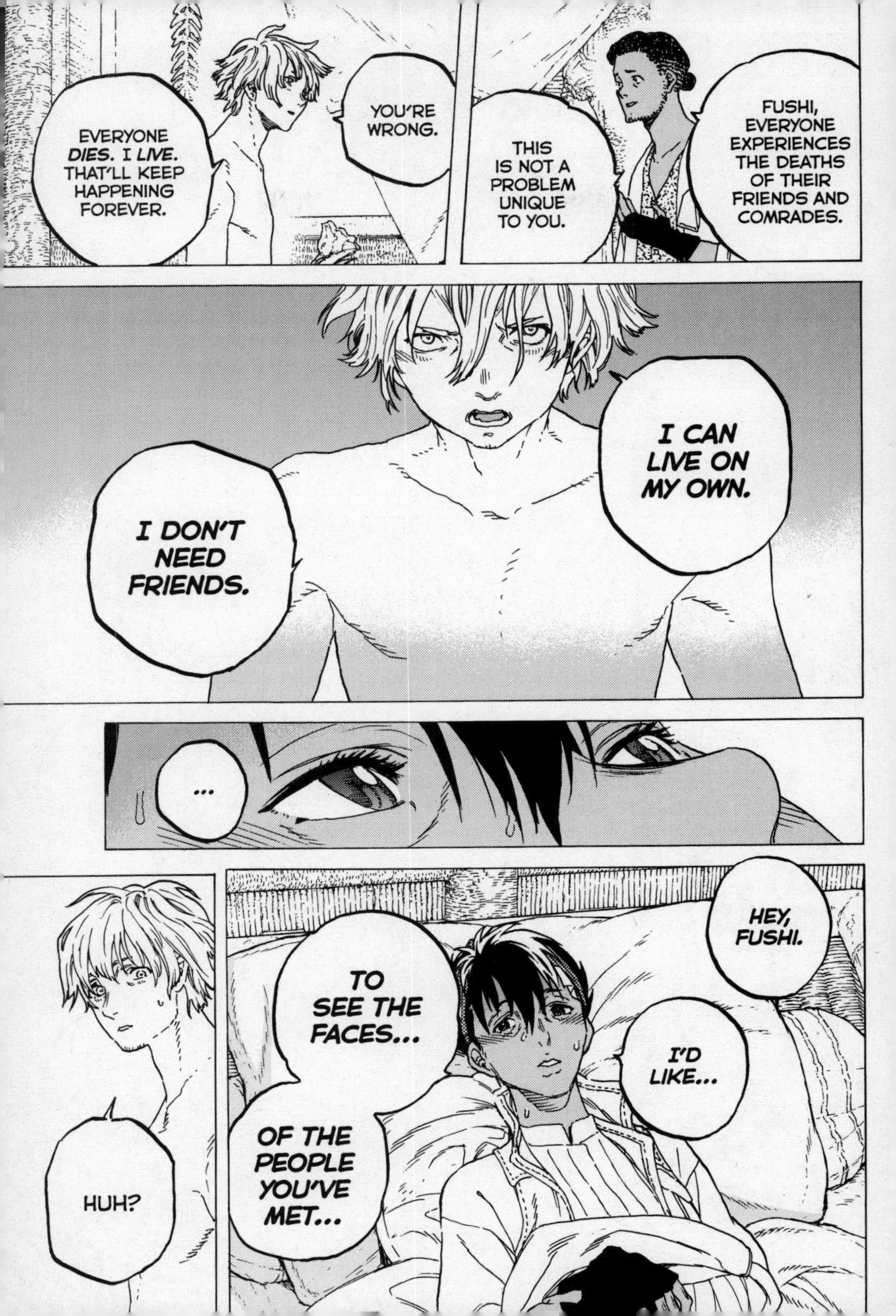
FUSHI, EVERYONE EXPERIENCES THE DEATHS OF THEIR FRIENDS AND COMRADES.
THIS IS NOT A PROBLEM UNIQUE TO YOU.
YOU'RE WRONG.
EVERYONE *DIES*. I *LIVE*. THAT'LL KEEP HAPPENING FOREVER.
I CAN LIVE ON MY OWN.
I DON'T NEED FRIENDS.
...
HEY, FUSHI.
I'D LIKE...
TO SEE THE FACES...
OF THE PEOPLE YOU'VE MET...
HUH?

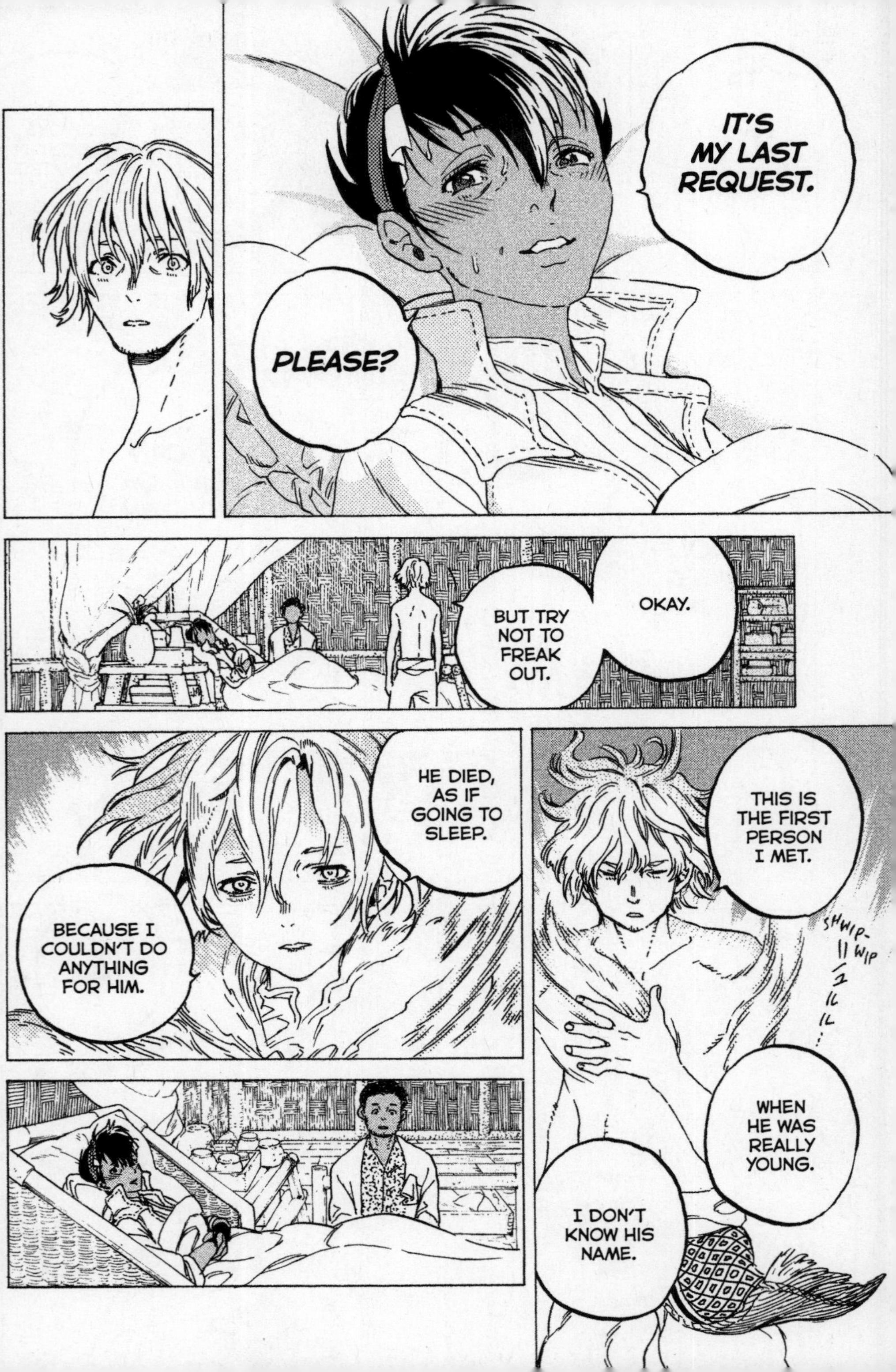
IT'S MY LAST REQUEST.
PLEASE?
OKAY.
BUT TRY NOT TO FREAK OUT.
THIS IS THE FIRST PERSON I MET.
SHWIP-WIP
WHEN HE WAS REALLY YOUNG.
I DON'T KNOW HIS NAME.
HE DIED, AS IF GOING TO SLEEP.
BECAUSE I COULDN'T DO ANYTHING FOR HIM.

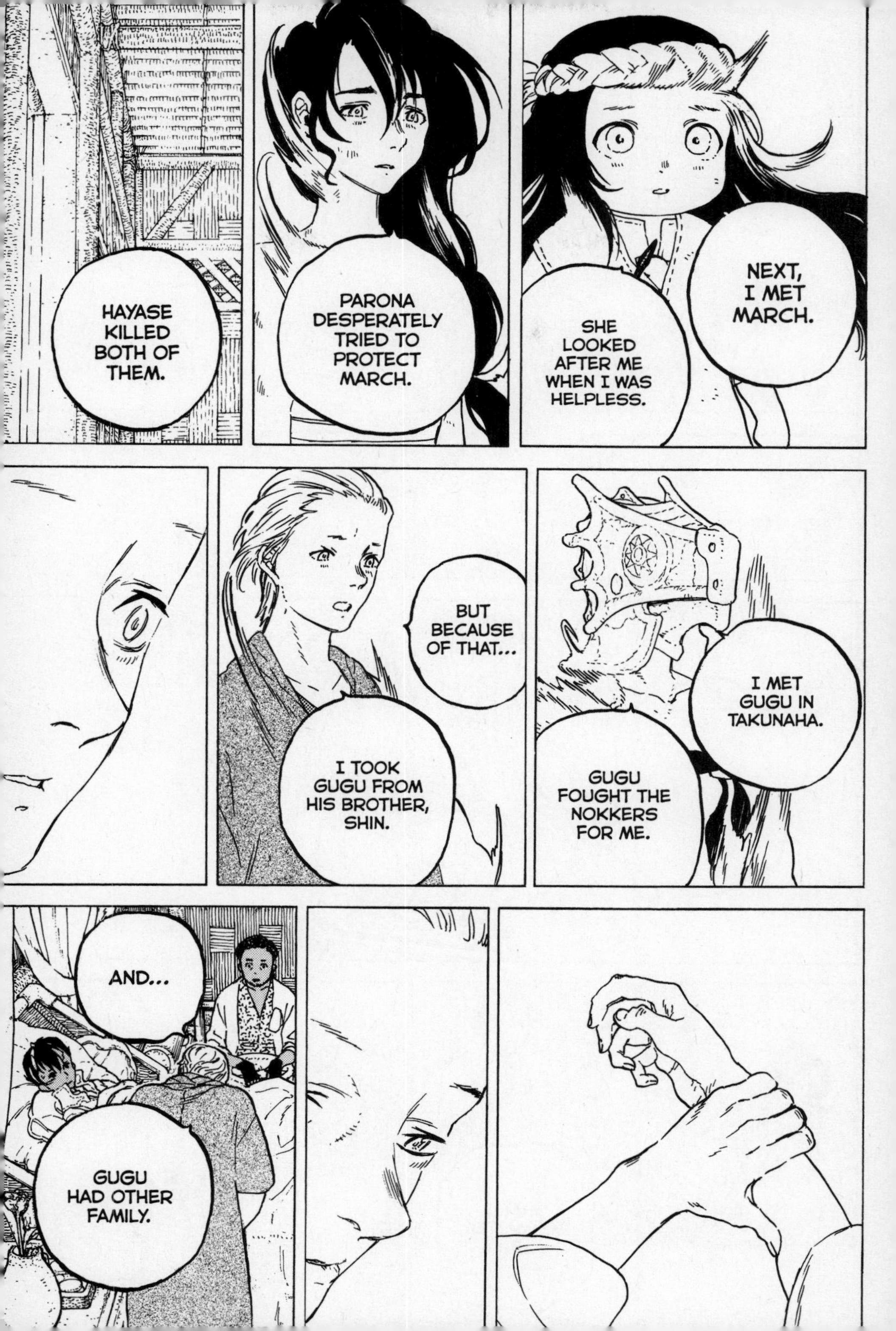
NEXT, I MET MARCH.
SHE LOOKED AFTER ME WHEN I WAS HELPLESS.
PARONA DESPERATELY TRIED TO PROTECT MARCH.
HAYASE KILLED BOTH OF THEM.
I MET GUGU IN TAKUNAHA.
GUGU FOUGHT THE NOKKERS FOR ME.
BUT BECAUSE OF THAT...
I TOOK GUGU FROM HIS BROTHER, SHIN.
AND...
GUGU HAD OTHER FAMILY.

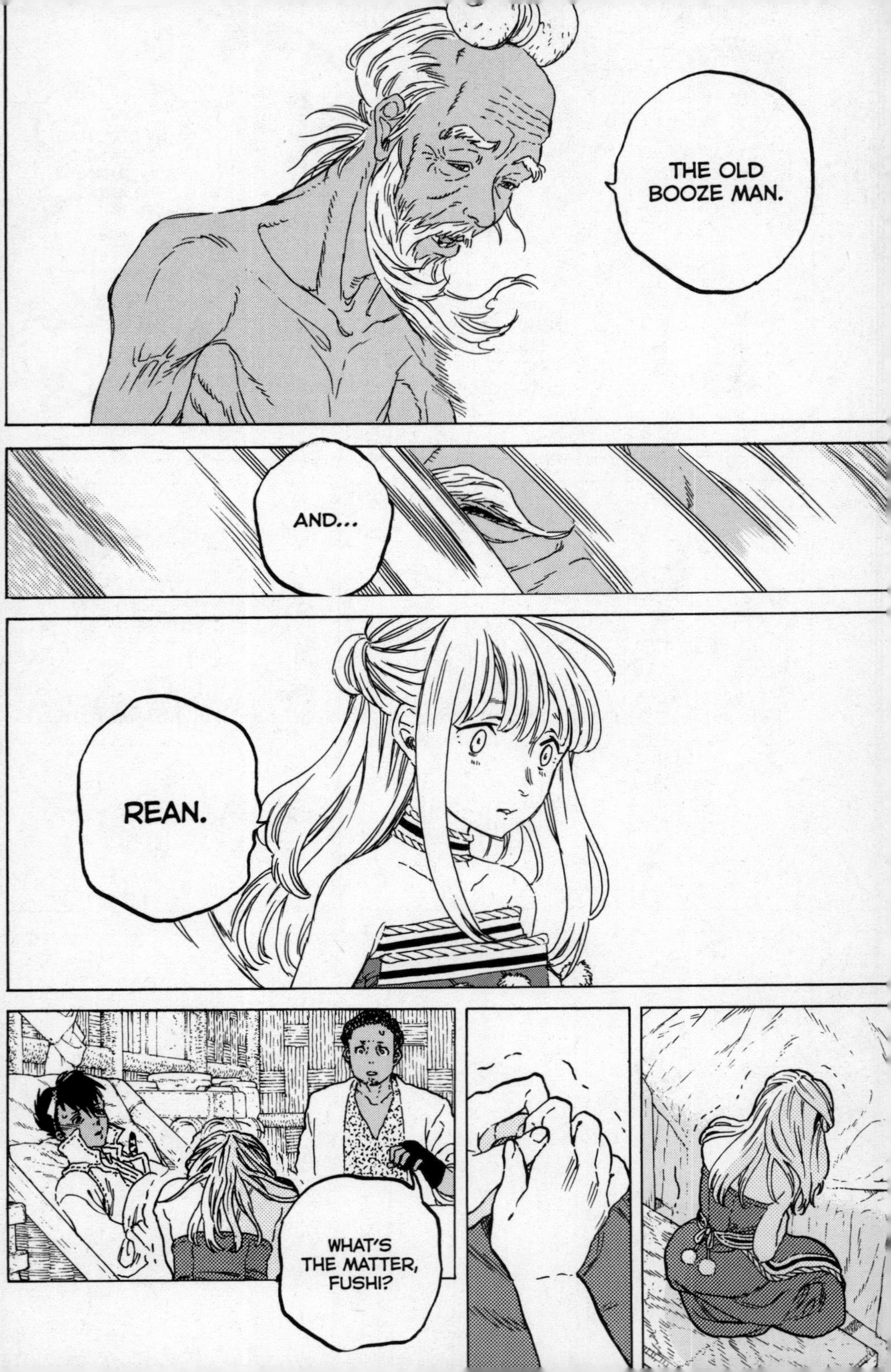
THE OLD BOOZE MAN.
AND...
REAN.
WHAT'S THE MATTER, FUSHI?

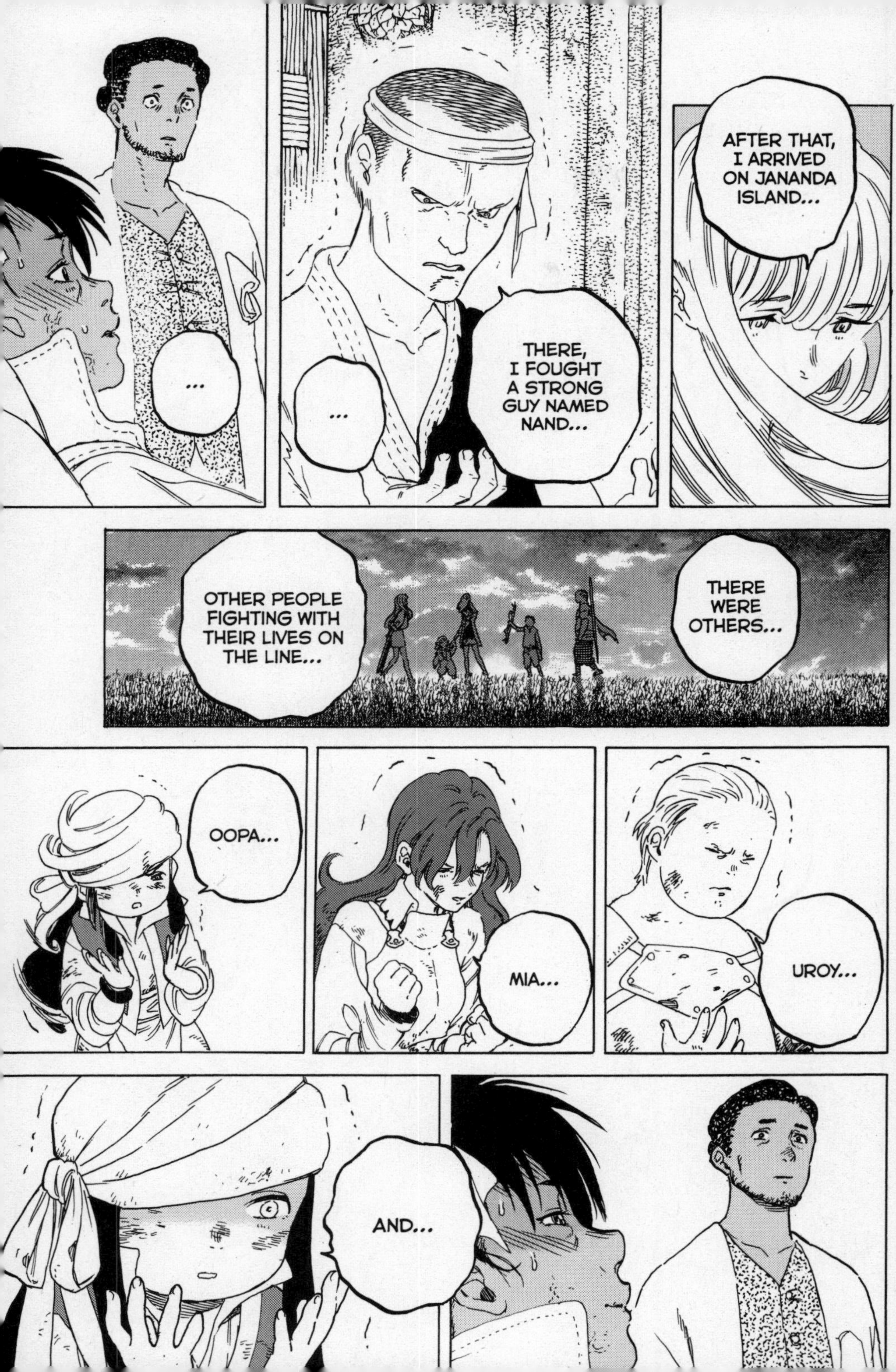
AFTER THAT, I ARRIVED ON JANANDA ISLAND...
THERE, I FOUGHT A STRONG GUY NAMED NAND...
...
...
THERE WERE OTHERS...
OTHER PEOPLE FIGHTING WITH THEIR LIVES ON THE LINE...
UROY...
MIA...
OOPA...
AND...

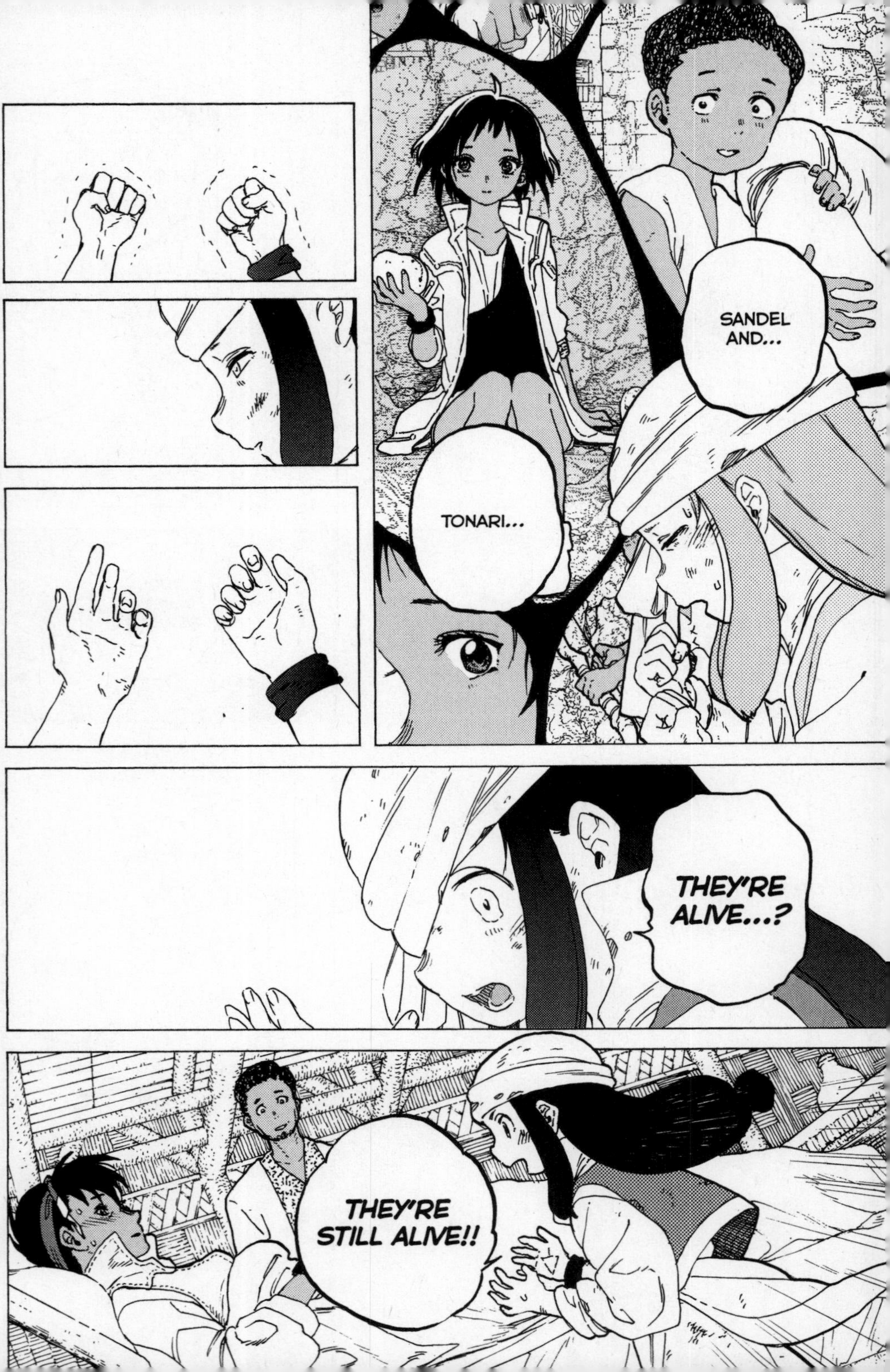
SANDEL AND...
TONARI...
THEY'RE ALIVE...?
THEY'RE STILL ALIVE!!

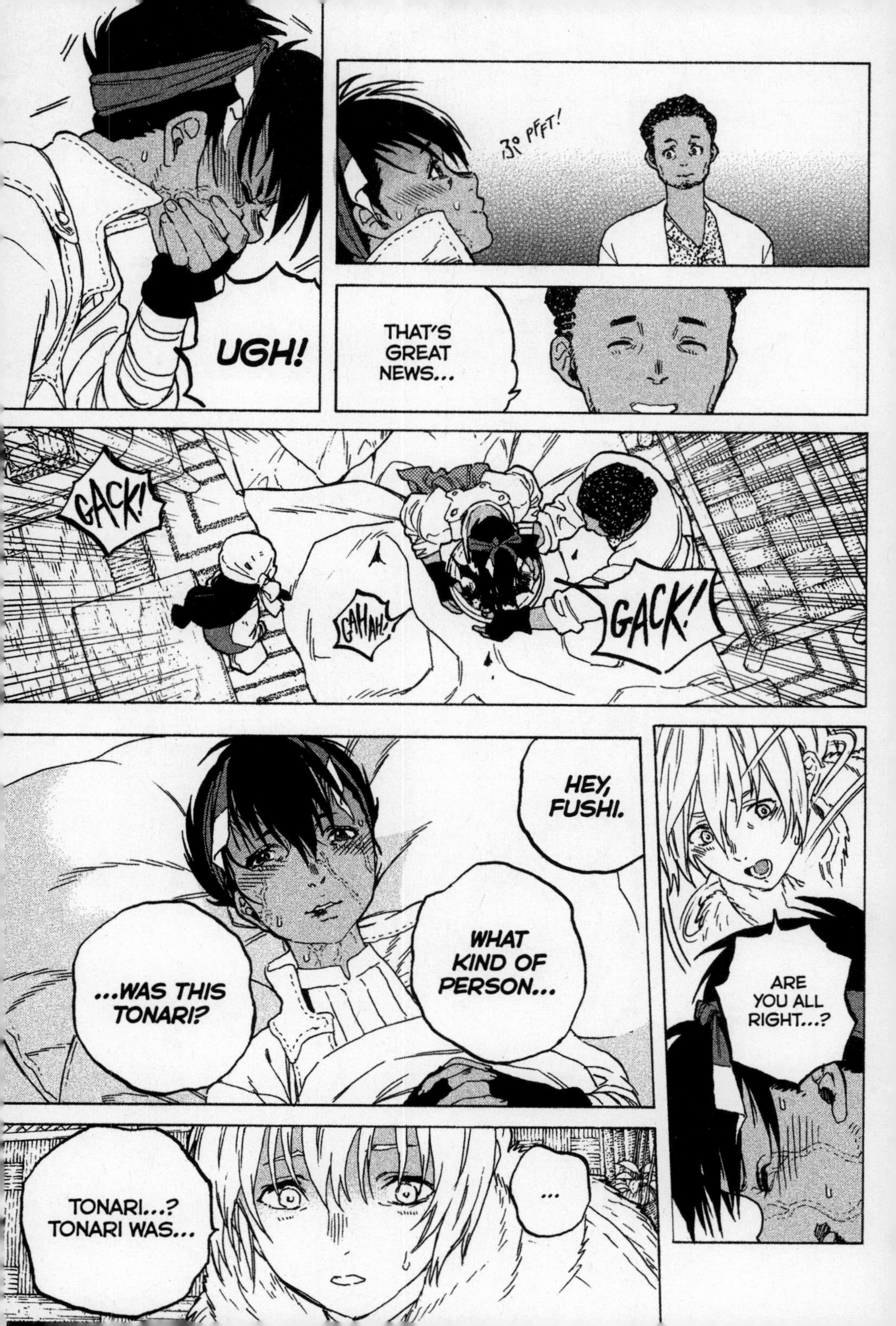
PFFT!
THAT'S GREAT NEWS...
UGH!
GACK!
GAHAH!
GACK!
ARE YOU ALL RIGHT...?
HEY, FUSHI.
WHAT KIND OF PERSON...
...WAS THIS TONARI?
...
TONARI...? TONARI WAS...

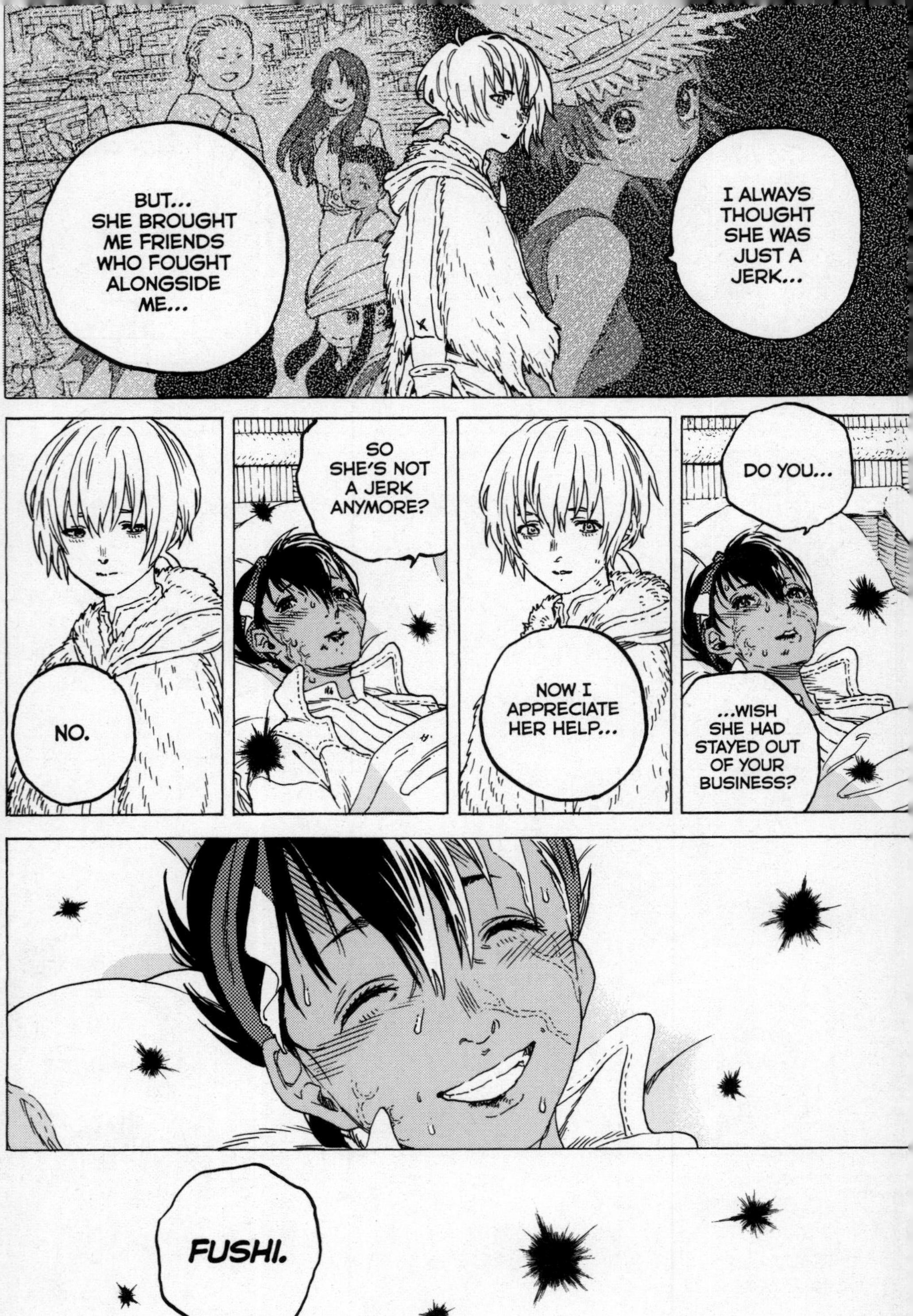
I ALWAYS THOUGHT SHE WAS JUST A JERK...
BUT... SHE BROUGHT ME FRIENDS WHO FOUGHT ALONGSIDE ME...
DO YOU...
...WISH SHE HAD STAYED OUT OF YOUR BUSINESS?
NOW I APPRECIATE HER HELP...
SO SHE'S NOT A JERK ANYMORE?
NO.
FUSHI.

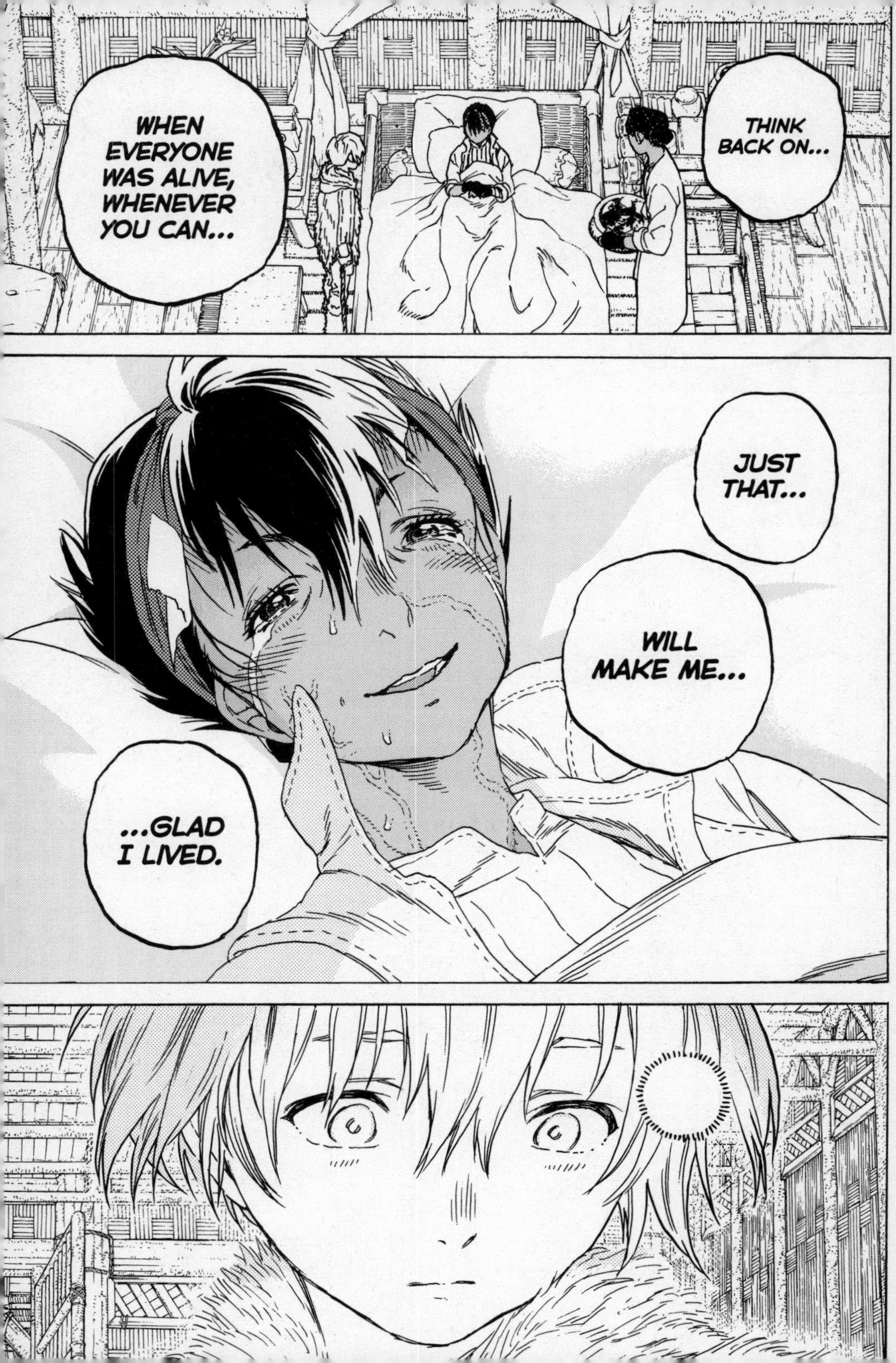
THINK BACK ON...
WHEN EVERYONE WAS ALIVE, WHENEVER YOU CAN...
JUST THAT...
WILL MAKE ME...
...GLAD I LIVED.

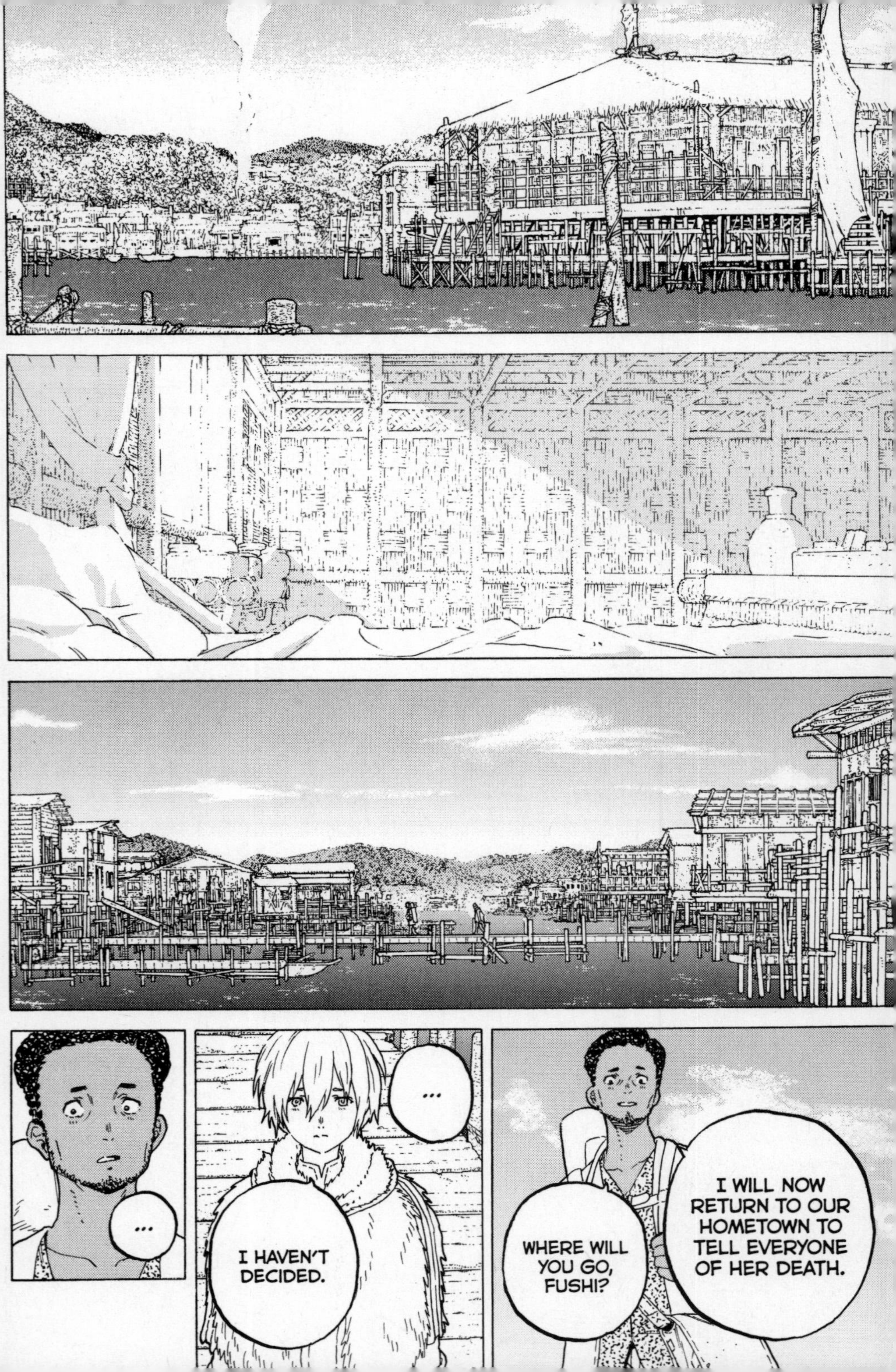
I WILL NOW RETURN TO OUR HOMETOWN TO TELL EVERYONE OF HER DEATH.
WHERE WILL YOU GO, FUSHI?
...
I HAVEN'T DECIDED.
...

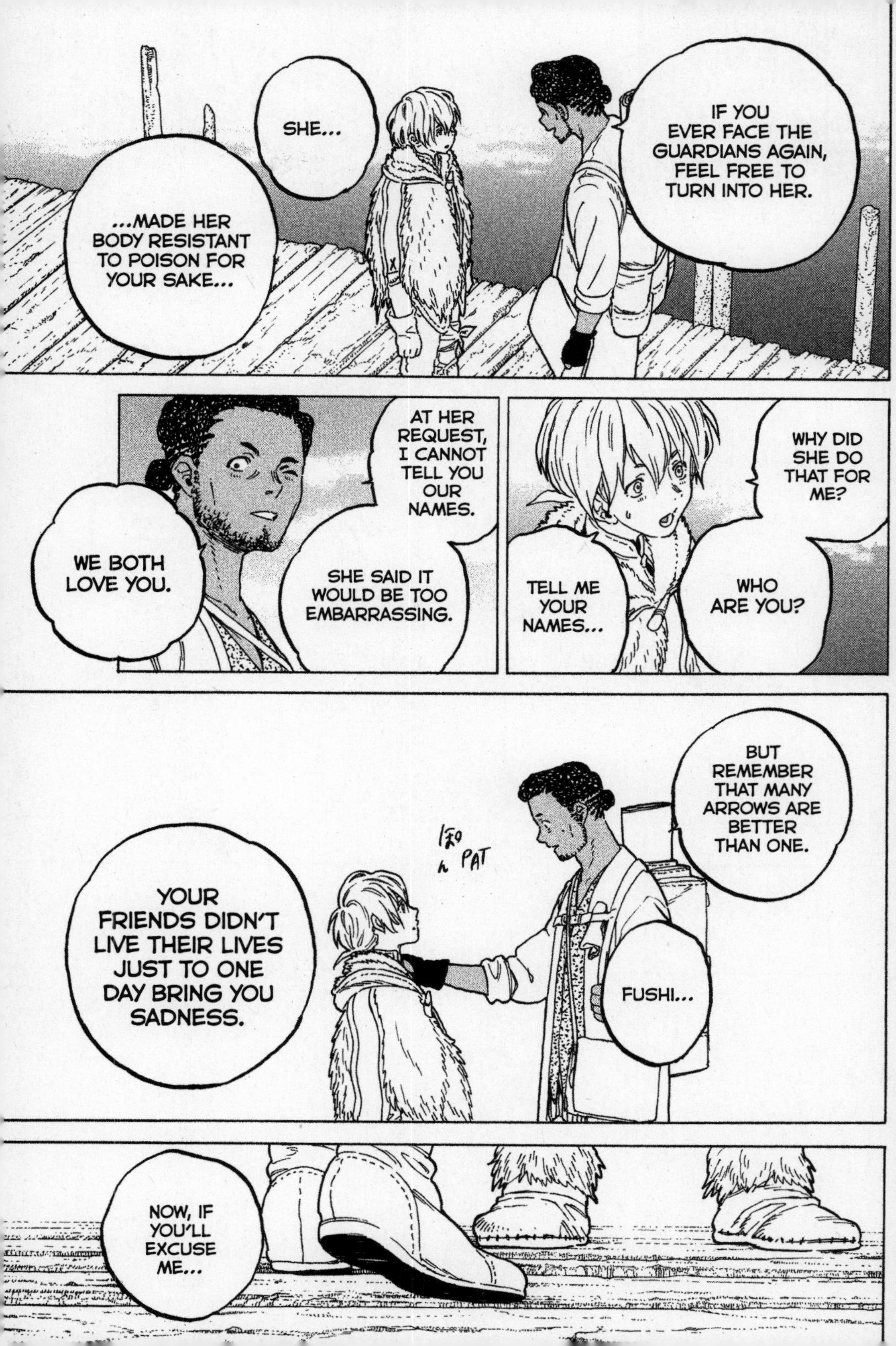

IF YOU EVER FACE THE GUARDIANS AGAIN, FEEL FREE TO TURN INTO HER.
SHE...
...MADE HER BODY RESISTANT TO POISON FOR YOUR SAKE...
WHY DID SHE DO THAT FOR ME?
WHO ARE YOU?
TELL ME YOUR NAMES...
AT HER REQUEST, I CANNOT TELL YOU OUR NAMES.
SHE SAID IT WOULD BE TOO EMBARRASSING.
WE BOTH LOVE YOU.
BUT REMEMBER THAT MANY ARROWS ARE BETTER THAN ONE.
PAT
FUSHI...
YOUR FRIENDS DIDN'T LIVE THEIR LIVES JUST TO ONE DAY BRING YOU SADNESS.
NOW, IF YOU'LL EXCUSE ME...

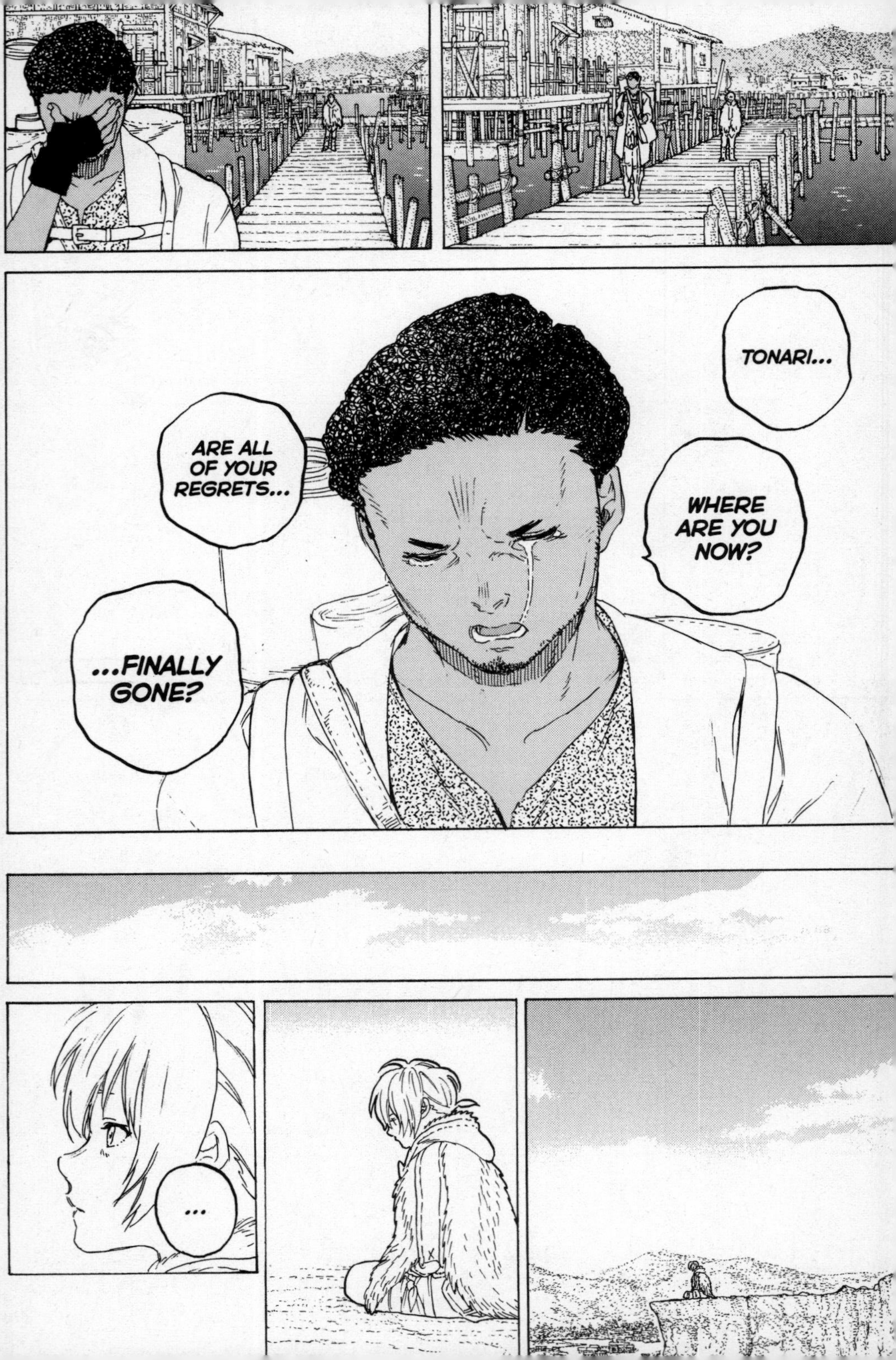
TONARI...
WHERE ARE YOU NOW?
ARE ALL OF YOUR REGRETS...
...FINALLY GONE?
...

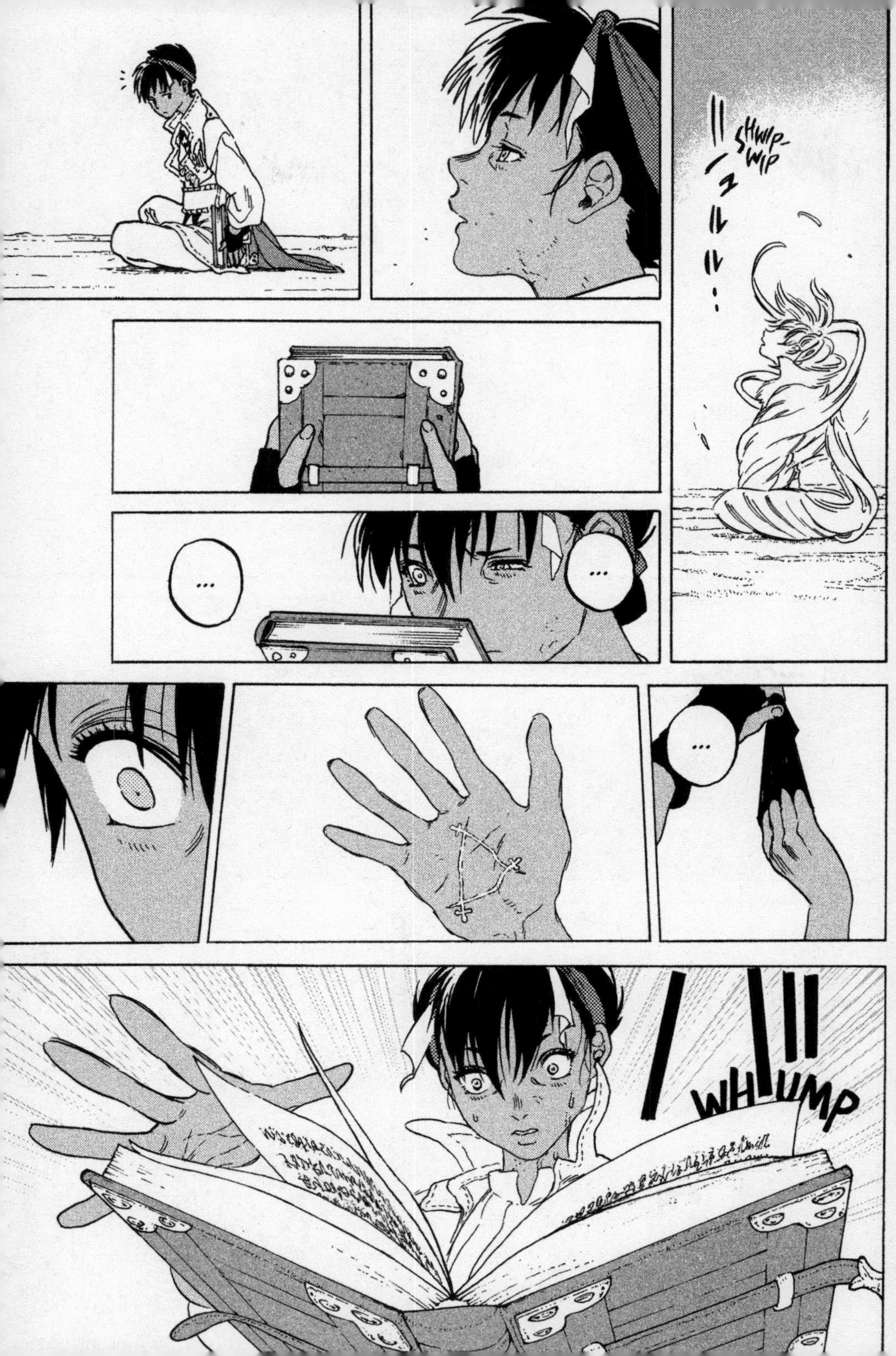

SHWIP-WIP
シュルル・・
...
...
...
WHUMP

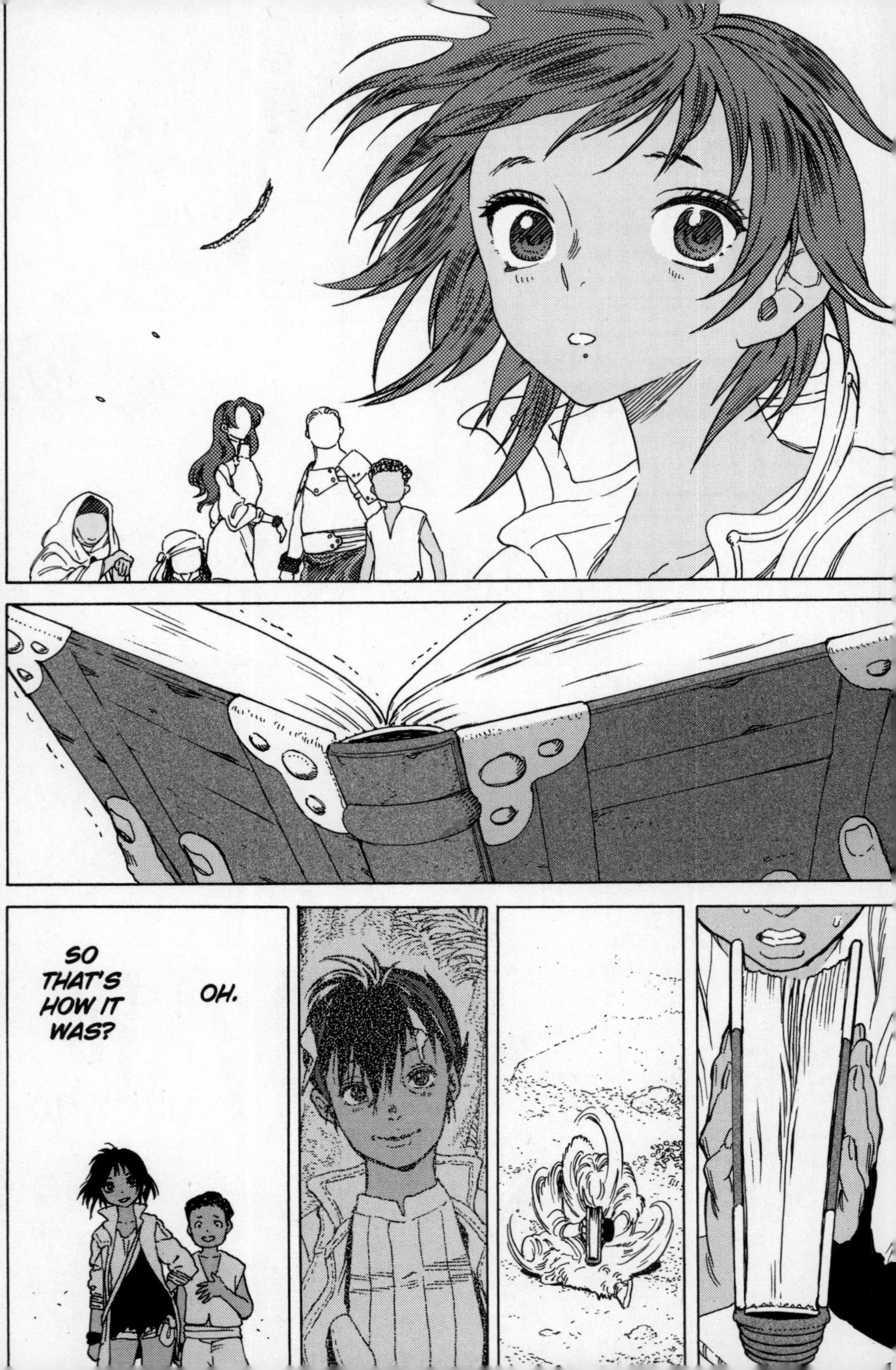
OH.
SO THAT'S HOW IT WAS?

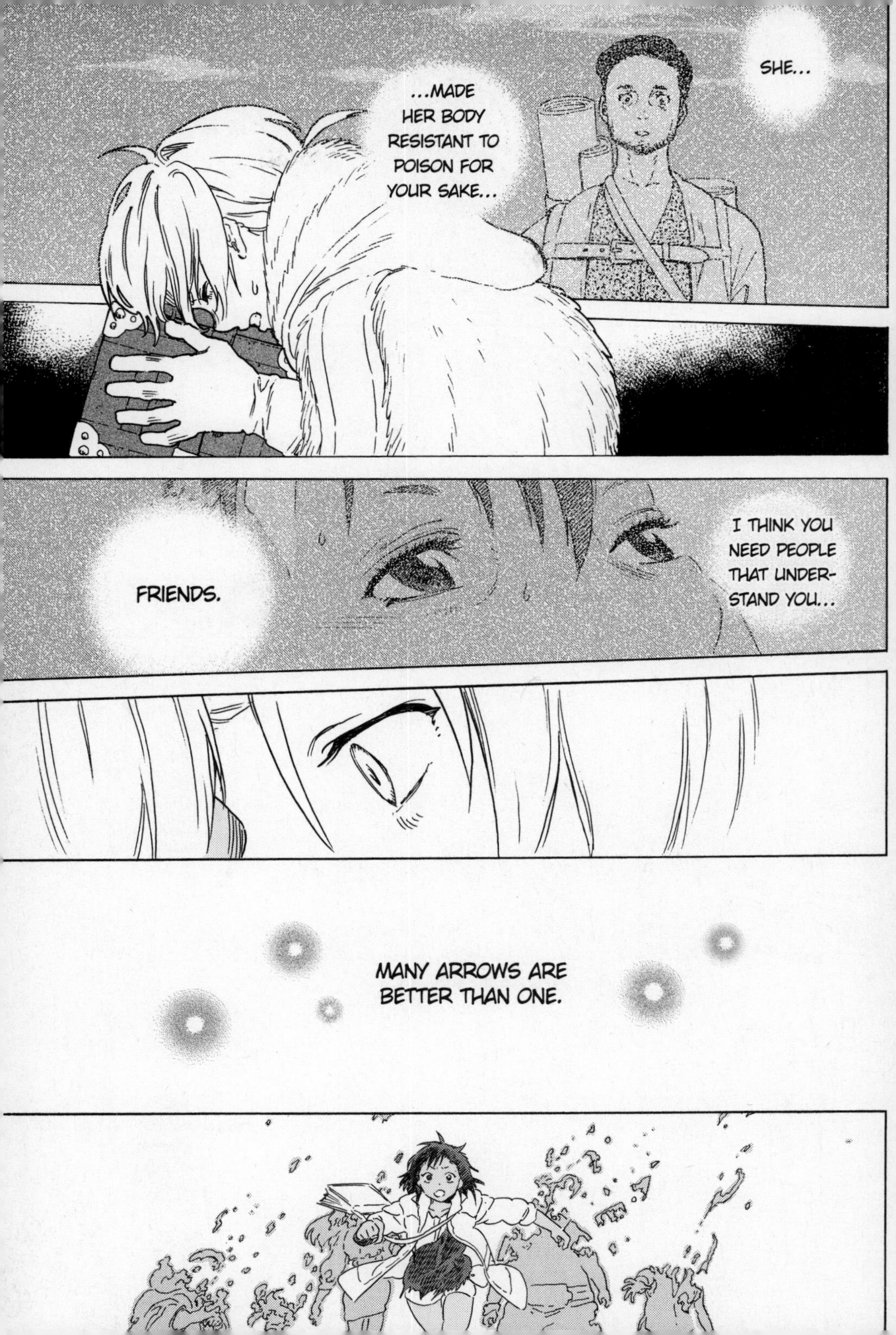
SHE...
...MADE HER BODY RESISTANT TO POISON FOR YOUR SAKE...
I THINK YOU NEED PEOPLE THAT UNDER-STAND YOU...
FRIENDS.
MANY ARROWS ARE BETTER THAN ONE.

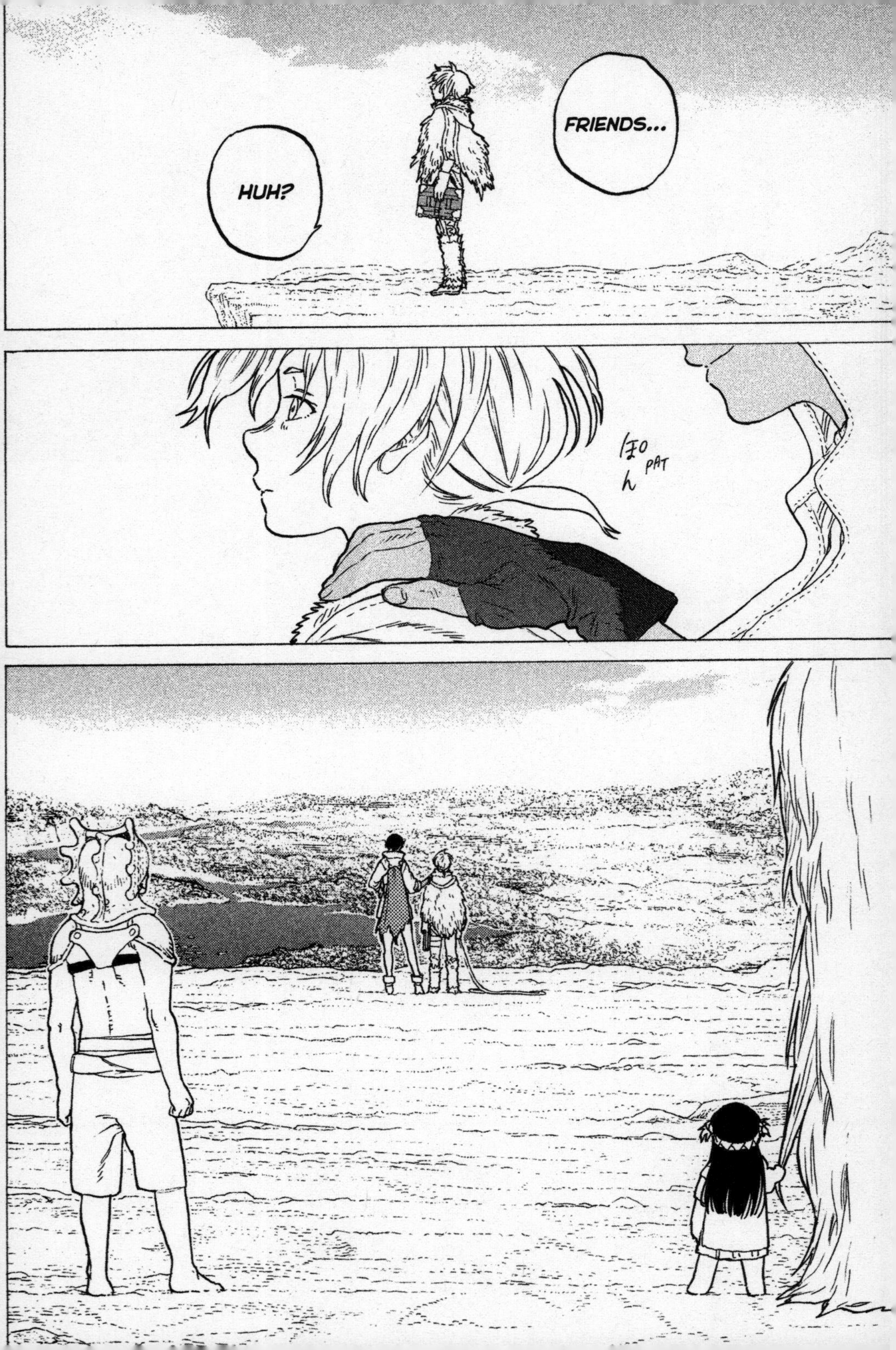
FRIENDS...
HUH?
ほん
PAT

TO YOUR
ETERNITY

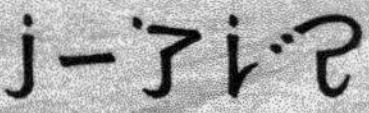

The Mark of the Jananda People

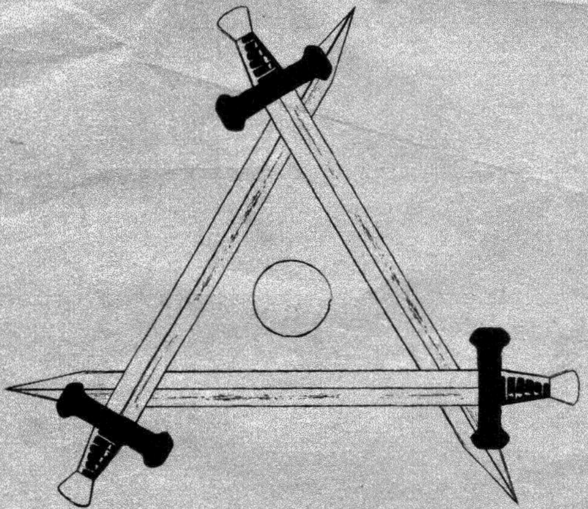

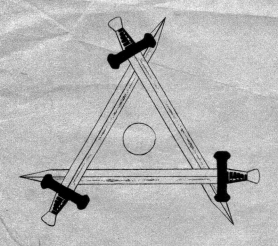

The Churches of Monjo, Bennett, and Zumla

Through battle, they all become one.
Their center is the arena.

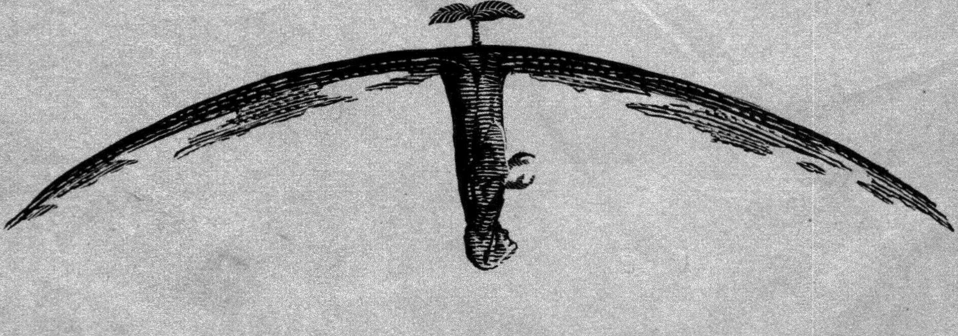

#60 Fate of a Long-Held Dream

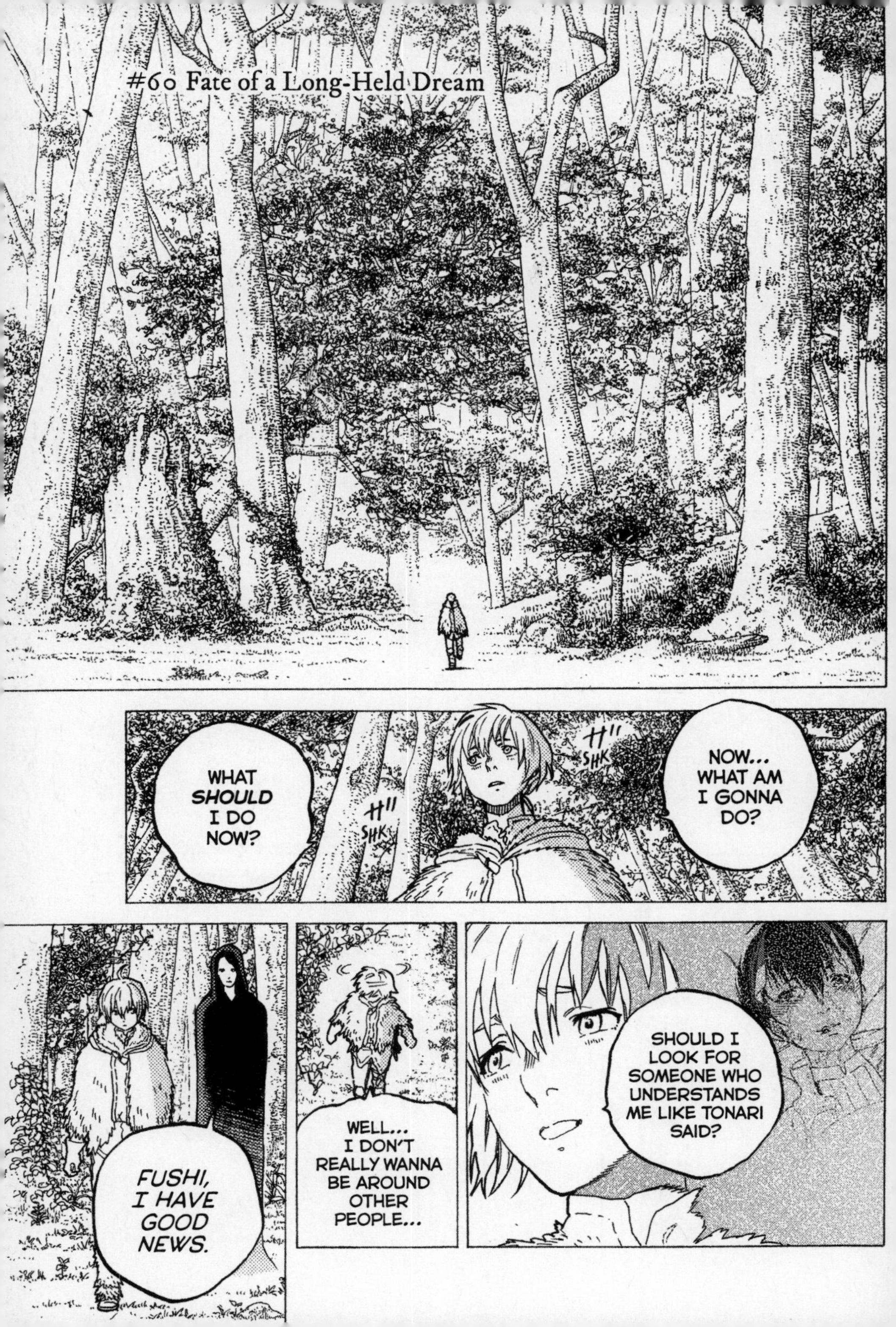
NOW... WHAT AM I GONNA DO?
SHK
SHK
WHAT *SHOULD* I DO NOW?
SHOULD I LOOK FOR SOMEONE WHO UNDERSTANDS ME LIKE TONARI SAID?
WELL... I DON'T REALLY WANNA BE AROUND OTHER PEOPLE...
FUSHI, I HAVE GOOD NEWS.

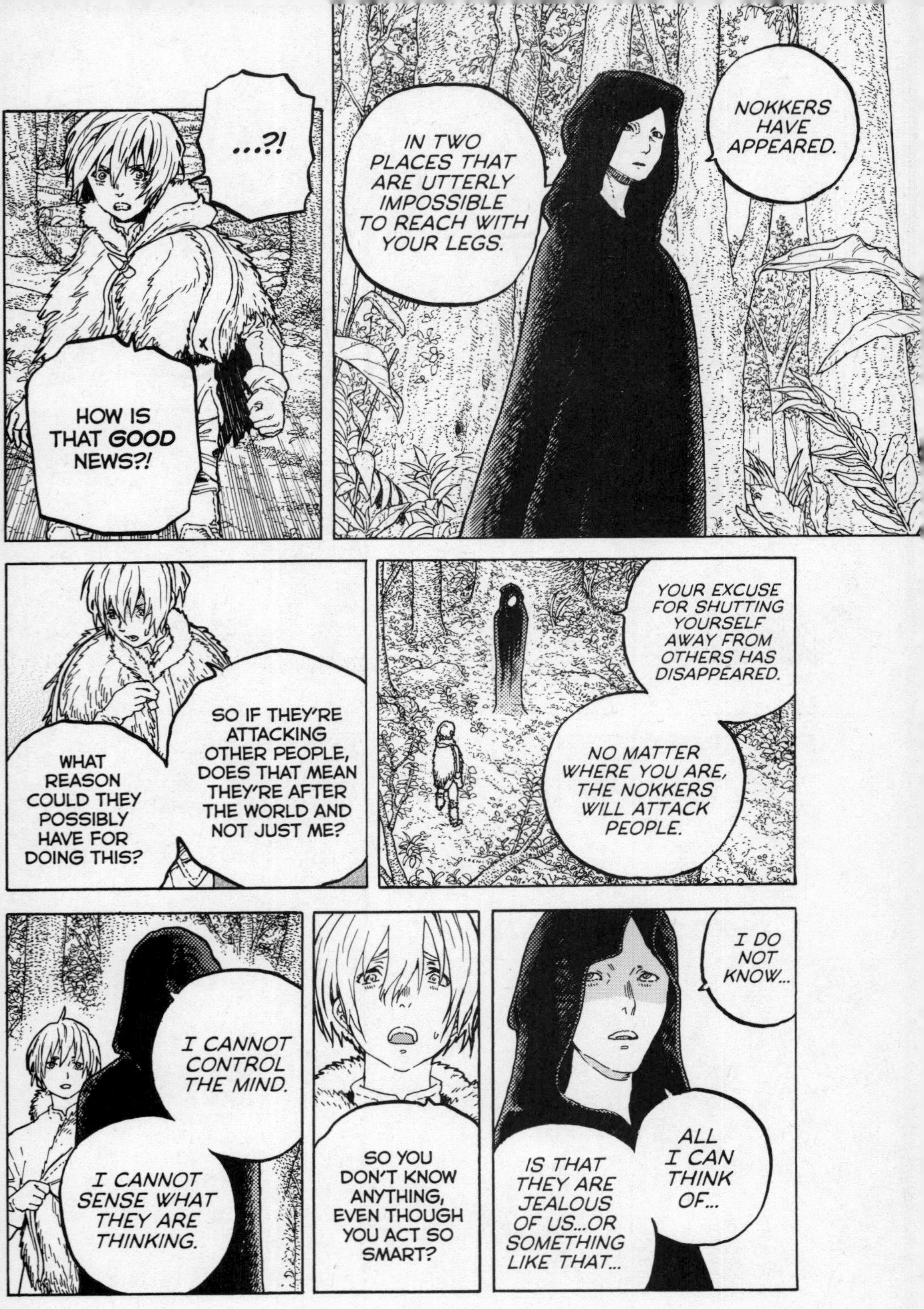
NOKKERS HAVE APPEARED.
IN TWO PLACES THAT ARE UTTERLY IMPOSSIBLE TO REACH WITH YOUR LEGS.
...?!
HOW IS THAT GOOD NEWS?!
YOUR EXCUSE FOR SHUTTING YOURSELF AWAY FROM OTHERS HAS DISAPPEARED.
NO MATTER WHERE YOU ARE, THE NOKKERS WILL ATTACK PEOPLE.
SO IF THEY'RE ATTACKING OTHER PEOPLE, DOES THAT MEAN THEY'RE AFTER THE WORLD AND NOT JUST ME?
WHAT REASON COULD THEY POSSIBLY HAVE FOR DOING THIS?
I DO NOT KNOW...
ALL I CAN THINK OF...
IS THAT THEY ARE JEALOUS OF US...OR SOMETHING LIKE THAT...
SO YOU DON'T KNOW ANYTHING, EVEN THOUGH YOU ACT SO SMART?
I CANNOT CONTROL THE MIND.
I CANNOT SENSE WHAT THEY ARE THINKING.

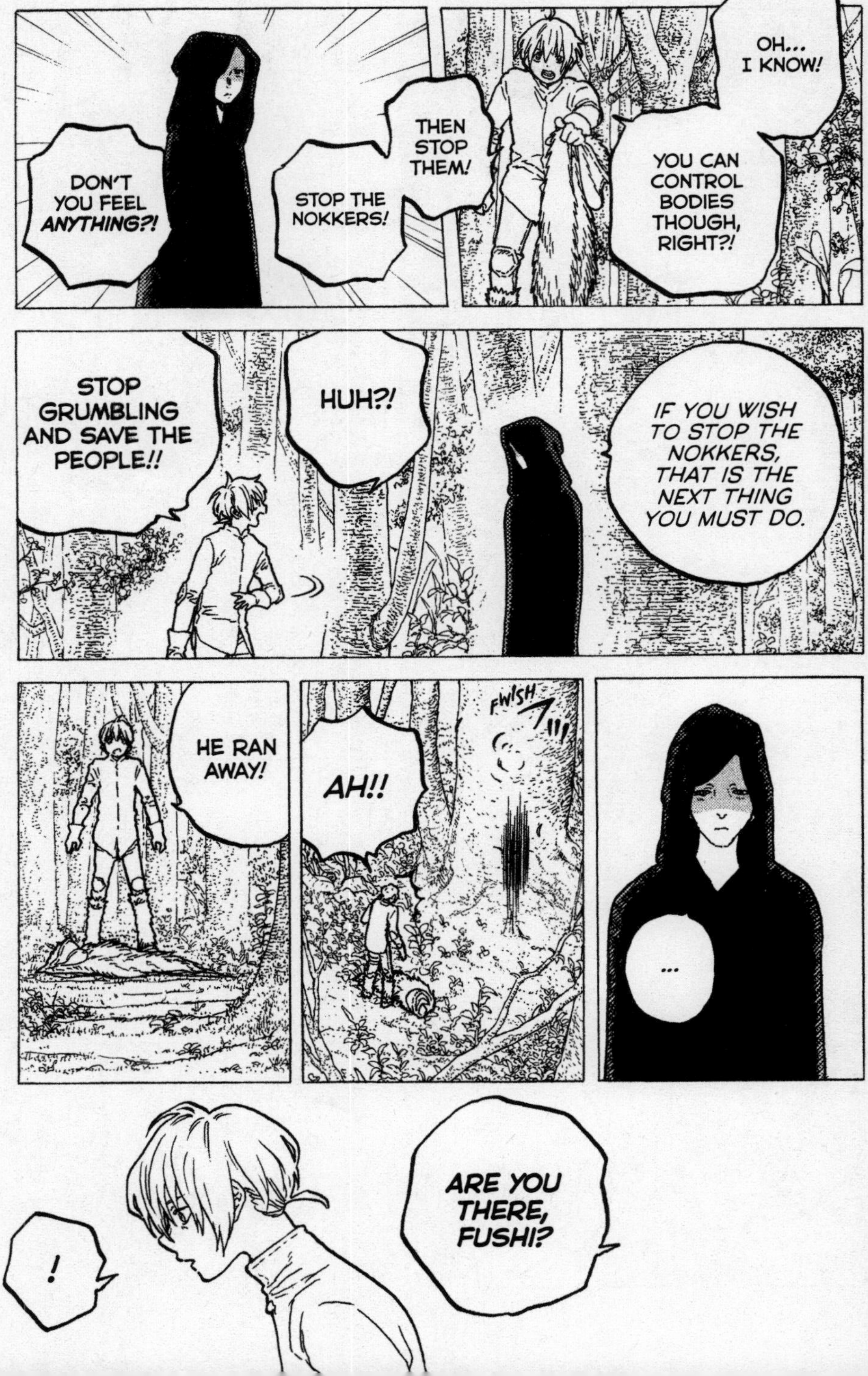
OH... I KNOW!
YOU CAN CONTROL BODIES THOUGH, RIGHT?!
THEN STOP THEM!
STOP THE NOKKERS!
DON'T YOU FEEL *ANYTHING?!*
IF YOU WISH TO STOP THE NOKKERS, THAT IS THE NEXT THING YOU MUST DO.
HUH?!
STOP GRUMBLING AND SAVE THE PEOPLE!!
...
FWISH
AH!!
HE RAN AWAY!
ARE YOU THERE, FUSHI?
!

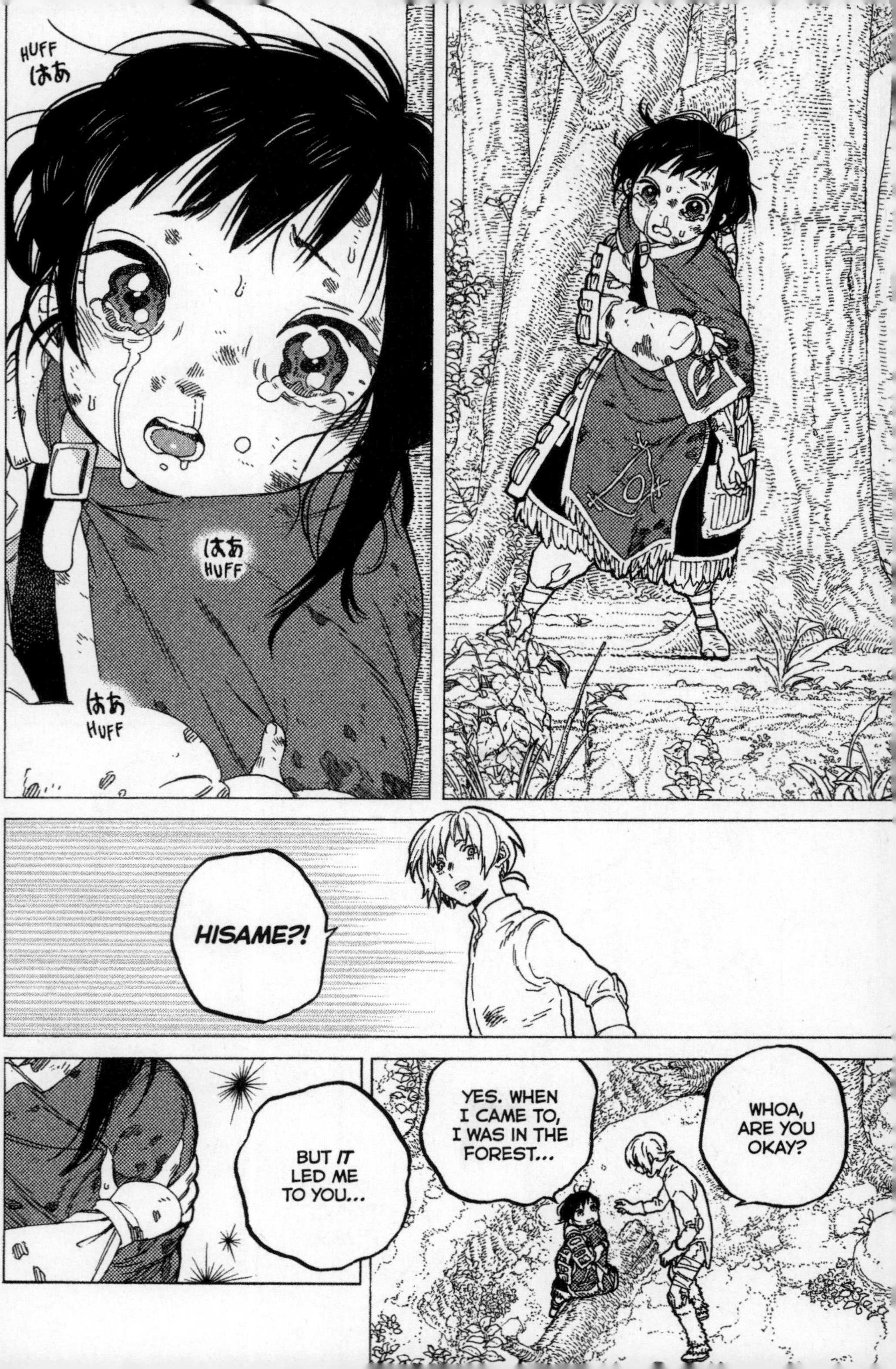
HUFF はあ
はあ HUFF
はあ HUFF
HISAME?!
WHOA, ARE YOU OKAY?
YES. WHEN I CAME TO, I WAS IN THE FOREST...
BUT *IT* LED ME TO YOU...

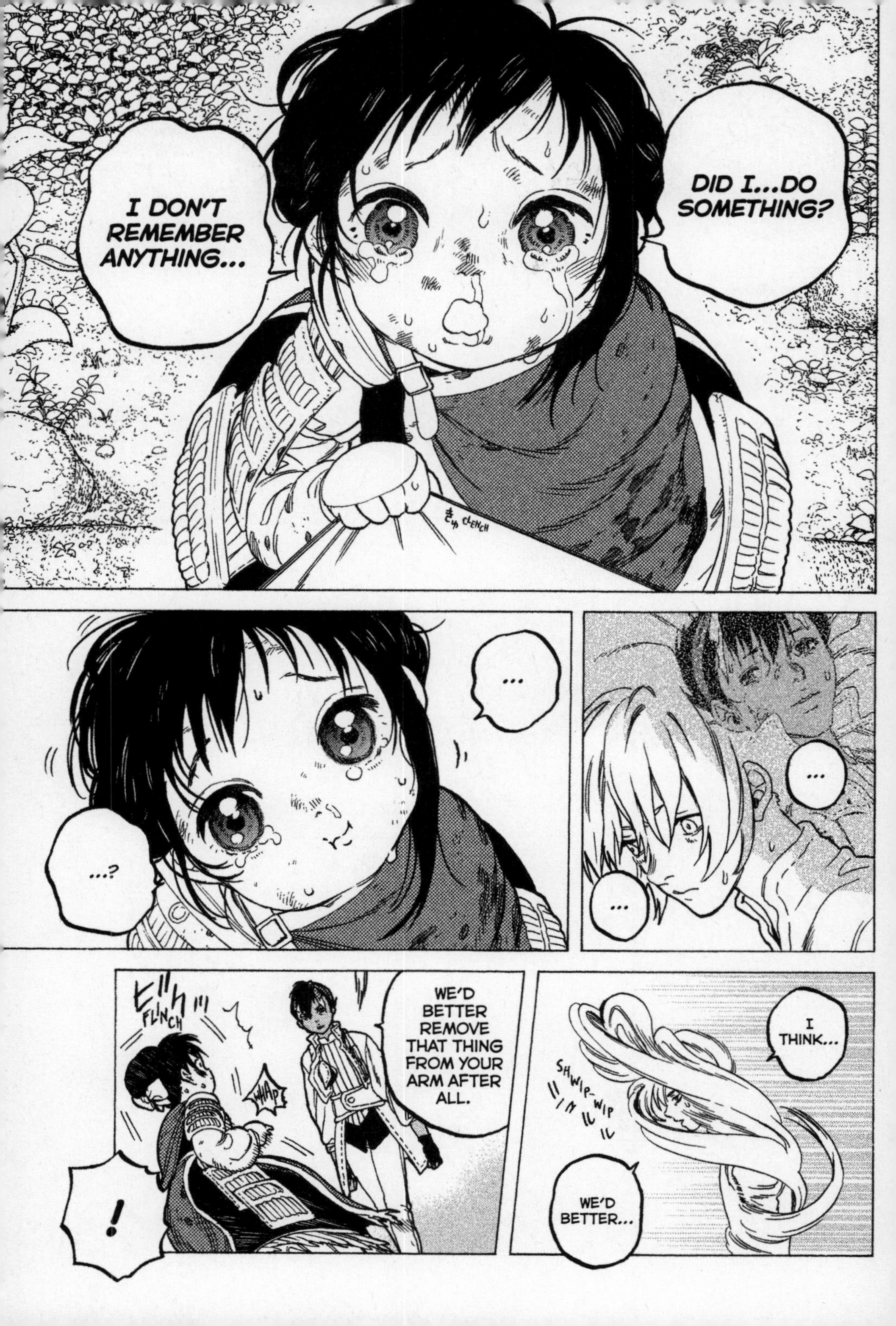
DID I...DO SOMETHING?
I DON'T REMEMBER ANYTHING...
CLENCH
...
...
...
...?
I THINK...
SHWIP-WIP
WE'D BETTER...
WE'D BETTER REMOVE THAT THING FROM YOUR ARM AFTER ALL.
WHAP
FLINCH
!

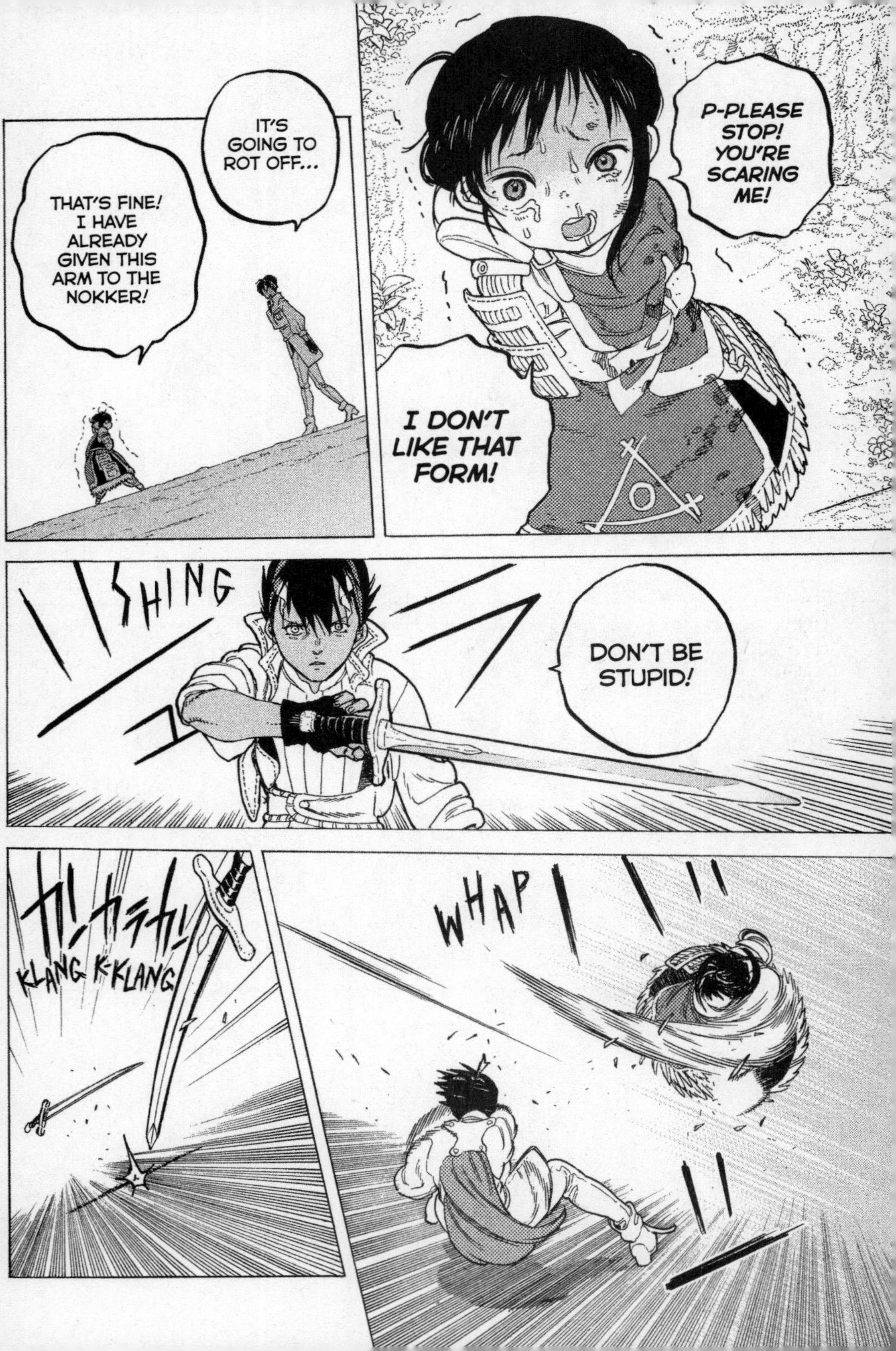
P-PLEASE STOP! YOU'RE SCARING ME!
I DON'T LIKE THAT FORM!
IT'S GOING TO ROT OFF...
THAT'S FINE! I HAVE ALREADY GIVEN THIS ARM TO THE NOKKER!
DON'T BE STUPID!
SHING
WHAP
カン カラカン!
KLANG K-KLANG

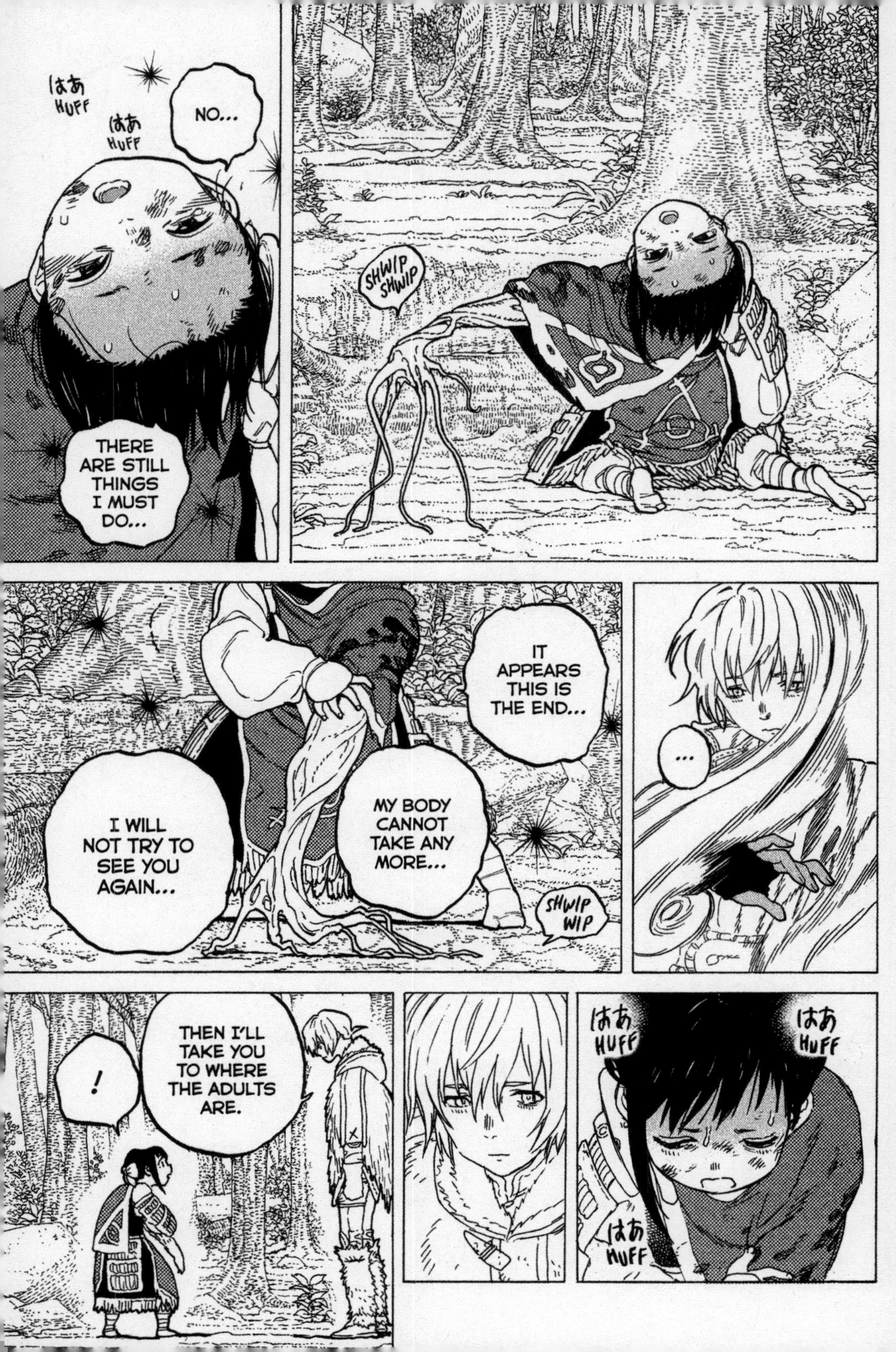
SHWIP SHWIP
はあ HUFF
はあ HUFF
NO...
THERE ARE STILL THINGS I MUST DO...
...
IT APPEARS THIS IS THE END...
MY BODY CANNOT TAKE ANY MORE...
SHWIP WIP
I WILL NOT TRY TO SEE YOU AGAIN...
はあ HUFF
はあ HUFF
はあ HUFF
THEN I'LL TAKE YOU TO WHERE THE ADULTS ARE.
!

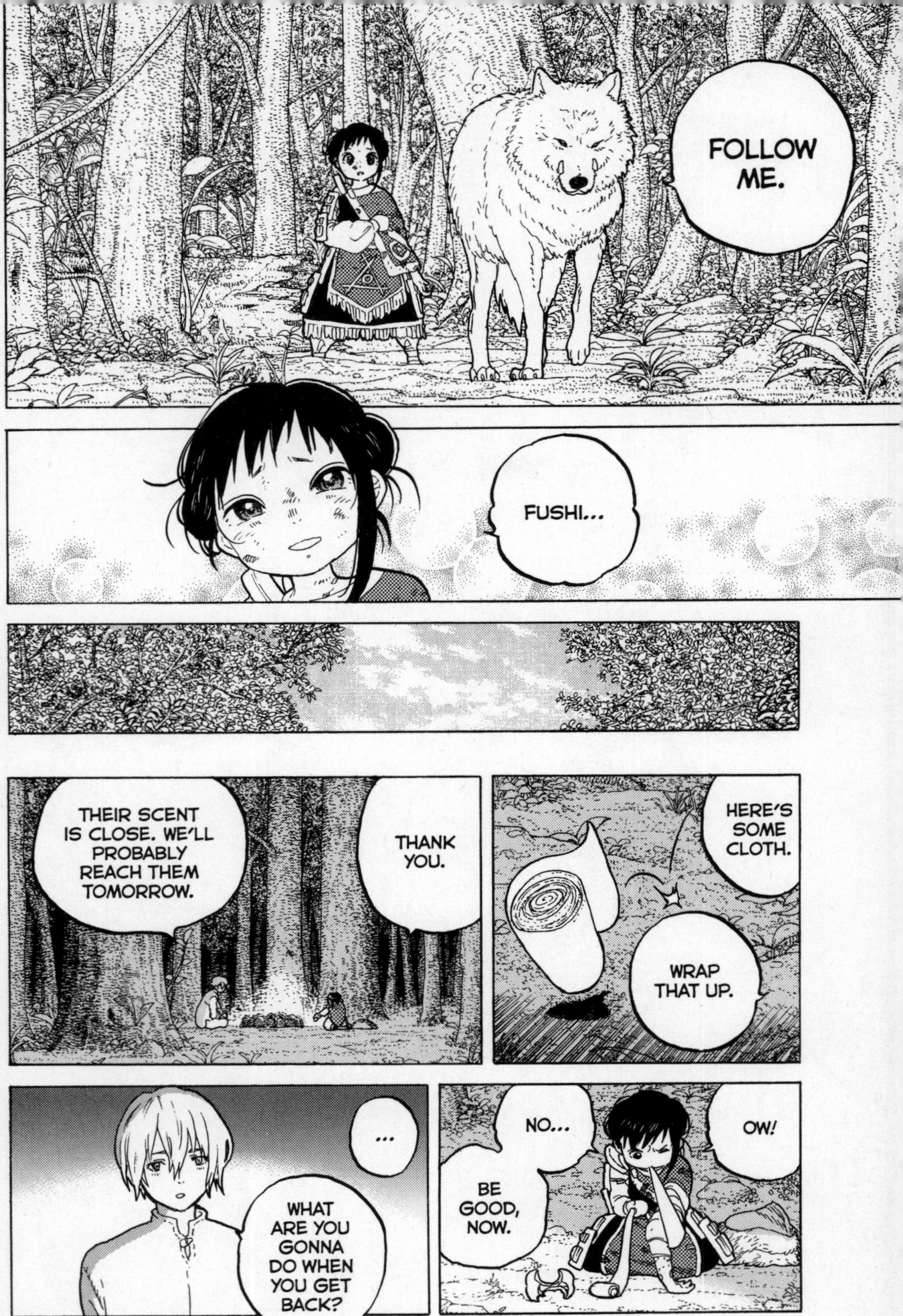
FOLLOW ME.
FUSHI...
HERE'S SOME CLOTH.
WRAP THAT UP.
THANK YOU.
THEIR SCENT IS CLOSE. WE'LL PROBABLY REACH THEM TOMORROW.
OW!
NO...
BE GOOD, NOW.
...
WHAT ARE YOU GONNA DO WHEN YOU GET BACK?

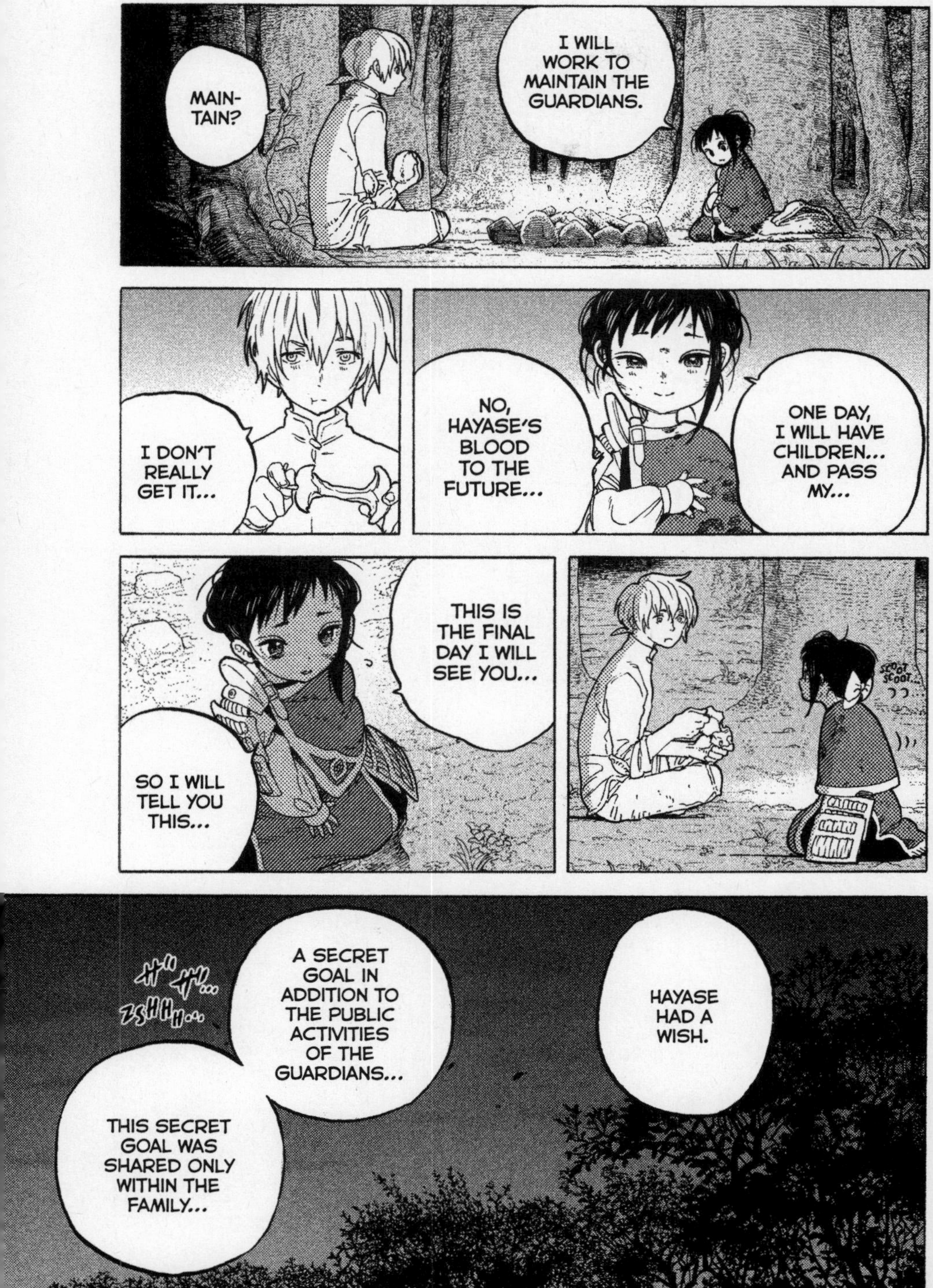
I WILL WORK TO MAINTAIN THE GUARDIANS.
MAIN-TAIN?
ONE DAY, I WILL HAVE CHILDREN... AND PASS MY...
NO, HAYASE'S BLOOD TO THE FUTURE...
I DON'T REALLY GET IT...
SCOOT SCOOT...
THIS IS THE FINAL DAY I WILL SEE YOU...
SO I WILL TELL YOU THIS...
HAYASE HAD A WISH.
A SECRET GOAL IN ADDITION TO THE PUBLIC ACTIVITIES OF THE GUARDIANS...
ZSHHH...
THIS SECRET GOAL WAS SHARED ONLY WITHIN THE FAMILY...

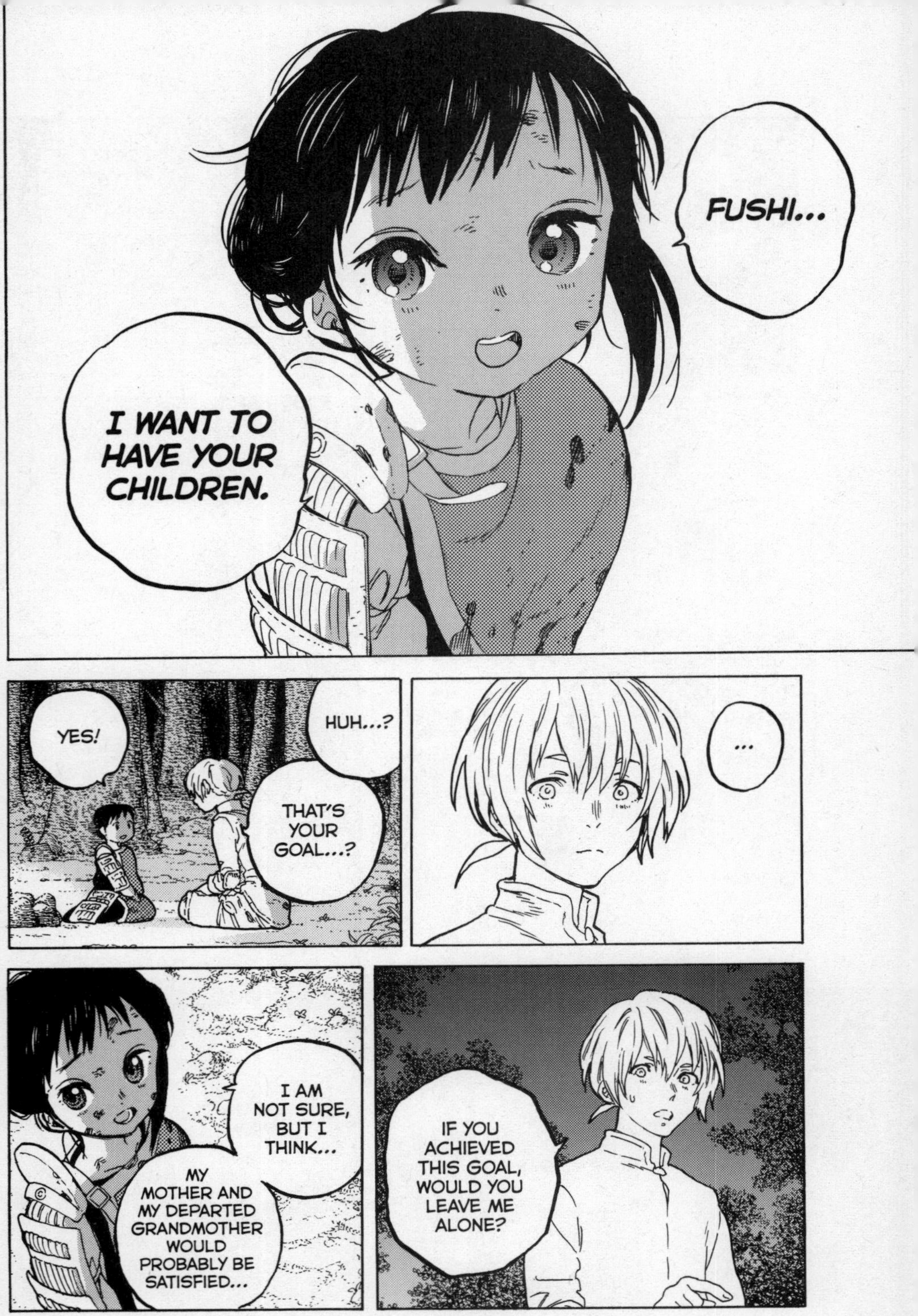
FUSHI...
I WANT TO HAVE YOUR CHILDREN.
...
HUH...?
THAT'S YOUR GOAL...?
YES!
IF YOU ACHIEVED THIS GOAL, WOULD YOU LEAVE ME ALONE?
I AM NOT SURE, BUT I THINK...
MY MOTHER AND MY DEPARTED GRANDMOTHER WOULD PROBABLY BE SATISFIED...

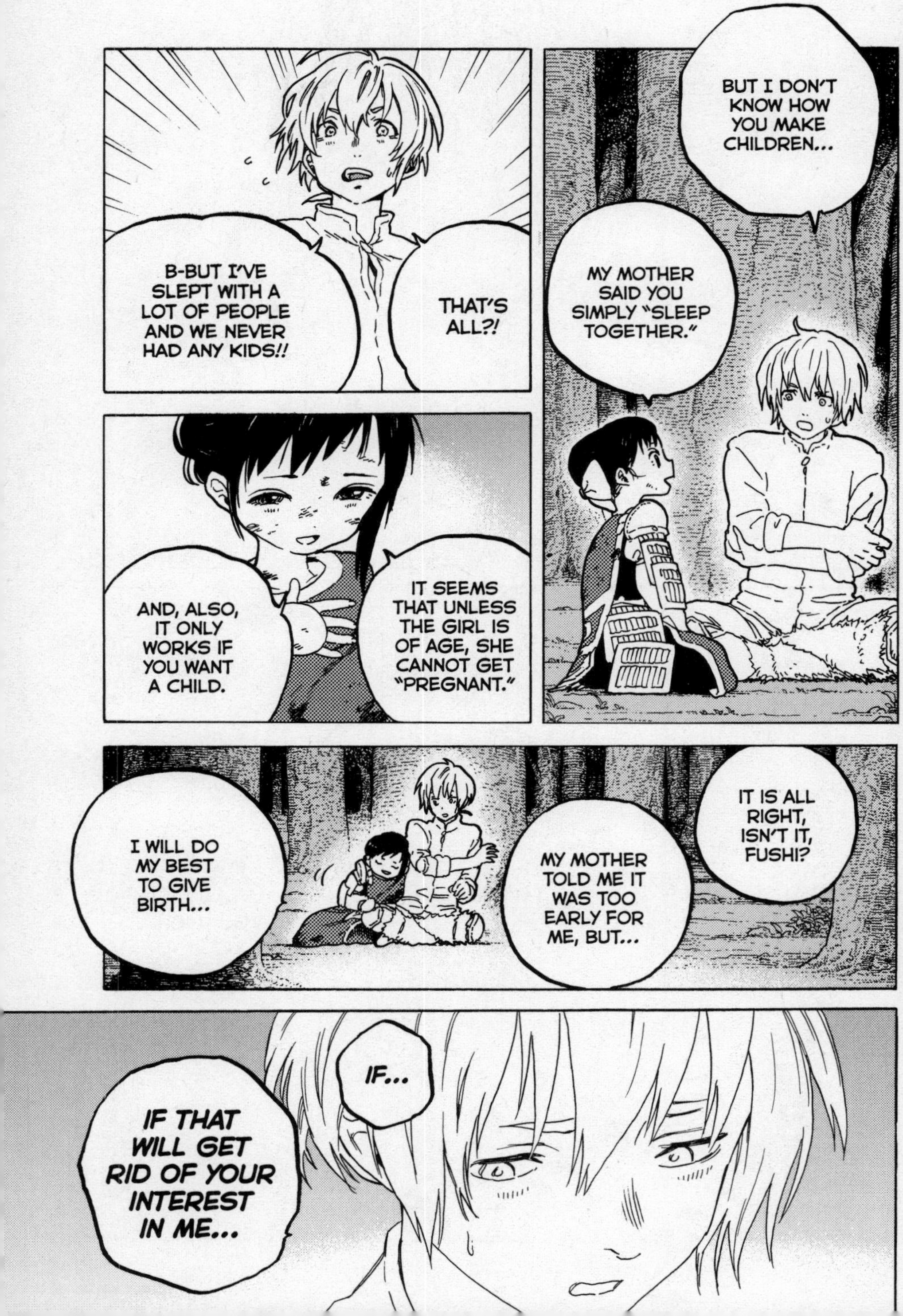
BUT I DON'T KNOW HOW YOU MAKE CHILDREN...
MY MOTHER SAID YOU SIMPLY "SLEEP TOGETHER."
THAT'S ALL?!
B-BUT I'VE SLEPT WITH A LOT OF PEOPLE AND WE NEVER HAD ANY KIDS!!
IT SEEMS THAT UNLESS THE GIRL IS OF AGE, SHE CANNOT GET "PREGNANT."
AND, ALSO, IT ONLY WORKS IF YOU WANT A CHILD.
IT IS ALL RIGHT, ISN'T IT, FUSHI?
MY MOTHER TOLD ME IT WAS TOO EARLY FOR ME, BUT...
I WILL DO MY BEST TO GIVE BIRTH...
IF...
IF THAT WILL GET RID OF YOUR INTEREST IN ME...

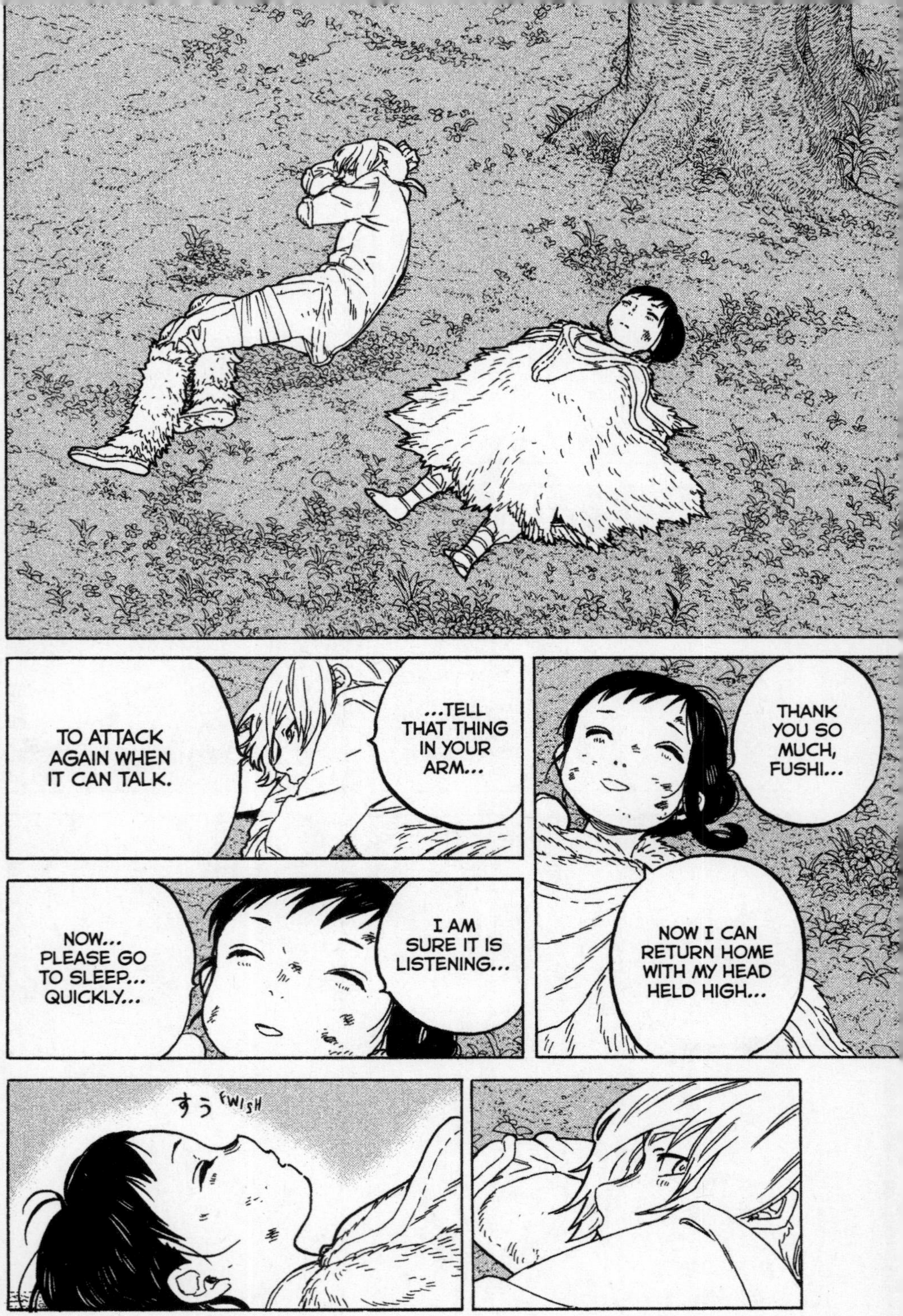
THANK YOU SO MUCH, FUSHI...
NOW I CAN RETURN HOME WITH MY HEAD HELD HIGH...
...TELL THAT THING IN YOUR ARM...
TO ATTACK AGAIN WHEN IT CAN TALK.
I AM SURE IT IS LISTENING...
NOW... PLEASE GO TO SLEEP... QUICKLY...
すう FWISH

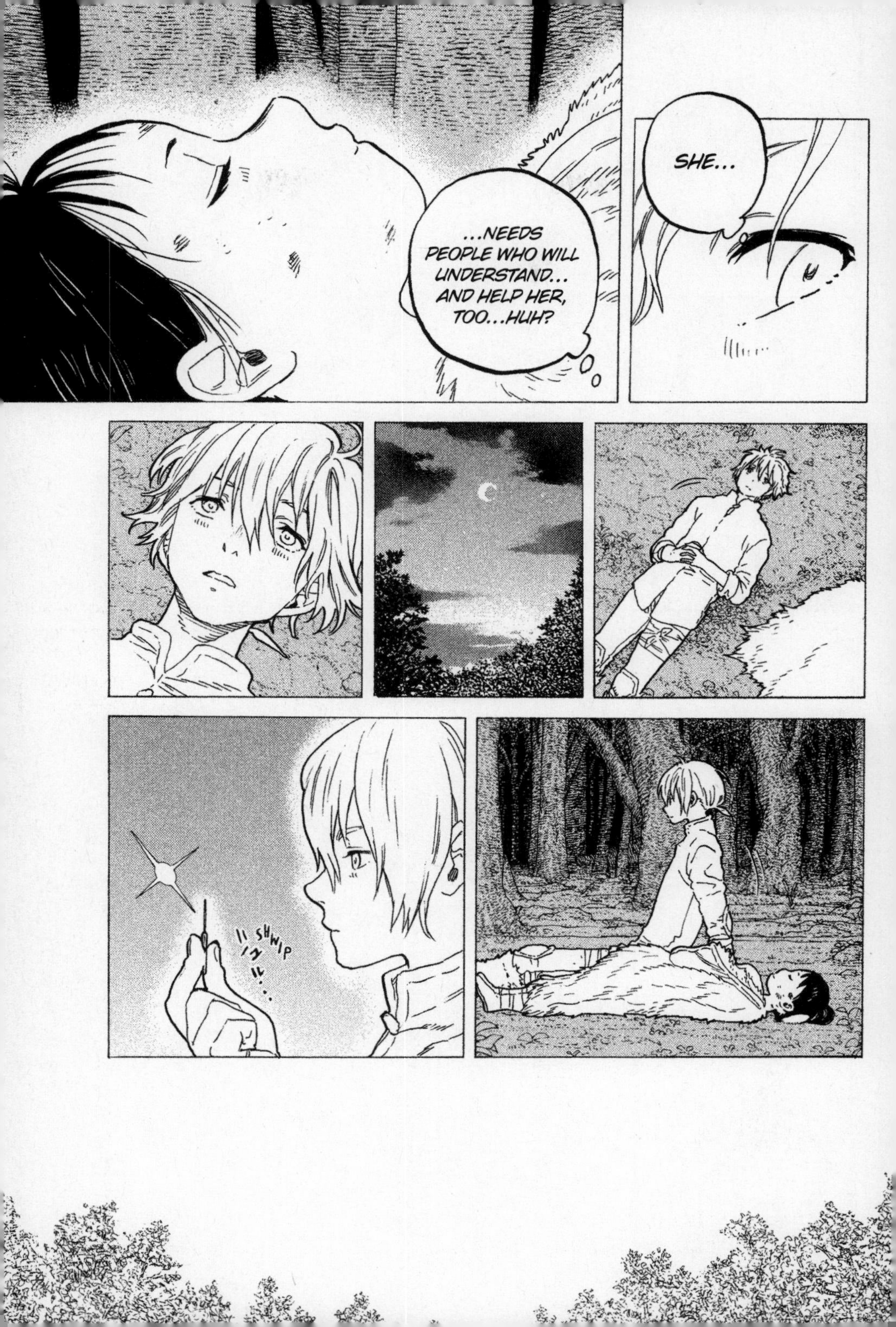
SHE...
...NEEDS PEOPLE WHO WILL UNDERSTAND... AND HELP HER, TOO...HUH?
SHWIP

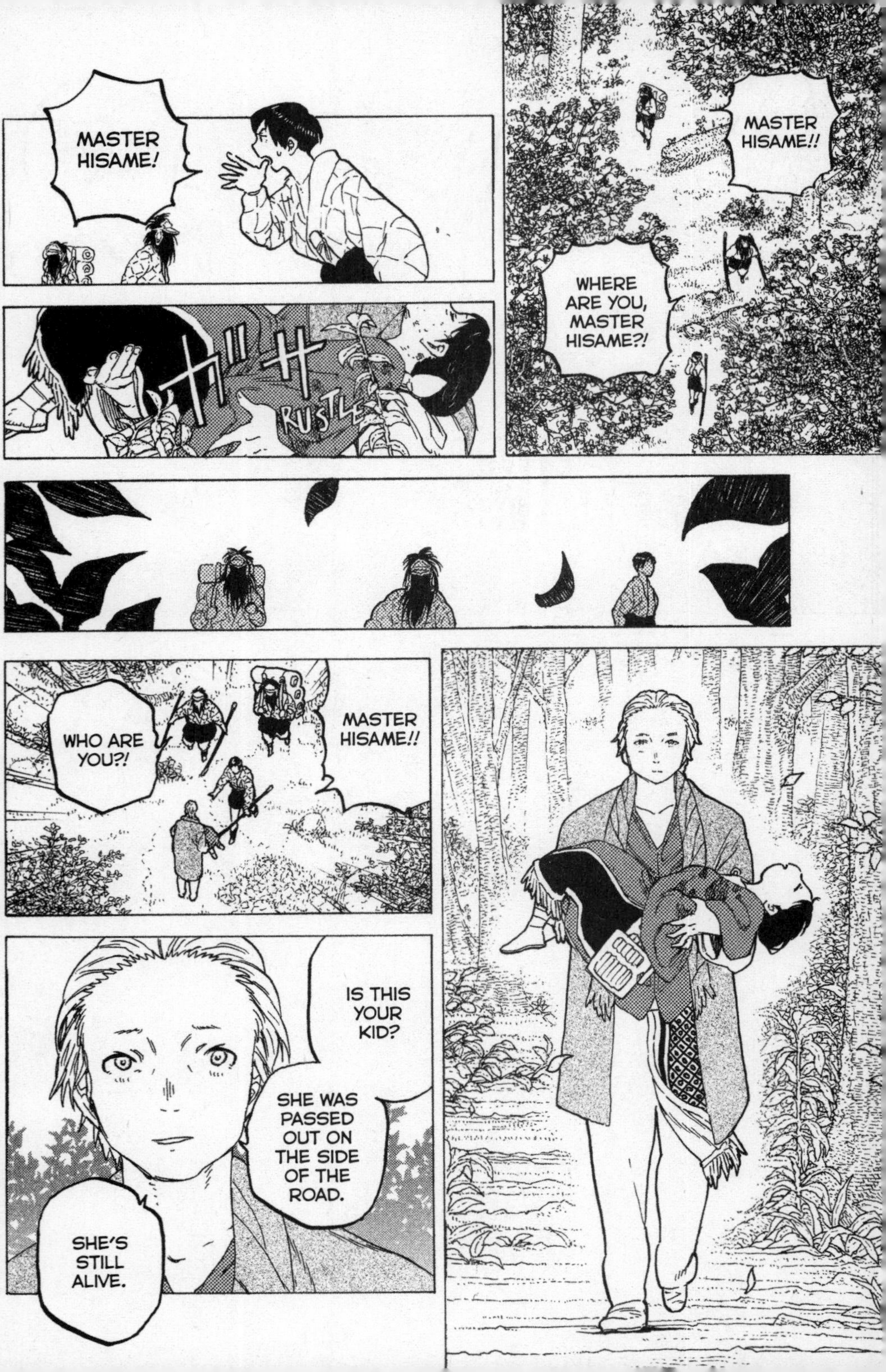
MASTER HISAME!!
WHERE ARE YOU, MASTER HISAME?!
MASTER HISAME!
RUSTLE
MASTER HISAME!!
WHO ARE YOU?!
IS THIS YOUR KID?
SHE WAS PASSED OUT ON THE SIDE OF THE ROAD.
SHE'S STILL ALIVE.

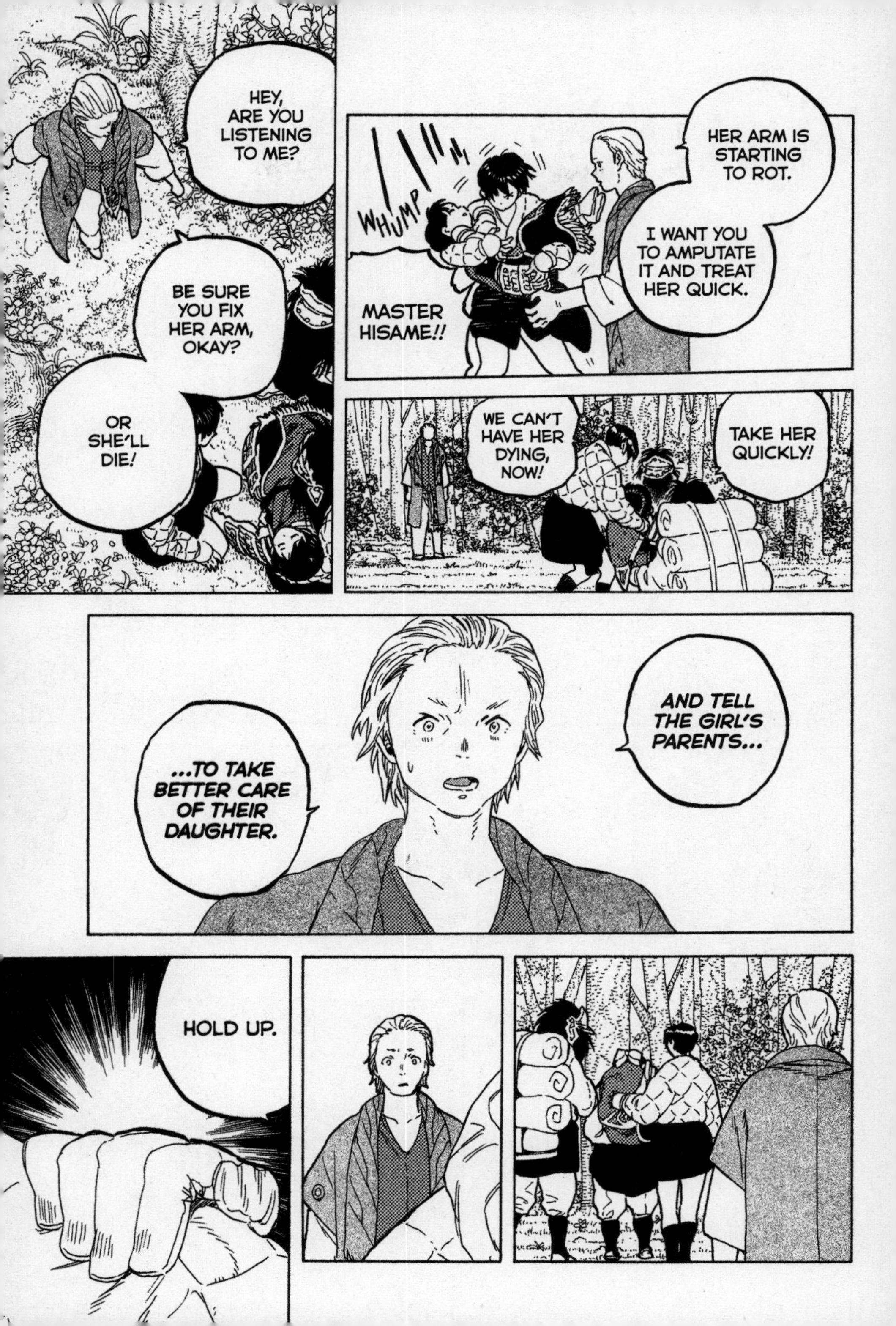
HER ARM IS STARTING TO ROT.
I WANT YOU TO AMPUTATE IT AND TREAT HER QUICK.
WHUMP
MASTER HISAME!!
TAKE HER QUICKLY!
WE CAN'T HAVE HER DYING, NOW!
HEY, ARE YOU LISTENING TO ME?
BE SURE YOU FIX HER ARM, OKAY?
OR SHE'LL DIE!
AND TELL THE GIRL'S PARENTS...
...TO TAKE BETTER CARE OF THEIR DAUGHTER.
HOLD UP.

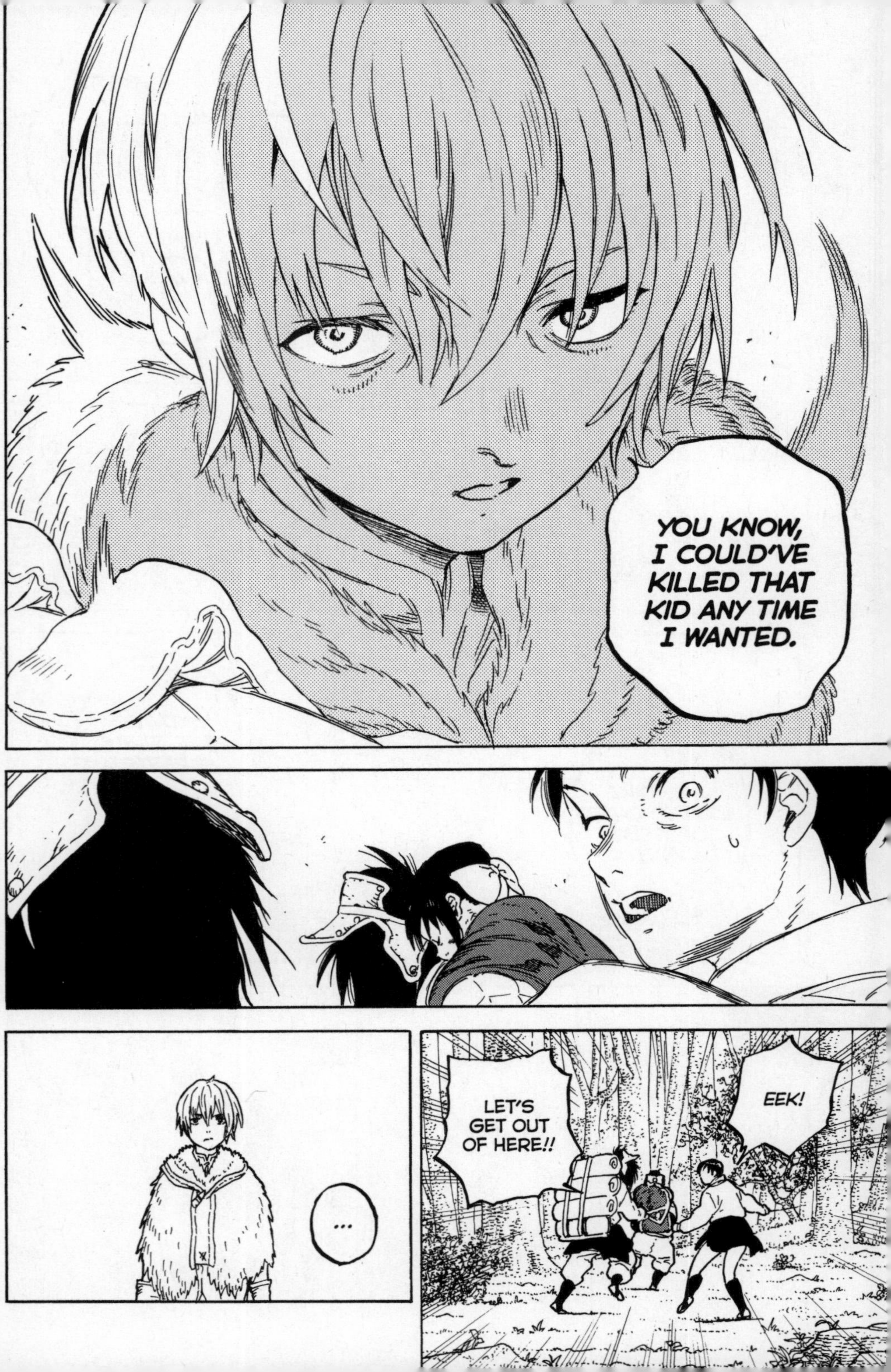
YOU KNOW, I COULD'VE KILLED THAT KID ANY TIME I WANTED.
EEK!
LET'S GET OUT OF HERE!!
...

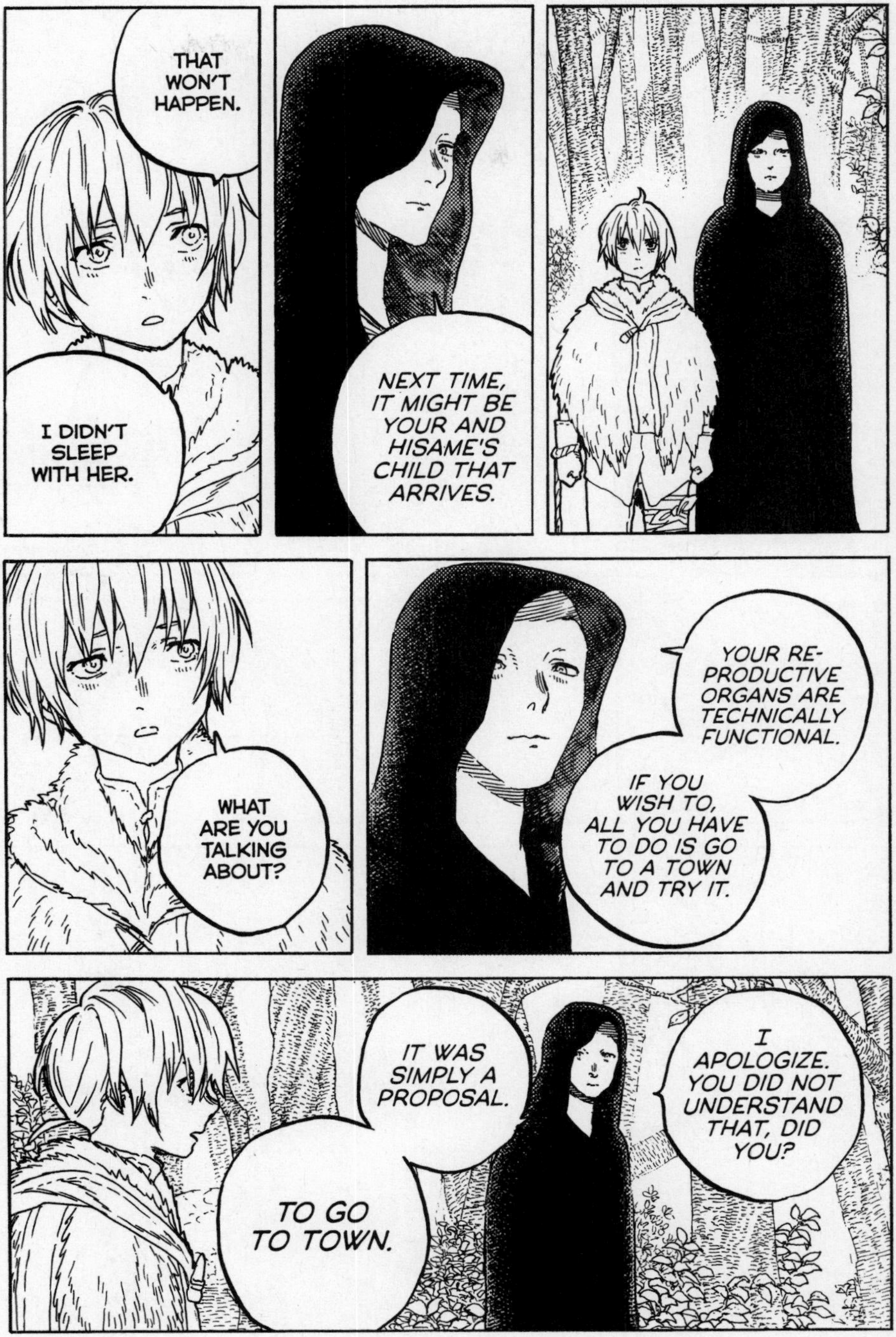
NEXT TIME, IT MIGHT BE YOUR AND HISAME'S CHILD THAT ARRIVES.
THAT WON'T HAPPEN.
I DIDN'T SLEEP WITH HER.
YOUR RE-PRODUCTIVE ORGANS ARE TECHNICALLY FUNCTIONAL.
IF YOU WISH TO, ALL YOU HAVE TO DO IS GO TO A TOWN AND TRY IT.
WHAT ARE YOU TALKING ABOUT?
I APOLOGIZE. YOU DID NOT UNDERSTAND THAT, DID YOU?
IT WAS SIMPLY A PROPOSAL.
TO GO TO TOWN.

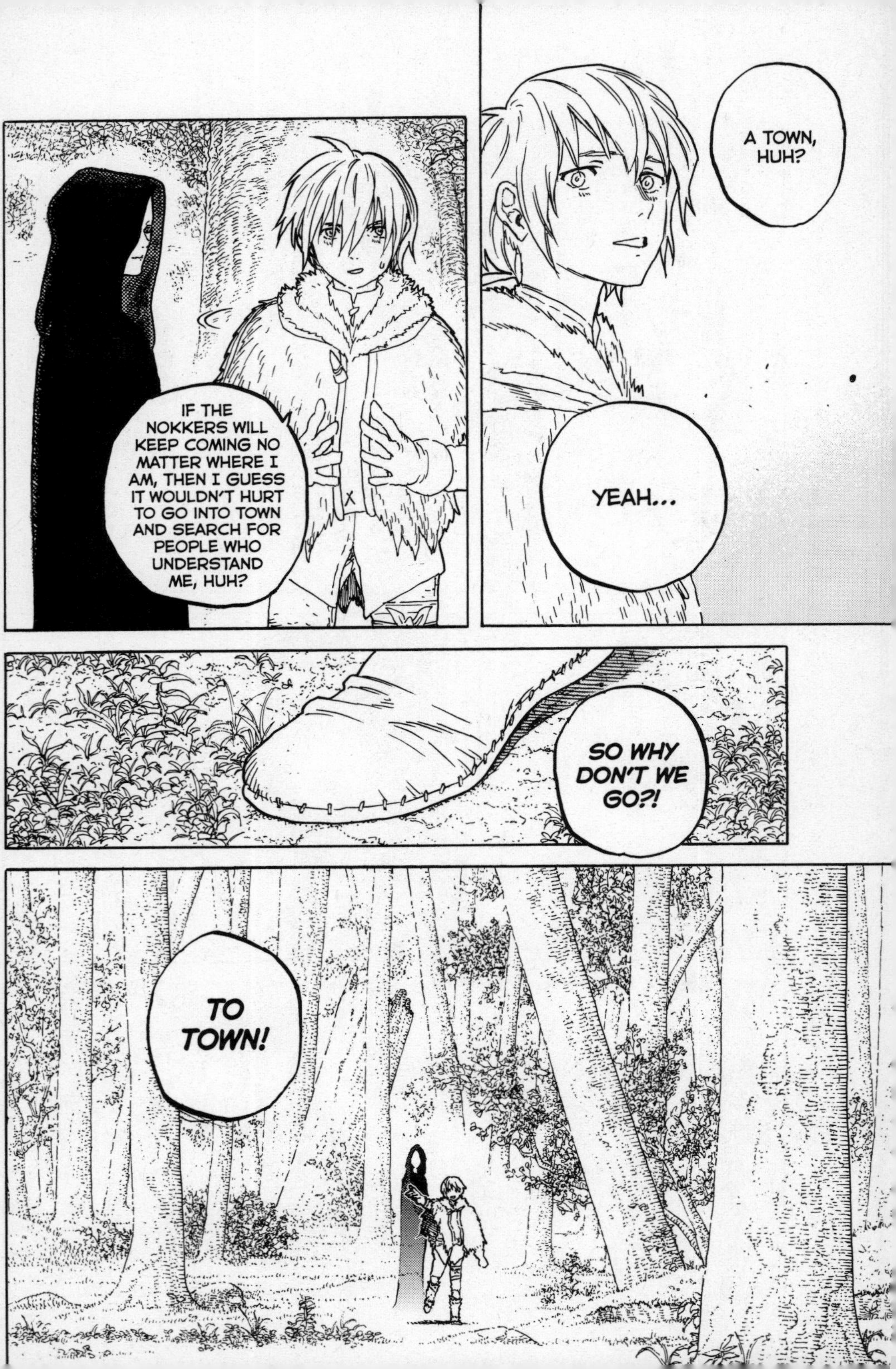
A TOWN, HUH?
YEAH...
IF THE NOKKERS WILL KEEP COMING NO MATTER WHERE I AM, THEN I GUESS IT WOULDN'T HURT TO GO INTO TOWN AND SEARCH FOR PEOPLE WHO UNDERSTAND ME, HUH?
SO WHY DON'T WE GO?!
TO TOWN!

TO YOUR
ETERNITY

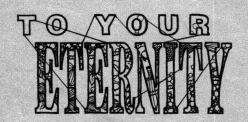

j–ʾʞˤ–j

HOW TO MAKE DRIED NOKKERS

1. Defeat a Nokker.

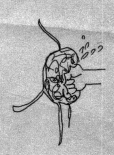

2. Remove the innards.

3. Wash the Nokker well with water.

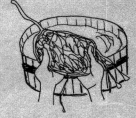

4. Soak in seawater.

5. Hang the Nokker in the sun.

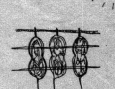

6. Once it has been dried for around three days, long enough to remove the water completely, the process is complete.

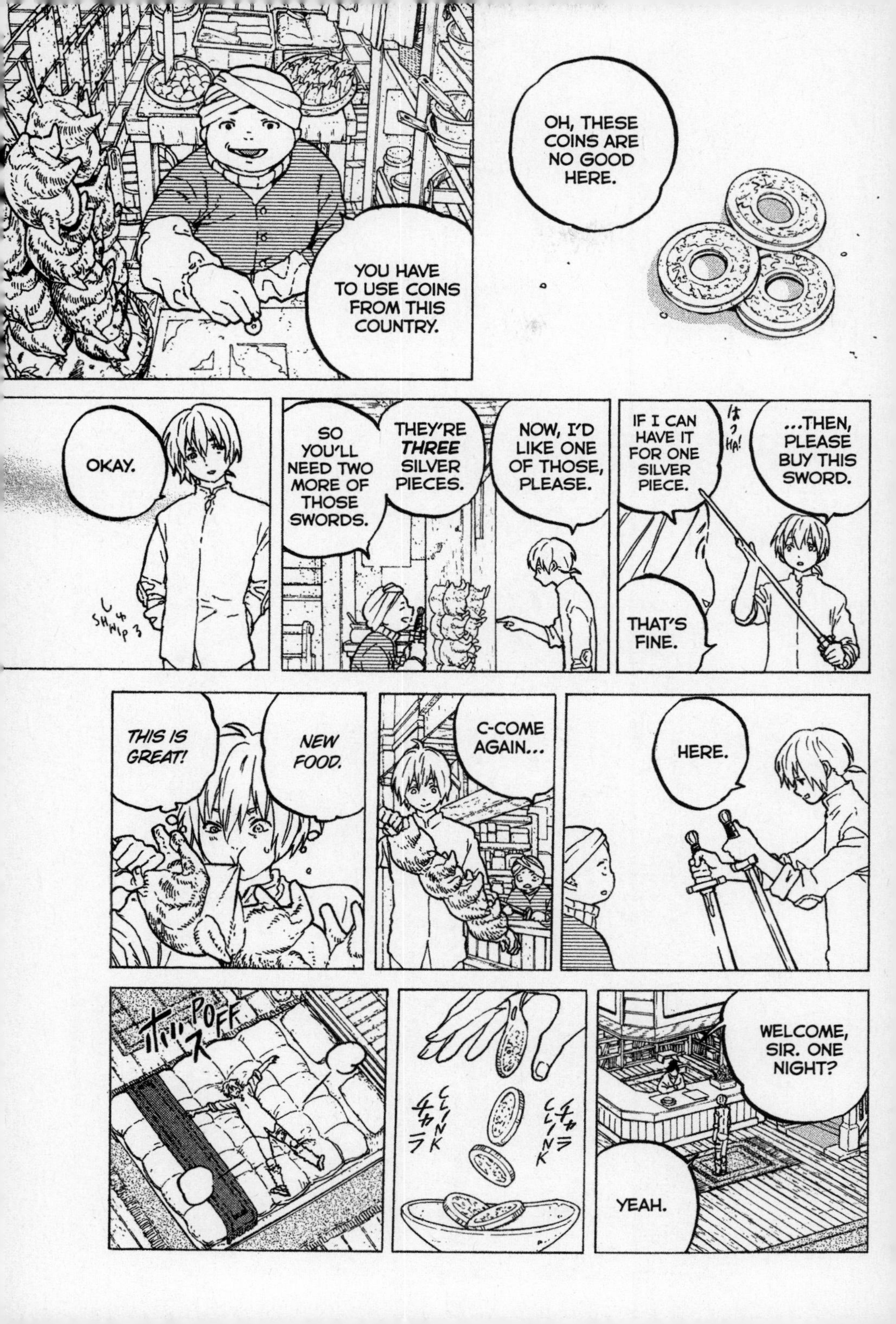
OH, THESE COINS ARE NO GOOD HERE.
YOU HAVE TO USE COINS FROM THIS COUNTRY.
...THEN, PLEASE BUY THIS SWORD.
はっ HA!
IF I CAN HAVE IT FOR ONE SILVER PIECE.
THAT'S FINE.
NOW, I'D LIKE ONE OF THOSE, PLEASE.
THEY'RE *THREE* SILVER PIECES.
SO YOU'LL NEED TWO MORE OF THOSE SWORDS.
OKAY.
しゅ
HERE.
C-COME AGAIN...
NEW FOOD.
THIS IS GREAT!
WELCOME, SIR. ONE NIGHT?
YEAH.
チャラ CLINK
チャラ CLINK
POFF

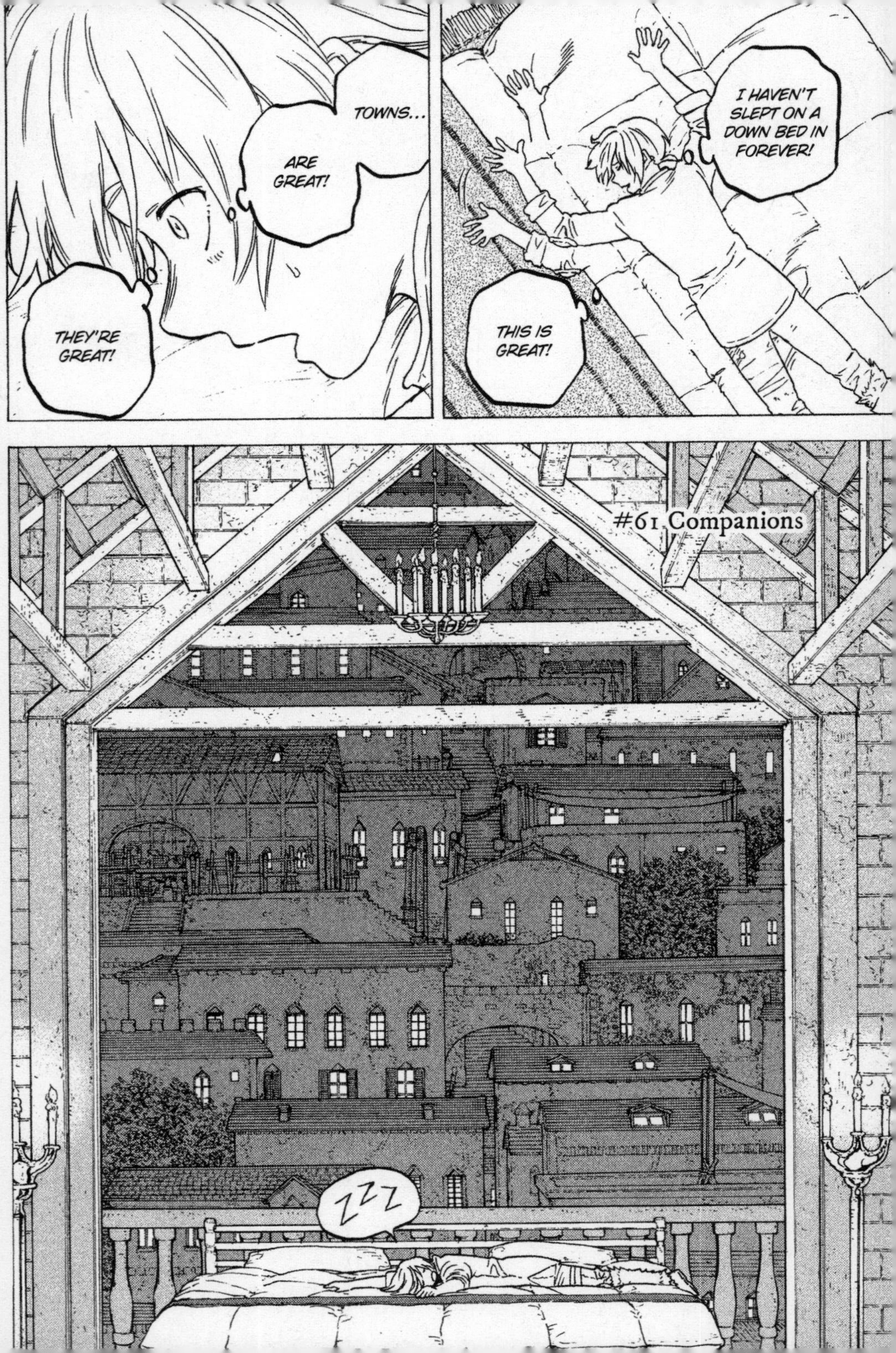
I HAVEN'T SLEPT ON A DOWN BED IN FOREVER!
THIS IS GREAT!
TOWNS...
ARE GREAT!
THEY'RE GREAT!
#61 Companions
ZZZ

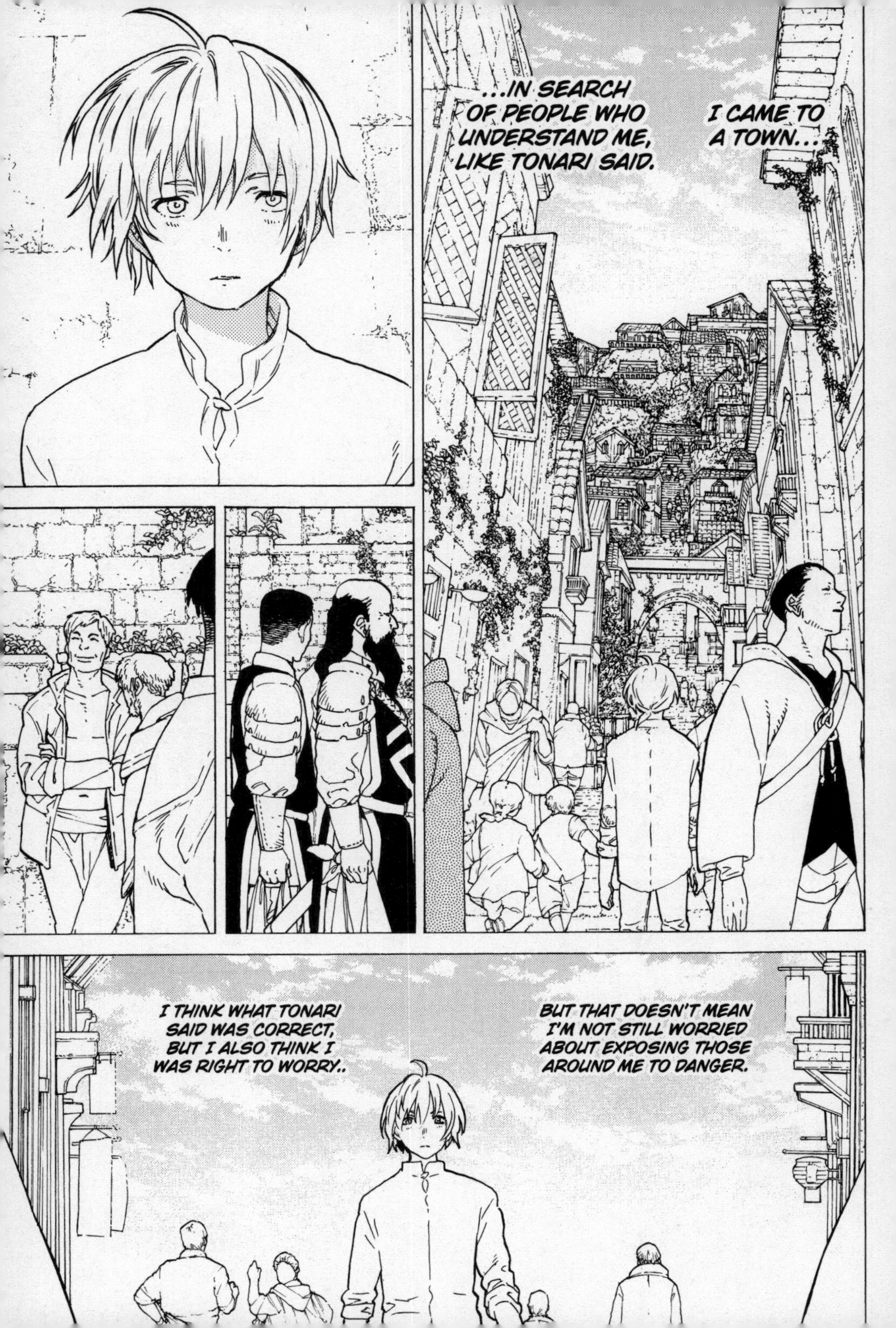
I CAME TO A TOWN...
...IN SEARCH OF PEOPLE WHO UNDERSTAND ME, LIKE TONARI SAID.
BUT THAT DOESN'T MEAN I'M NOT STILL WORRIED ABOUT EXPOSING THOSE AROUND ME TO DANGER.
I THINK WHAT TONARI SAID WAS CORRECT, BUT I ALSO THINK I WAS RIGHT TO WORRY..

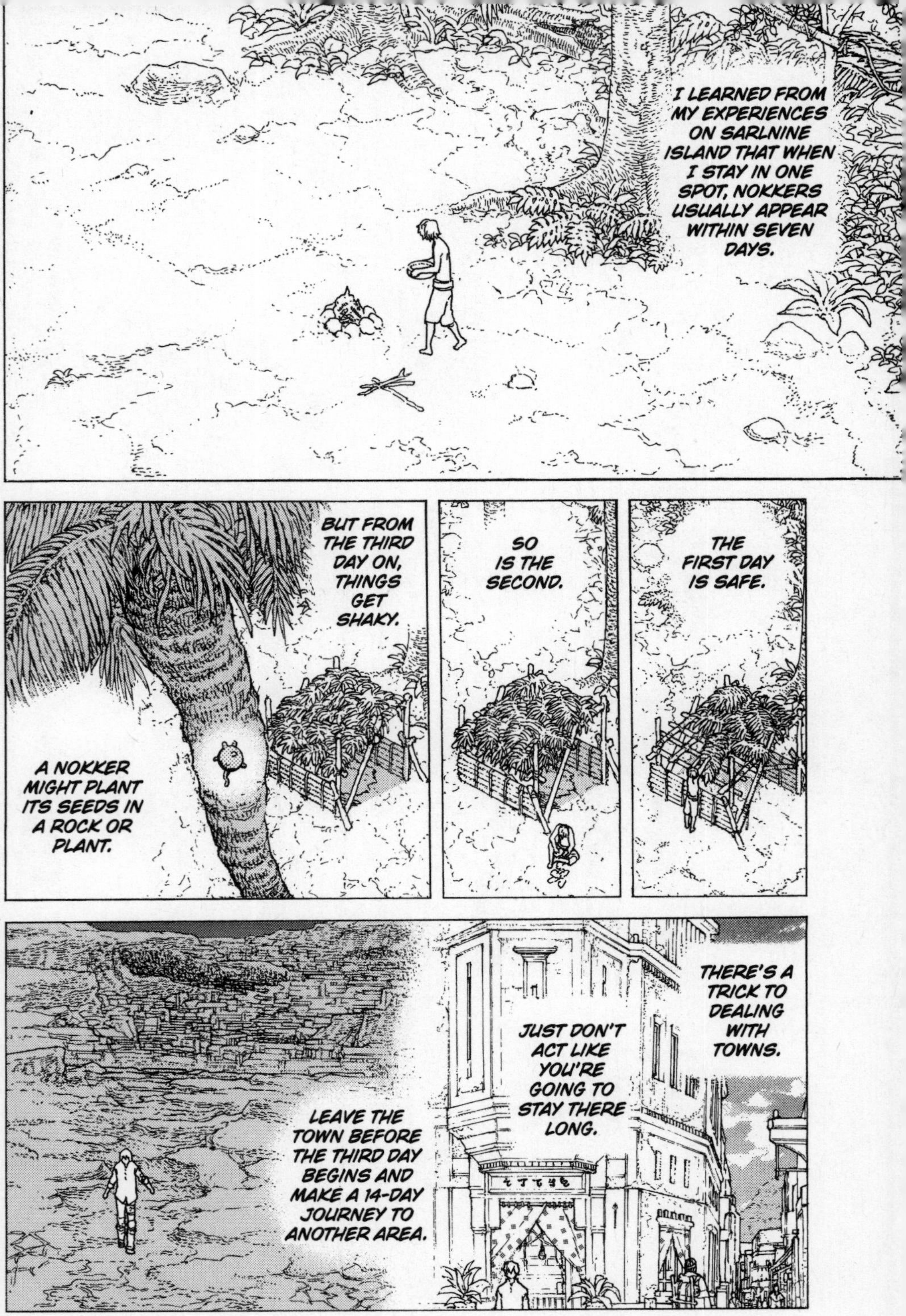
I LEARNED FROM MY EXPERIENCES ON SARLNINE ISLAND THAT WHEN I STAY IN ONE SPOT, NOKKERS USUALLY APPEAR WITHIN SEVEN DAYS.
THE FIRST DAY IS SAFE.
SO IS THE SECOND.
BUT FROM THE THIRD DAY ON, THINGS GET SHAKY.
A NOKKER MIGHT PLANT ITS SEEDS IN A ROCK OR PLANT.
THERE'S A TRICK TO DEALING WITH TOWNS.
JUST DON'T ACT LIKE YOU'RE GOING TO STAY THERE LONG.
LEAVE THE TOWN BEFORE THE THIRD DAY BEGINS AND MAKE A 14-DAY JOURNEY TO ANOTHER AREA.

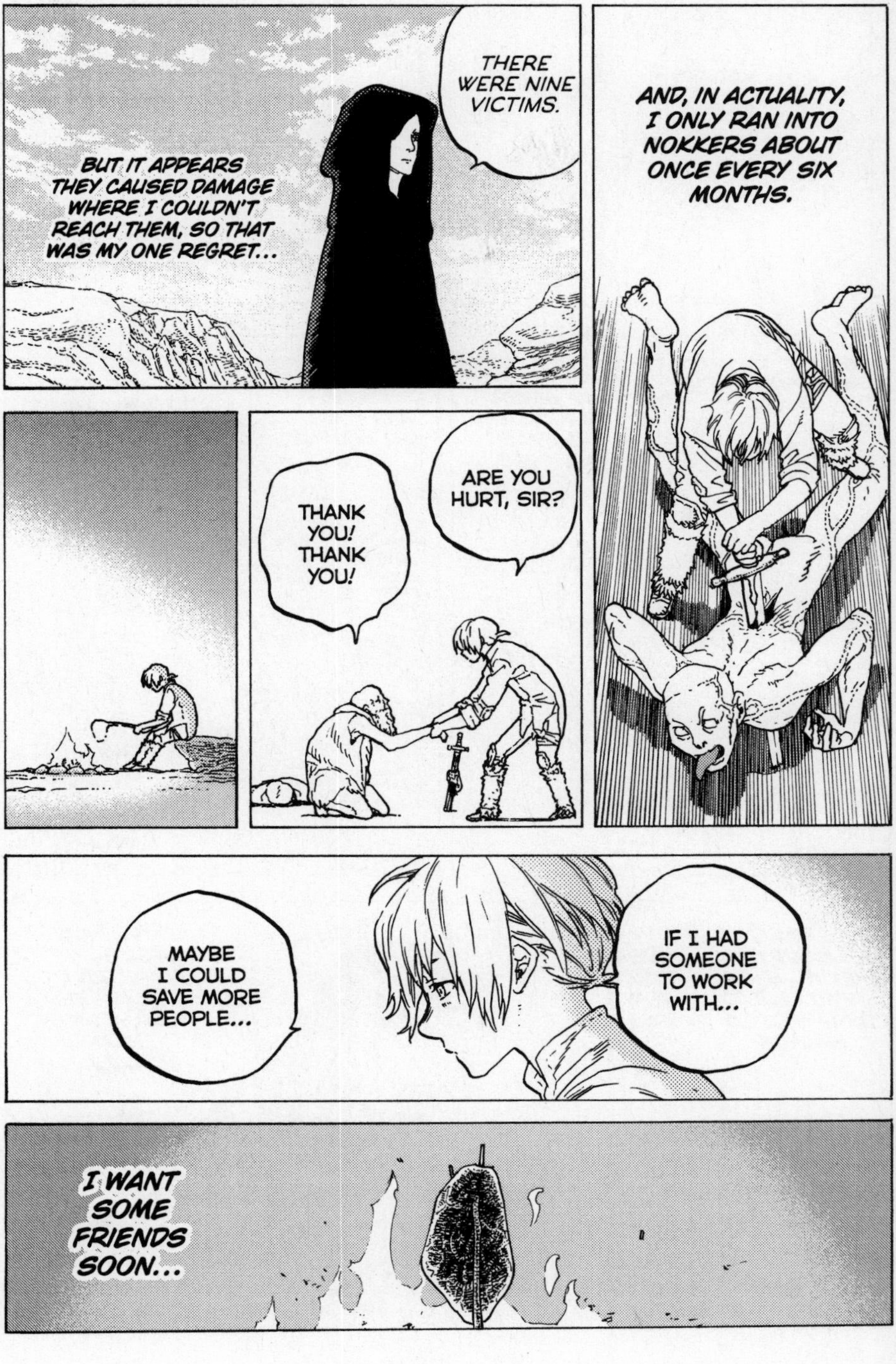
AND, IN ACTUALITY, I ONLY RAN INTO NOKKERS ABOUT ONCE EVERY SIX MONTHS.
THERE WERE NINE VICTIMS.
BUT IT APPEARS THEY CAUSED DAMAGE WHERE I COULDN'T REACH THEM, SO THAT WAS MY ONE REGRET...
ARE YOU HURT, SIR?
THANK YOU! THANK YOU!
IF I HAD SOMEONE TO WORK WITH...
MAYBE I COULD SAVE MORE PEOPLE...
I WANT SOME FRIENDS SOON...

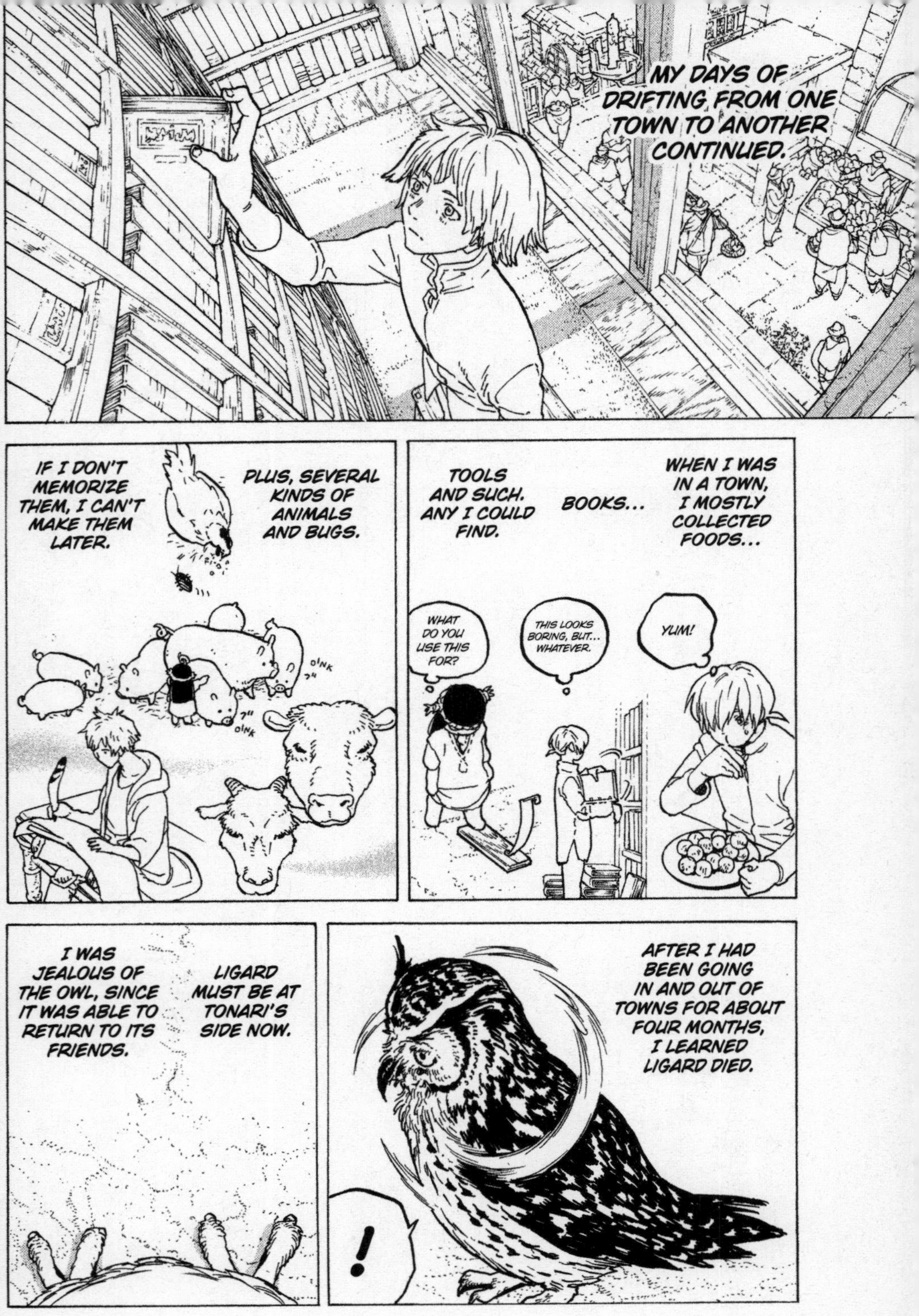
MY DAYS OF DRIFTING FROM ONE TOWN TO ANOTHER CONTINUED.
WHEN I WAS IN A TOWN, I MOSTLY COLLECTED FOODS...
BOOKS...
TOOLS AND SUCH. ANY I COULD FIND.
YUM!
THIS LOOKS BORING, BUT... WHATEVER.
WHAT DO YOU USE THIS FOR?
PLUS, SEVERAL KINDS OF ANIMALS AND BUGS.
IF I DON'T MEMORIZE THEM, I CAN'T MAKE THEM LATER.
OINK
OINK
AFTER I HAD BEEN GOING IN AND OUT OF TOWNS FOR ABOUT FOUR MONTHS, I LEARNED LIGARD DIED.
!
LIGARD MUST BE AT TONARI'S SIDE NOW.
I WAS JEALOUS OF THE OWL, SINCE IT WAS ABLE TO RETURN TO ITS FRIENDS.

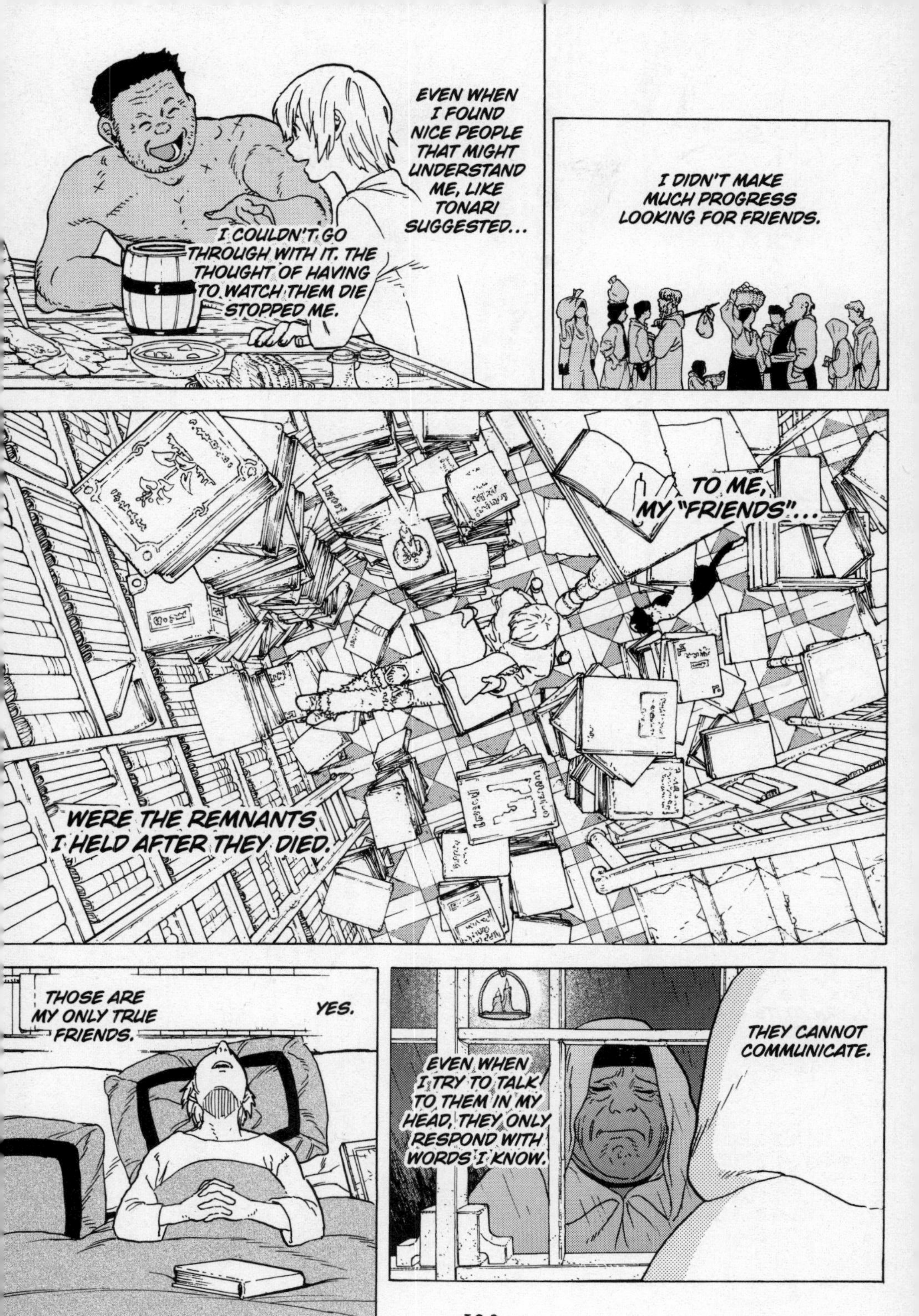
I DIDN'T MAKE MUCH PROGRESS LOOKING FOR FRIENDS.
EVEN WHEN I FOUND NICE PEOPLE THAT MIGHT UNDERSTAND ME, LIKE TONARI SUGGESTED...
I COULDN'T GO THROUGH WITH IT. THE THOUGHT OF HAVING TO WATCH THEM DIE STOPPED ME.
TO ME, MY "FRIENDS"...
WERE THE REMNANTS I HELD AFTER THEY DIED.
THEY CANNOT COMMUNICATE.
EVEN WHEN I TRY TO TALK TO THEM IN MY HEAD, THEY ONLY RESPOND WITH WORDS I KNOW.
YES.
THOSE ARE MY ONLY TRUE FRIENDS.

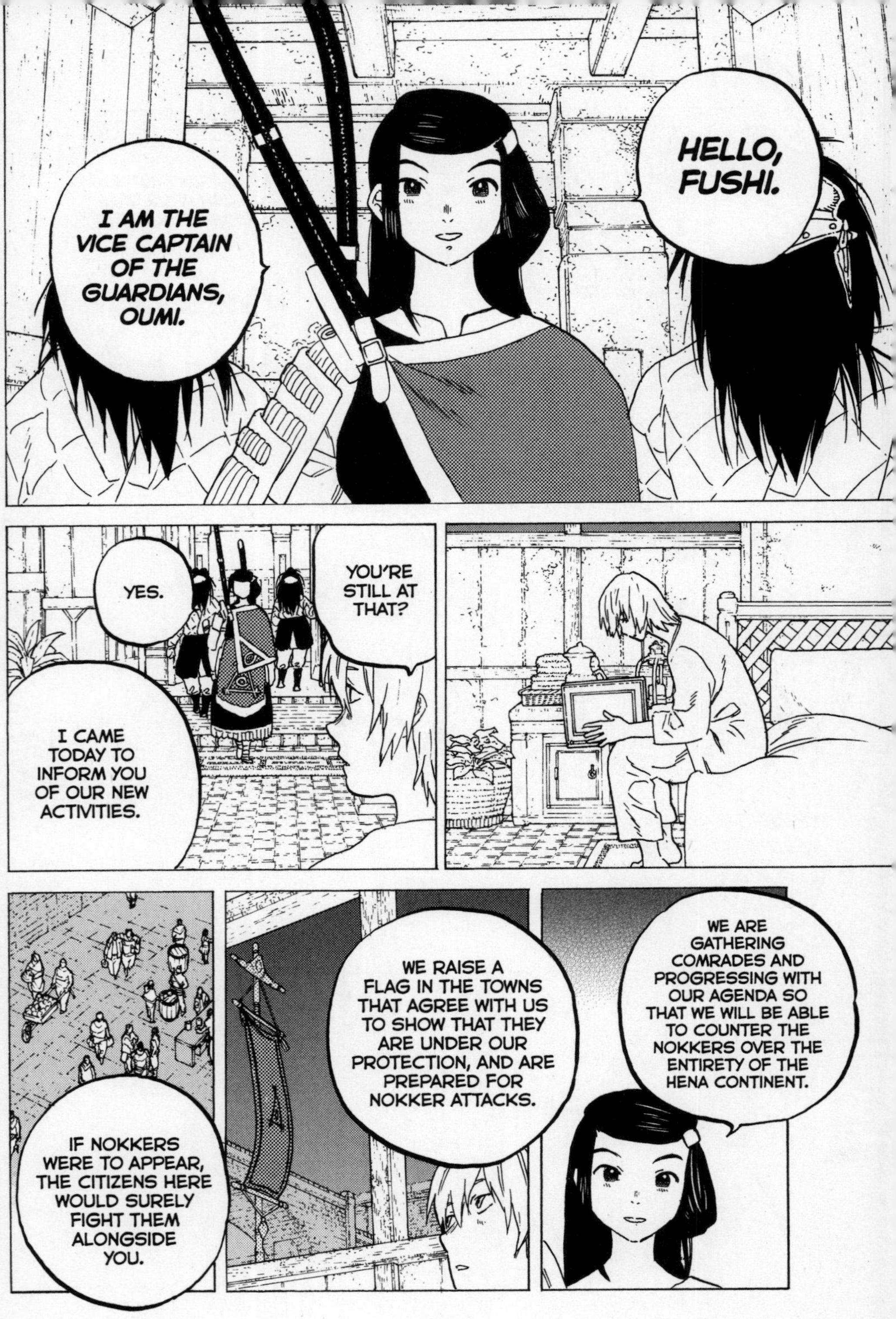
HELLO, FUSHI.
I AM THE VICE CAPTAIN OF THE GUARDIANS, OUMI.
YOU'RE STILL AT THAT?
YES.
I CAME TODAY TO INFORM YOU OF OUR NEW ACTIVITIES.
WE ARE GATHERING COMRADES AND PROGRESSING WITH OUR AGENDA SO THAT WE WILL BE ABLE TO COUNTER THE NOKKERS OVER THE ENTIRETY OF THE HENA CONTINENT.
WE RAISE A FLAG IN THE TOWNS THAT AGREE WITH US TO SHOW THAT THEY ARE UNDER OUR PROTECTION, AND ARE PREPARED FOR NOKKER ATTACKS.
IF NOKKERS WERE TO APPEAR, THE CITIZENS HERE WOULD SURELY FIGHT THEM ALONGSIDE YOU.

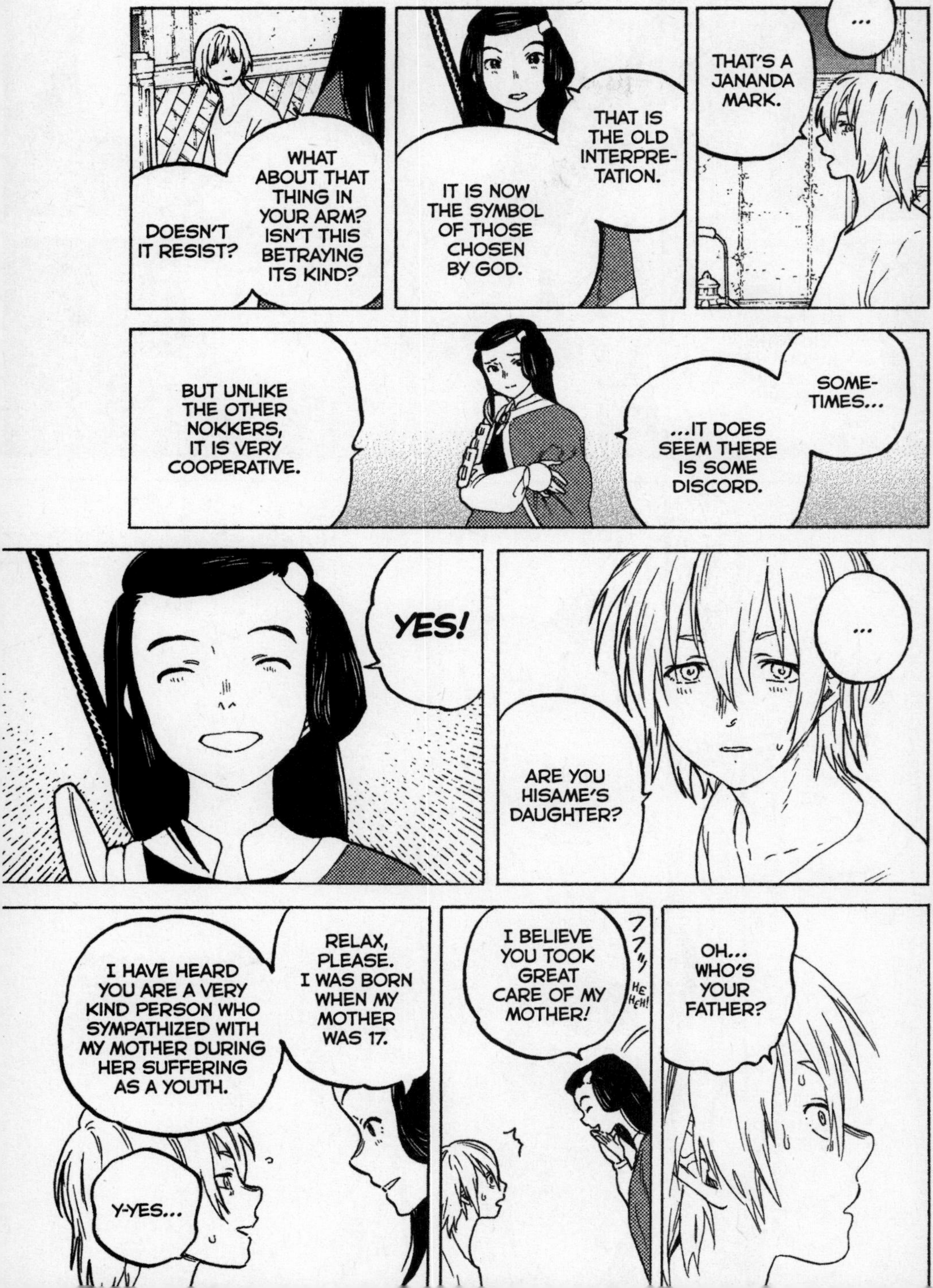
...
THAT'S A JANANDA MARK.
THAT IS THE OLD INTERPRETATION.
IT IS NOW THE SYMBOL OF THOSE CHOSEN BY GOD.
WHAT ABOUT THAT THING IN YOUR ARM? ISN'T THIS BETRAYING ITS KIND?
DOESN'T IT RESIST?
SOME-TIMES...
...IT DOES SEEM THERE IS SOME DISCORD.
BUT UNLIKE THE OTHER NOKKERS, IT IS VERY COOPERATIVE.
...
ARE YOU HISAME'S DAUGHTER?
YES!
OH... WHO'S YOUR FATHER?
HE HEH!
I BELIEVE YOU TOOK GREAT CARE OF MY MOTHER!
RELAX, PLEASE. I WAS BORN WHEN MY MOTHER WAS 17.
I HAVE HEARD YOU ARE A VERY KIND PERSON WHO SYMPATHIZED WITH MY MOTHER DURING HER SUFFERING AS A YOUTH.
Y-YES...

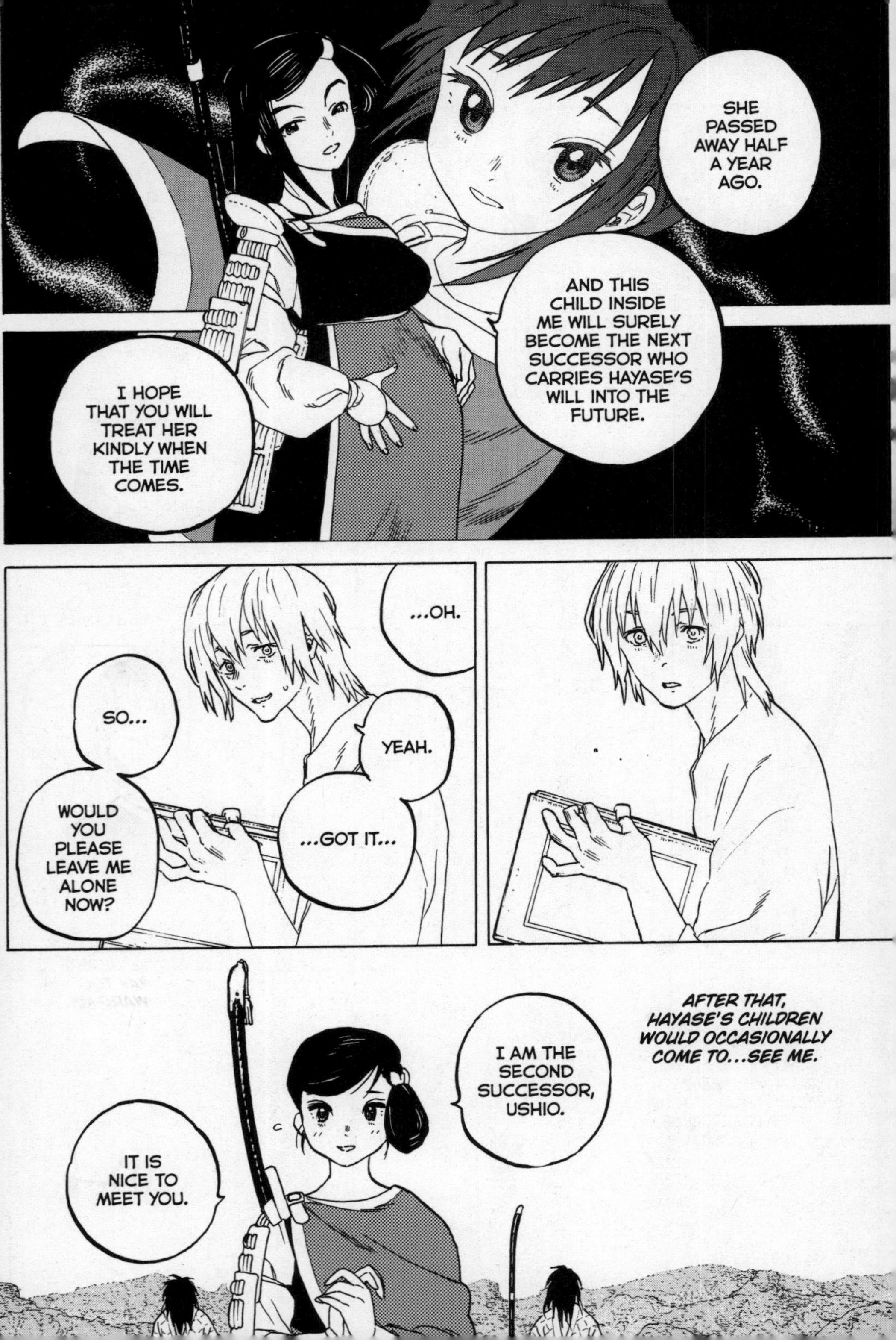
SHE PASSED AWAY HALF A YEAR AGO.
AND THIS CHILD INSIDE ME WILL SURELY BECOME THE NEXT SUCCESSOR WHO CARRIES HAYASE'S WILL INTO THE FUTURE.
I HOPE THAT YOU WILL TREAT HER KINDLY WHEN THE TIME COMES.
...OH.
YEAH.
...GOT IT...
SO...
WOULD YOU PLEASE LEAVE ME ALONE NOW?
AFTER THAT, HAYASE'S CHILDREN WOULD OCCASIONALLY COME TO...SEE ME.
I AM THE SECOND SUCCESSOR, USHIO.
IT IS NICE TO MEET YOU.

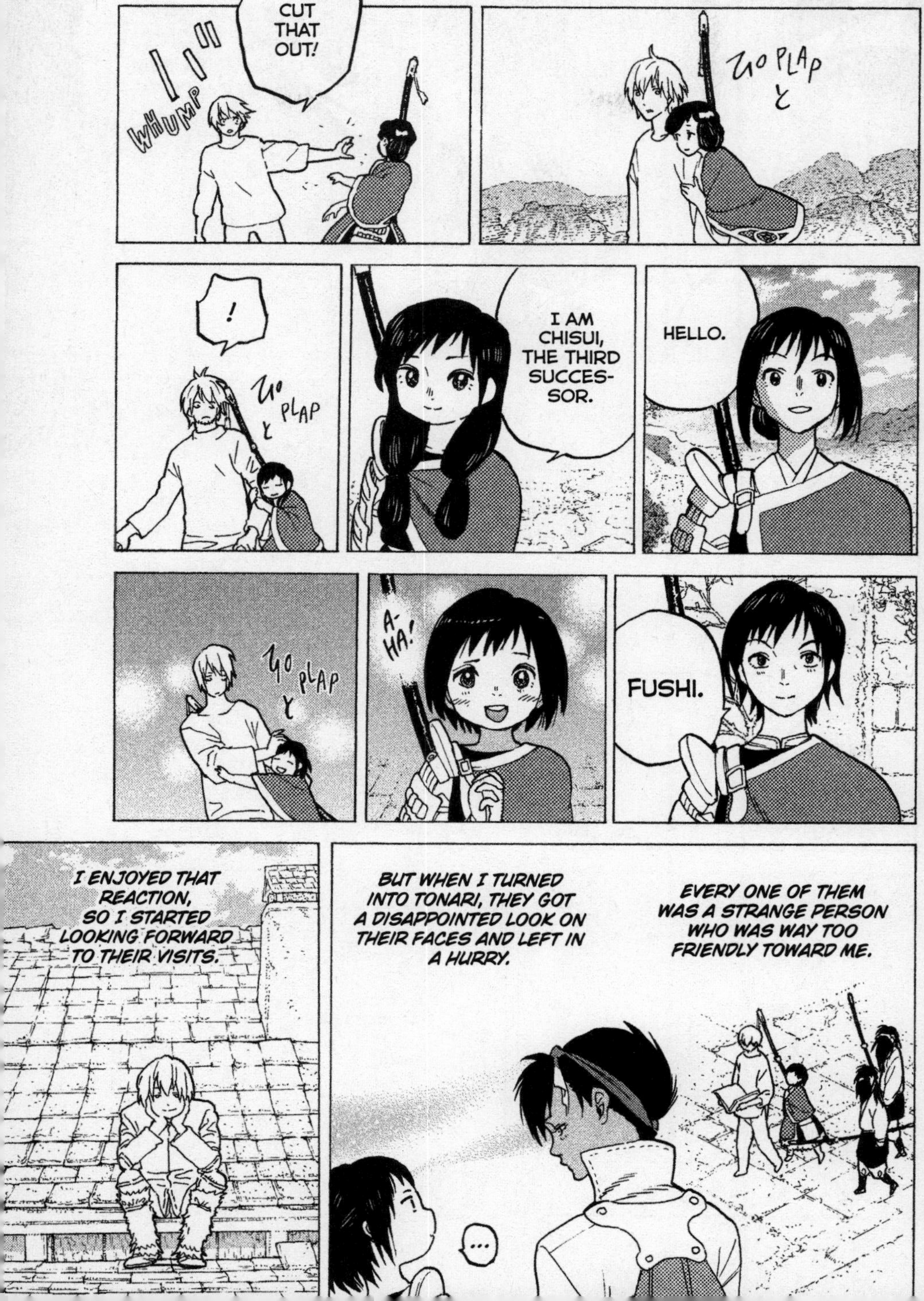
PLAP
WHUMP
CUT THAT OUT!
HELLO.
I AM CHISUI, THE THIRD SUCCES-SOR.
!
PLAP
FUSHI.
A-HA!
PLAP
EVERY ONE OF THEM WAS A STRANGE PERSON WHO WAS WAY TOO FRIENDLY TOWARD ME.
BUT WHEN I TURNED INTO TONARI, THEY GOT A DISAPPOINTED LOOK ON THEIR FACES AND LEFT IN A HURRY.
...
I ENJOYED THAT REACTION, SO I STARTED LOOKING FORWARD TO THEIR VISITS.

AND WHILE I WAS WANDERING AROUND TOWNS, A FRUSTRATING TRUTH EMERGED.

TEN NOKKERS APPEARED IN THE MOUNTAINS TO THE NORTH, BUT THE GUARDIANS APPEAR TO HAVE DEFEATED THEM ALL.

I WASN'T THE ONE WHO ACTUALLY COUNTERED THE NOKKERS. IT WAS THOSE WOMEN...

O-OH...

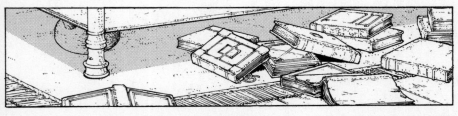

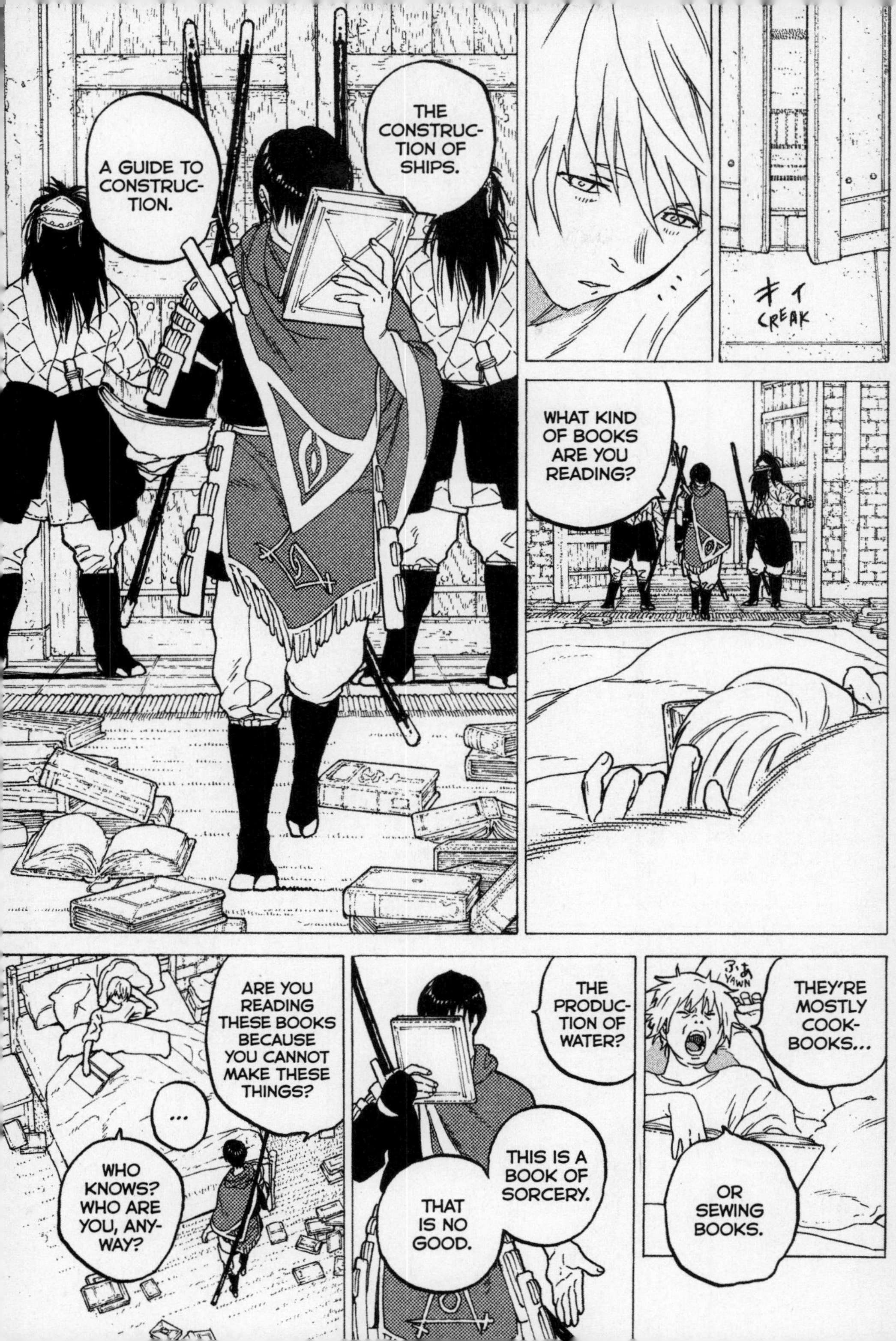
キイ
CREAK
WHAT KIND OF BOOKS ARE YOU READING?
THE CONSTRUCTION OF SHIPS.
A GUIDE TO CONSTRUCTION.
ふあ
YAWN
THEY'RE MOSTLY COOKBOOKS...
OR SEWING BOOKS.
THE PRODUCTION OF WATER?
THIS IS A BOOK OF SORCERY.
THAT IS NO GOOD.
ARE YOU READING THESE BOOKS BECAUSE YOU CANNOT MAKE THESE THINGS?
...
WHO KNOWS? WHO ARE YOU, ANYWAY?

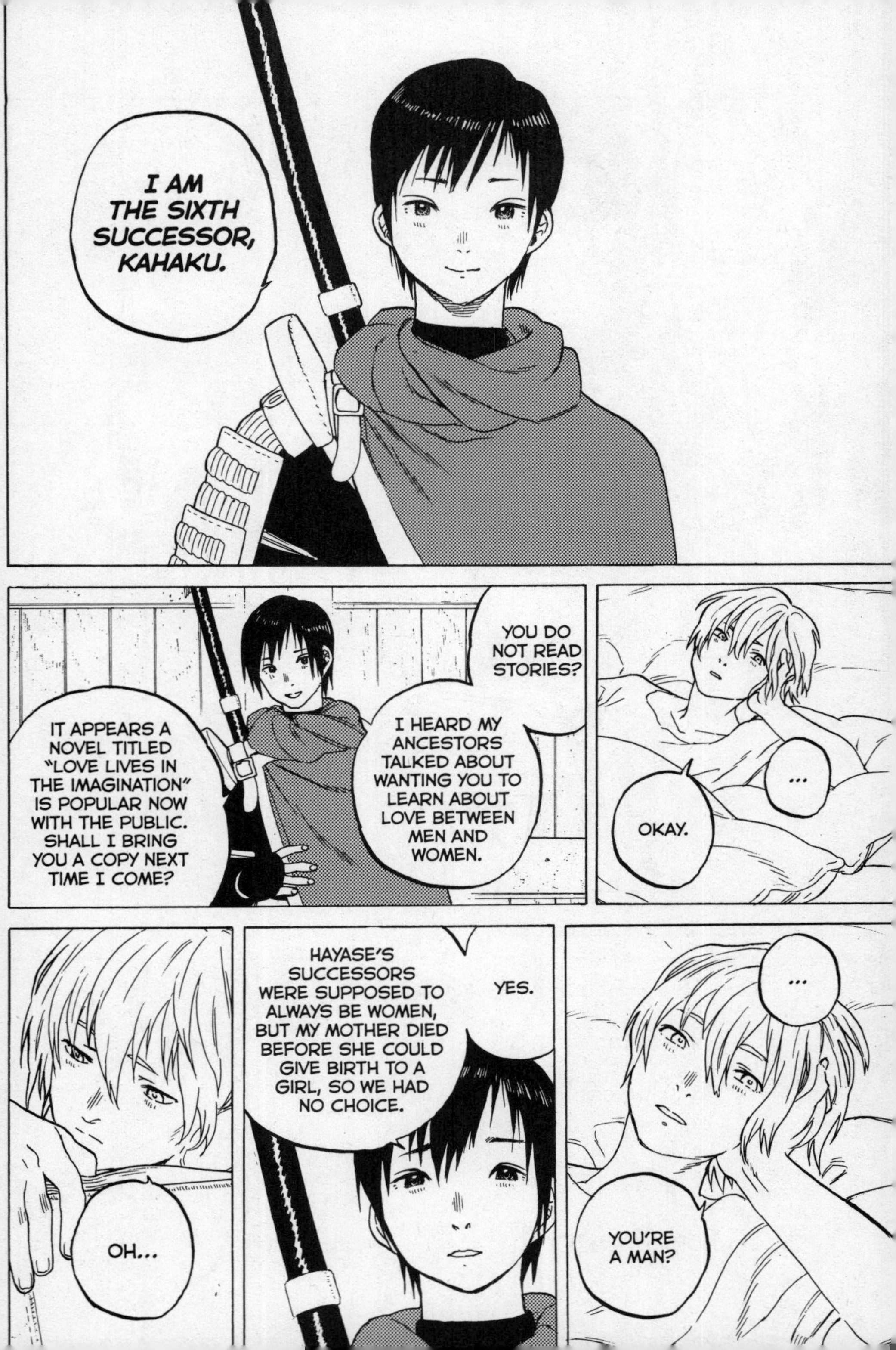
I AM THE SIXTH SUCCESSOR, KAHAKU.
...
OKAY.
YOU DO NOT READ STORIES?
I HEARD MY ANCESTORS TALKED ABOUT WANTING YOU TO LEARN ABOUT LOVE BETWEEN MEN AND WOMEN.
IT APPEARS A NOVEL TITLED "LOVE LIVES IN THE IMAGINATION" IS POPULAR NOW WITH THE PUBLIC. SHALL I BRING YOU A COPY NEXT TIME I COME?
...
YOU'RE A MAN?
YES.
HAYASE'S SUCCESSORS WERE SUPPOSED TO ALWAYS BE WOMEN, BUT MY MOTHER DIED BEFORE SHE COULD GIVE BIRTH TO A GIRL, SO WE HAD NO CHOICE.
OH...

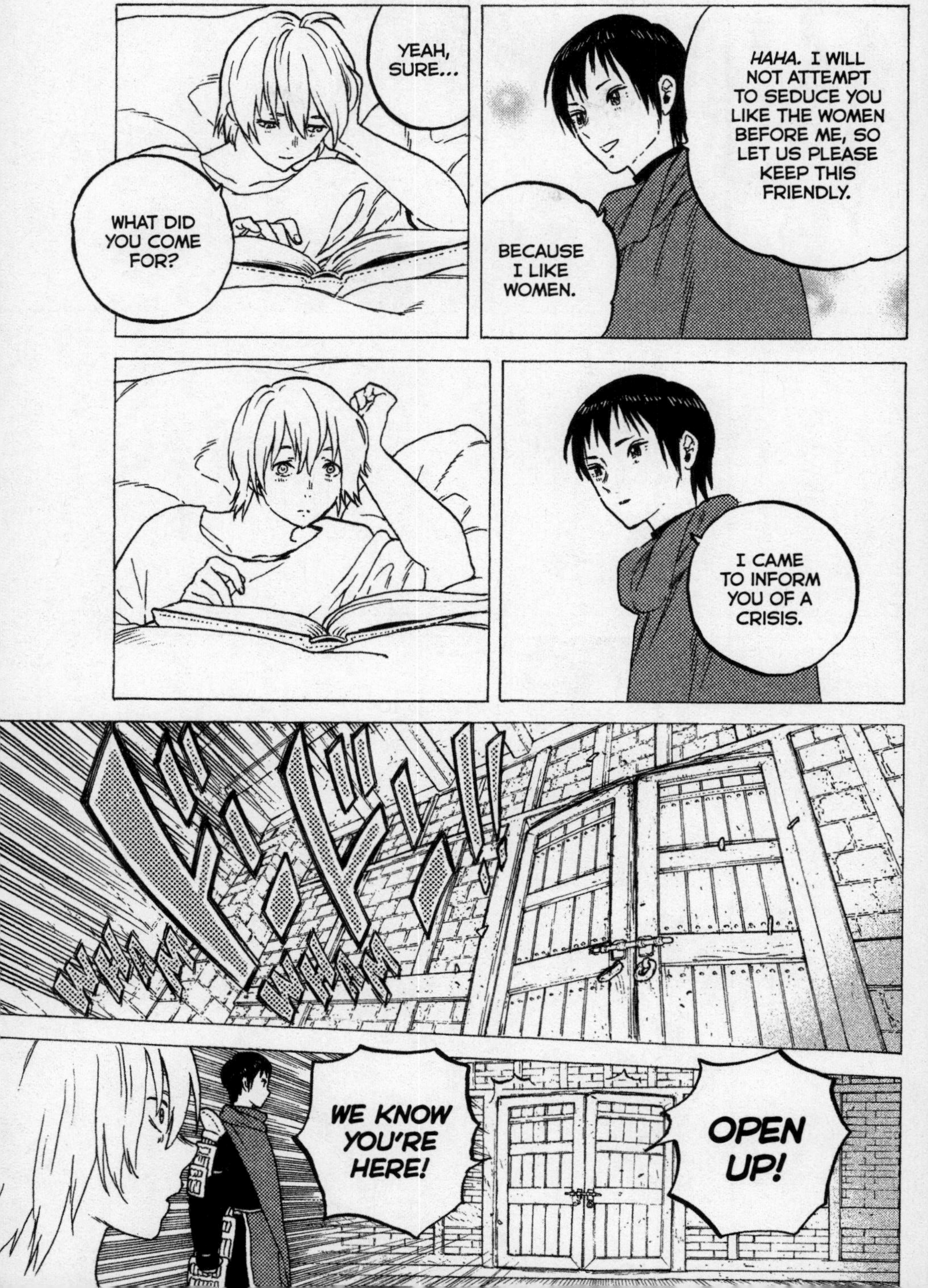
HAHA. I WILL NOT ATTEMPT TO SEDUCE YOU LIKE THE WOMEN BEFORE ME, SO LET US PLEASE KEEP THIS FRIENDLY.
BECAUSE I LIKE WOMEN.
YEAH, SURE...
WHAT DID YOU COME FOR?
I CAME TO INFORM YOU OF A CRISIS.
OPEN UP!
WE KNOW YOU'RE HERE!

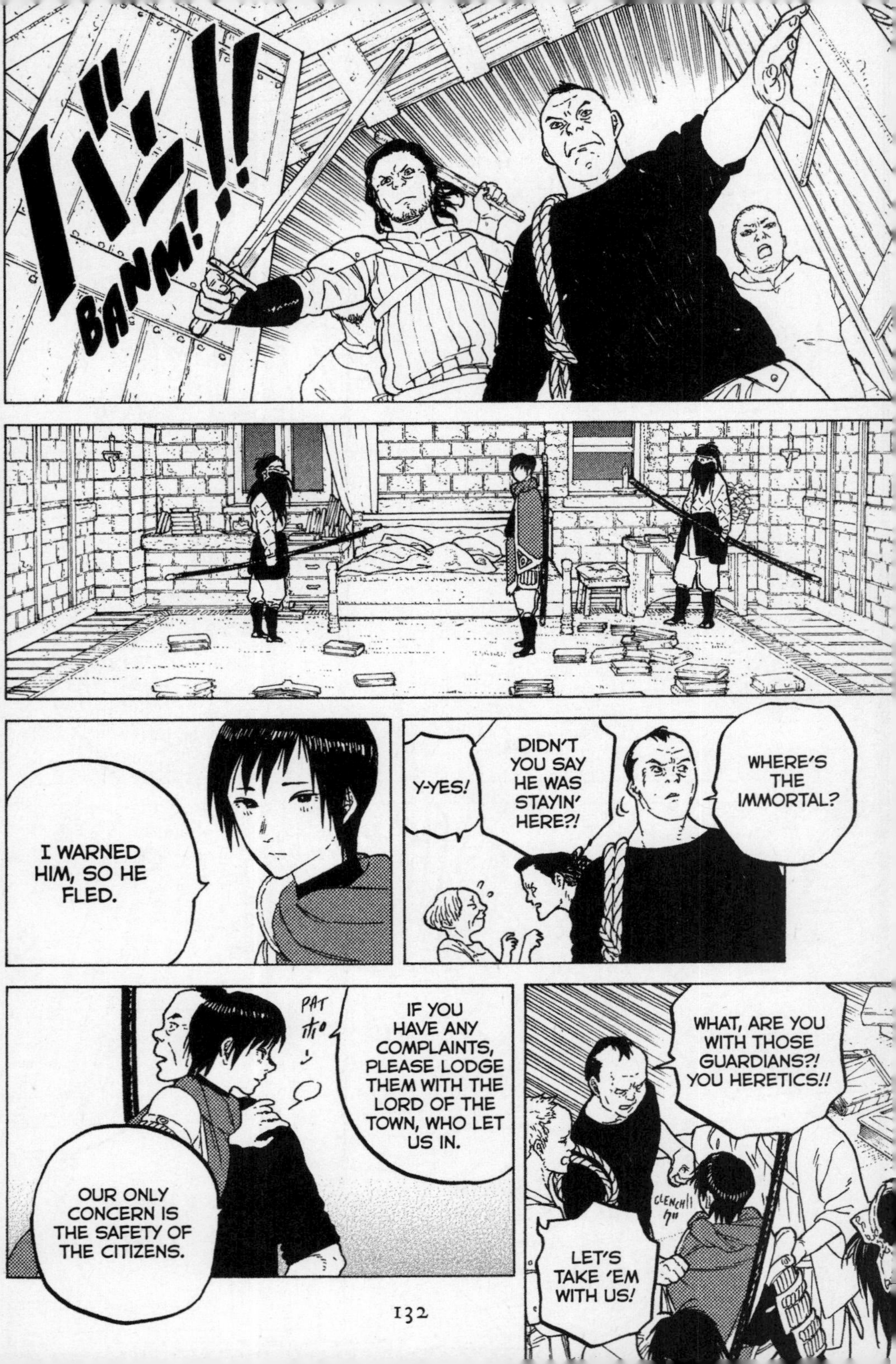
BANM!!
WHERE'S THE IMMORTAL?
DIDN'T YOU SAY HE WAS STAYIN' HERE?!
Y-YES!
I WARNED HIM, SO HE FLED.
WHAT, ARE YOU WITH THOSE GUARDIANS?! YOU HERETICS!!
CLENCH
LET'S TAKE 'EM WITH US!
PAT
IF YOU HAVE ANY COMPLAINTS, PLEASE LODGE THEM WITH THE LORD OF THE TOWN, WHO LET US IN.
OUR ONLY CONCERN IS THE SAFETY OF THE CITIZENS.

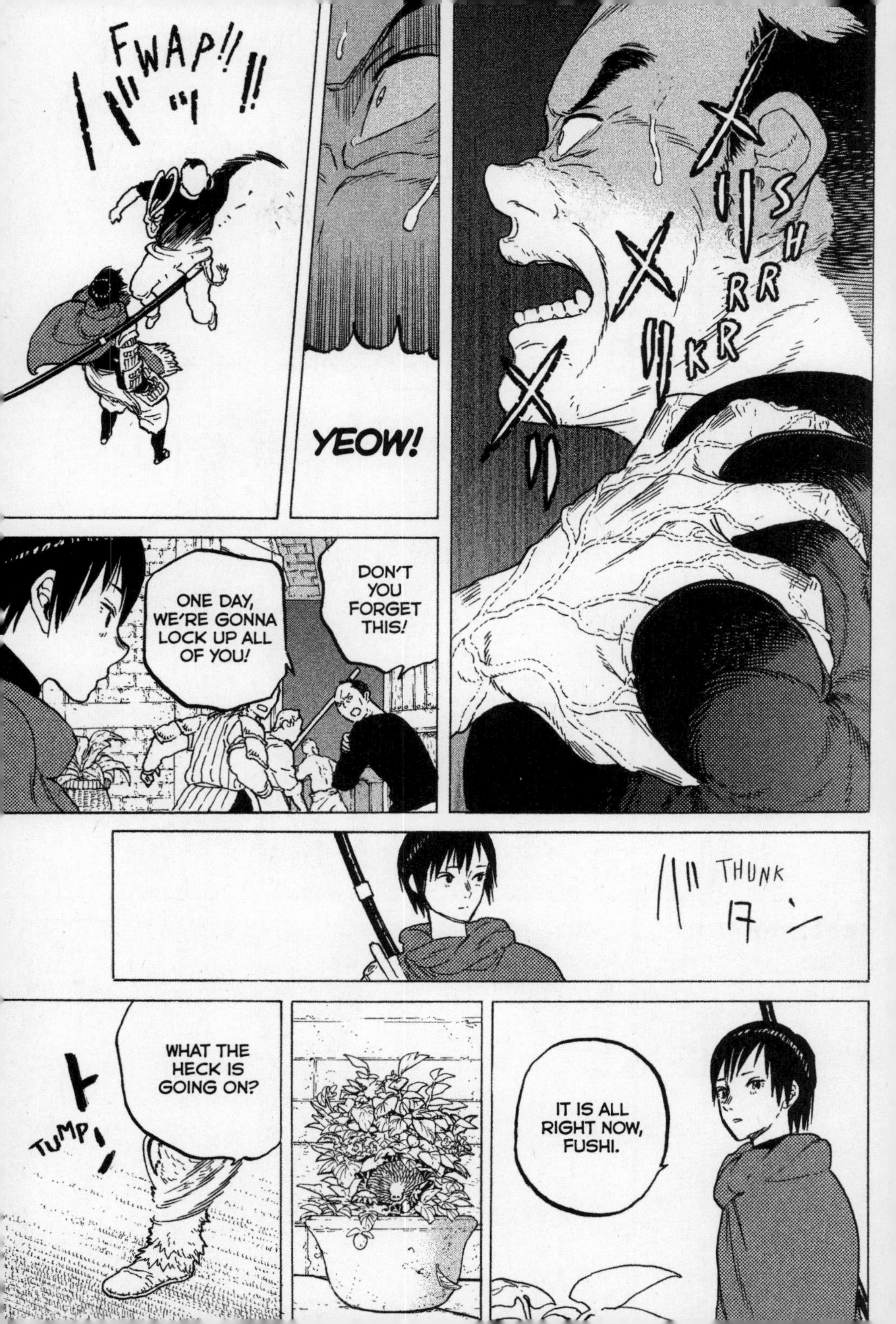
SHRRKR
YEOW!
FWAP!!
DON'T YOU FORGET THIS!
ONE DAY, WE'RE GONNA LOCK UP ALL OF YOU!
THUNK
IT IS ALL RIGHT NOW, FUSHI.
WHAT THE HECK IS GOING ON?
TUMP

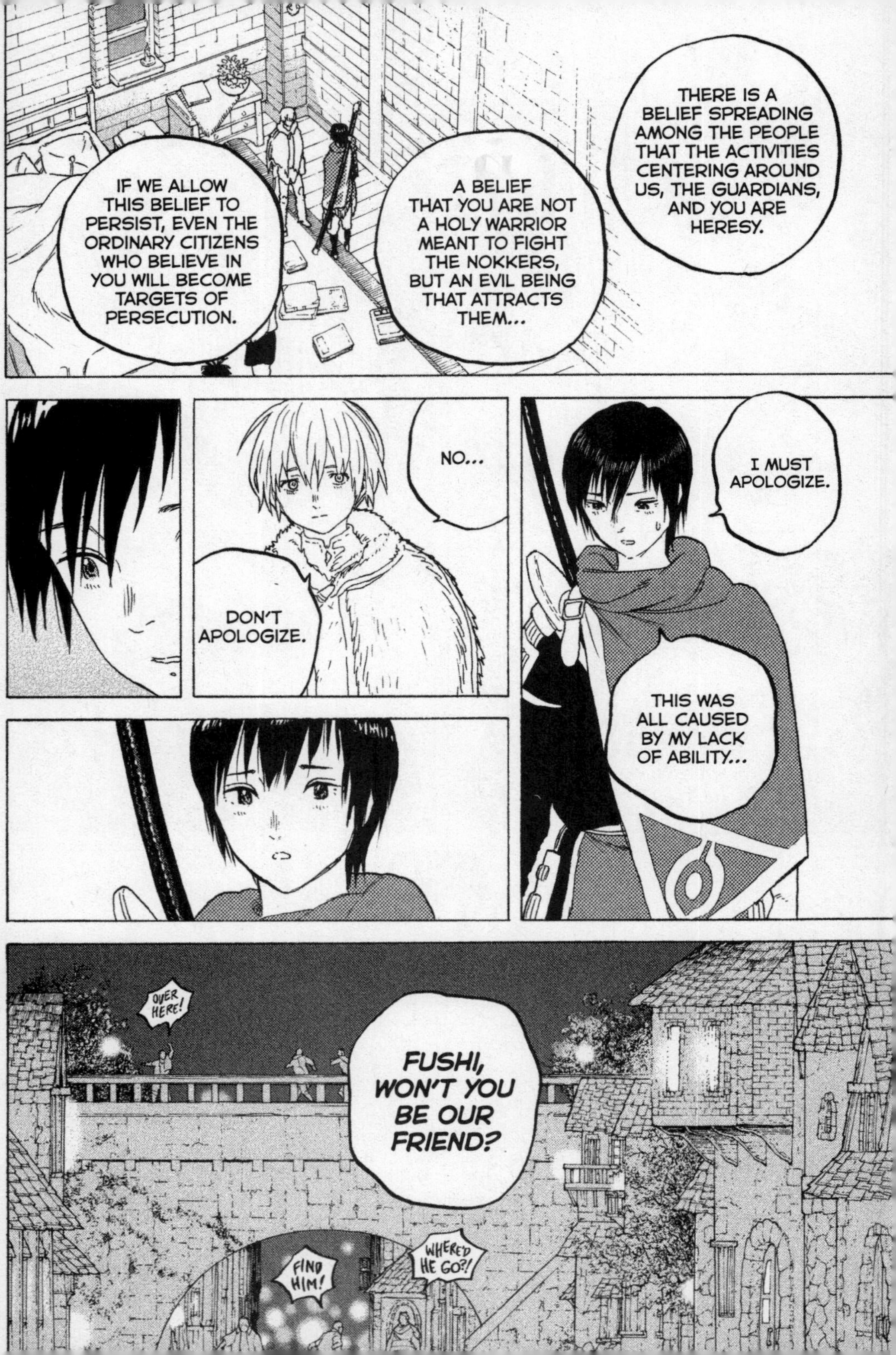
THERE IS A BELIEF SPREADING AMONG THE PEOPLE THAT THE ACTIVITIES CENTERING AROUND US, THE GUARDIANS, AND YOU ARE HERESY.
A BELIEF THAT YOU ARE NOT A HOLY WARRIOR MEANT TO FIGHT THE NOKKERS, BUT AN EVIL BEING THAT ATTRACTS THEM...
IF WE ALLOW THIS BELIEF TO PERSIST, EVEN THE ORDINARY CITIZENS WHO BELIEVE IN YOU WILL BECOME TARGETS OF PERSECUTION.
I MUST APOLOGIZE.
THIS WAS ALL CAUSED BY MY LACK OF ABILITY...
NO...
DON'T APOLOGIZE.
FUSHI, WON'T YOU BE OUR FRIEND?
OVER HERE!
WHERE'D HE GO?!
FIND HIM!

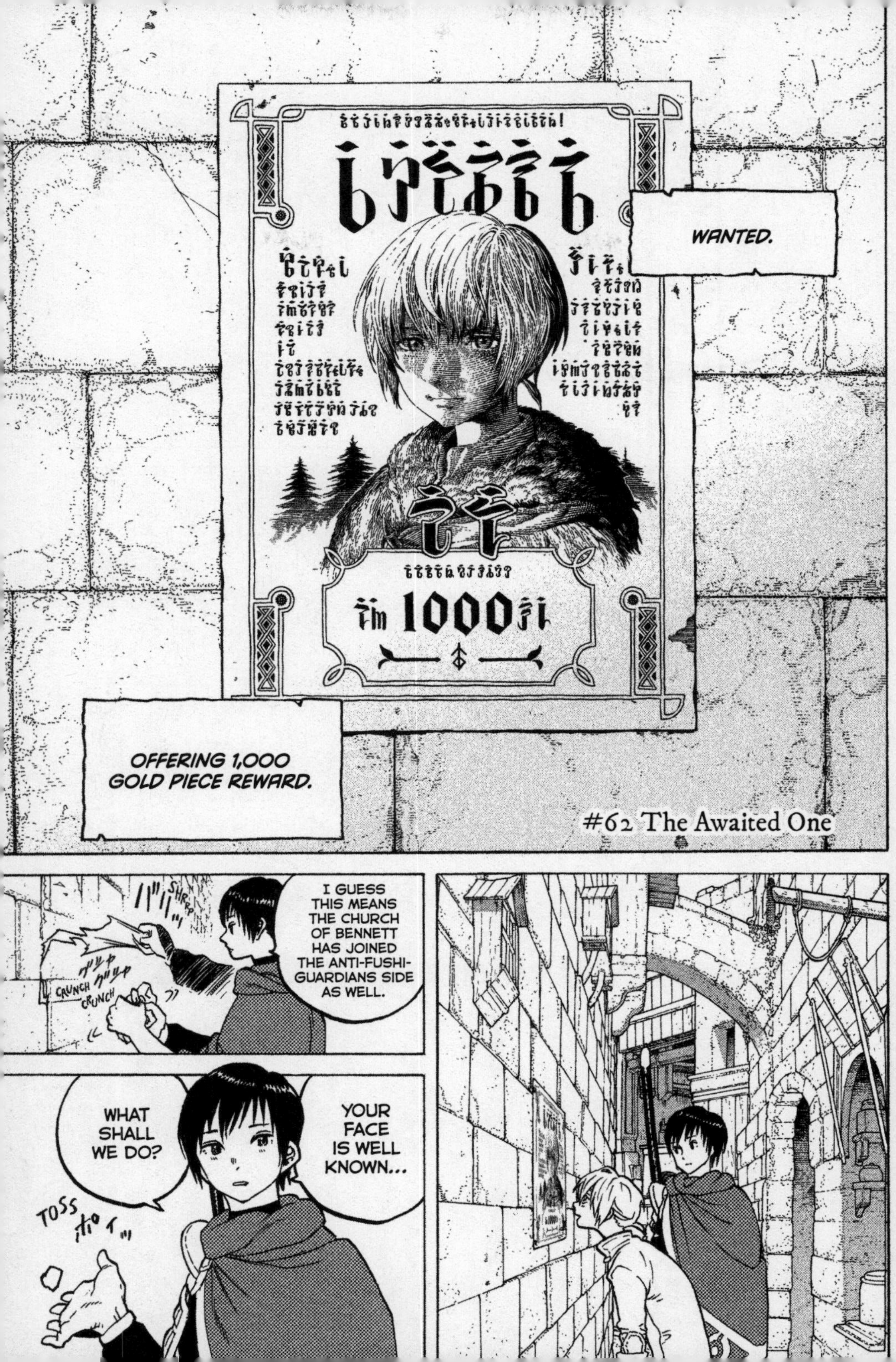
WANTED.
OFFERING 1,000 GOLD PIECE REWARD.
#62 The Awaited One
SHRRP
I GUESS THIS MEANS THE CHURCH OF BENNETT HAS JOINED THE ANTI-FUSHI-GUARDIANS SIDE AS WELL.
CRUNCH CRUNCH
YOUR FACE IS WELL KNOWN...
WHAT SHALL WE DO?
TOSS

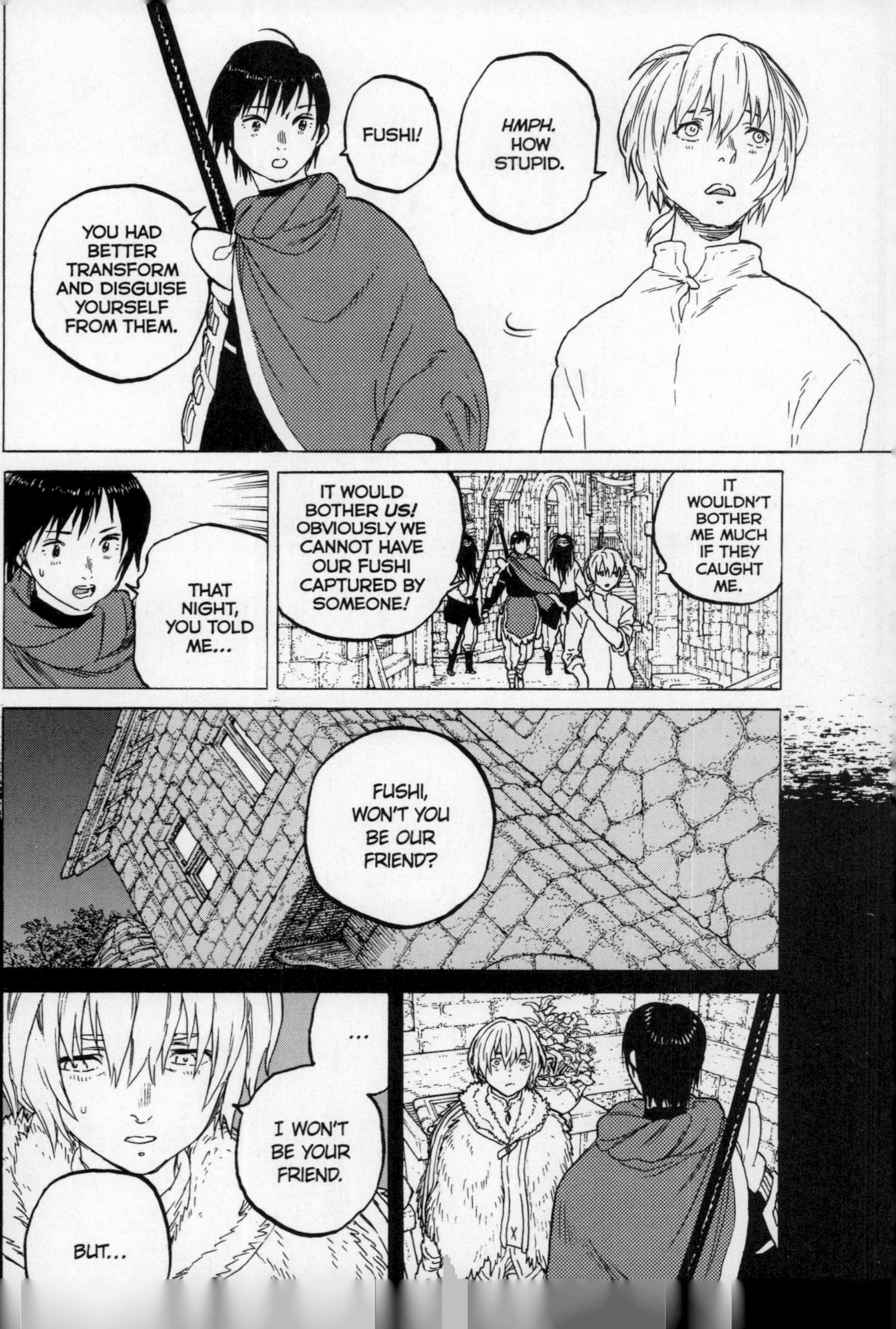
HMPH. HOW STUPID.
FUSHI!
YOU HAD BETTER TRANSFORM AND DISGUISE YOURSELF FROM THEM.
IT WOULDN'T BOTHER ME MUCH IF THEY CAUGHT ME.
IT WOULD BOTHER US! OBVIOUSLY WE CANNOT HAVE OUR FUSHI CAPTURED BY SOMEONE!
THAT NIGHT, YOU TOLD ME...
FUSHI, WON'T YOU BE OUR FRIEND?
...
I WON'T BE YOUR FRIEND.
BUT...

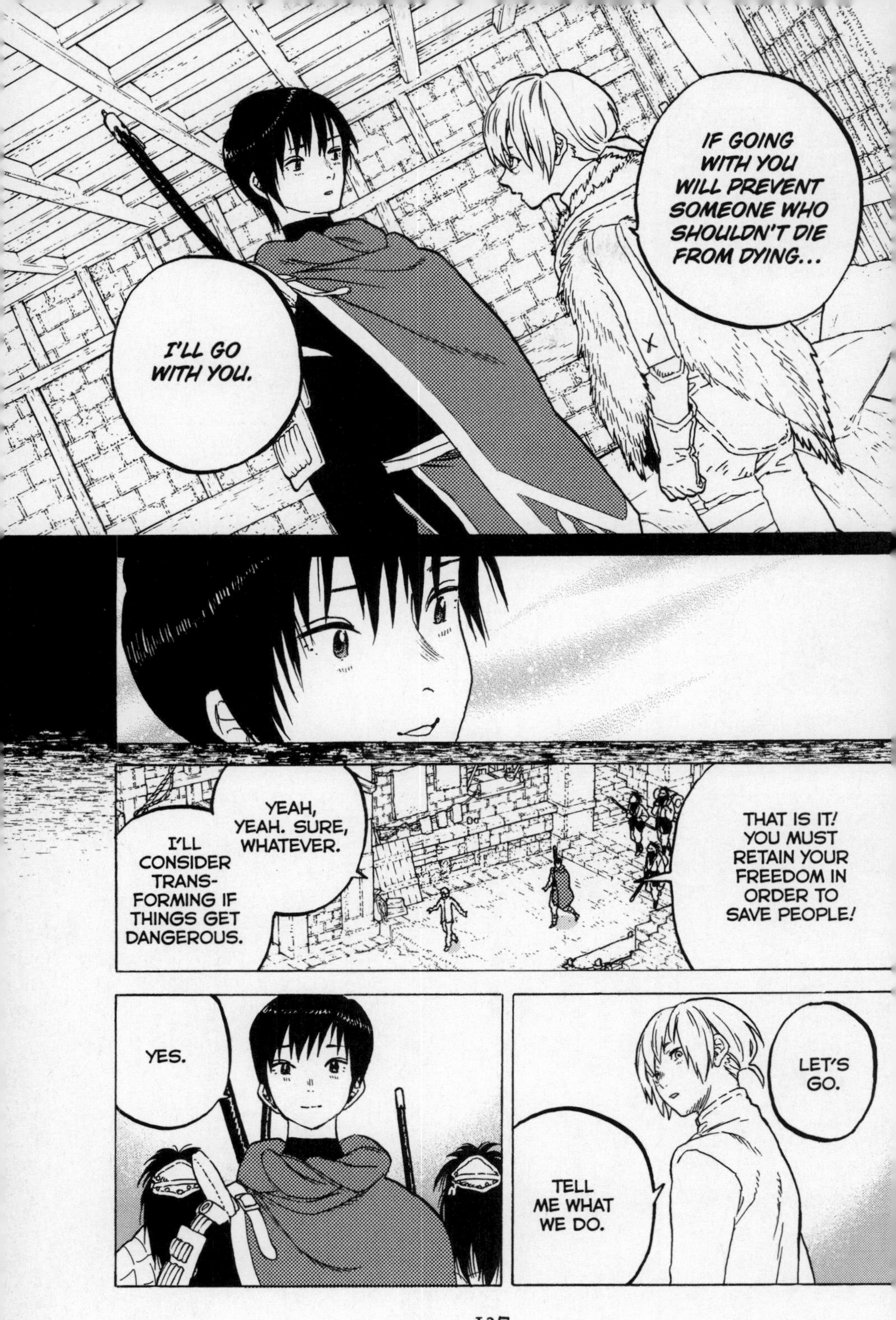
IF GOING WITH YOU WILL PREVENT SOMEONE WHO SHOULDN'T DIE FROM DYING...
I'LL GO WITH YOU.
THAT IS IT! YOU MUST RETAIN YOUR FREEDOM IN ORDER TO SAVE PEOPLE!
YEAH, YEAH. SURE, WHATEVER.
I'LL CONSIDER TRANS-FORMING IF THINGS GET DANGEROUS.
LET'S GO.
TELL ME WHAT WE DO.
YES.

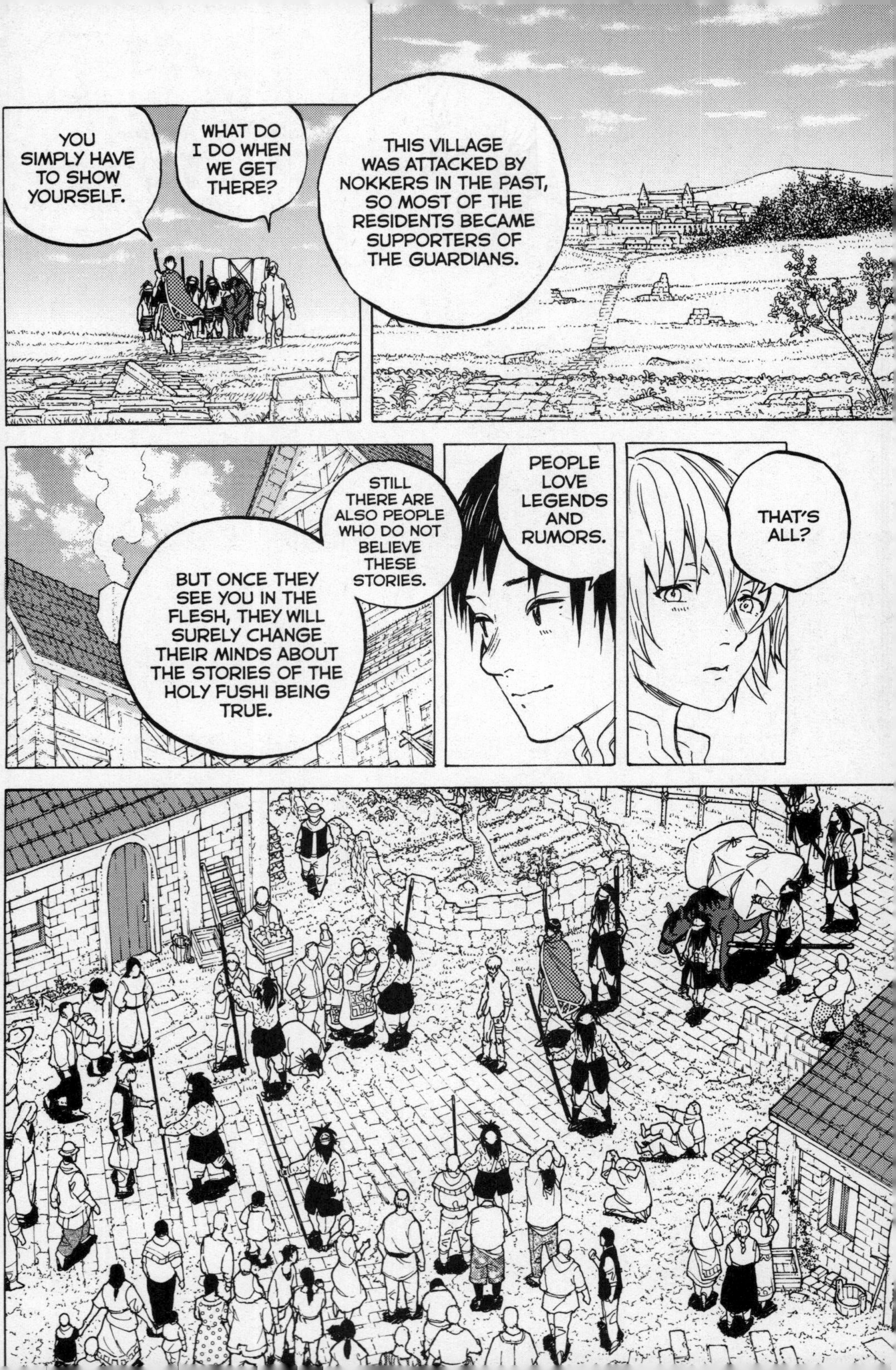
THIS VILLAGE WAS ATTACKED BY NOKKERS IN THE PAST, SO MOST OF THE RESIDENTS BECAME SUPPORTERS OF THE GUARDIANS.
WHAT DO I DO WHEN WE GET THERE?
YOU SIMPLY HAVE TO SHOW YOURSELF.
THAT'S ALL?
PEOPLE LOVE LEGENDS AND RUMORS.
STILL THERE ARE ALSO PEOPLE WHO DO NOT BELIEVE THESE STORIES.
BUT ONCE THEY SEE YOU IN THE FLESH, THEY WILL SURELY CHANGE THEIR MINDS ABOUT THE STORIES OF THE HOLY FUSHI BEING TRUE.

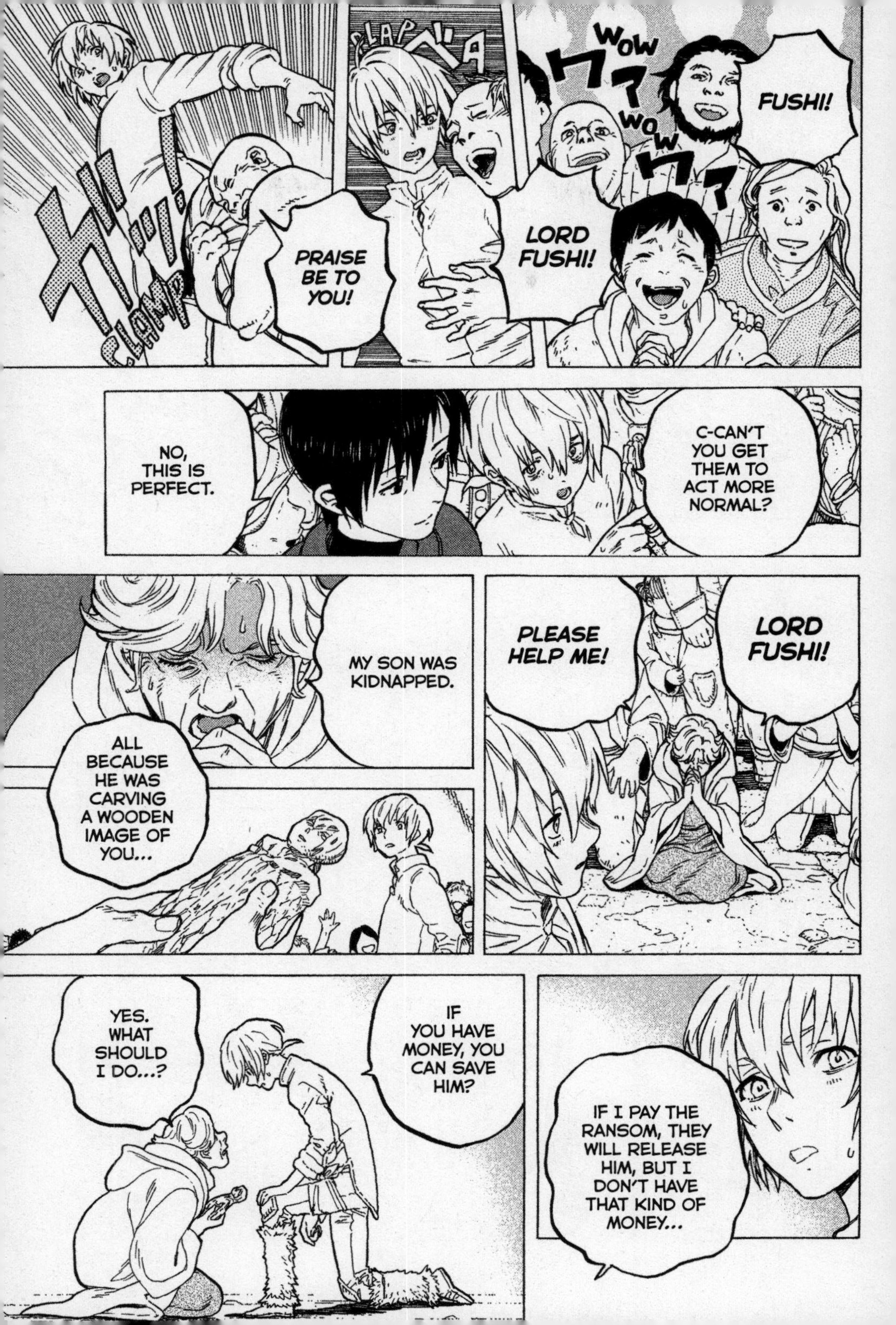
WOW
WOW
FUSHI!
LORD FUSHI!
SLAP
PRAISE BE TO YOU!
CLAMP
C-CAN'T YOU GET THEM TO ACT MORE NORMAL?
NO, THIS IS PERFECT.
LORD FUSHI!
PLEASE HELP ME!
MY SON WAS KIDNAPPED.
ALL BECAUSE HE WAS CARVING A WOODEN IMAGE OF YOU...
IF I PAY THE RANSOM, THEY WILL RELEASE HIM, BUT I DON'T HAVE THAT KIND OF MONEY...
IF YOU HAVE MONEY, YOU CAN SAVE HIM?
YES. WHAT SHOULD I DO...?

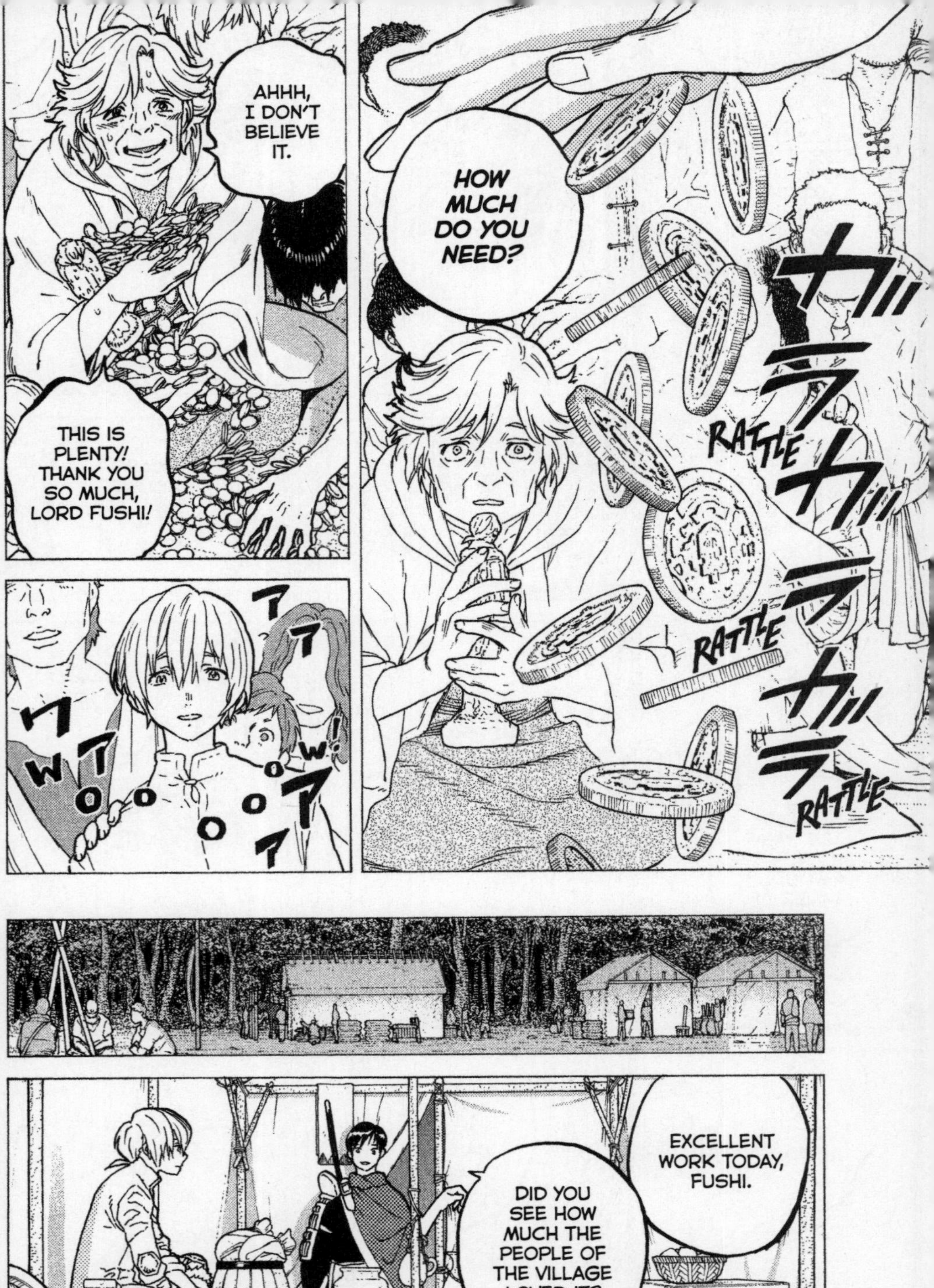
HOW MUCH DO YOU NEED?
ガラガラ
RATTLE
RATTLE
ガラガラ
RATTLE
AHHH, I DON'T BELIEVE IT.
THIS IS PLENTY! THANK YOU SO MUCH, LORD FUSHI!
アアア
WOOOW!
ワアア
WOOOO
EXCELLENT WORK TODAY, FUSHI.
DID YOU SEE HOW MUCH THE PEOPLE OF THE VILLAGE LOVED IT?

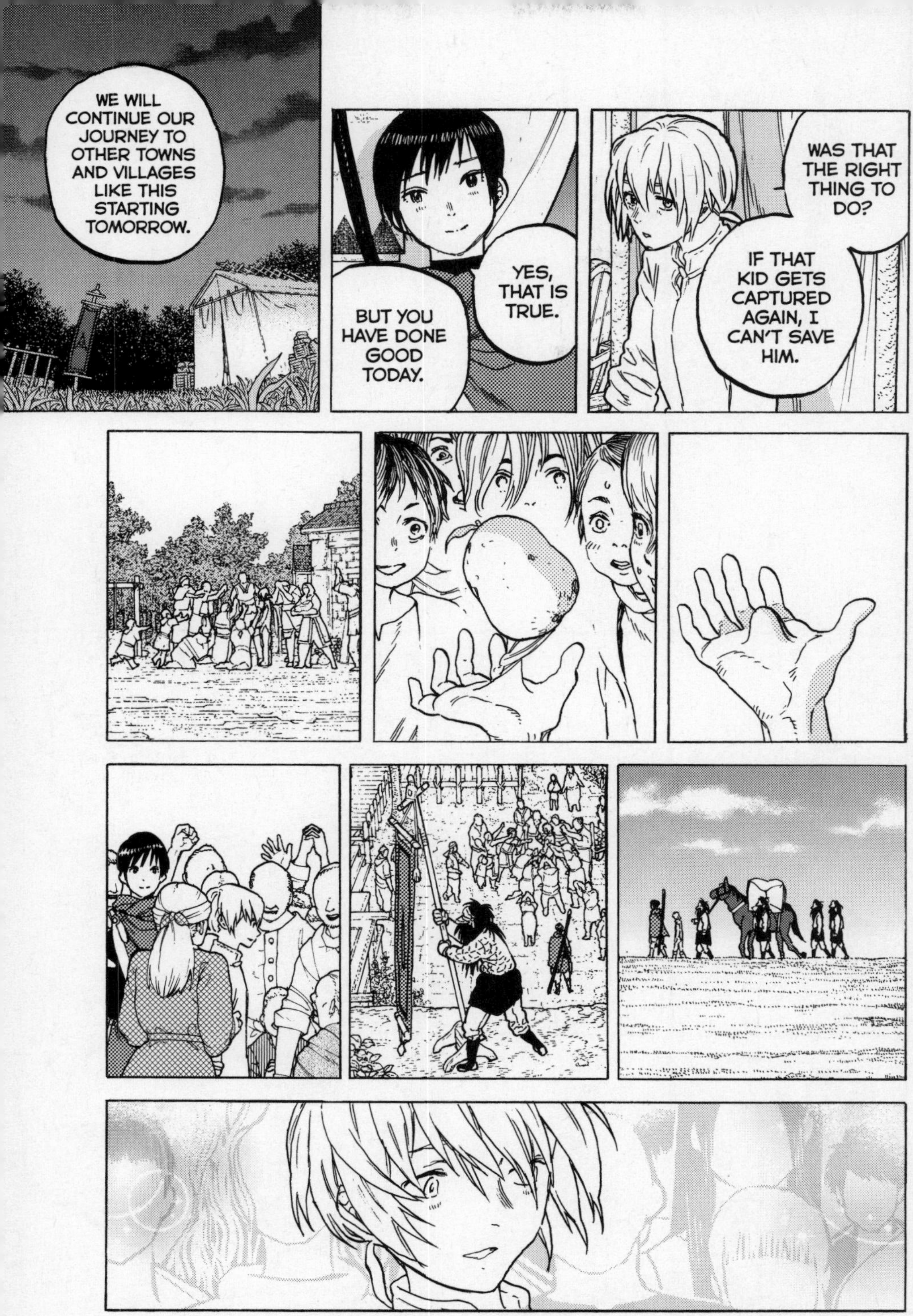
WAS THAT THE RIGHT THING TO DO?
IF THAT KID GETS CAPTURED AGAIN, I CAN'T SAVE HIM.
YES, THAT IS TRUE.
BUT YOU HAVE DONE GOOD TODAY.
WE WILL CONTINUE OUR JOURNEY TO OTHER TOWNS AND VILLAGES LIKE THIS STARTING TOMORROW.

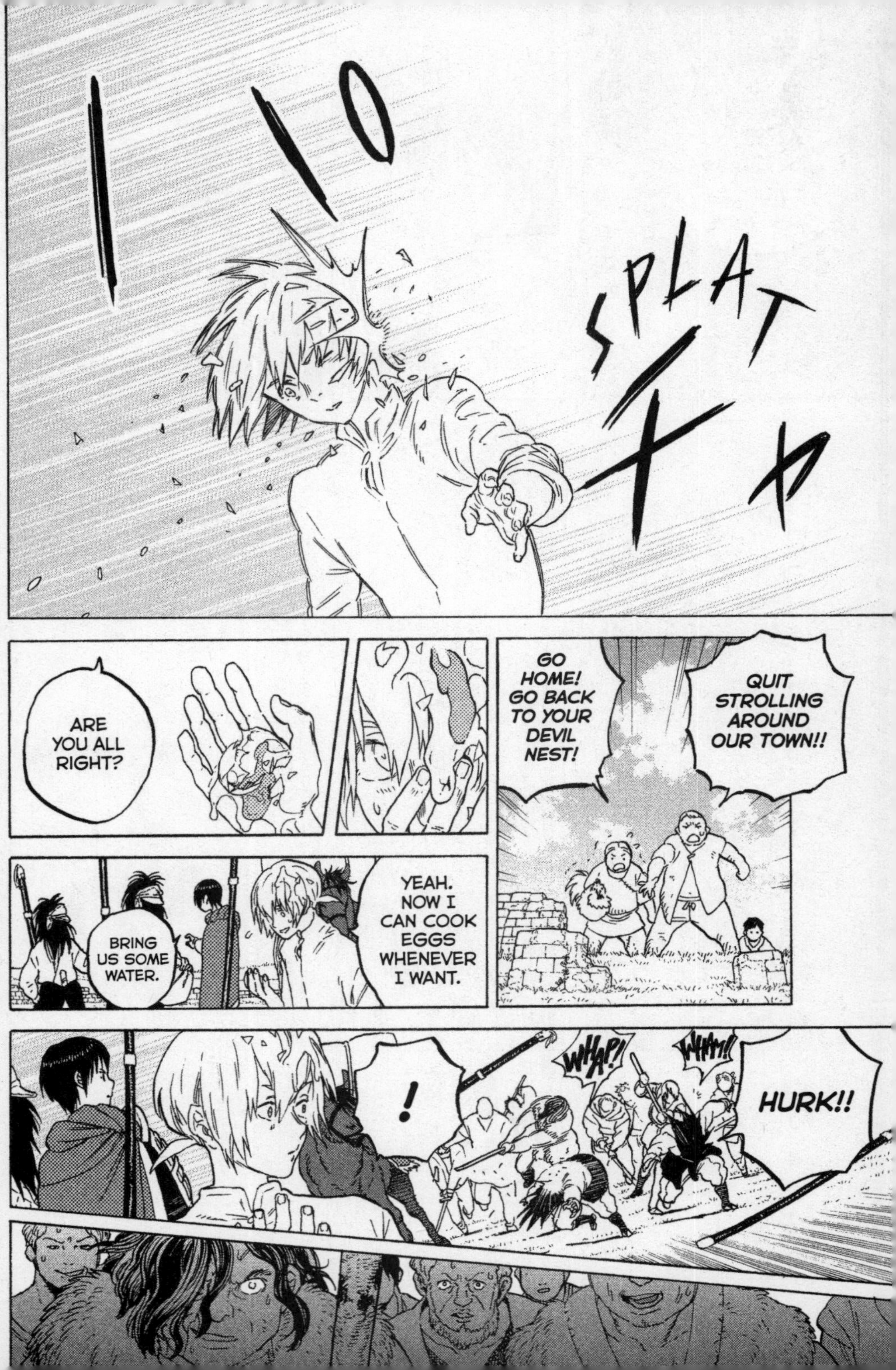
SPLAT
QUIT STROLLING AROUND OUR TOWN!!
GO HOME! GO BACK TO YOUR DEVIL NEST!
ARE YOU ALL RIGHT?
YEAH. NOW I CAN COOK EGGS WHENEVER I WANT.
BRING US SOME WATER.
HURK!!
WHAM!!
WHAP!!
!

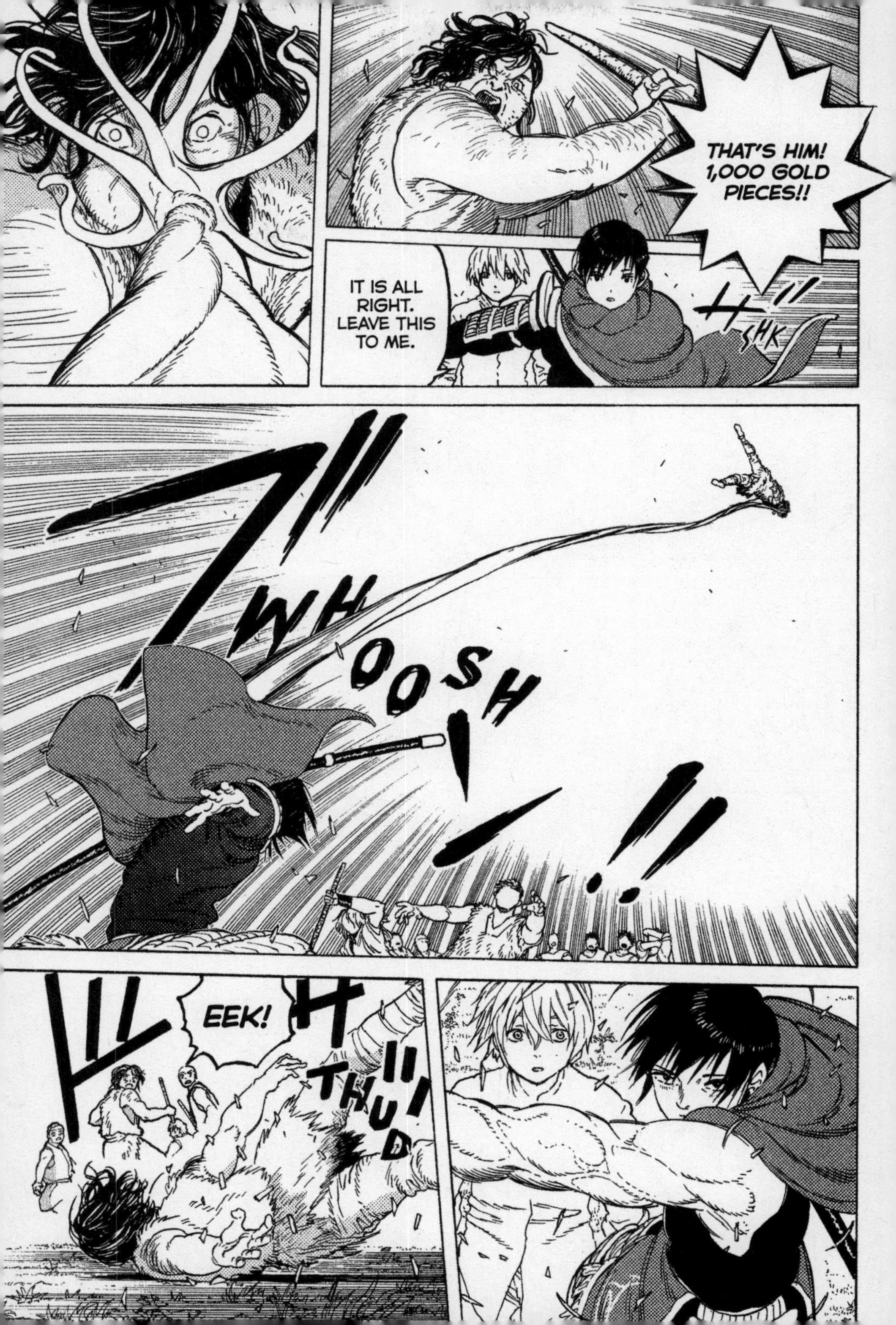
THAT'S HIM! 1,000 GOLD PIECES!!
IT IS ALL RIGHT. LEAVE THIS TO ME.
SHK
WHOOSH!!
EEK!
THUD

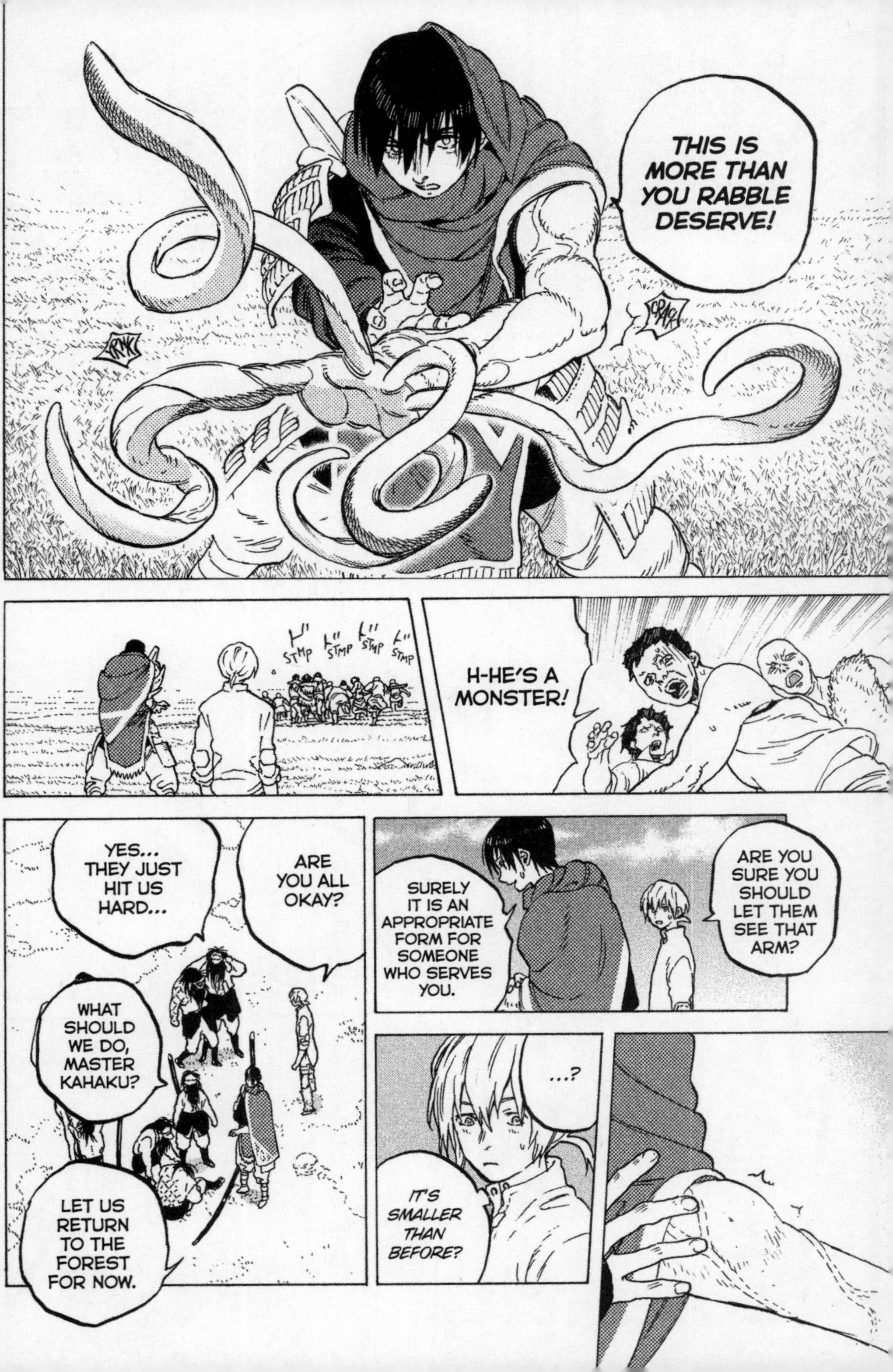
THIS IS MORE THAN YOU RABBLE DESERVE!
H-HE'S A MONSTER!
STMP STMP STMP STMP
ARE YOU SURE YOU SHOULD LET THEM SEE THAT ARM?
SURELY IT IS AN APPROPRIATE FORM FOR SOMEONE WHO SERVES YOU.
...?
IT'S SMALLER THAN BEFORE?
ARE YOU ALL OKAY?
YES... THEY JUST HIT US HARD...
WHAT SHOULD WE DO, MASTER KAHAKU?
LET US RETURN TO THE FOREST FOR NOW.

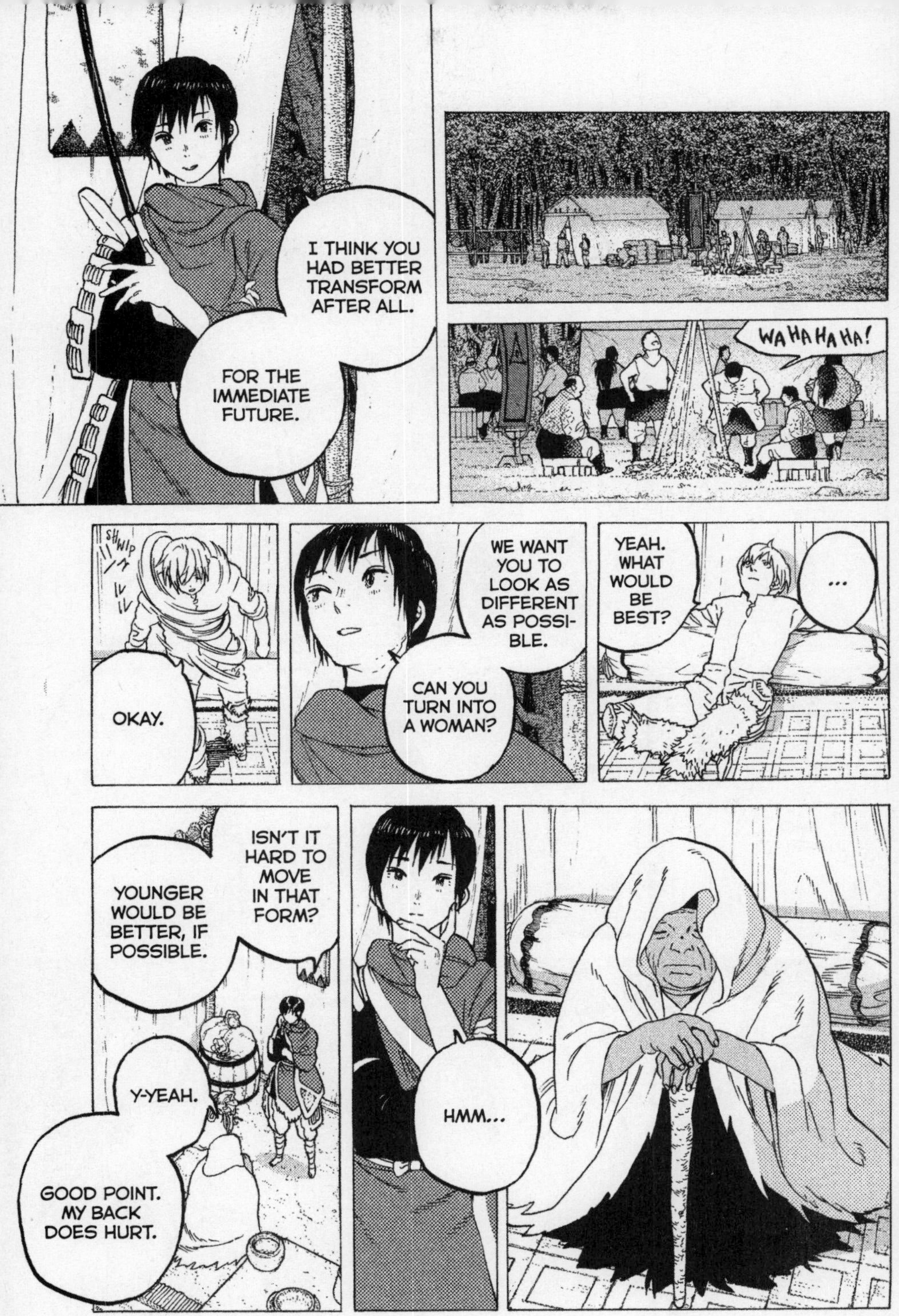
WA HA HA HA HA!
I THINK YOU HAD BETTER TRANSFORM AFTER ALL.
FOR THE IMMEDIATE FUTURE.
...
YEAH. WHAT WOULD BE BEST?
WE WANT YOU TO LOOK AS DIFFERENT AS POSSI-BLE.
CAN YOU TURN INTO A WOMAN?
SHWIP
OKAY.
HMM...
ISN'T IT HARD TO MOVE IN THAT FORM?
YOUNGER WOULD BE BETTER, IF POSSIBLE.
Y-YEAH.
GOOD POINT. MY BACK DOES HURT.

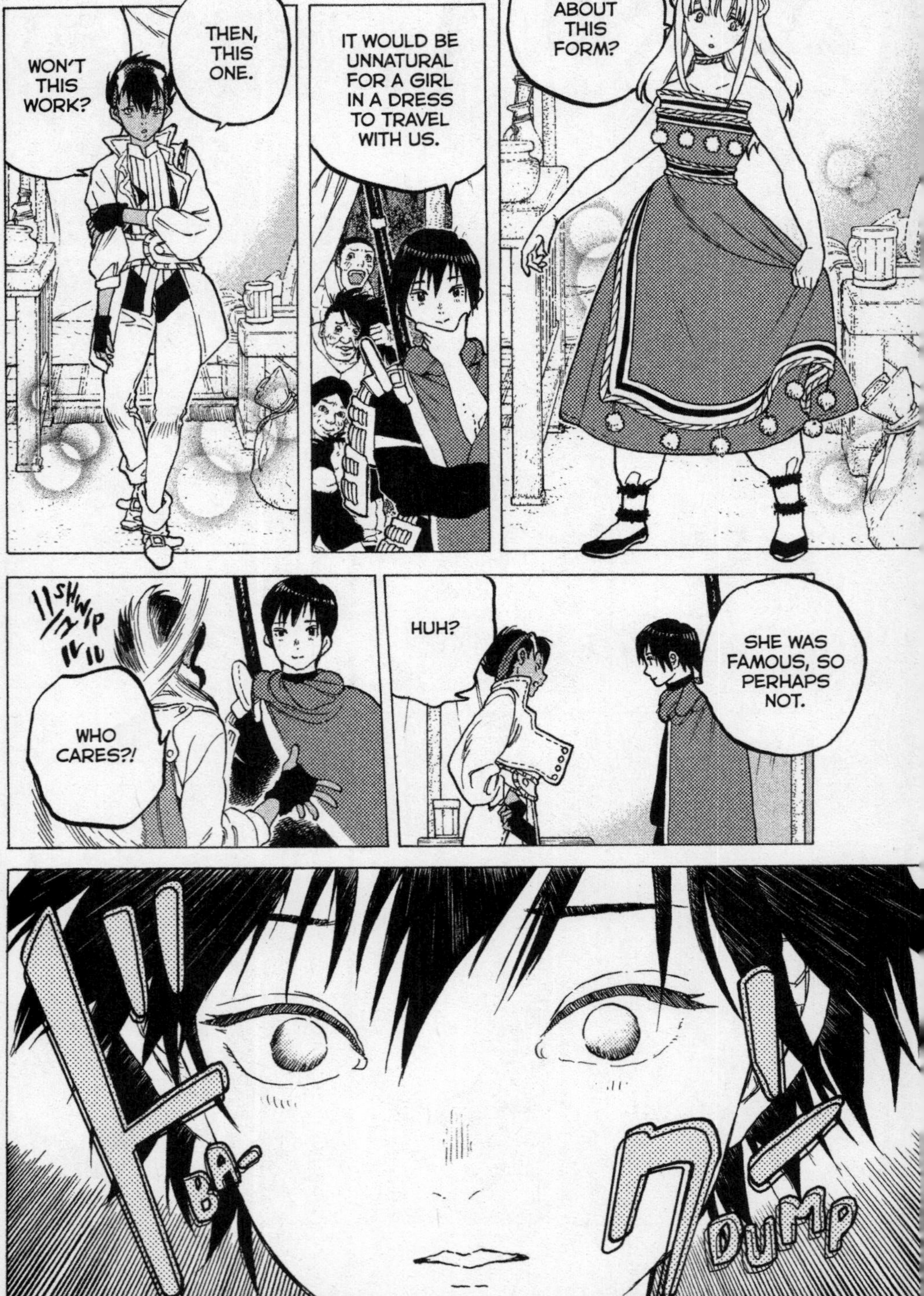
HOW ABOUT THIS FORM?
IT WOULD BE UNNATURAL FOR A GIRL IN A DRESS TO TRAVEL WITH US.
THEN, THIS ONE.
WON'T THIS WORK?
SHE WAS FAMOUS, SO PERHAPS NOT.
HUH?
SHWIP
WHO CARES?!
BA-
DUMP

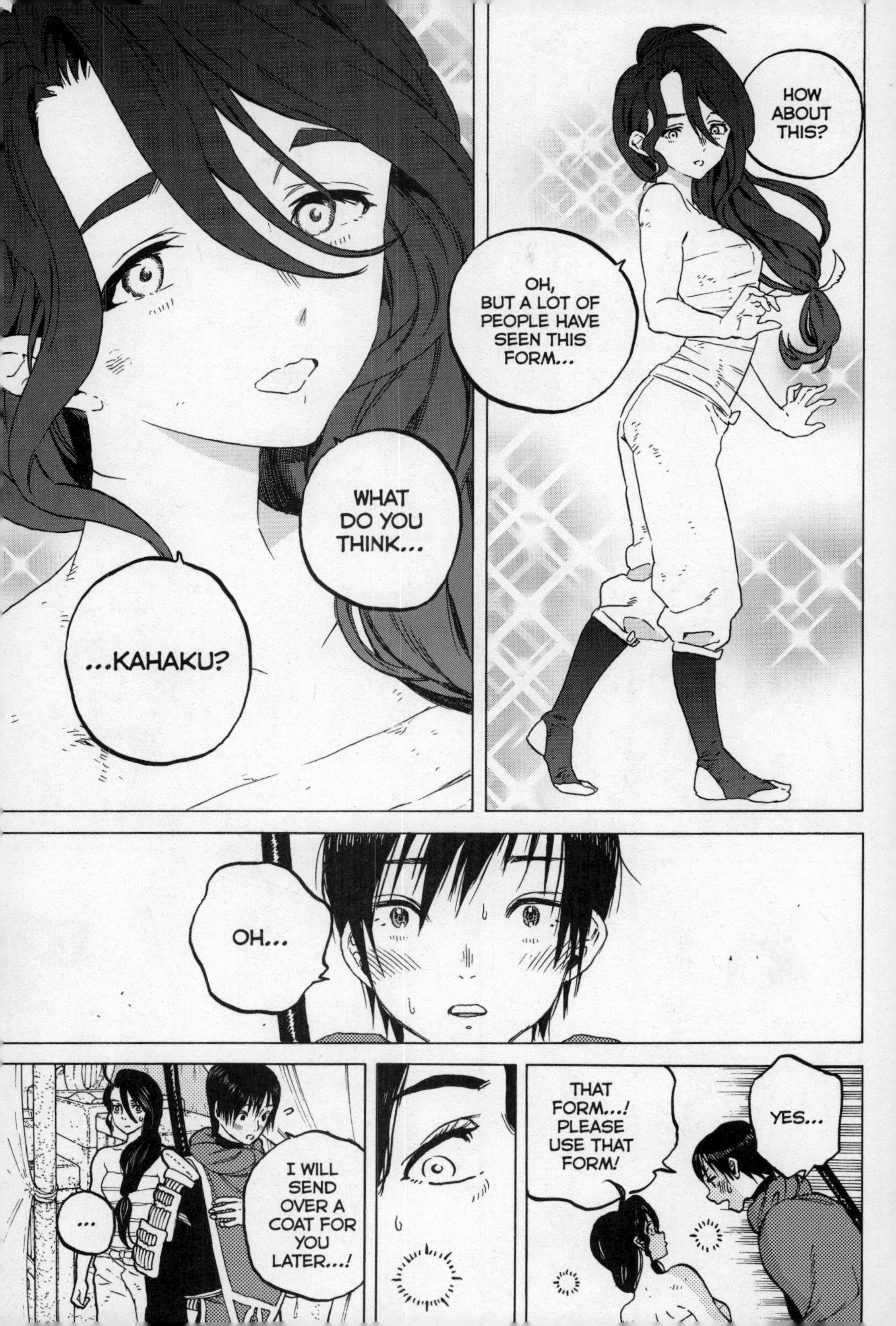
HOW ABOUT THIS?
OH, BUT A LOT OF PEOPLE HAVE SEEN THIS FORM...
WHAT DO YOU THINK...
...KAHAKU?
OH...
YES...
THAT FORM...! PLEASE USE THAT FORM!
I WILL SEND OVER A COAT FOR YOU LATER...!
...

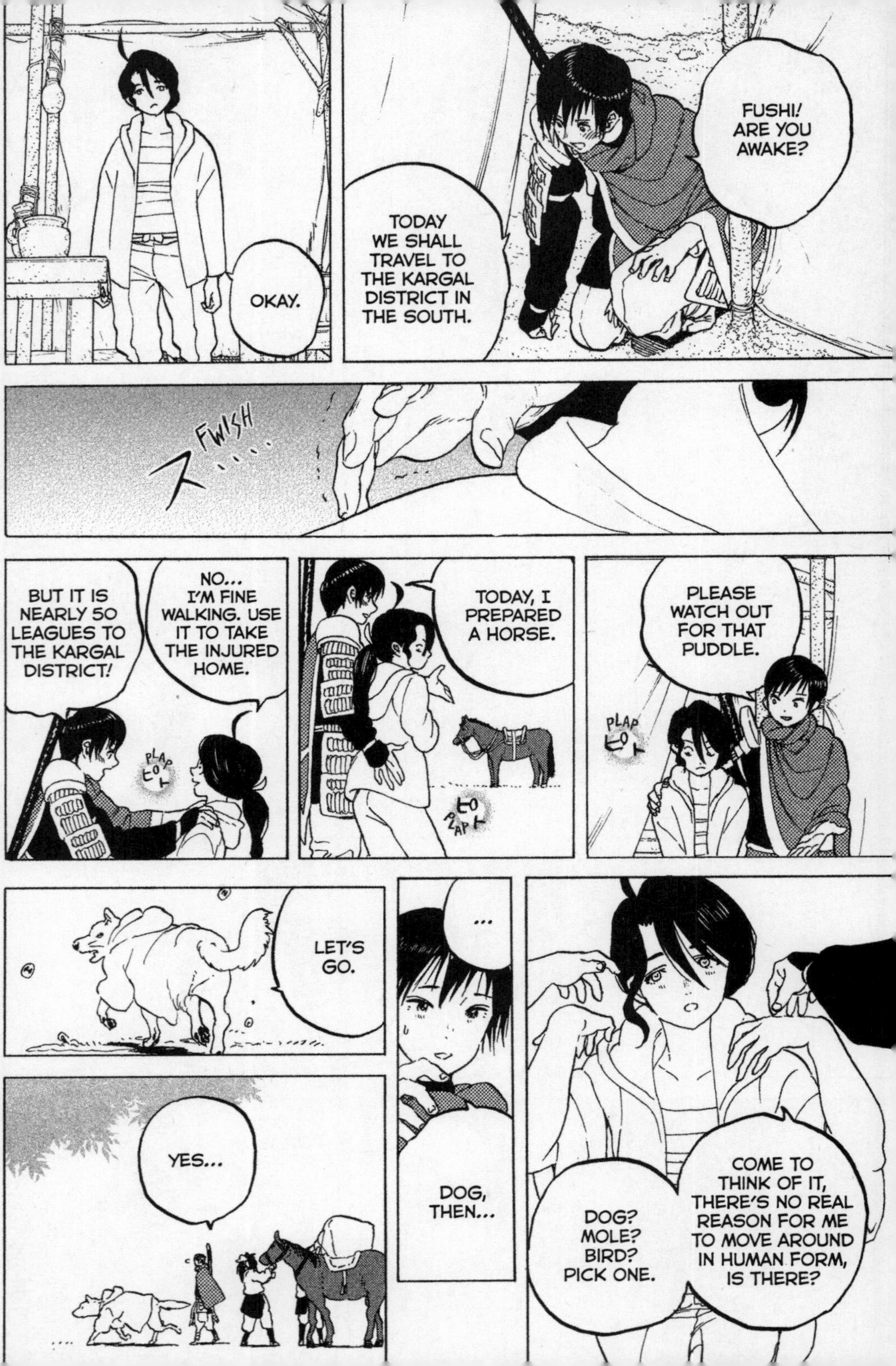
FUSHI! ARE YOU AWAKE?
TODAY WE SHALL TRAVEL TO THE KARGAL DISTRICT IN THE SOUTH.
OKAY.
FWISH
ス....
PLEASE WATCH OUT FOR THAT PUDDLE.
PLAP
TODAY, I PREPARED A HORSE.
PLAP
NO... I'M FINE WALKING. USE IT TO TAKE THE INJURED HOME.
BUT IT IS NEARLY 50 LEAGUES TO THE KARGAL DISTRICT!
PLAP
COME TO THINK OF IT, THERE'S NO REAL REASON FOR ME TO MOVE AROUND IN HUMAN FORM, IS THERE?
DOG? MOLE? BIRD? PICK ONE.
...
DOG, THEN...
LET'S GO.
YES...

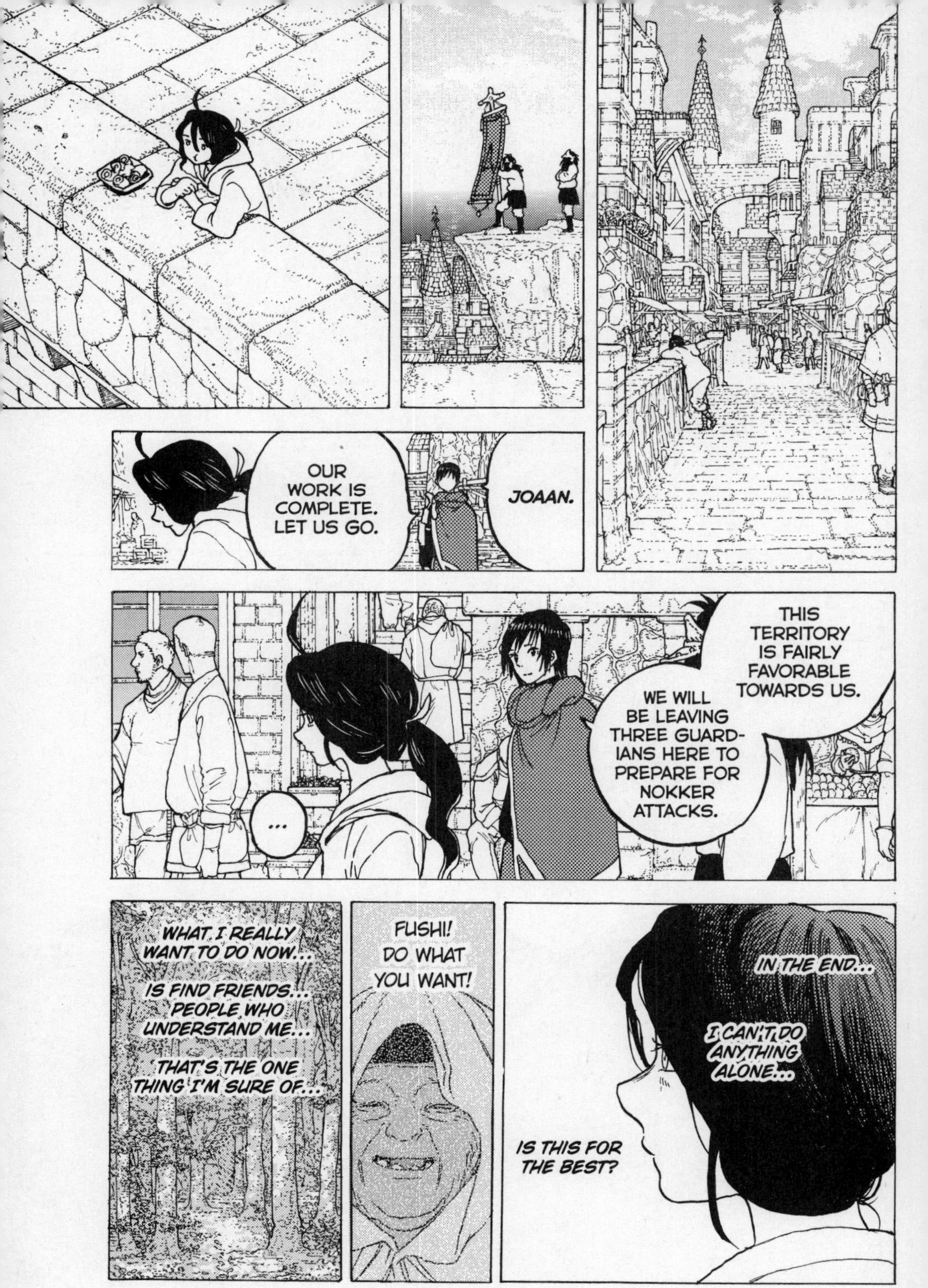
JOAAN.
OUR WORK IS COMPLETE. LET US GO.
THIS TERRITORY IS FAIRLY FAVORABLE TOWARDS US.
WE WILL BE LEAVING THREE GUARDIANS HERE TO PREPARE FOR NOKKER ATTACKS.
...
IN THE END...
I CAN'T DO ANYTHING ALONE...
IS THIS FOR THE BEST?
FUSHI! DO WHAT YOU WANT!
WHAT I REALLY WANT TO DO NOW...
IS FIND FRIENDS... PEOPLE WHO UNDERSTAND ME...
THAT'S THE ONE THING I'M SURE OF...

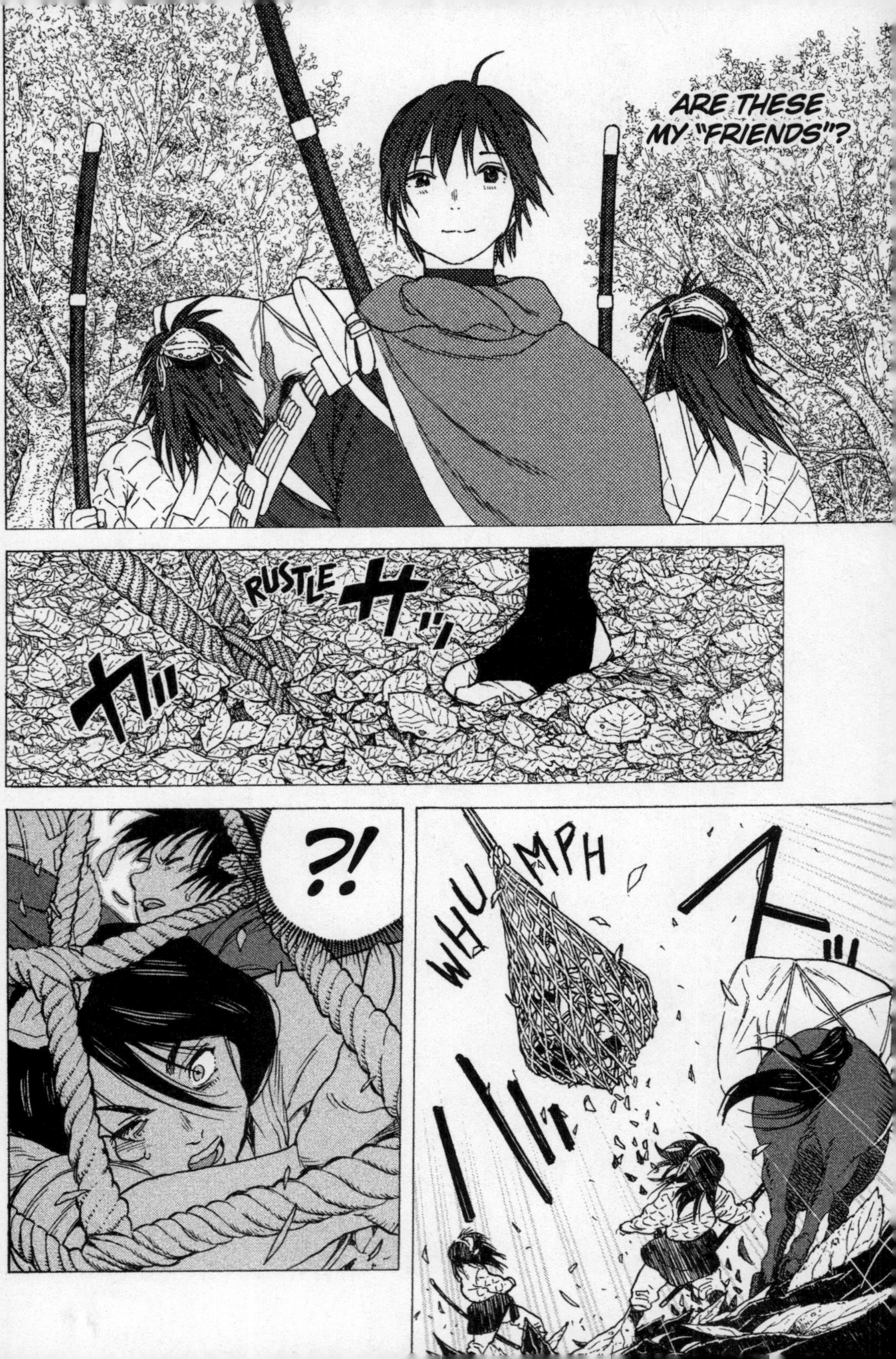
ARE THESE MY "FRIENDS"?
RUSTLE
WHUMPH
?!

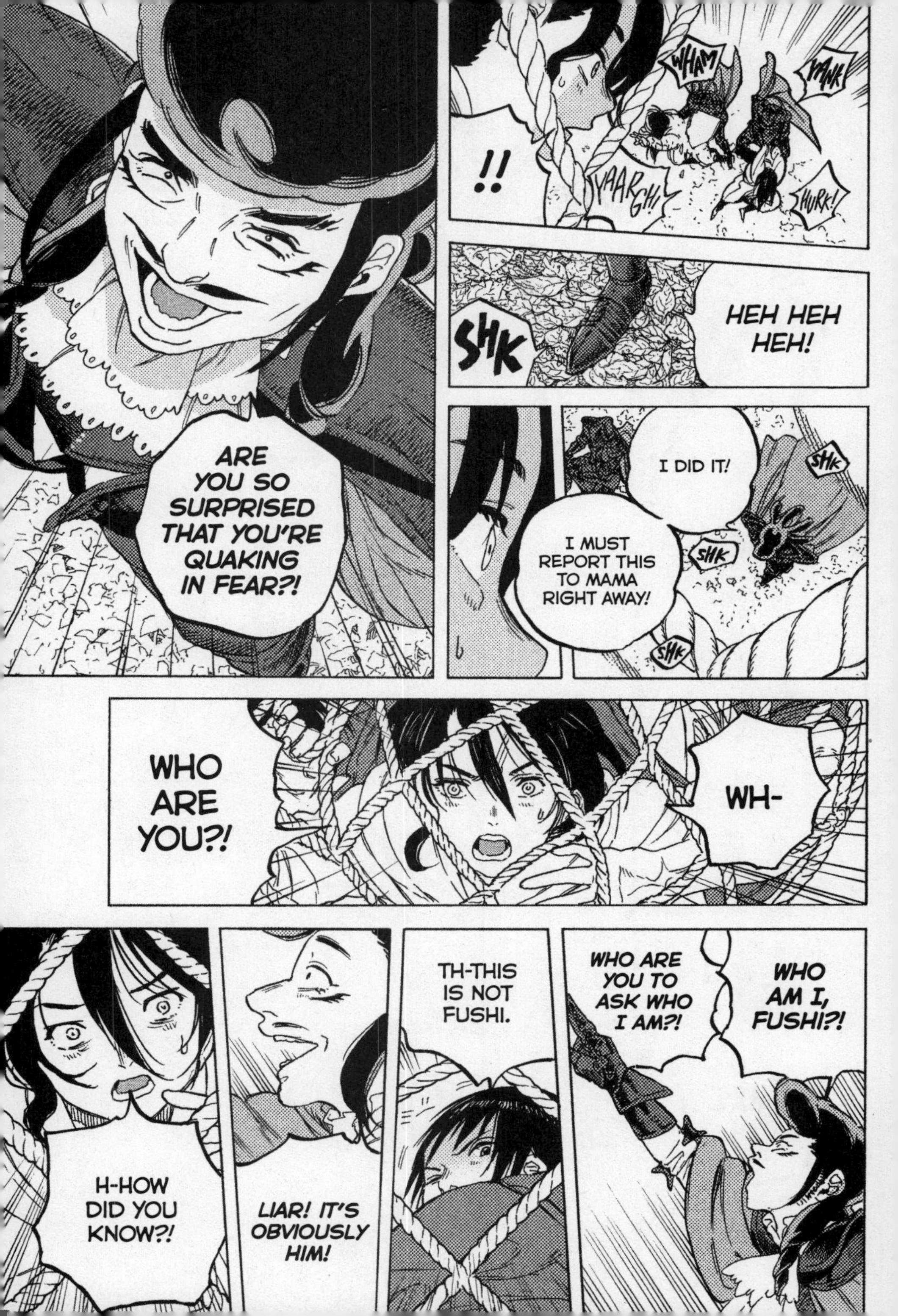
YANK
WHAM
HURK!
YAARGH!
!!
HEH HEH HEH!
SHK
I DID IT!
SHK
I MUST REPORT THIS TO MAMA RIGHT AWAY!
SHK
SHK
ARE YOU SO SURPRISED THAT YOU'RE QUAKING IN FEAR?!
WH-
WHO ARE YOU?!
WHO AM I, FUSHI?!
WHO ARE YOU TO ASK WHO I AM?!
TH-THIS IS NOT FUSHI.
LIAR! IT'S OBVIOUSLY HIM!
H-HOW DID YOU KNOW?!

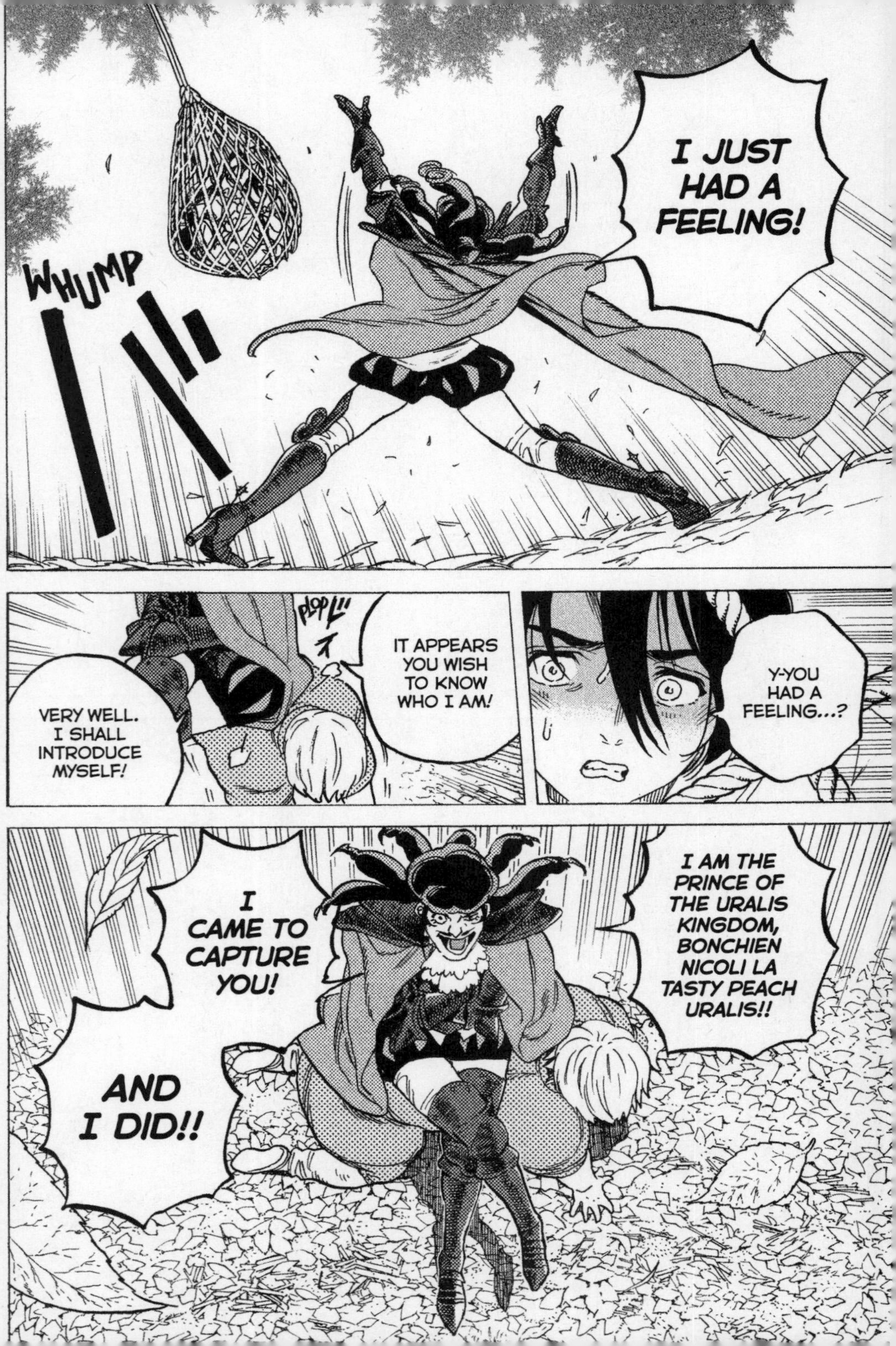
I JUST HAD A FEELING!
WHUMP
Y-YOU HAD A FEELING...?
PLOP
IT APPEARS YOU WISH TO KNOW WHO I AM!
VERY WELL. I SHALL INTRODUCE MYSELF!
I AM THE PRINCE OF THE URALIS KINGDOM, BONCHIEN NICOLI LA TASTY PEACH URALIS!!
I CAME TO CAPTURE YOU!
AND I DID!!

#63 The Merry Prince

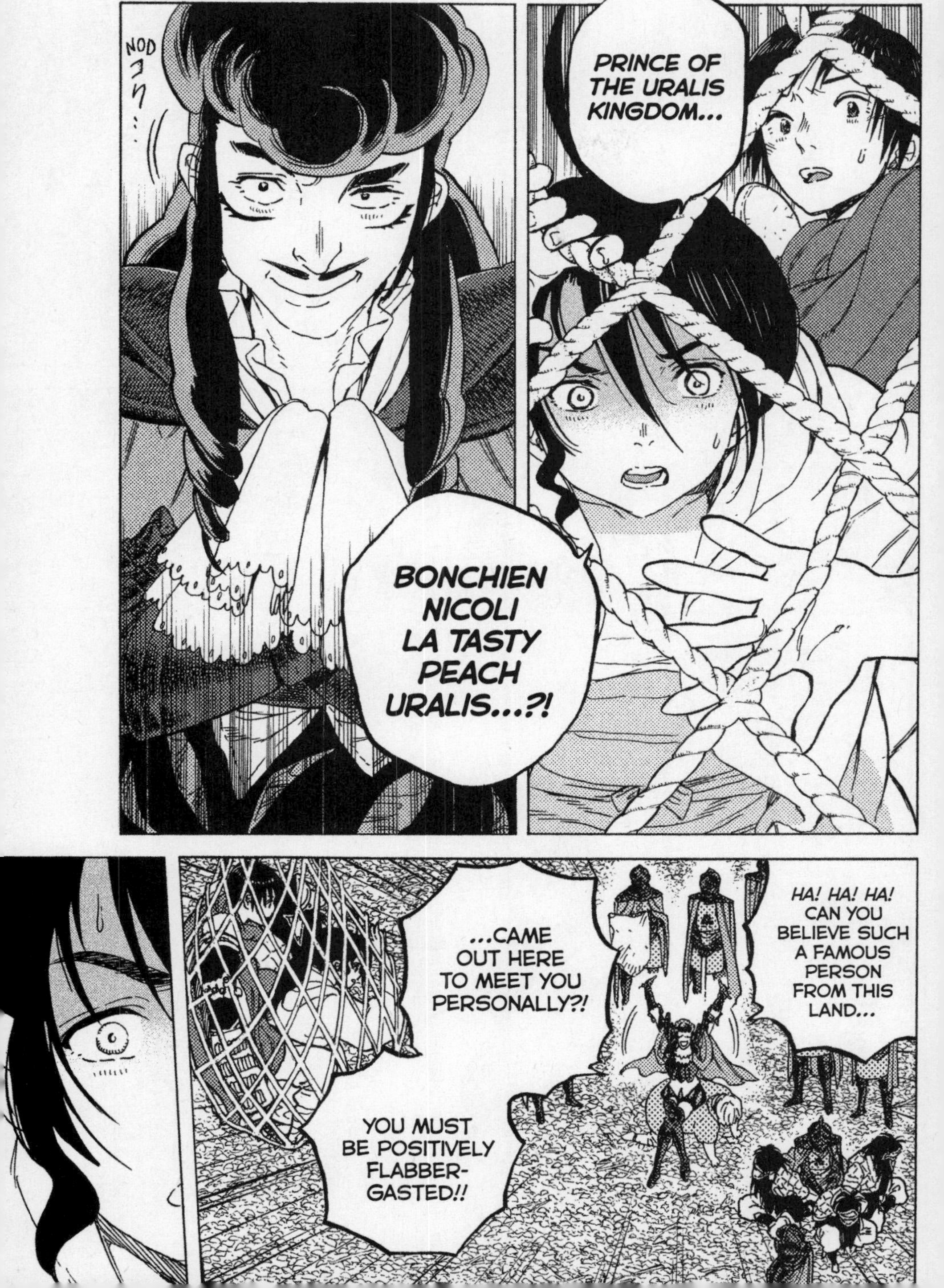
PRINCE OF THE URALIS KINGDOM...
BONCHIEN NICOLI LA TASTY PEACH URALIS...?!
NOD
コク…
HA! HA! HA! CAN YOU BELIEVE SUCH A FAMOUS PERSON FROM THIS LAND...
...CAME OUT HERE TO MEET YOU PERSONALLY?!
YOU MUST BE POSITIVELY FLABBERGASTED!!

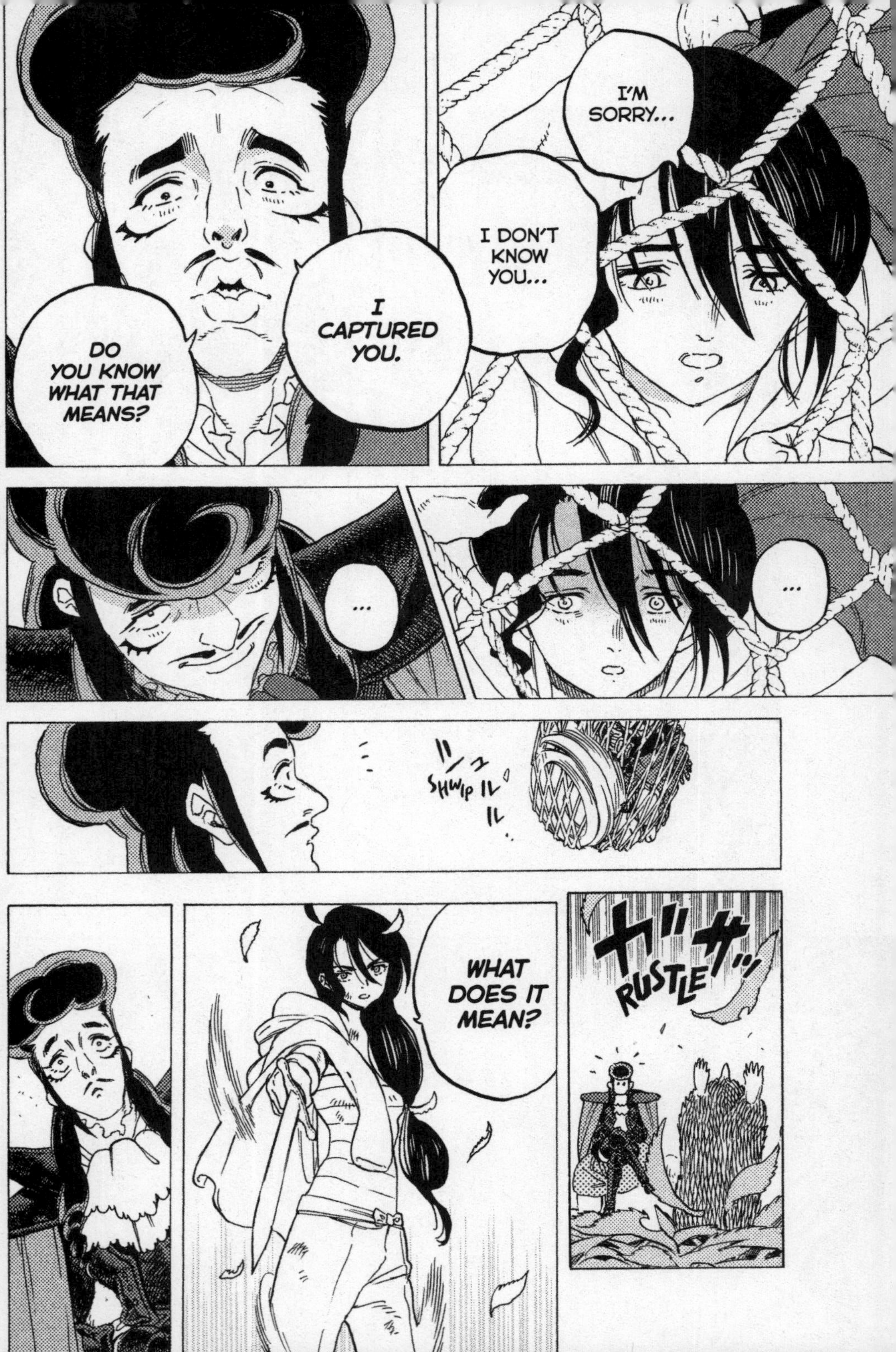
I'M SORRY...
I DON'T KNOW YOU...
I CAPTURED YOU.
DO YOU KNOW WHAT THAT MEANS?
...
...
SHWIP
RUSTLE
WHAT DOES IT MEAN?

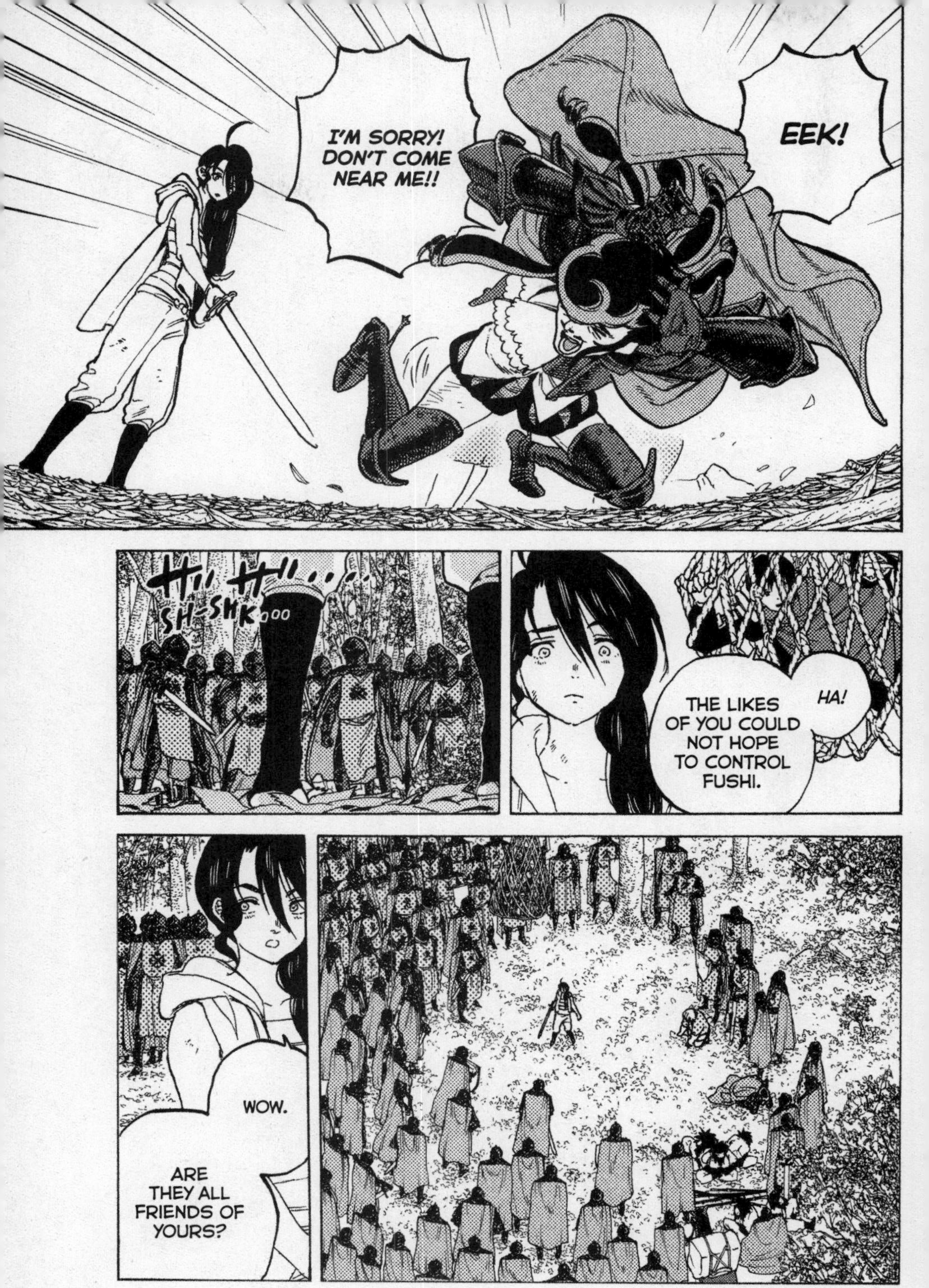
EEK!
I'M SORRY! DON'T COME NEAR ME!!
HA!
THE LIKES OF YOU COULD NOT HOPE TO CONTROL FUSHI.
SH-SHK...
WOW.
ARE THEY ALL FRIENDS OF YOURS?

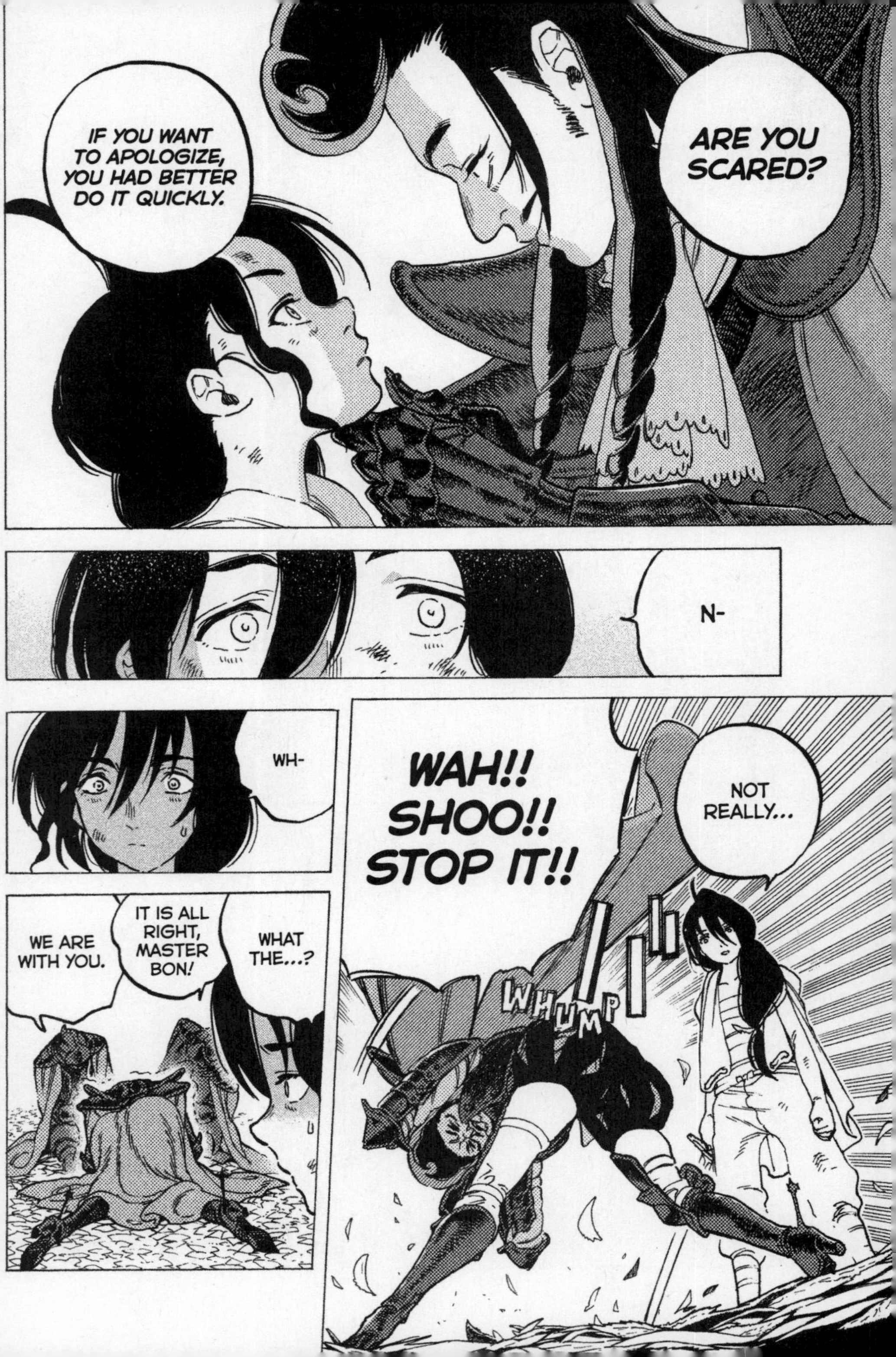
ARE YOU SCARED?
IF YOU WANT TO APOLOGIZE, YOU HAD BETTER DO IT QUICKLY.
N-
NOT REALLY...
WAH!! SHOO!! STOP IT!!
WHUMP
WH-
WHAT THE...?
IT IS ALL RIGHT, MASTER BON!
WE ARE WITH YOU.

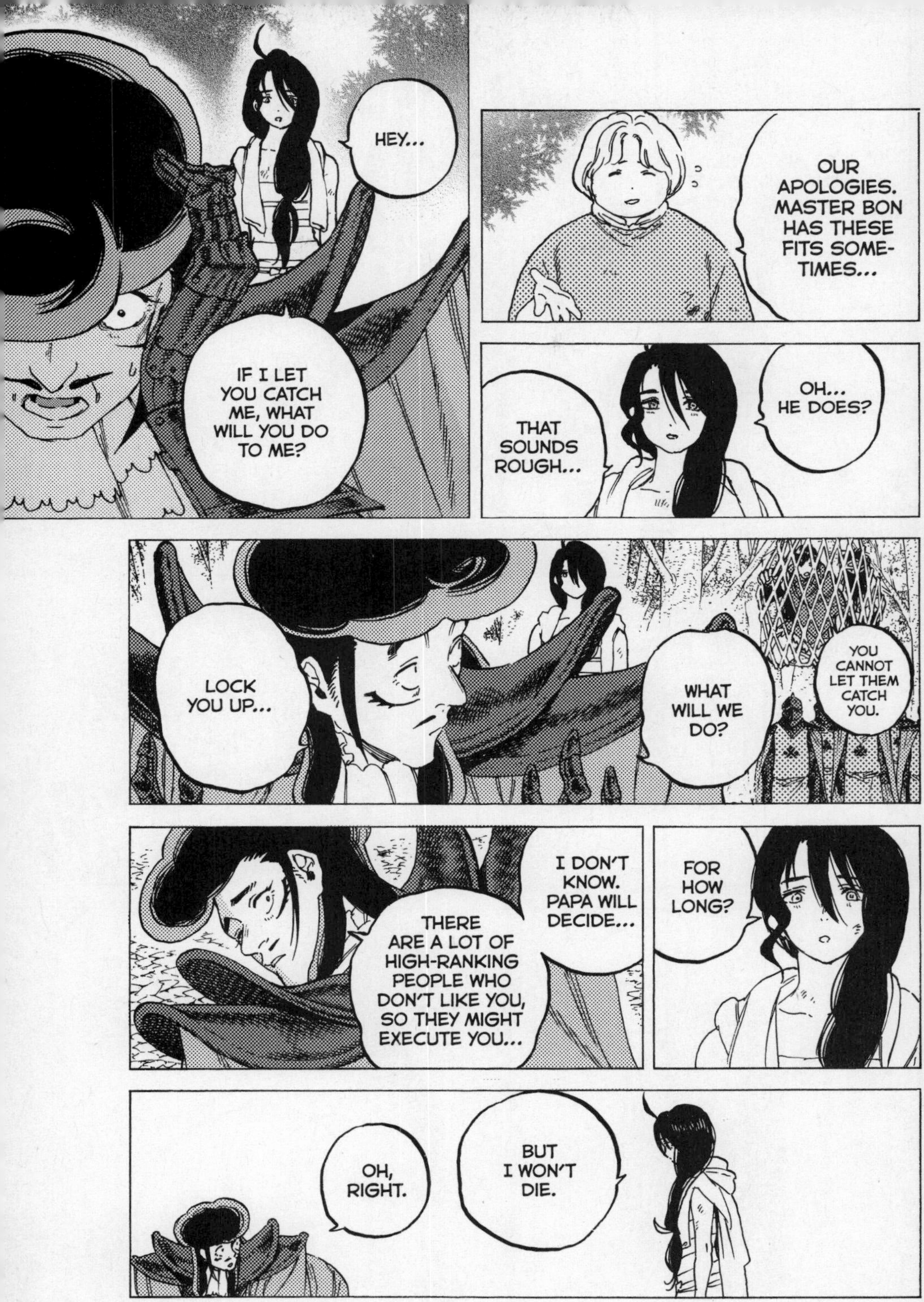
OUR APOLOGIES. MASTER BON HAS THESE FITS SOME-TIMES...
OH... HE DOES?
THAT SOUNDS ROUGH...
HEY...
IF I LET YOU CATCH ME, WHAT WILL YOU DO TO ME?
YOU CANNOT LET THEM CATCH YOU.
WHAT WILL WE DO?
LOCK YOU UP...
FOR HOW LONG?
I DON'T KNOW. PAPA WILL DECIDE...
THERE ARE A LOT OF HIGH-RANKING PEOPLE WHO DON'T LIKE YOU, SO THEY MIGHT EXECUTE YOU...
BUT I WON'T DIE.
OH, RIGHT.

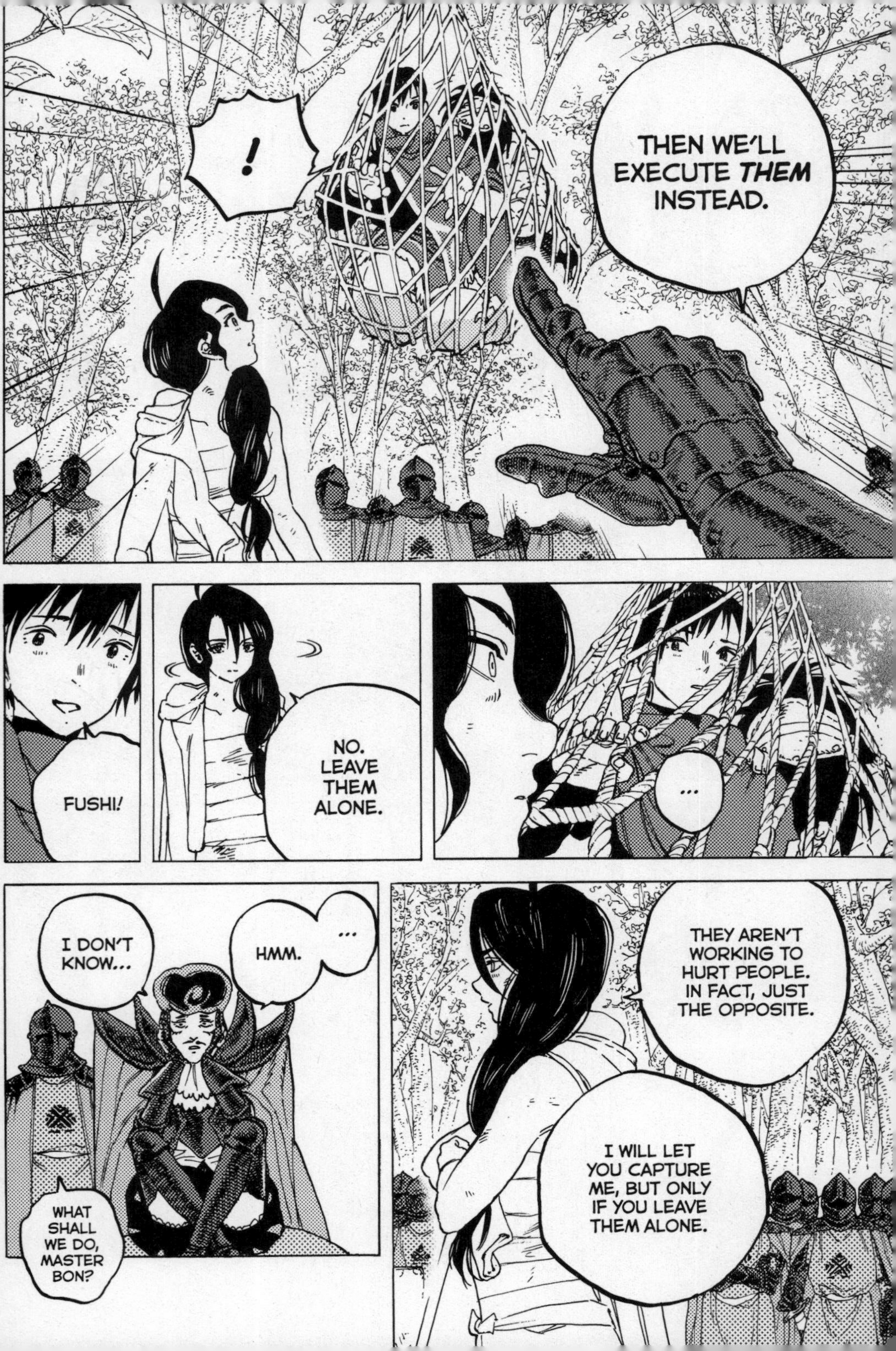
THEN WE'LL EXECUTE *THEM* INSTEAD.
!
...
NO. LEAVE THEM ALONE.
FUSHI!
THEY AREN'T WORKING TO HURT PEOPLE. IN FACT, JUST THE OPPOSITE.
I WILL LET YOU CAPTURE ME, BUT ONLY IF YOU LEAVE THEM ALONE.
...
HMM.
I DON'T KNOW...
WHAT SHALL WE DO, MASTER BON?

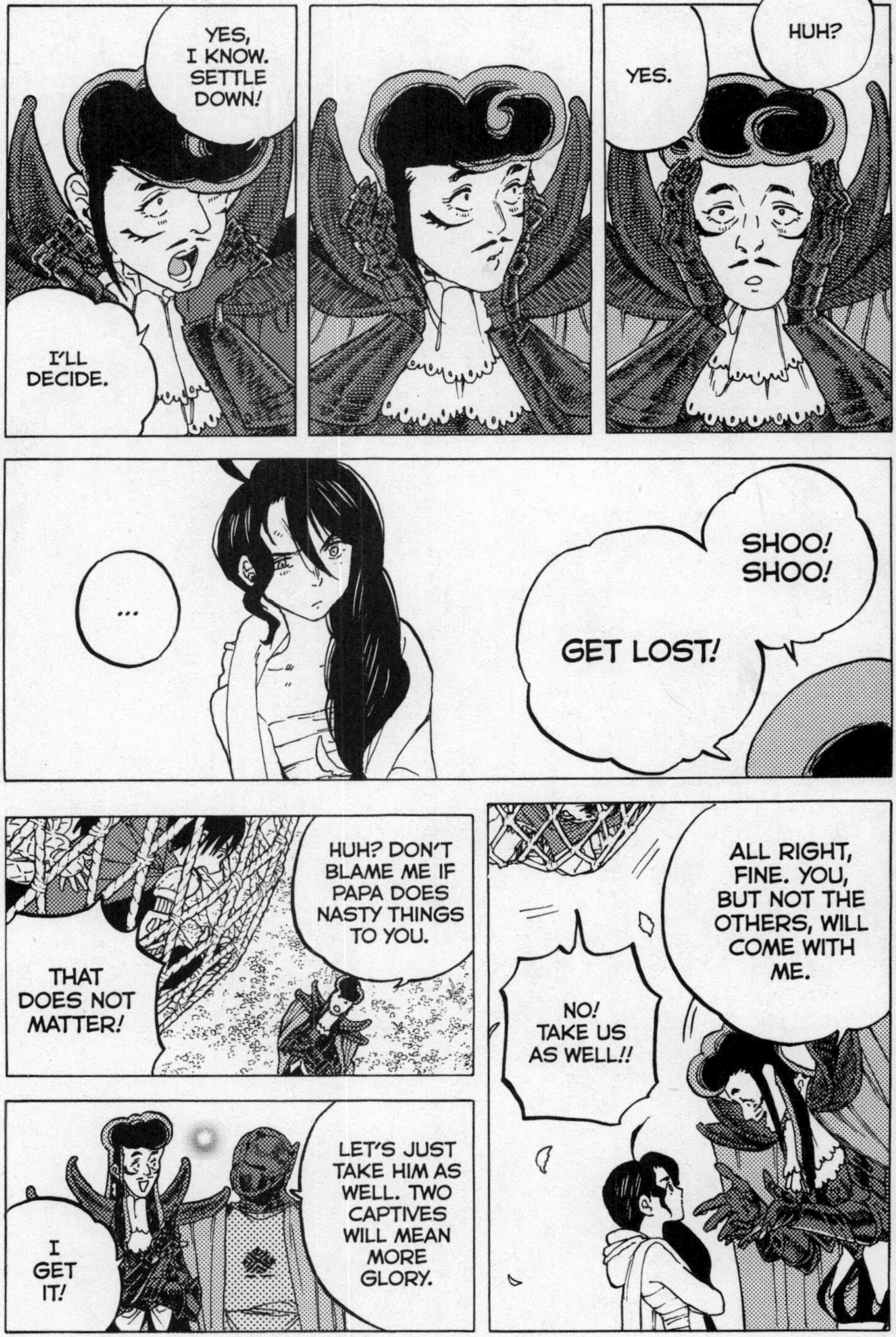
HUH?
YES.
YES, I KNOW. SETTLE DOWN!
I'LL DECIDE.
SHOO! SHOO!
GET LOST!
...
ALL RIGHT, FINE. YOU, BUT NOT THE OTHERS, WILL COME WITH ME.
NO! TAKE US AS WELL!!
HUH? DON'T BLAME ME IF PAPA DOES NASTY THINGS TO YOU.
THAT DOES NOT MATTER!
LET'S JUST TAKE HIM AS WELL. TWO CAPTIVES WILL MEAN MORE GLORY.
I GET IT!

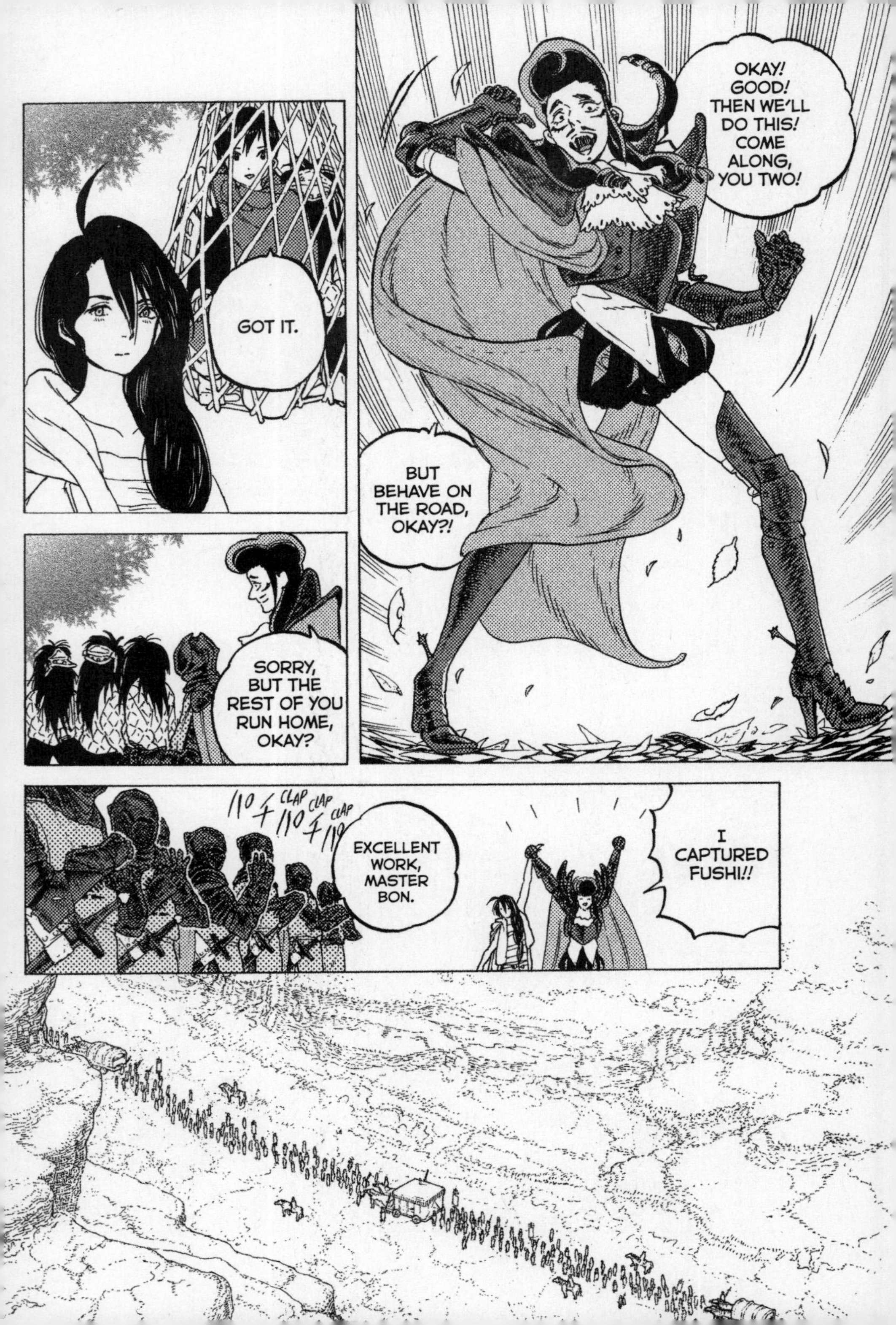
OKAY! GOOD! THEN WE'LL DO THIS! COME ALONG, YOU TWO!
BUT BEHAVE ON THE ROAD, OKAY?!
GOT IT.
SORRY, BUT THE REST OF YOU RUN HOME, OKAY?
I CAPTURED FUSHI!!
EXCELLENT WORK, MASTER BON.
CLAP CLAP CLAP

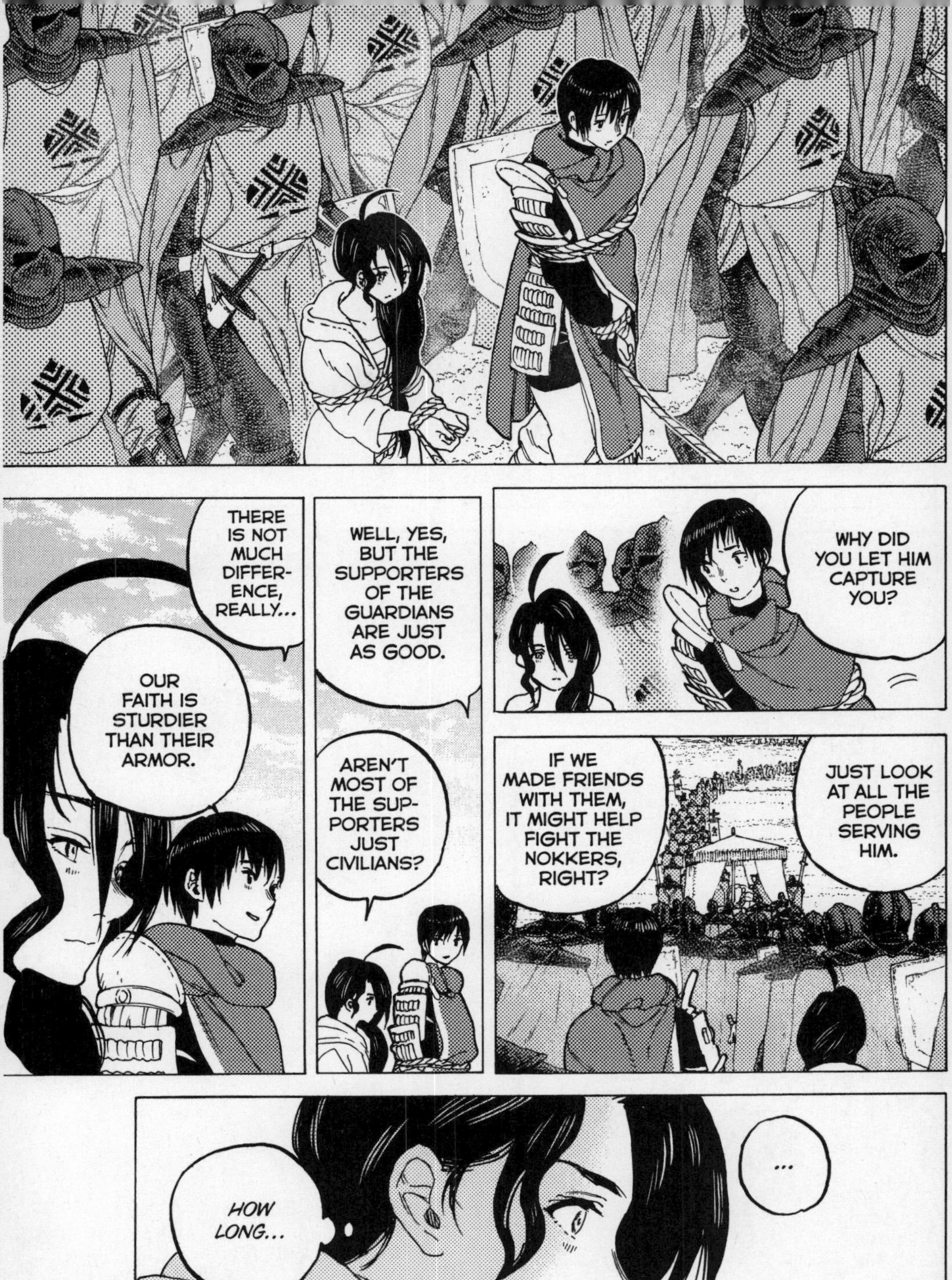
WHY DID YOU LET HIM CAPTURE YOU?
JUST LOOK AT ALL THE PEOPLE SERVING HIM.
IF WE MADE FRIENDS WITH THEM, IT MIGHT HELP FIGHT THE NOKKERS, RIGHT?
WELL, YES, BUT THE SUPPORTERS OF THE GUARDIANS ARE JUST AS GOOD.
AREN'T MOST OF THE SUP-PORTERS JUST CIVILIANS?
THERE IS NOT MUCH DIFFER-ENCE, REALLY...
OUR FAITH IS STURDIER THAN THEIR ARMOR.
...
HOW LONG...

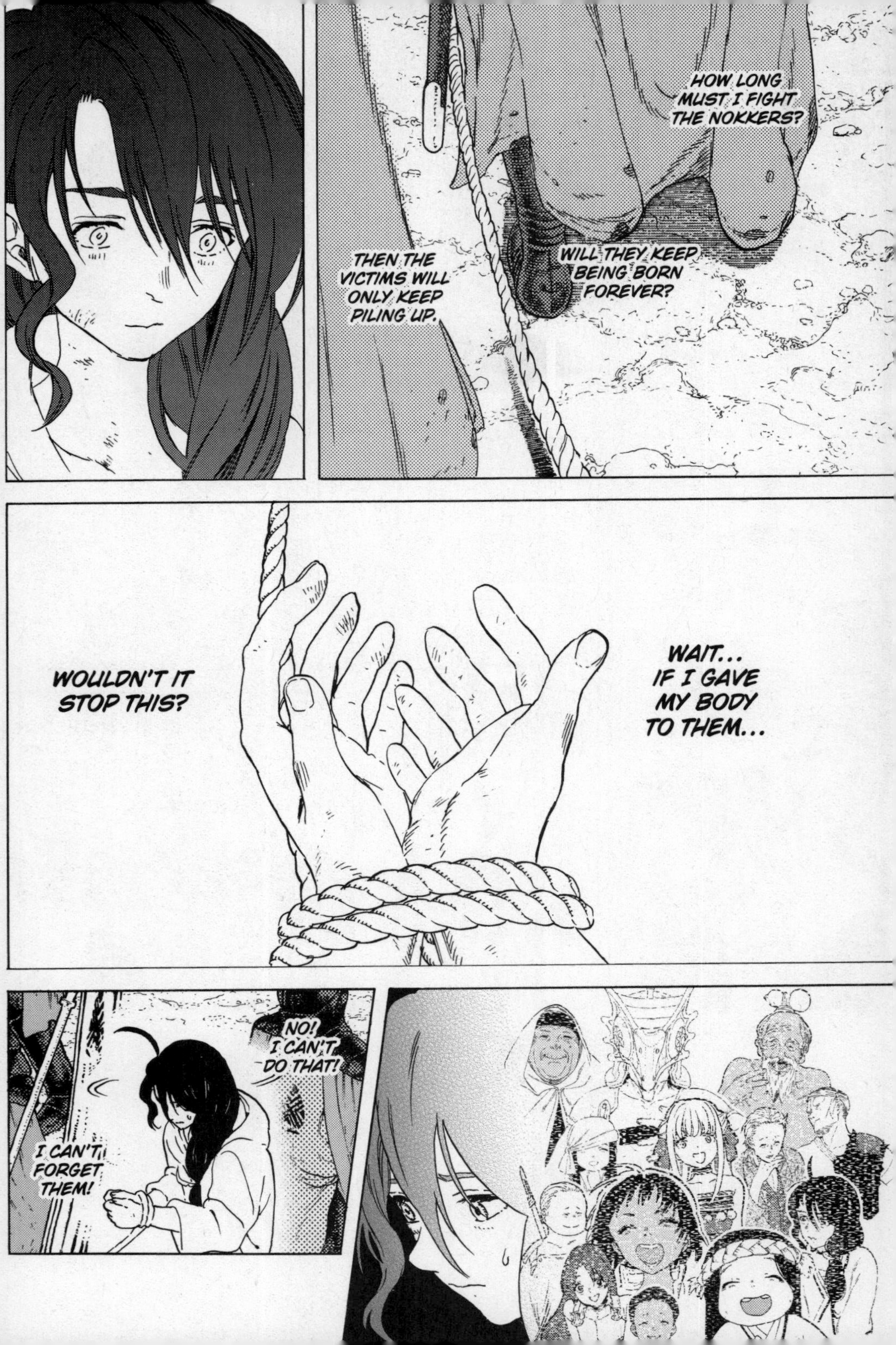
HOW LONG MUST I FIGHT THE NOKKERS?
WILL THEY KEEP BEING BORN FOREVER?
THEN THE VICTIMS WILL ONLY KEEP PILING UP.
WAIT... IF I GAVE MY BODY TO THEM...
WOULDN'T IT STOP THIS?
NO! I CAN'T DO THAT!
I CAN'T FORGET THEM!

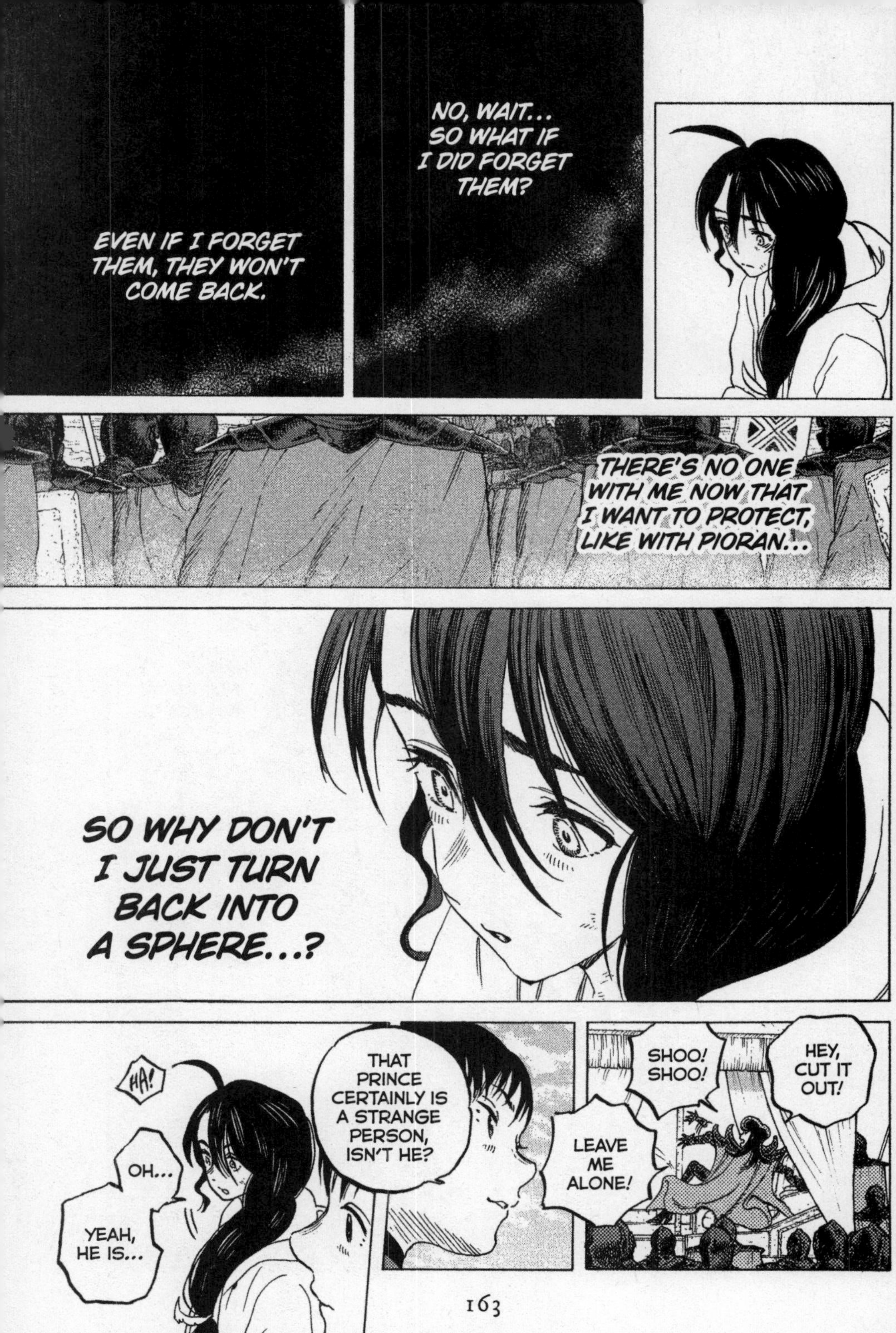
NO, WAIT... SO WHAT IF I DID FORGET THEM?
EVEN IF I FORGET THEM, THEY WON'T COME BACK.
THERE'S NO ONE WITH ME NOW THAT I WANT TO PROTECT, LIKE WITH PIORAN...
SO WHY DON'T I JUST TURN BACK INTO A SPHERE...?
HEY, CUT IT OUT!
SHOO! SHOO!
LEAVE ME ALONE!
THAT PRINCE CERTAINLY IS A STRANGE PERSON, ISN'T HE?
HA!
OH...
YEAH, HE IS...

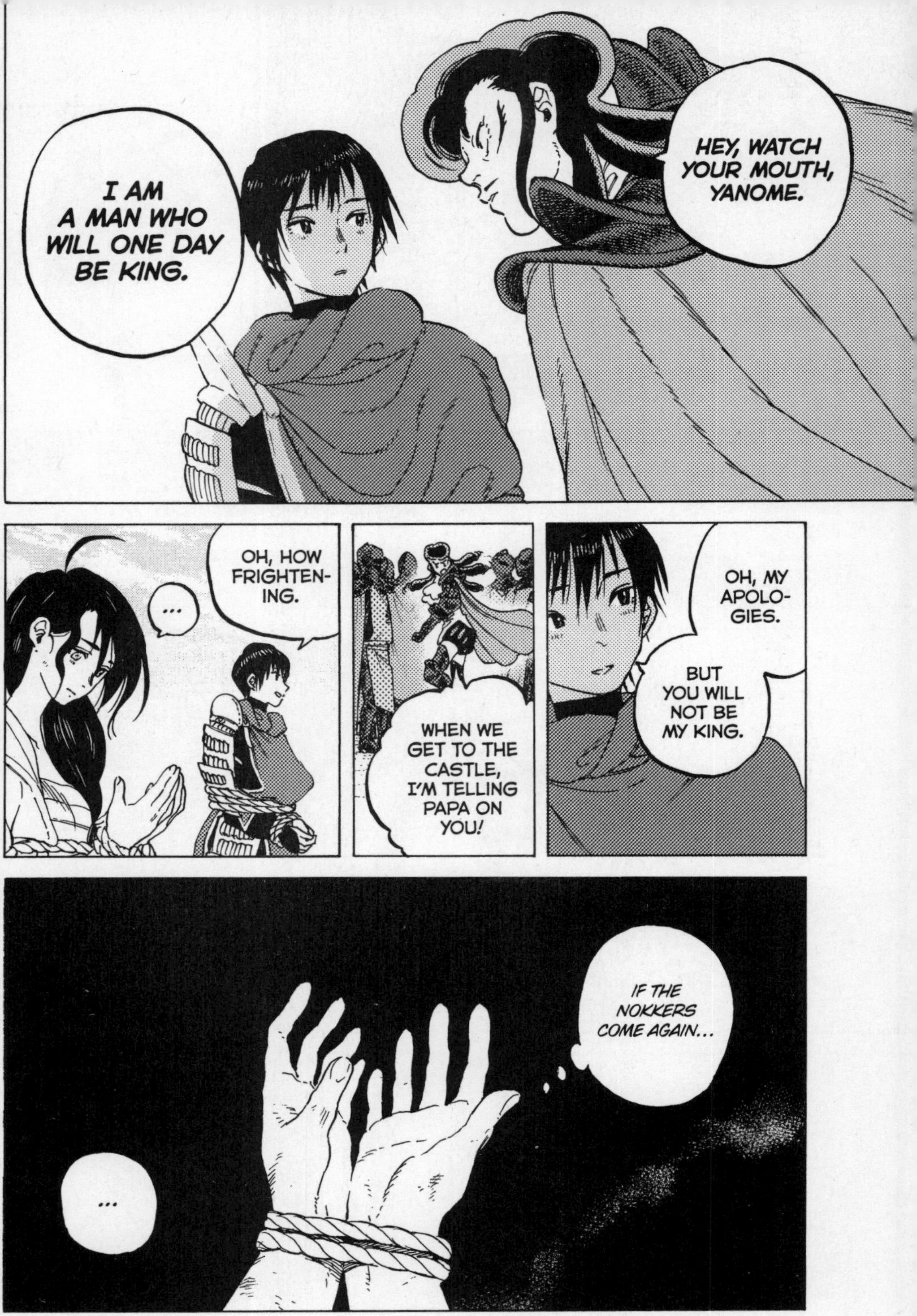
HEY, WATCH YOUR MOUTH, YANOME.
I AM A MAN WHO WILL ONE DAY BE KING.
OH, MY APOLOGIES.
BUT YOU WILL NOT BE MY KING.
WHEN WE GET TO THE CASTLE, I'M TELLING PAPA ON YOU!
OH, HOW FRIGHTEN-ING.
...
IF THE NOKKERS COME AGAIN...
...

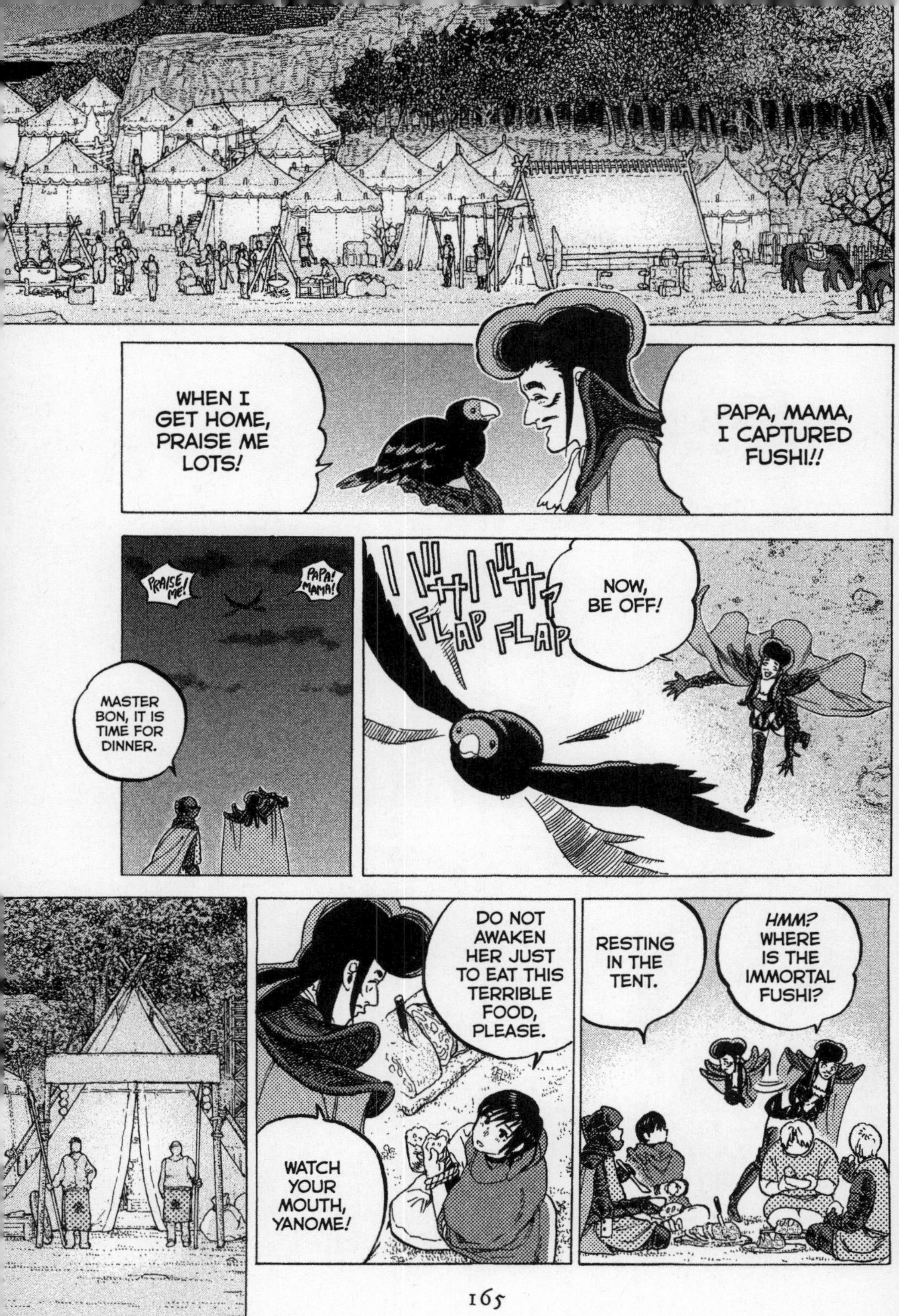
PAPA, MAMA, I CAPTURED FUSHI!!
WHEN I GET HOME, PRAISE ME LOTS!
NOW, BE OFF!
FLAP FLAP
PAPA! MAMA!
PRAISE ME!
MASTER BON, IT IS TIME FOR DINNER.
HMM? WHERE IS THE IMMORTAL FUSHI?
RESTING IN THE TENT.
DO NOT AWAKEN HER JUST TO EAT THIS TERRIBLE FOOD, PLEASE.
WATCH YOUR MOUTH, YANOME!

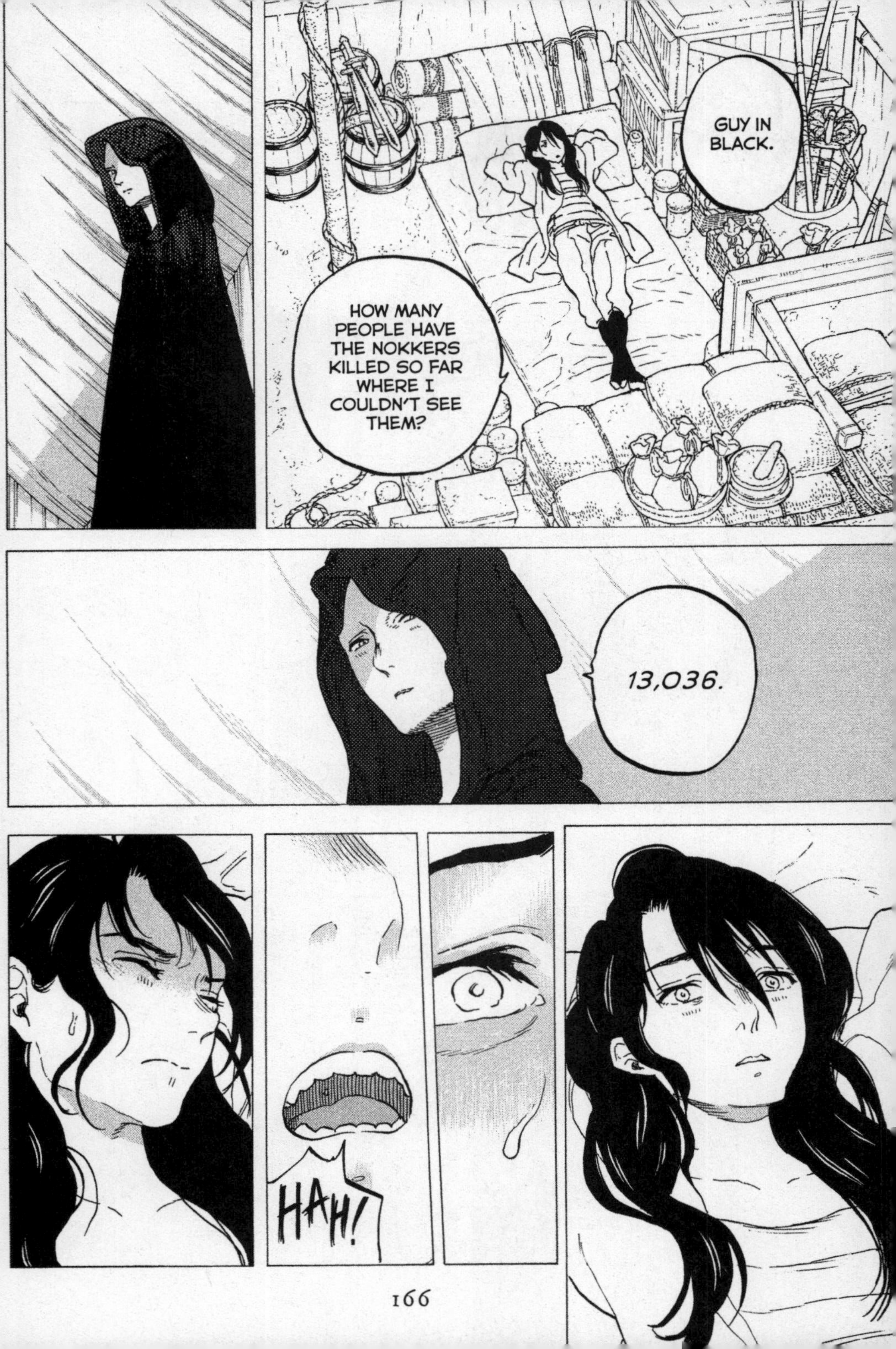
GUY IN BLACK.
HOW MANY PEOPLE HAVE THE NOKKERS KILLED SO FAR WHERE I COULDN'T SEE THEM?
13,036.
HAH!

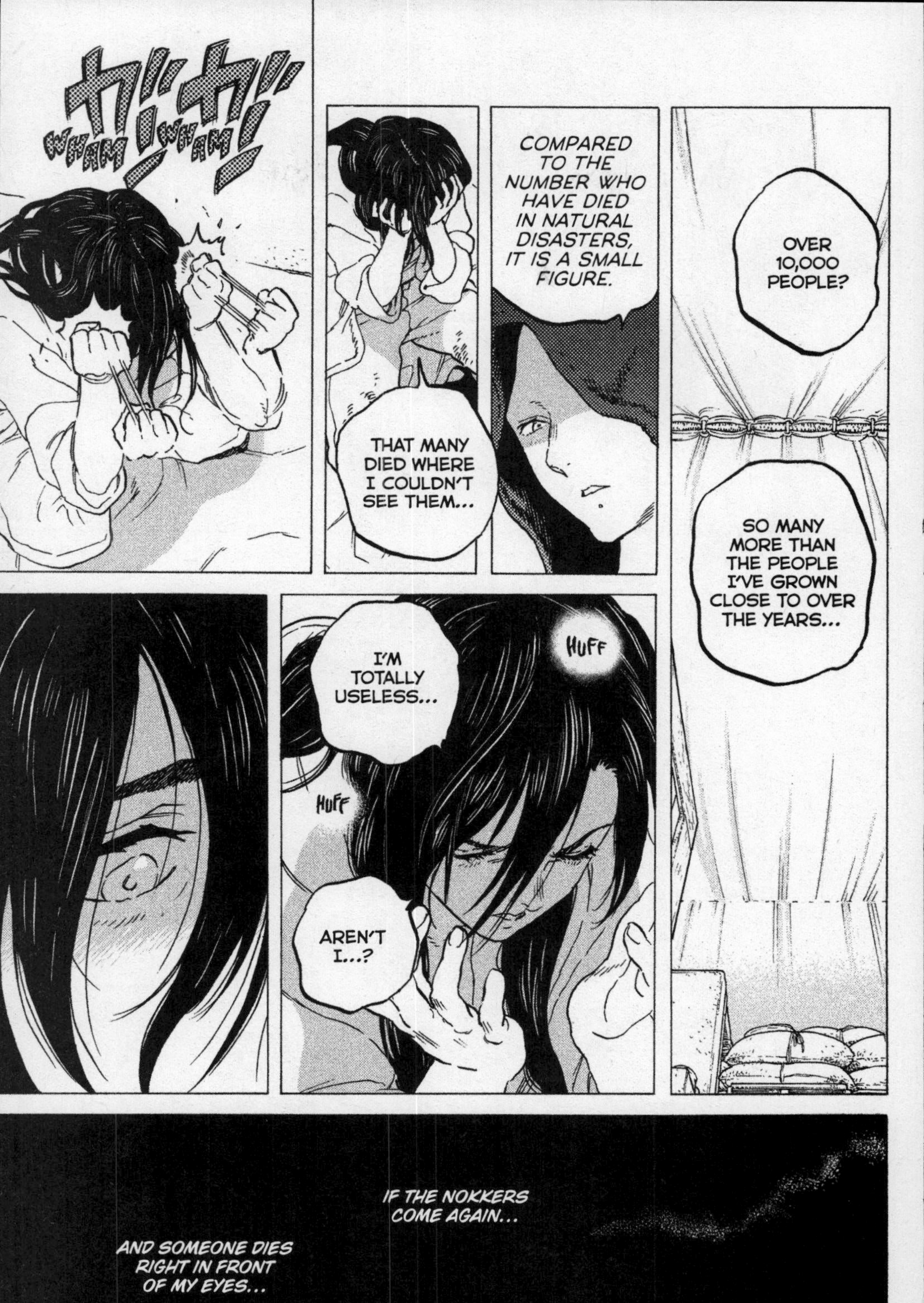
OVER 10,000 PEOPLE?
SO MANY MORE THAN THE PEOPLE I'VE GROWN CLOSE TO OVER THE YEARS...
COMPARED TO THE NUMBER WHO HAVE DIED IN NATURAL DISASTERS, IT IS A SMALL FIGURE.
THAT MANY DIED WHERE I COULDN'T SEE THEM...
WHAM WHAM
I'M TOTALLY USELESS...
HUFF
HUFF
AREN'T I...?
IF THE NOKKERS COME AGAIN...
AND SOMEONE DIES RIGHT IN FRONT OF MY EYES...

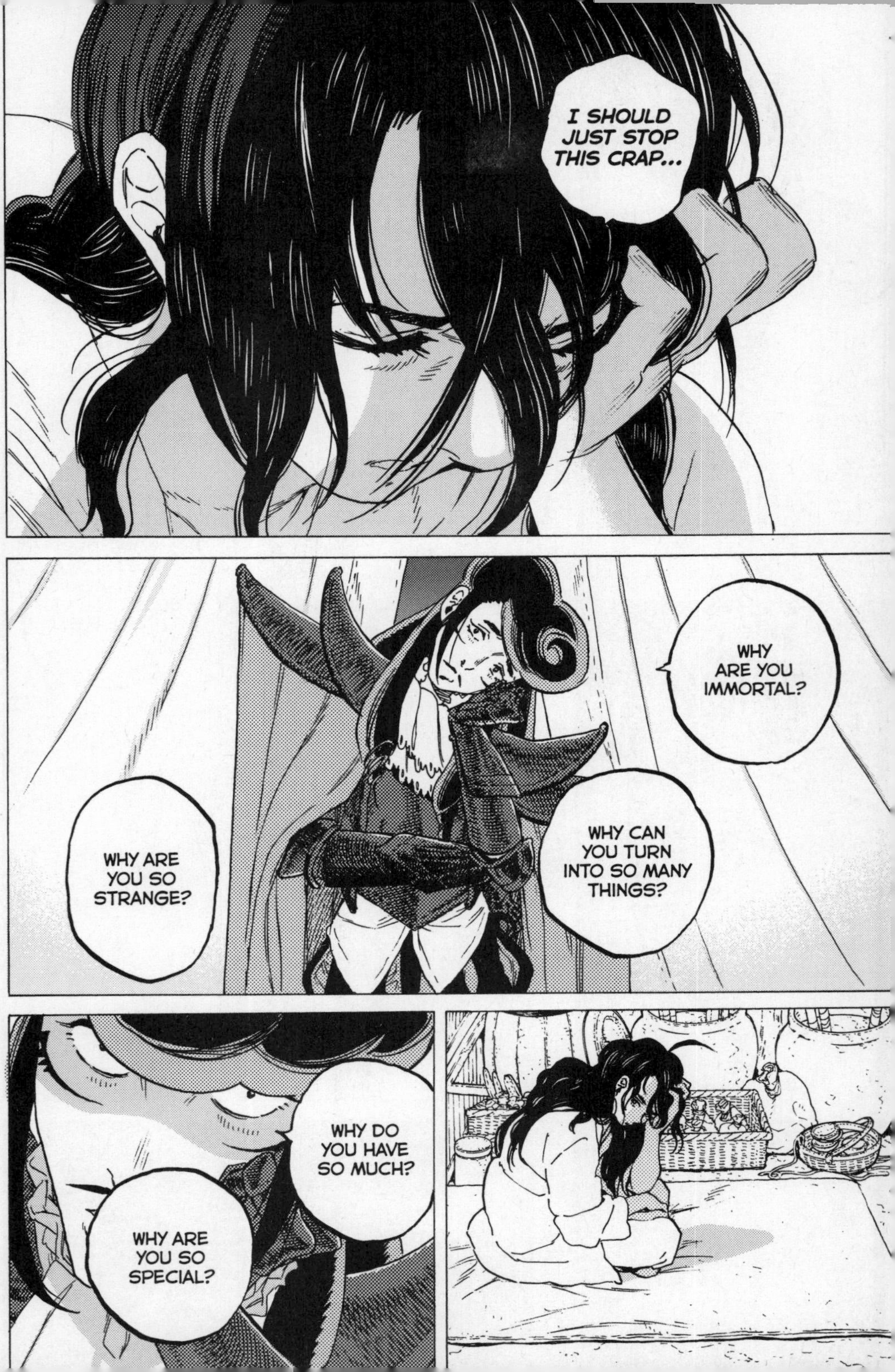
I SHOULD JUST STOP THIS CRAP...
WHY ARE YOU IMMORTAL?
WHY CAN YOU TURN INTO SO MANY THINGS?
WHY ARE YOU SO STRANGE?
WHY DO YOU HAVE SO MUCH?
WHY ARE YOU SO SPECIAL?

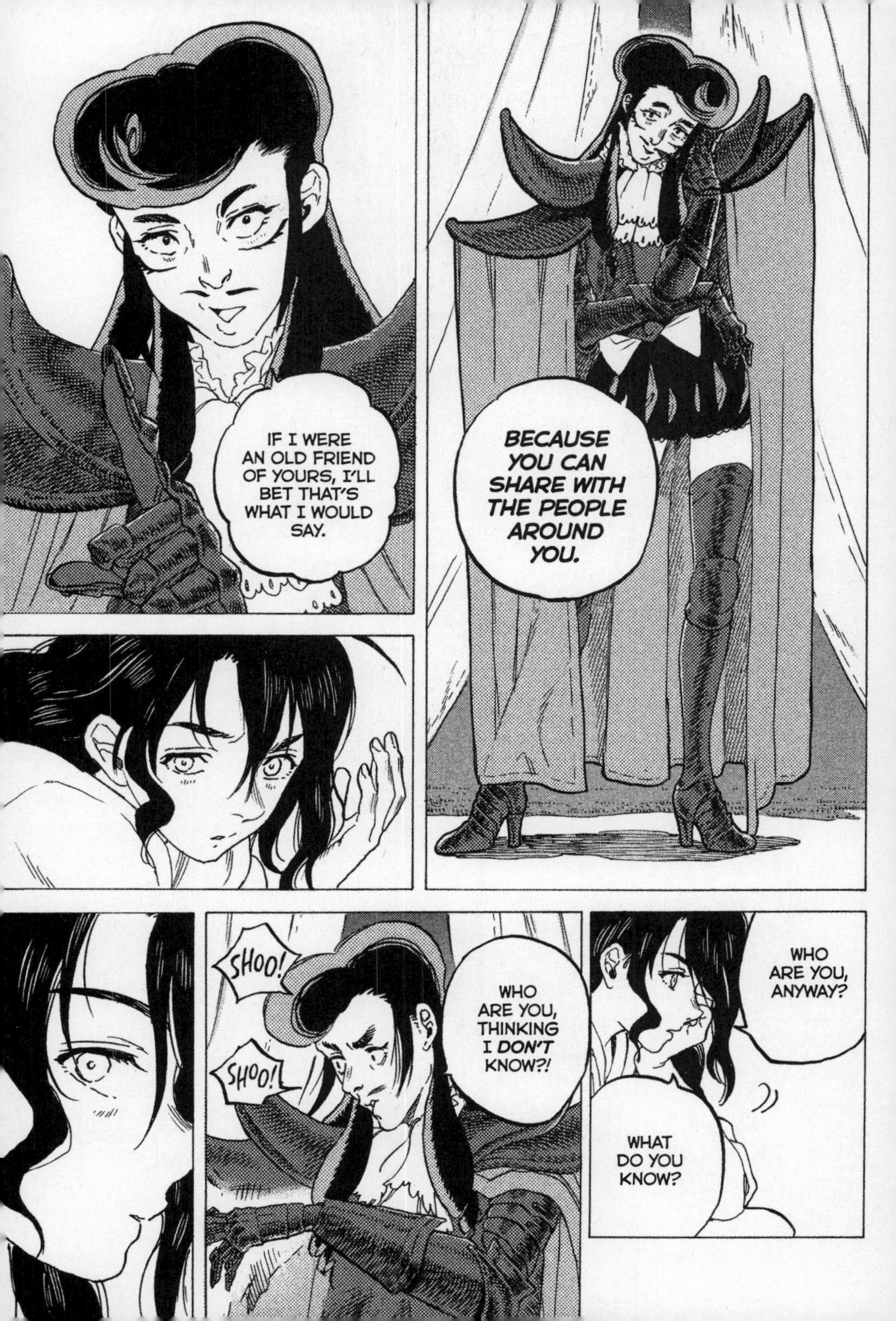
BECAUSE YOU CAN SHARE WITH THE PEOPLE AROUND YOU.
IF I WERE AN OLD FRIEND OF YOURS, I'LL BET THAT'S WHAT I WOULD SAY.
WHO ARE YOU, ANYWAY?
WHAT DO YOU KNOW?
WHO ARE YOU, THINKING I DON'T KNOW?!
SHOO!
SHOO!

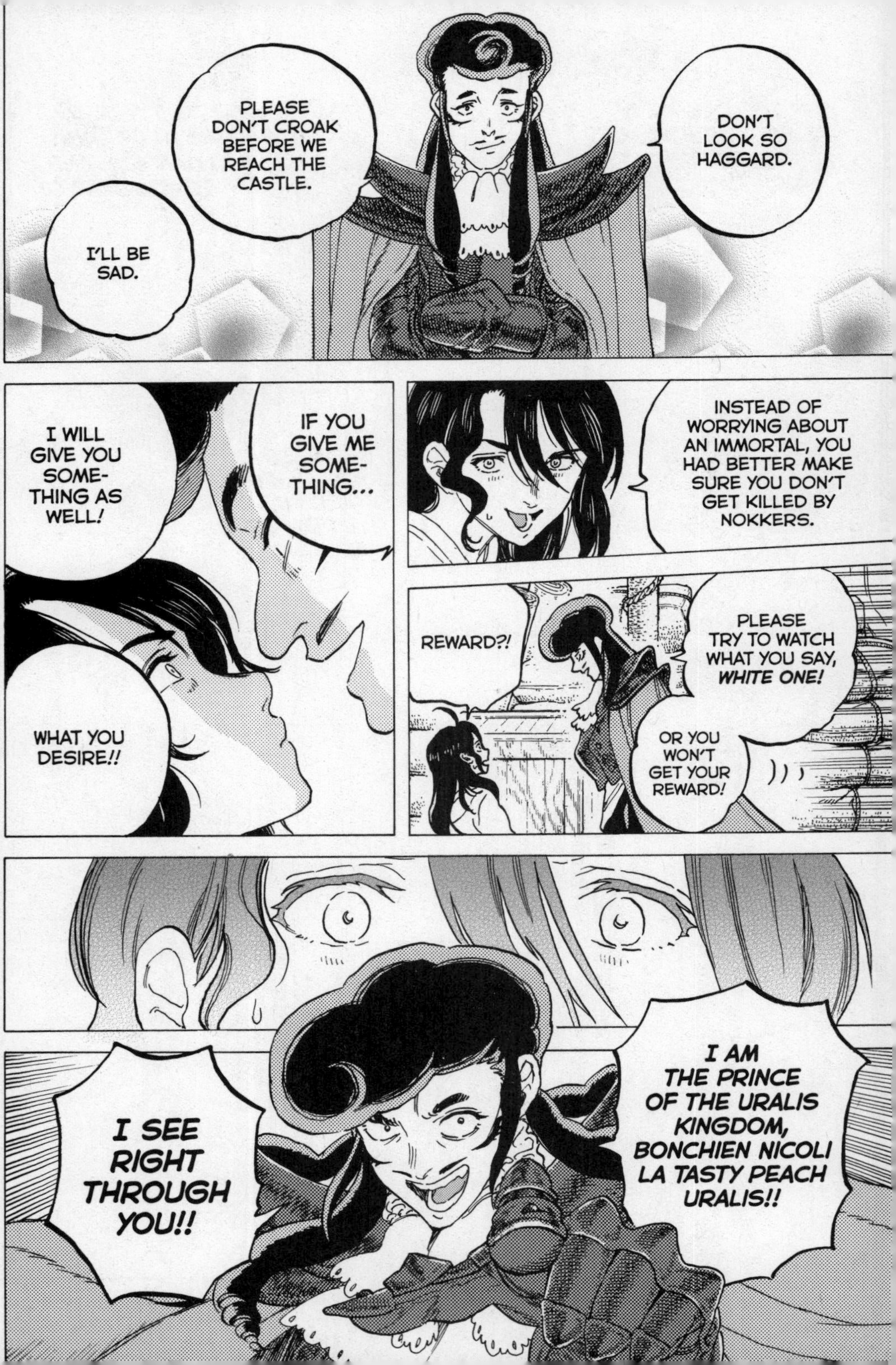
DON'T LOOK SO HAGGARD.
PLEASE DON'T CROAK BEFORE WE REACH THE CASTLE.
I'LL BE SAD.
INSTEAD OF WORRYING ABOUT AN IMMORTAL, YOU HAD BETTER MAKE SURE YOU DON'T GET KILLED BY NOKKERS.
PLEASE TRY TO WATCH WHAT YOU SAY, *WHITE ONE!*
OR YOU WON'T GET YOUR REWARD!
REWARD?!
IF YOU GIVE ME SOME-THING...
I WILL GIVE YOU SOME-THING AS WELL!
WHAT YOU DESIRE!!
I AM THE PRINCE OF THE URALIS KINGDOM, BONCHIEN NICOLI LA TASTY PEACH URALIS!!
I SEE RIGHT THROUGH YOU!!

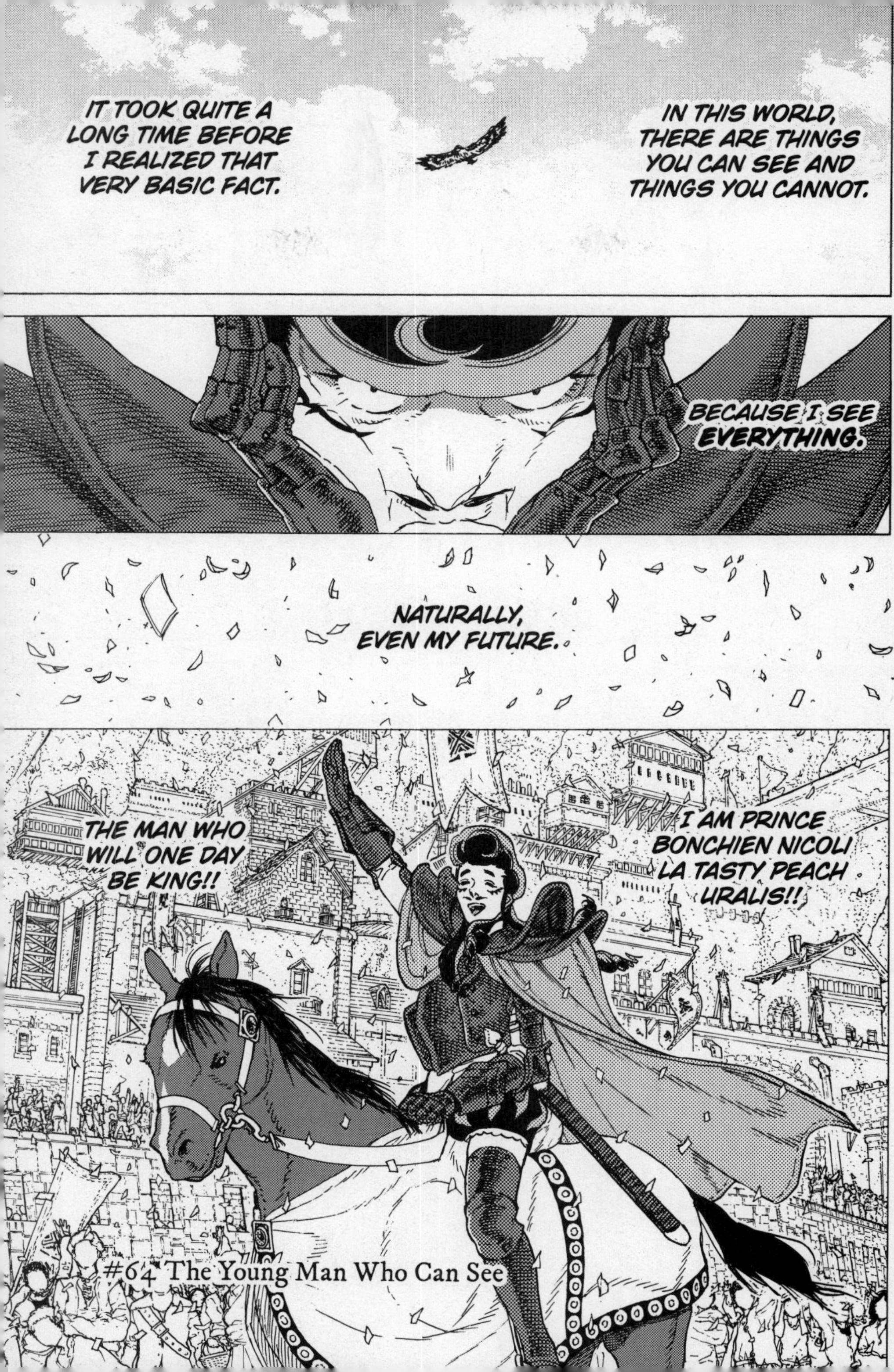
IN THIS WORLD, THERE ARE THINGS YOU CAN SEE AND THINGS YOU CANNOT.
IT TOOK QUITE A LONG TIME BEFORE I REALIZED THAT VERY BASIC FACT.
BECAUSE I SEE EVERYTHING.
NATURALLY, EVEN MY FUTURE.
I AM PRINCE BONCHIEN NICOLI LA TASTY PEACH URALIS!!
THE MAN WHO WILL ONE DAY BE KING!!
#64 The Young Man Who Can See

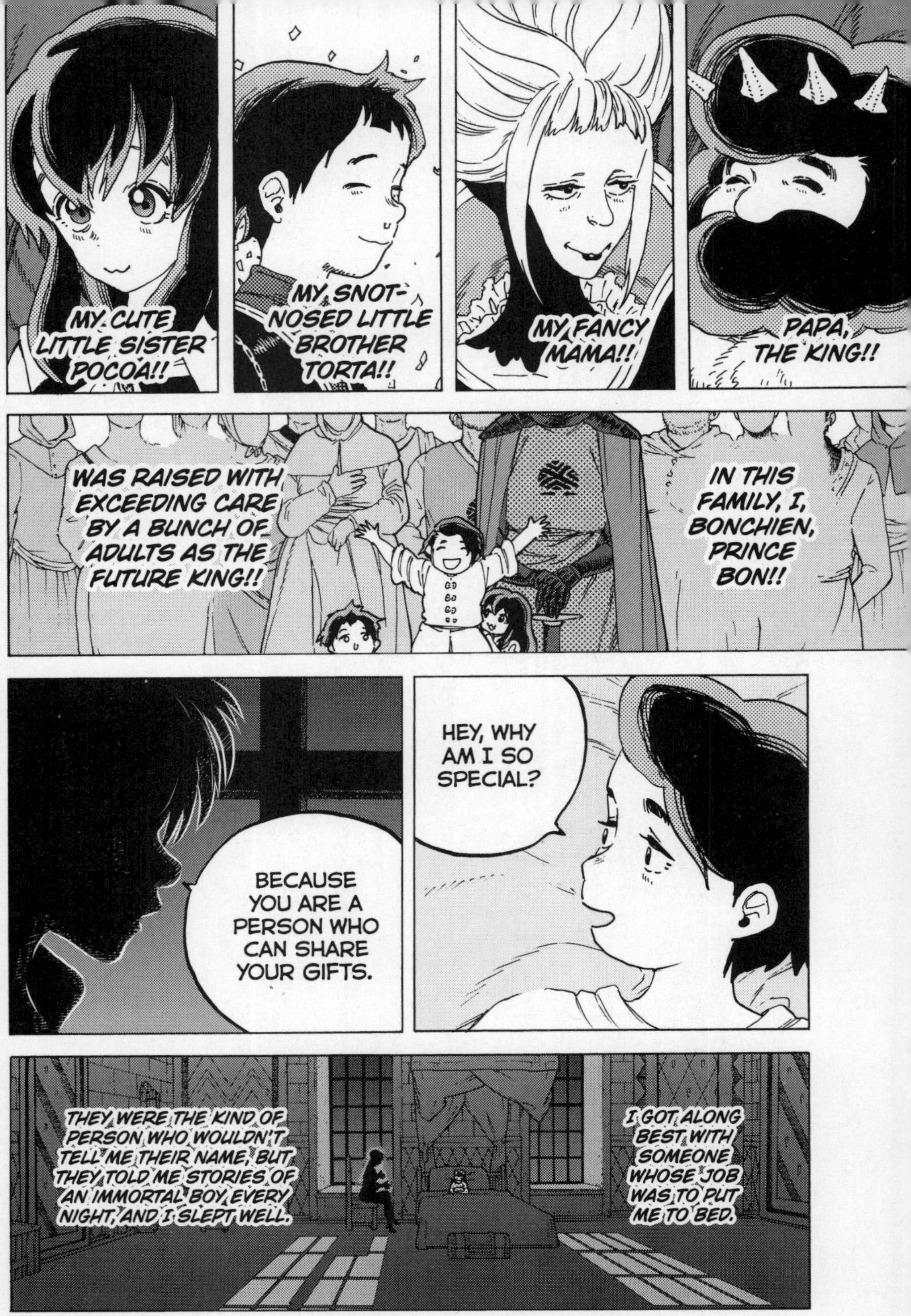
PAPA, THE KING!!
MY FANCY MAMA!!
MY SNOT-NOSED LITTLE BROTHER TORTA!!
MY CUTE LITTLE SISTER POCOA!!
IN THIS FAMILY, I, BONCHIEN, PRINCE BON!!
WAS RAISED WITH EXCEEDING CARE BY A BUNCH OF ADULTS AS THE FUTURE KING!!
HEY, WHY AM I SO SPECIAL?
BECAUSE YOU ARE A PERSON WHO CAN SHARE YOUR GIFTS.
I GOT ALONG BEST WITH SOMEONE WHOSE JOB WAS TO PUT ME TO BED.
THEY WERE THE KIND OF PERSON WHO WOULDN'T TELL ME THEIR NAME, BUT THEY TOLD ME STORIES OF AN IMMORTAL BOY EVERY NIGHT, AND I SLEPT WELL.

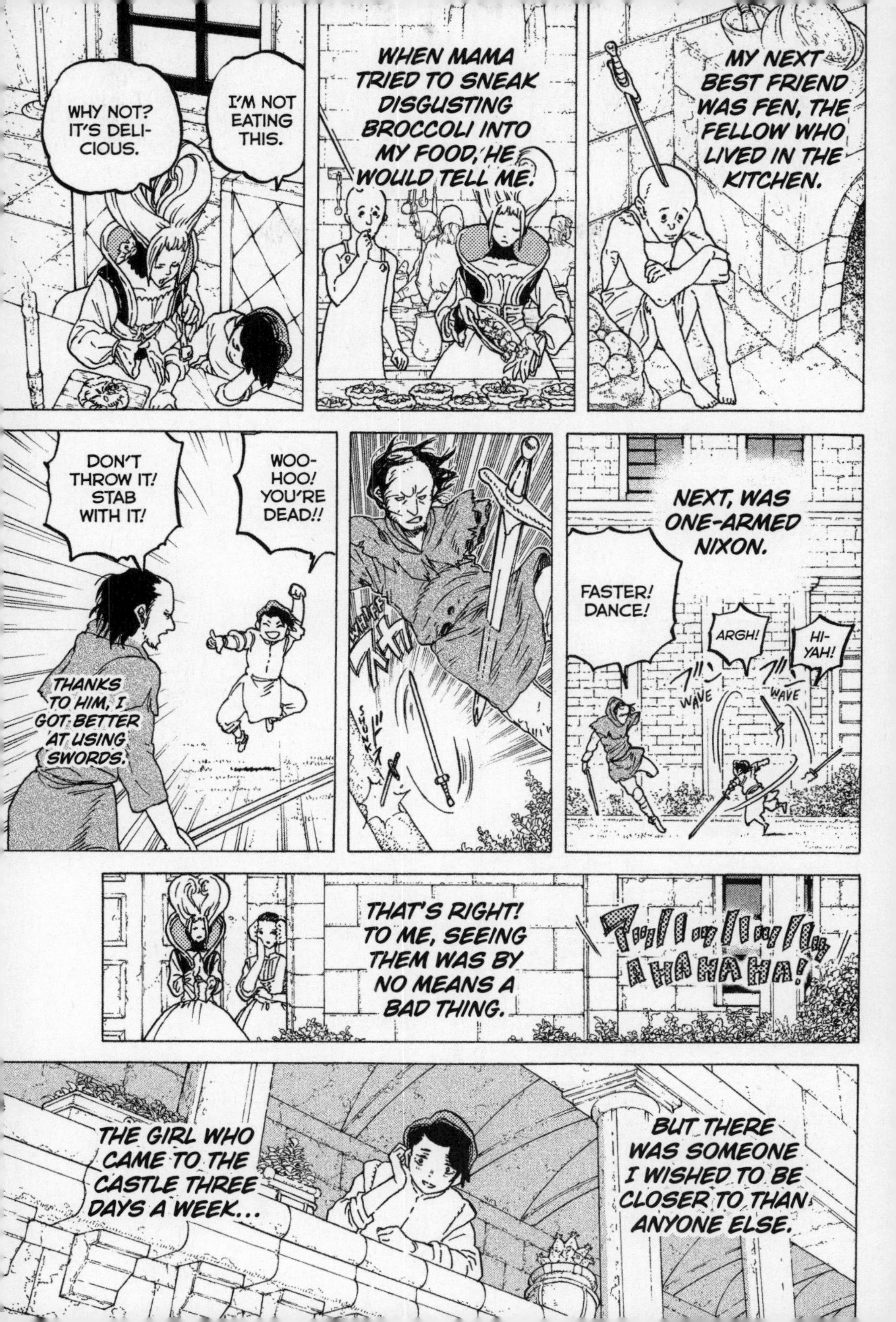
MY NEXT BEST FRIEND WAS FEN, THE FELLOW WHO LIVED IN THE KITCHEN.
WHEN MAMA TRIED TO SNEAK DISGUSTING BROCCOLI INTO MY FOOD, HE WOULD TELL ME.
I'M NOT EATING THIS.
WHY NOT? IT'S DELICIOUS.
NEXT, WAS ONE-ARMED NIXON.
HI-YAH!
ARGH!
FASTER! DANCE!
WAVE
WAVE
WHIFF
SHUNK
WOO-HOO! YOU'RE DEAD!!
DON'T THROW IT! STAB WITH IT!
THANKS TO HIM, I GOT BETTER AT USING SWORDS.
AHAHAHA!
THAT'S RIGHT! TO ME, SEEING THEM WAS BY NO MEANS A BAD THING.
BUT THERE WAS SOMEONE I WISHED TO BE CLOSER TO THAN ANYONE ELSE.
THE GIRL WHO CAME TO THE CASTLE THREE DAYS A WEEK...

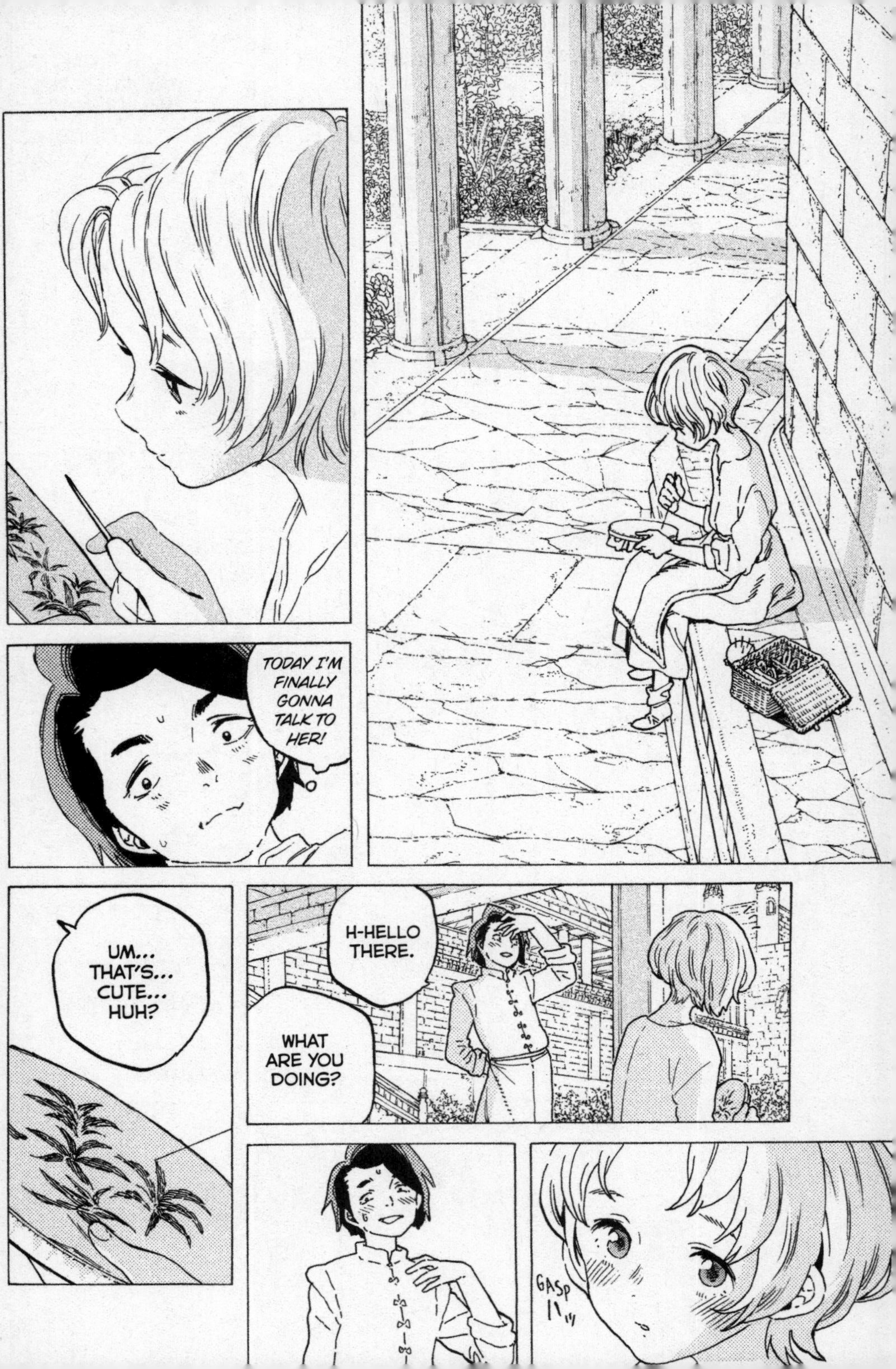
TODAY I'M FINALLY GONNA TALK TO HER!
H-HELLO THERE.
WHAT ARE YOU DOING?
GASP
UM... THAT'S... CUTE... HUH?

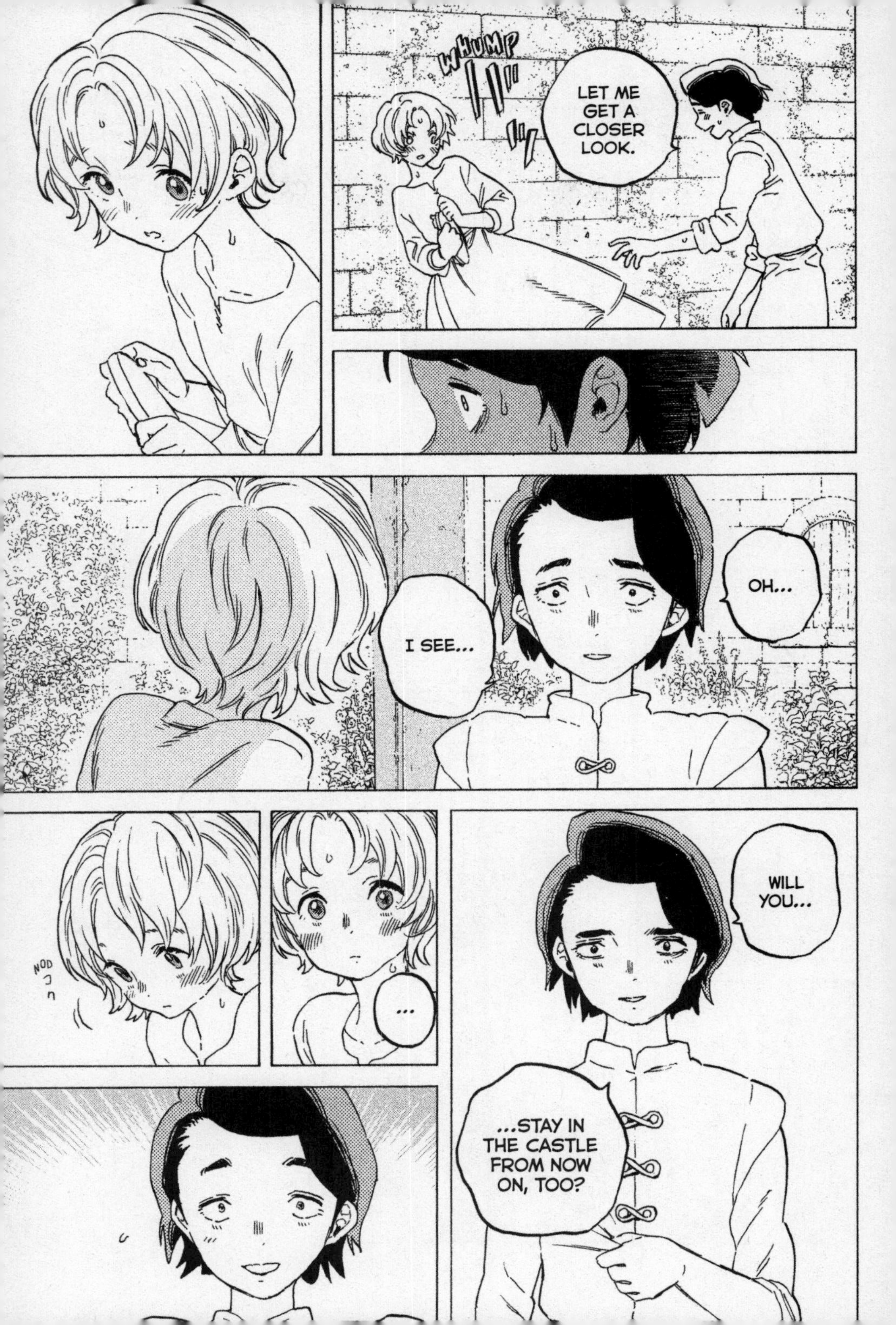
WHUMP
LET ME GET A CLOSER LOOK.
OH...
I SEE...
WILL YOU...
...STAY IN THE CASTLE FROM NOW ON, TOO?
...
NOD

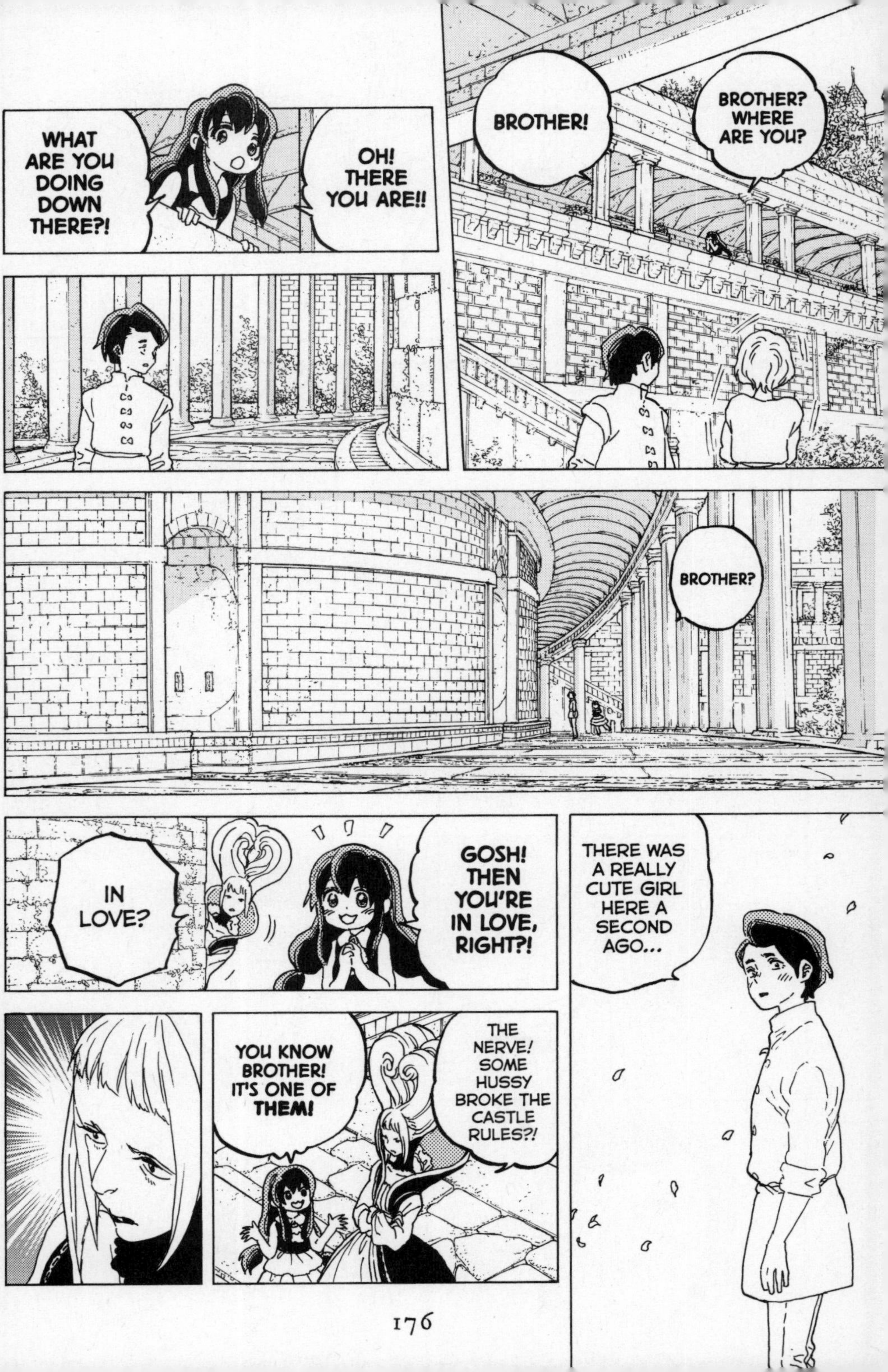
BROTHER? WHERE ARE YOU?
BROTHER!
OH! THERE YOU ARE!!
WHAT ARE YOU DOING DOWN THERE?!
BROTHER?
THERE WAS A REALLY CUTE GIRL HERE A SECOND AGO...
GOSH! THEN YOU'RE IN LOVE, RIGHT?!
IN LOVE?
THE NERVE! SOME HUSSY BROKE THE CASTLE RULES?!
YOU KNOW BROTHER! IT'S ONE OF **THEM!**

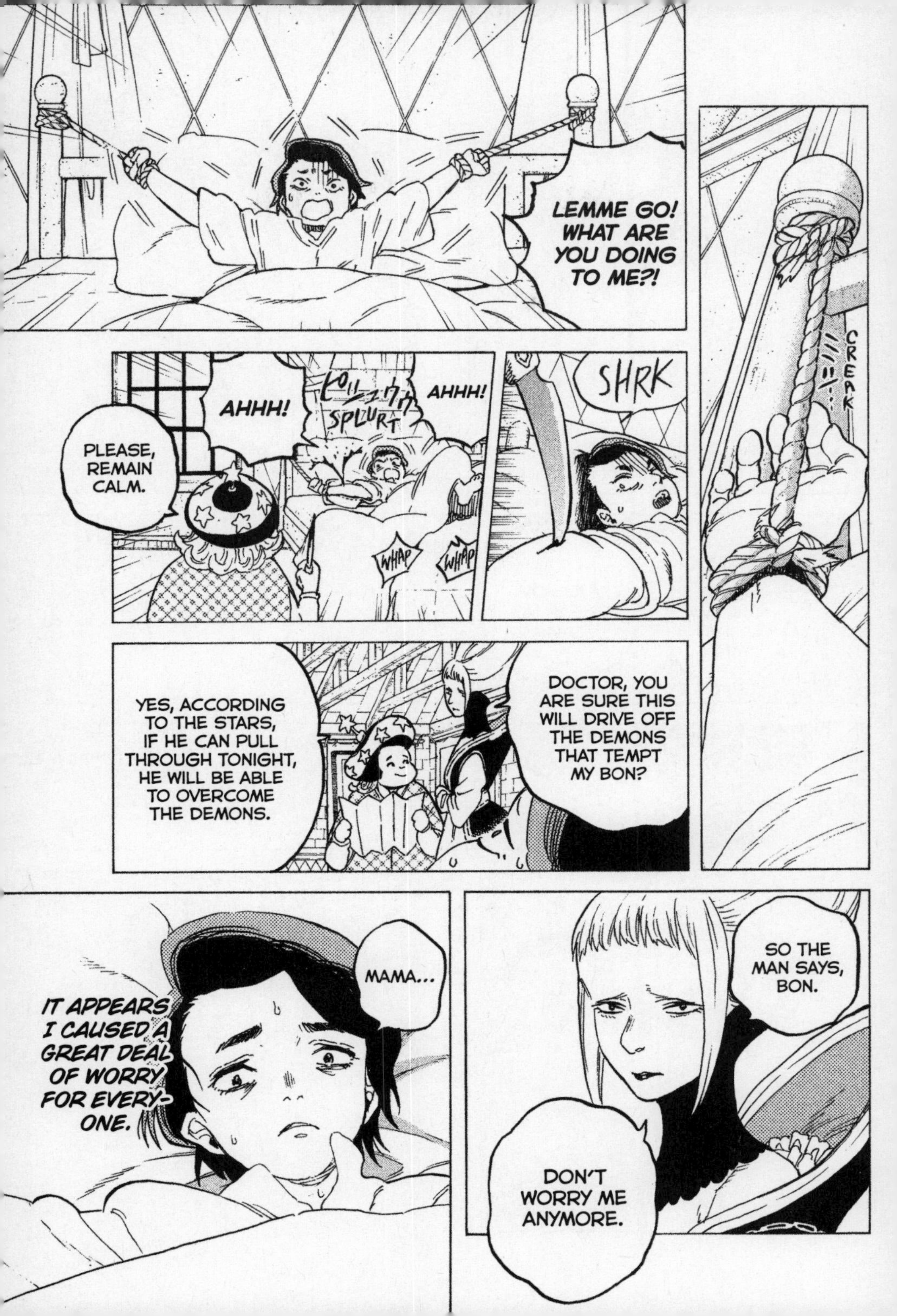
LEMME GO! WHAT ARE YOU DOING TO ME?!
CREAK
SHRK
AHHH!
SPLURT
AHHH!
PLEASE, REMAIN CALM.
WHAP
WHAP
DOCTOR, YOU ARE SURE THIS WILL DRIVE OFF THE DEMONS THAT TEMPT MY BON?
YES, ACCORDING TO THE STARS, IF HE CAN PULL THROUGH TONIGHT, HE WILL BE ABLE TO OVERCOME THE DEMONS.
SO THE MAN SAYS, BON.
DON'T WORRY ME ANYMORE.
MAMA...
IT APPEARS I CAUSED A GREAT DEAL OF WORRY FOR EVERY-ONE.

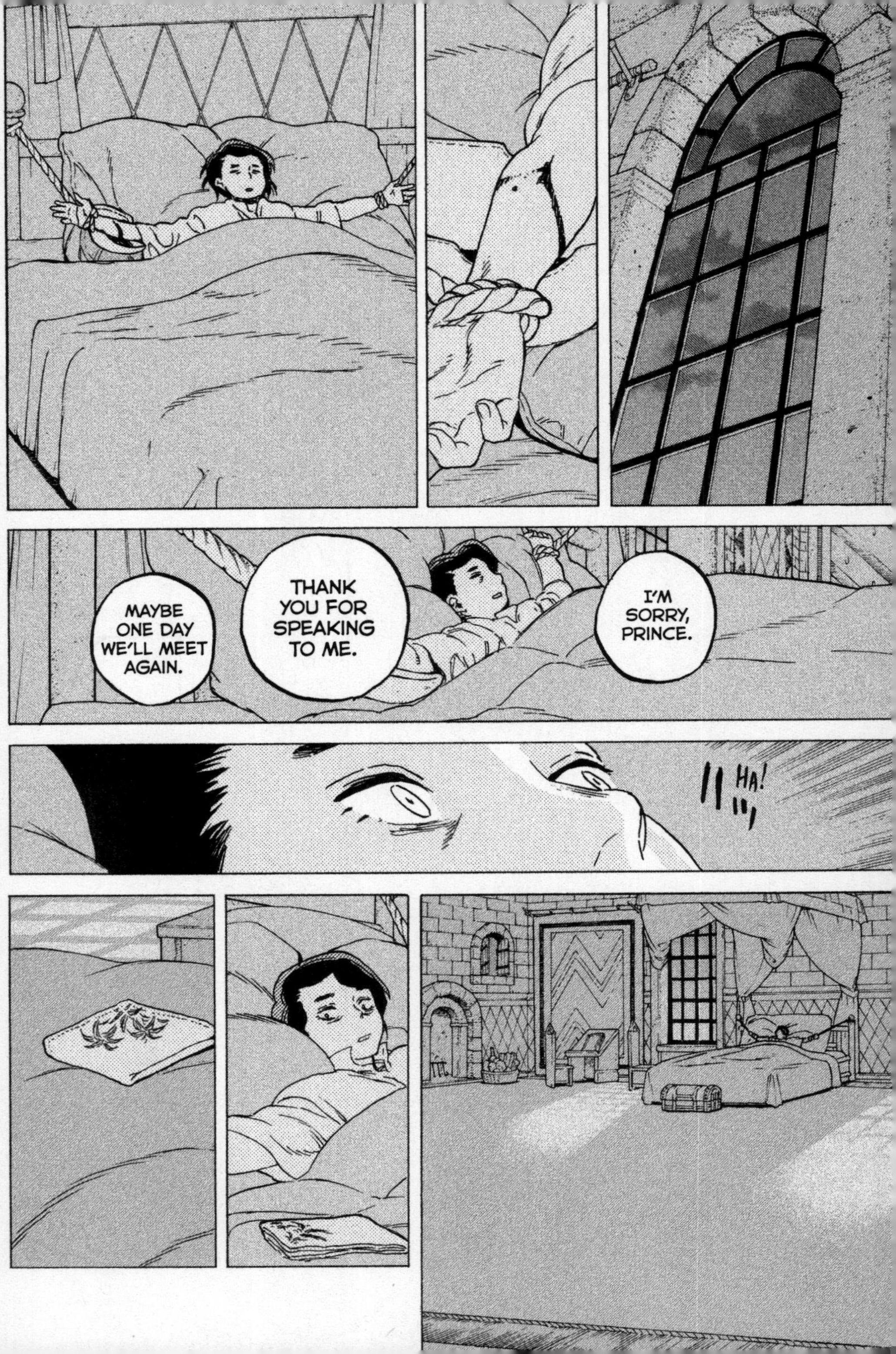
I'M SORRY, PRINCE.
THANK YOU FOR SPEAKING TO ME.
MAYBE ONE DAY WE'LL MEET AGAIN.
HA!

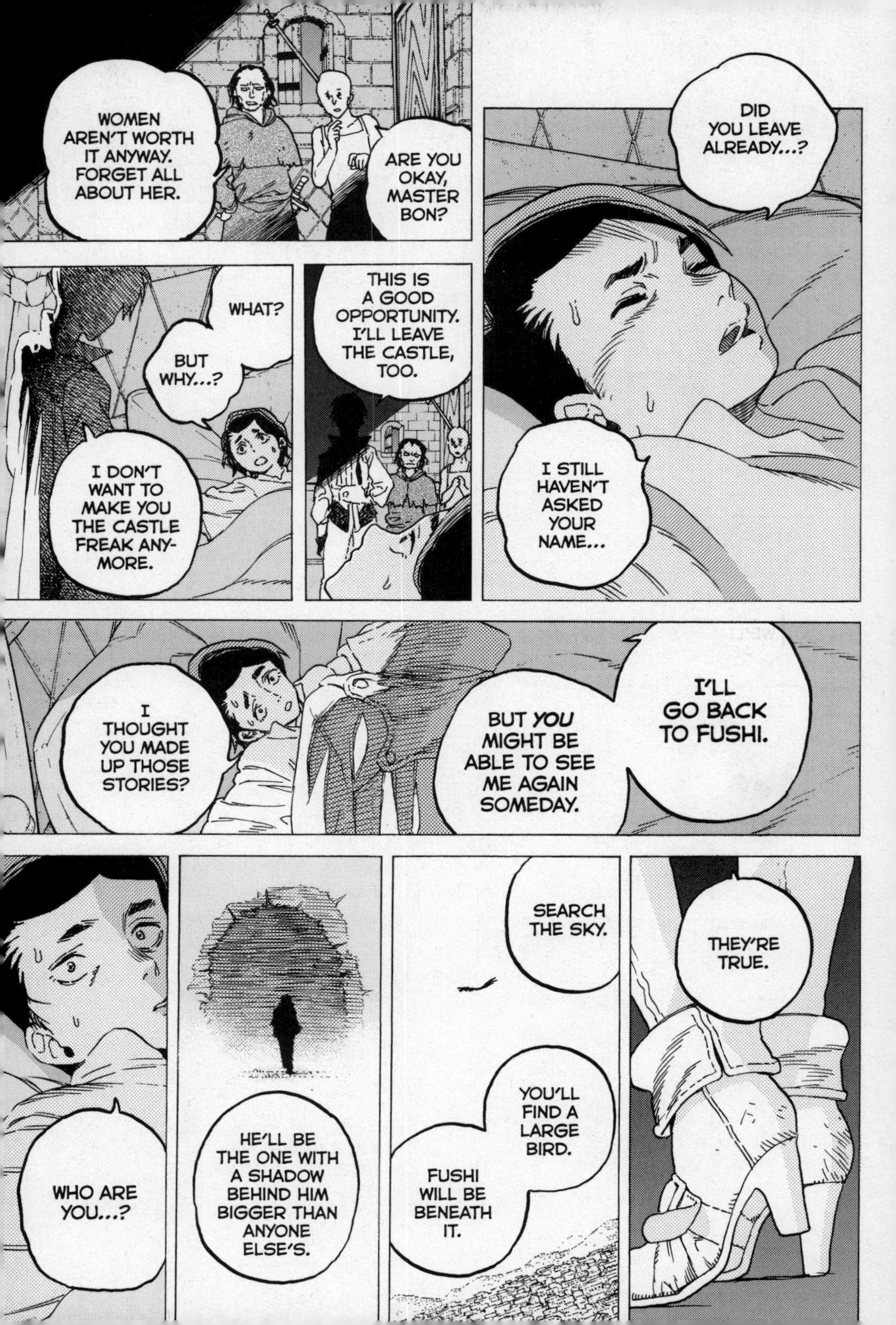
DID YOU LEAVE ALREADY...?
I STILL HAVEN'T ASKED YOUR NAME...
ARE YOU OKAY, MASTER BON?
WOMEN AREN'T WORTH IT ANYWAY. FORGET ALL ABOUT HER.
THIS IS A GOOD OPPORTUNITY. I'LL LEAVE THE CASTLE, TOO.
WHAT?
BUT WHY...?
I DON'T WANT TO MAKE YOU THE CASTLE FREAK ANY-MORE.
I'LL GO BACK TO FUSHI.
BUT *YOU* MIGHT BE ABLE TO SEE ME AGAIN SOMEDAY.
I THOUGHT YOU MADE UP THOSE STORIES?
THEY'RE TRUE.
SEARCH THE SKY.
YOU'LL FIND A LARGE BIRD.
FUSHI WILL BE BENEATH IT.
HE'LL BE THE ONE WITH A SHADOW BEHIND HIM BIGGER THAN ANYONE ELSE'S.
WHO ARE YOU...?

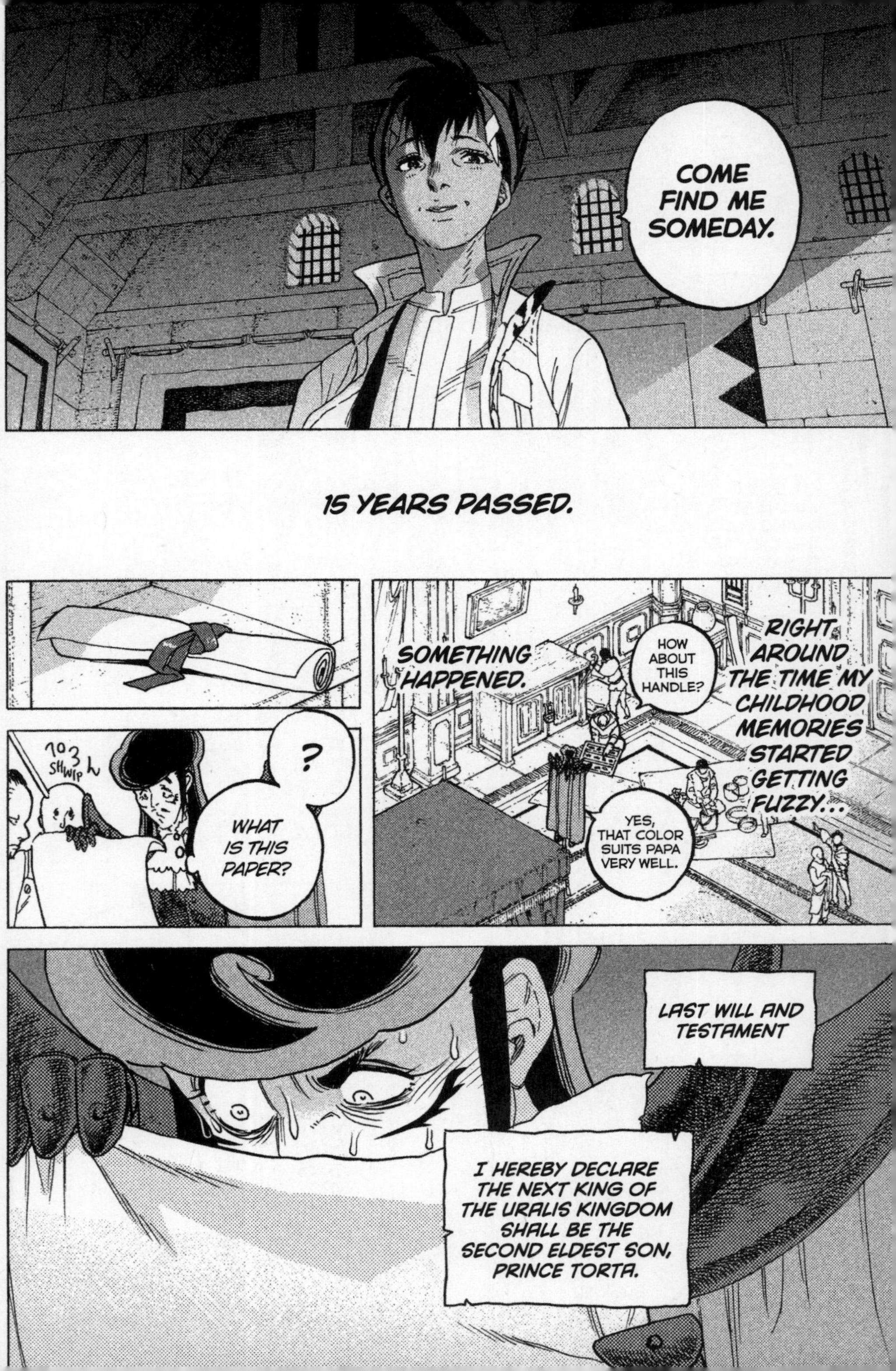
COME FIND ME SOMEDAY.
15 YEARS PASSED.
RIGHT AROUND THE TIME MY CHILDHOOD MEMORIES STARTED GETTING FUZZY...
HOW ABOUT THIS HANDLE?
SOMETHING HAPPENED.
YES, THAT COLOR SUITS PAPA VERY WELL.
?
WHAT IS THIS PAPER?
SHWIP
LAST WILL AND TESTAMENT
I HEREBY DECLARE THE NEXT KING OF THE URALIS KINGDOM SHALL BE THE SECOND ELDEST SON, PRINCE TORTA.

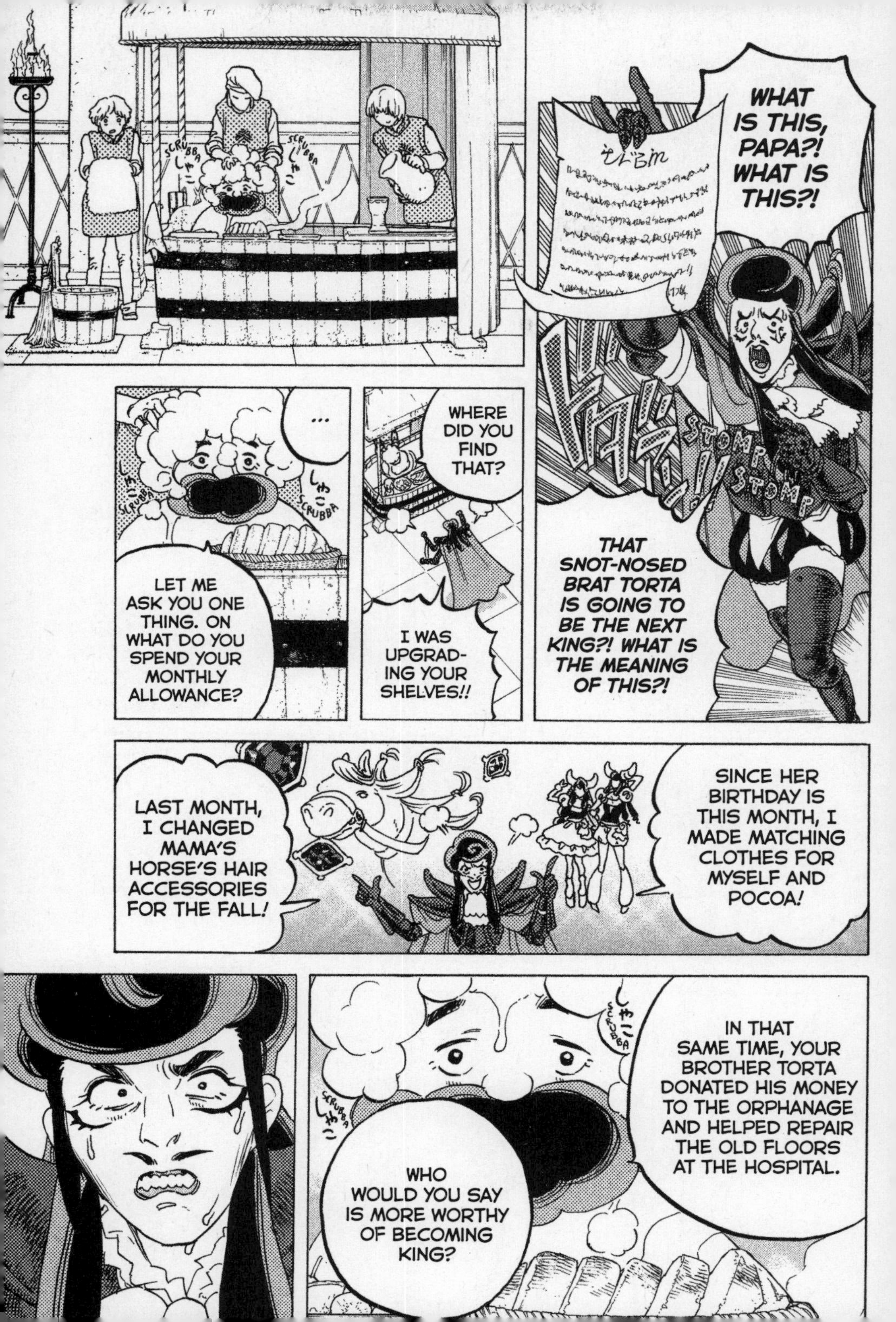
WHAT IS THIS, PAPA?! WHAT IS THIS?!
STOMP STOMP
THAT SNOT-NOSED BRAT TORTA IS GOING TO BE THE NEXT KING?! WHAT IS THE MEANING OF THIS?!
SCRUBBA
SCRUBBA
WHERE DID YOU FIND THAT?
I WAS UPGRADING YOUR SHELVES!!
...
SCRUBBA
SCRUBBA
LET ME ASK YOU ONE THING. ON WHAT DO YOU SPEND YOUR MONTHLY ALLOWANCE?
SINCE HER BIRTHDAY IS THIS MONTH, I MADE MATCHING CLOTHES FOR MYSELF AND POCOA!
LAST MONTH, I CHANGED MAMA'S HORSE'S HAIR ACCESSORIES FOR THE FALL!
SCRUBBA
IN THAT SAME TIME, YOUR BROTHER TORTA DONATED HIS MONEY TO THE ORPHANAGE AND HELPED REPAIR THE OLD FLOORS AT THE HOSPITAL.
SCRUBBA
WHO WOULD YOU SAY IS MORE WORTHY OF BECOMING KING?

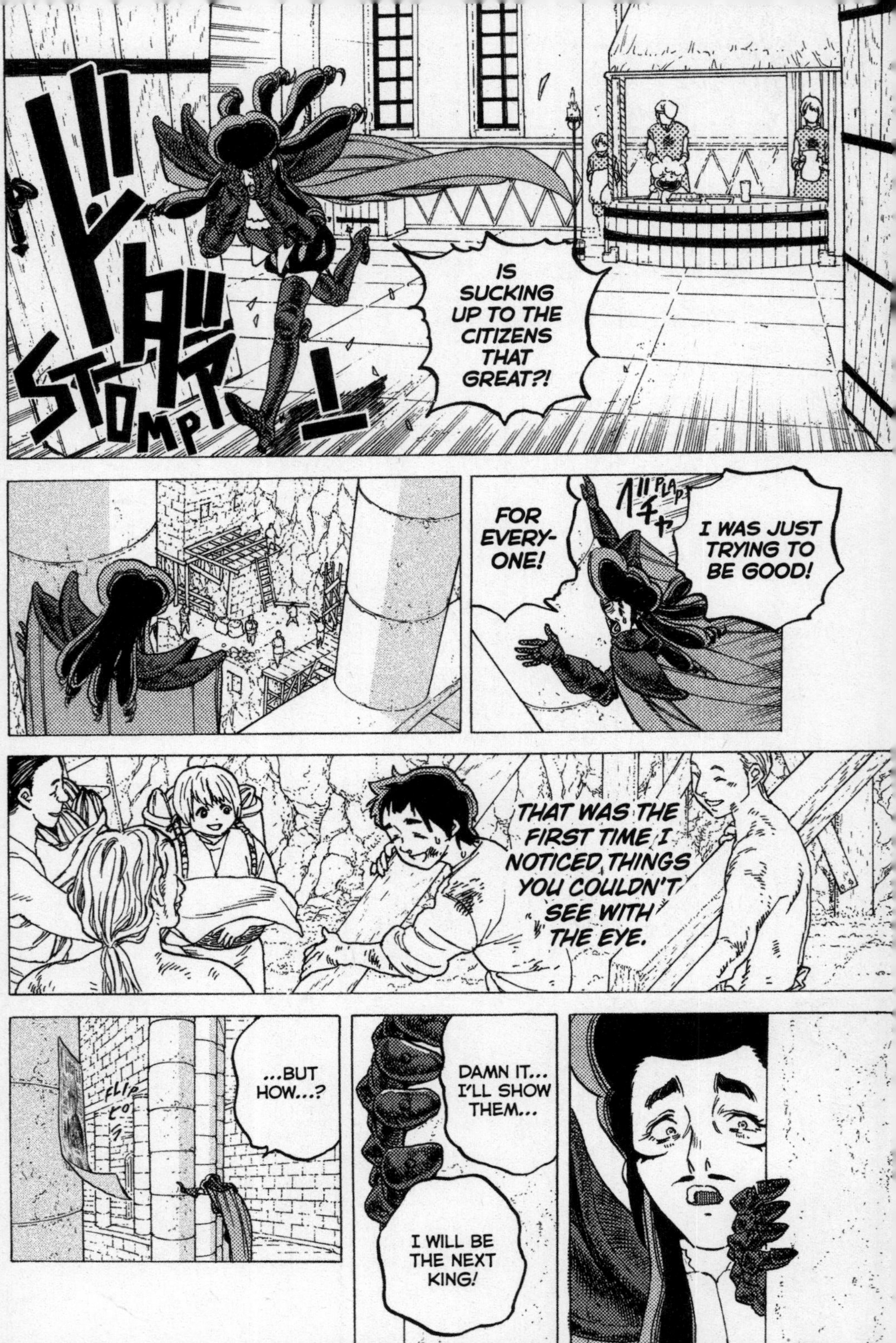
IS SUCKING UP TO THE CITIZENS THAT GREAT?!
STOMP
PLAP
I WAS JUST TRYING TO BE GOOD!
FOR EVERY-ONE!
THAT WAS THE FIRST TIME I NOTICED THINGS YOU COULDN'T SEE WITH THE EYE.
DAMN IT... I'LL SHOW THEM...
I WILL BE THE NEXT KING!
...BUT HOW...?
FLIP

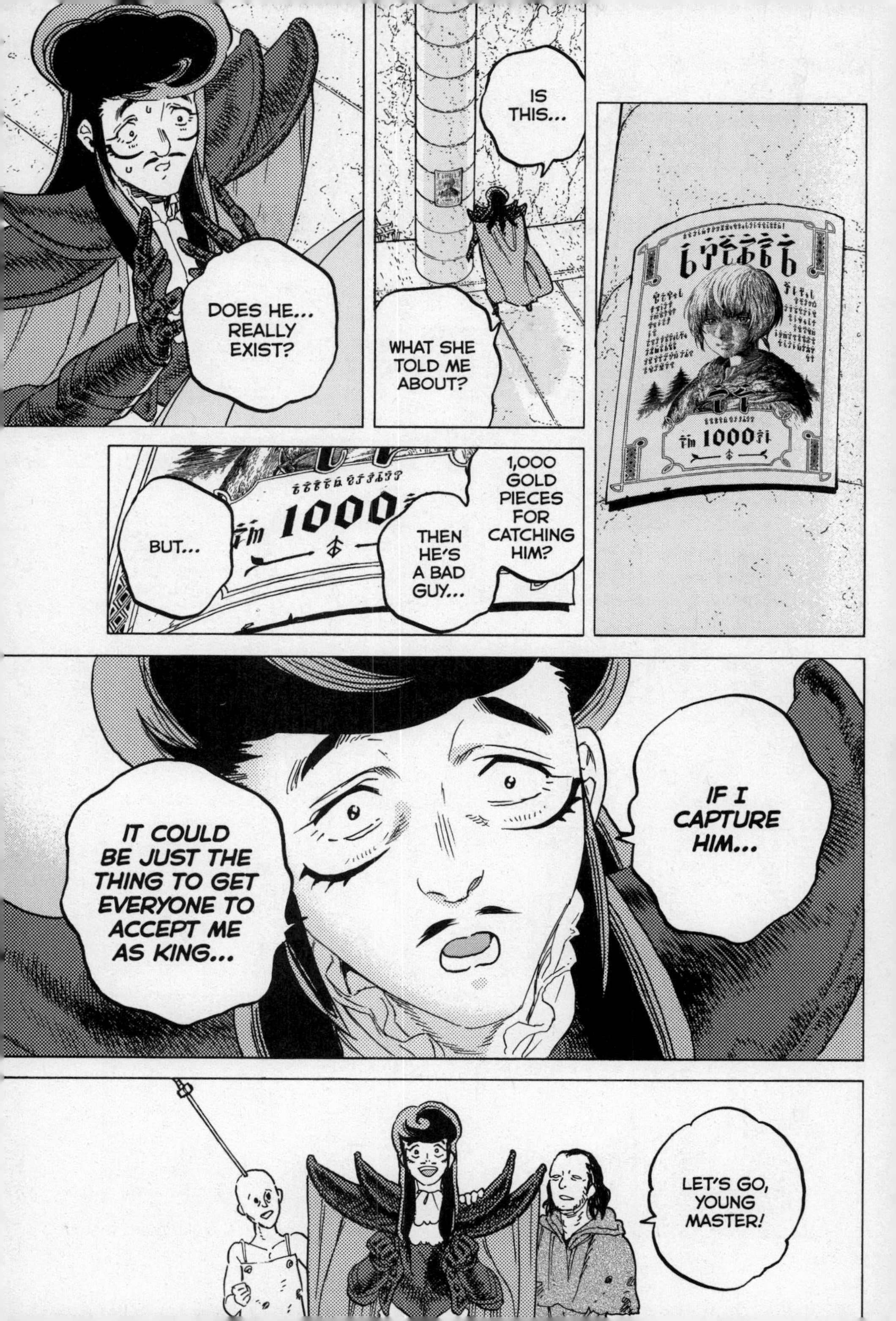
1000
IS THIS...
WHAT SHE TOLD ME ABOUT?
DOES HE... REALLY EXIST?
1,000 GOLD PIECES FOR CATCHING HIM?
THEN HE'S A BAD GUY...
BUT...
1000
IF I CAPTURE HIM...
IT COULD BE JUST THE THING TO GET EVERYONE TO ACCEPT ME AS KING...
LET'S GO, YOUNG MASTER!

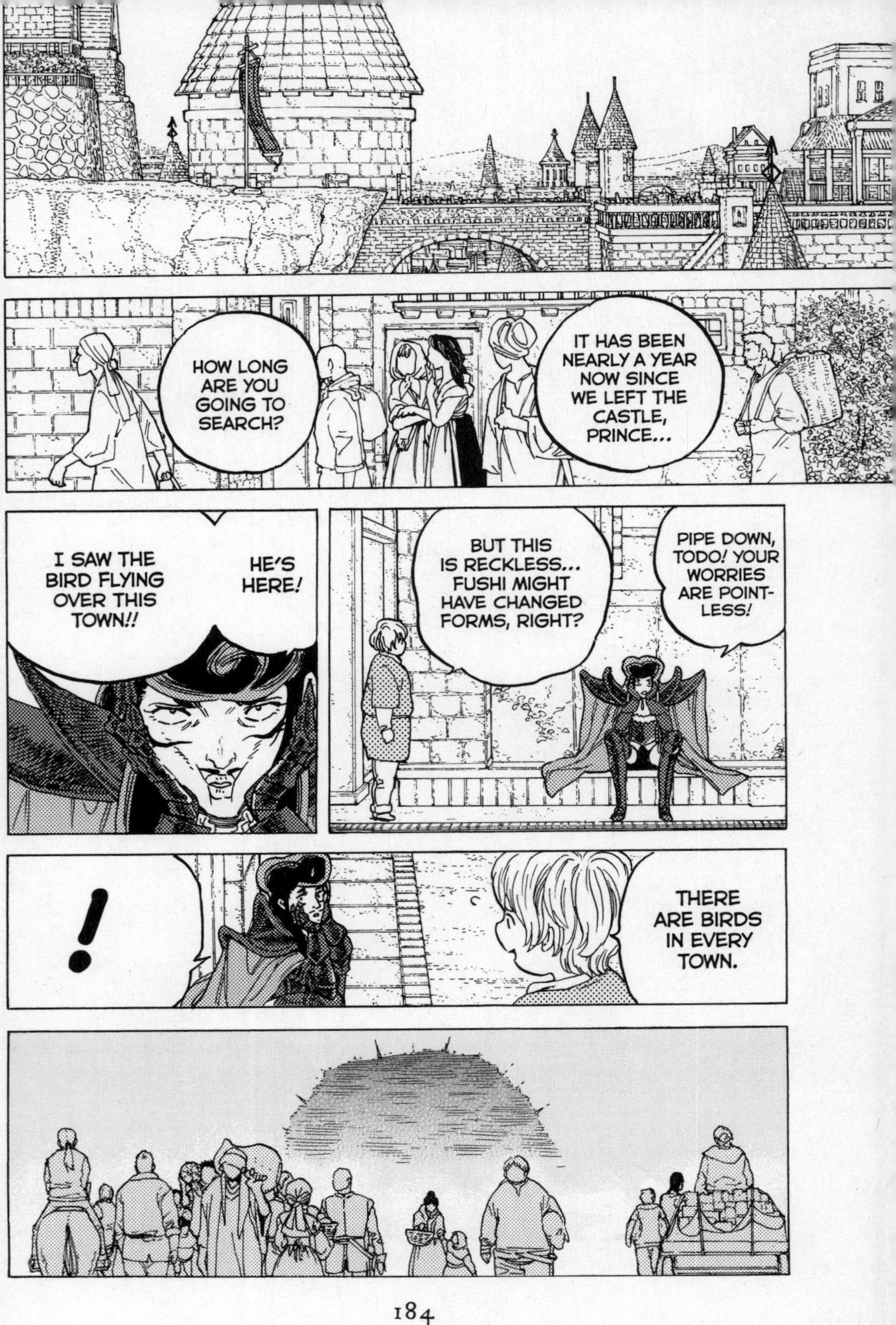

IT HAS BEEN NEARLY A YEAR NOW SINCE WE LEFT THE CASTLE, PRINCE...
HOW LONG ARE YOU GOING TO SEARCH?
BUT THIS IS RECKLESS... FUSHI MIGHT HAVE CHANGED FORMS, RIGHT?
PIPE DOWN, TODO! YOUR WORRIES ARE POINT-LESS!
HE'S HERE!
I SAW THE BIRD FLYING OVER THIS TOWN!!
THERE ARE BIRDS IN EVERY TOWN.
!

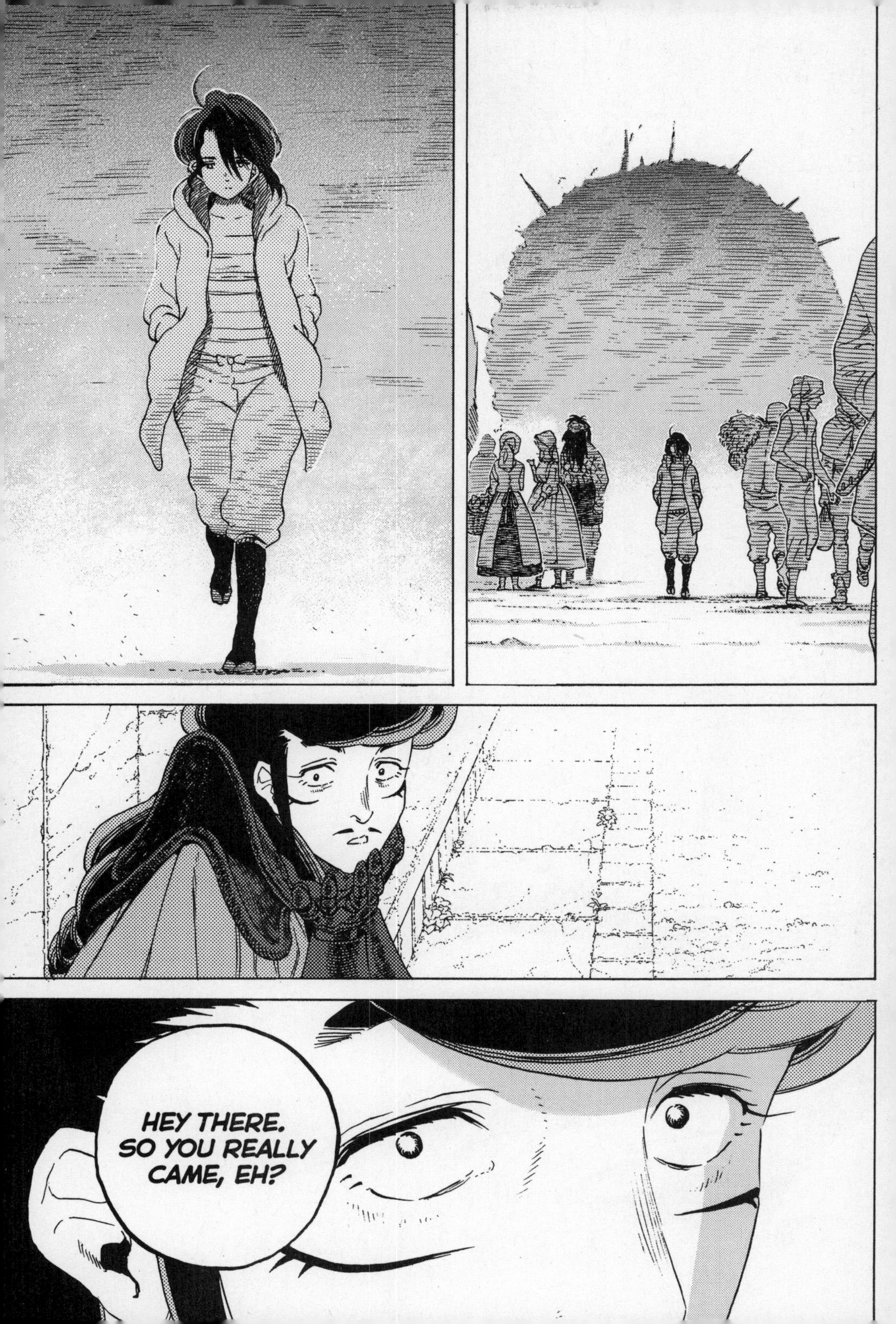
HEY THERE. SO YOU REALLY CAME, EH?

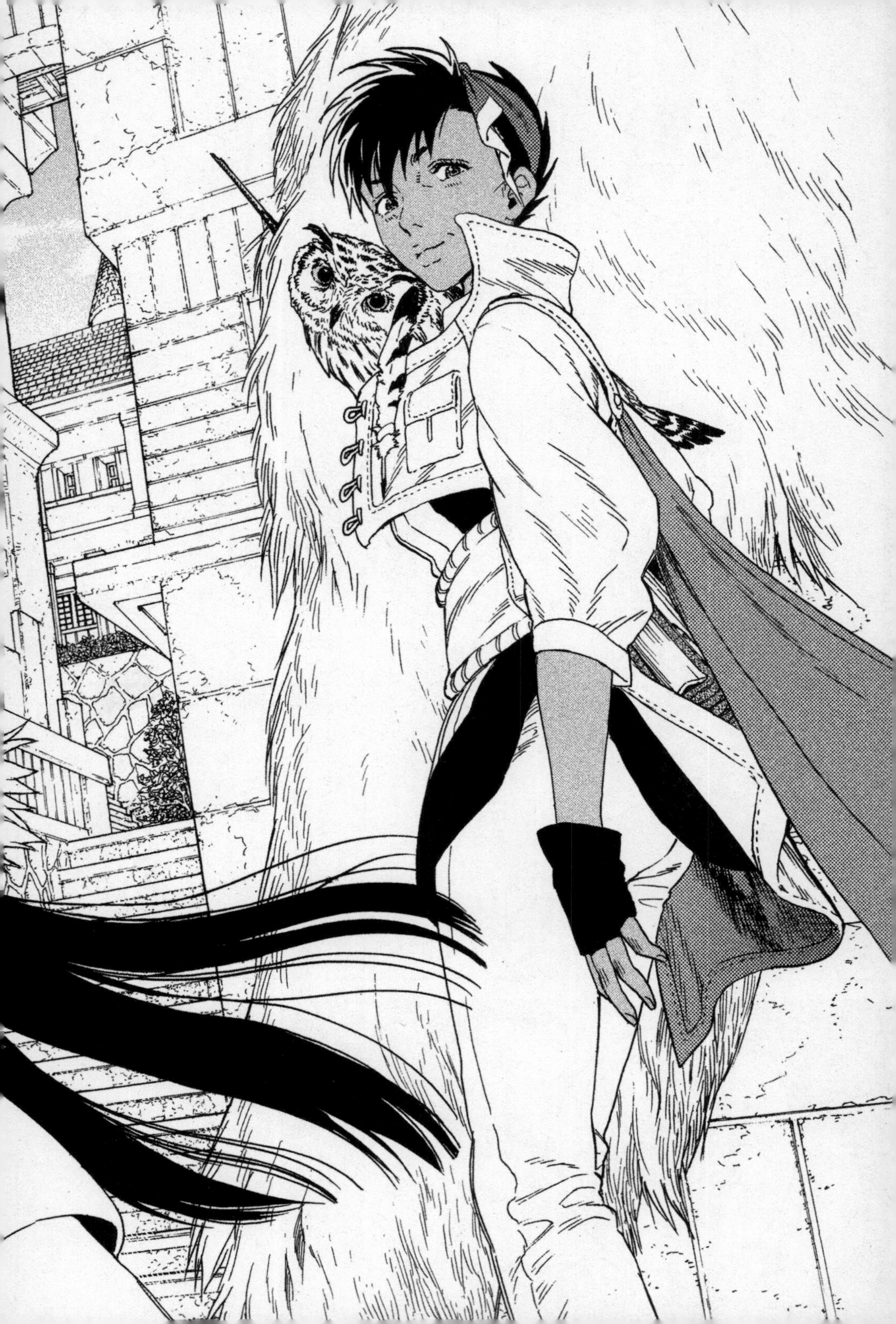

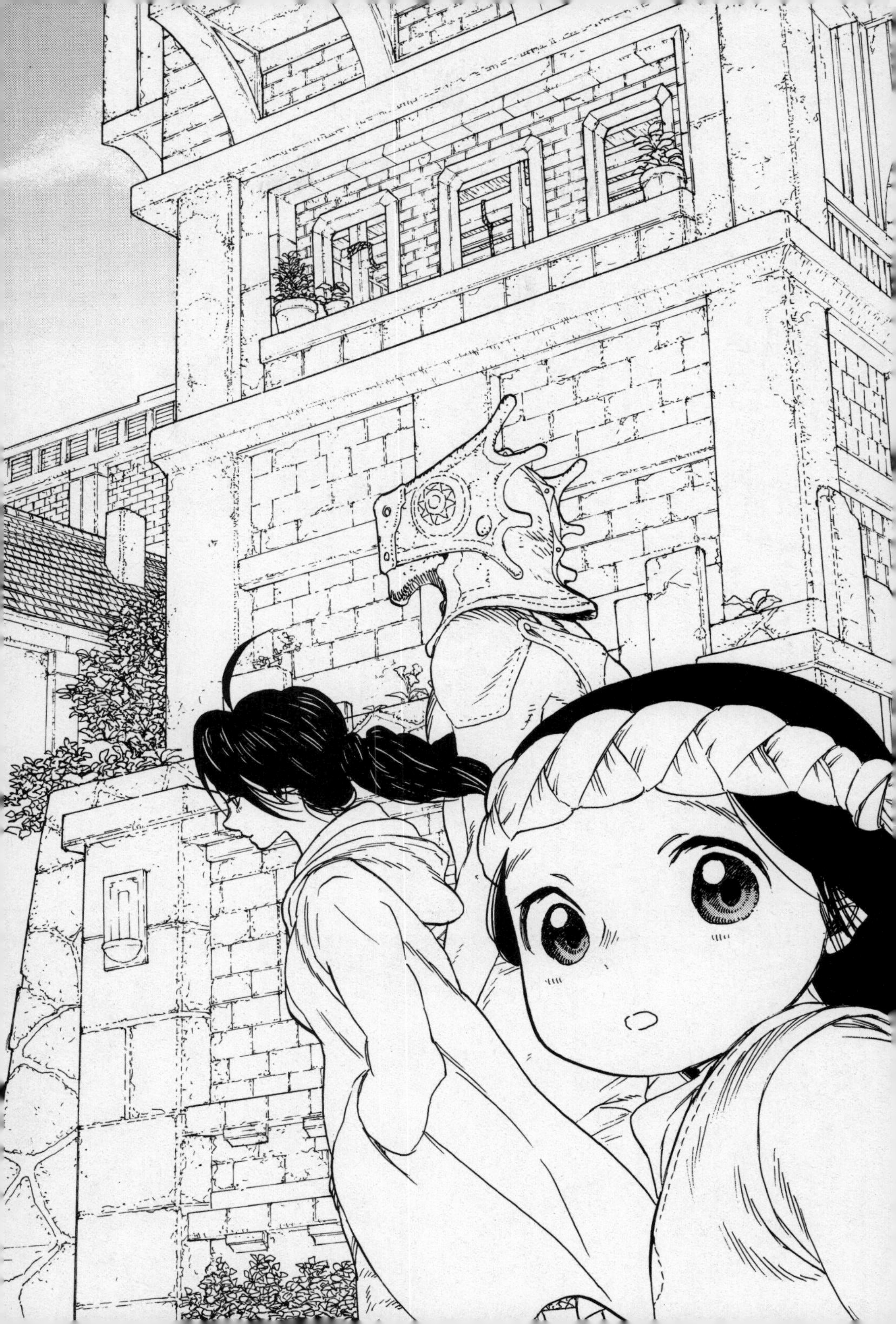

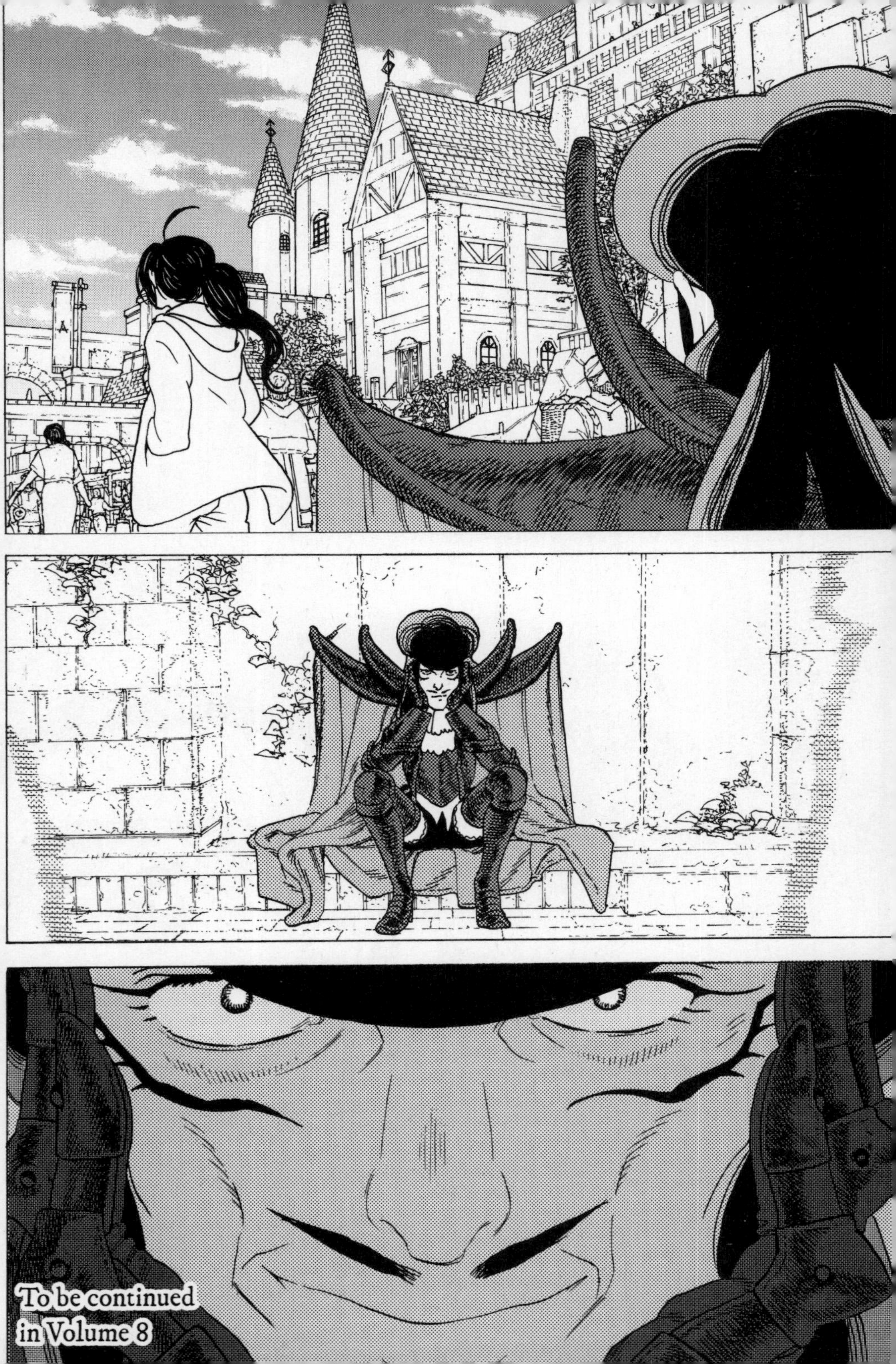
To be continued in Volume 8

TO YOUR ETERNITY

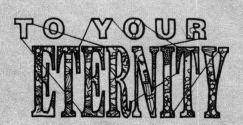

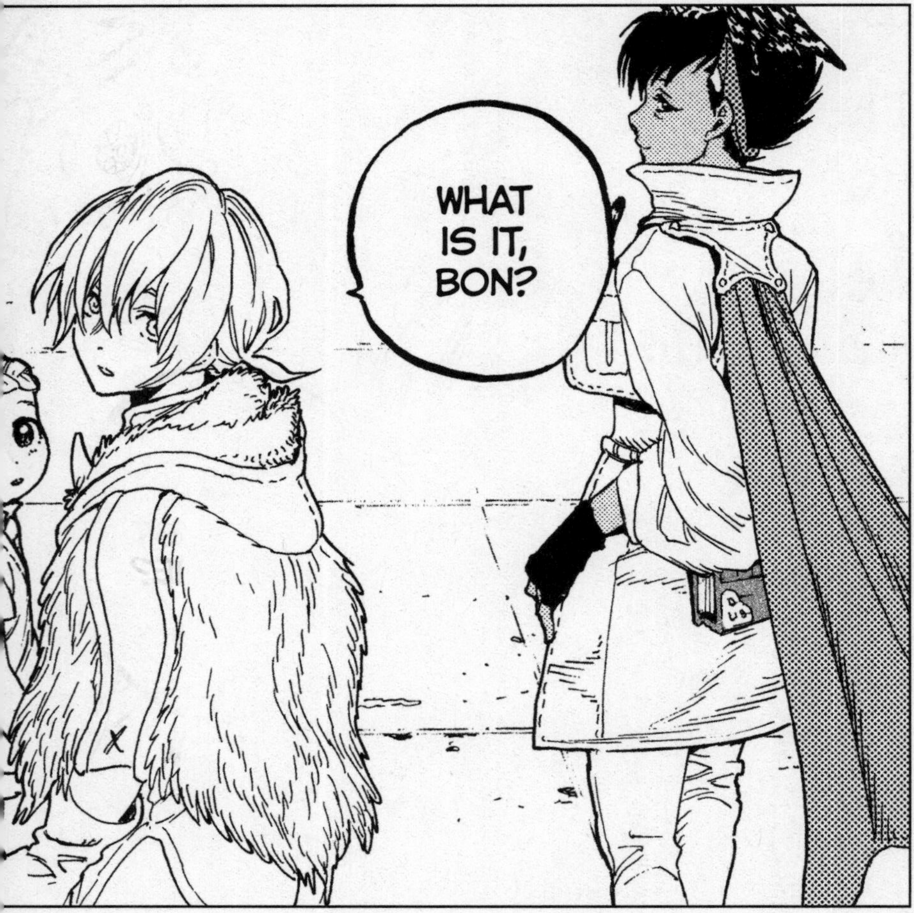
WHAT IS IT, BON?

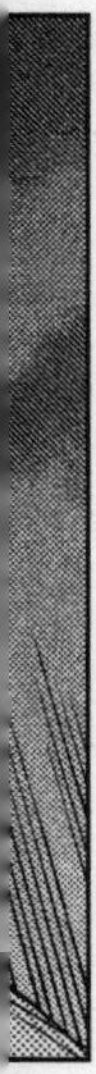

The young man
who has the ability to see,
brings forth an invisible world,
and along with it...friends.

NEXT VOLUME PREVIEW

The Uralis arc begins.

Volume 8 coming soon.

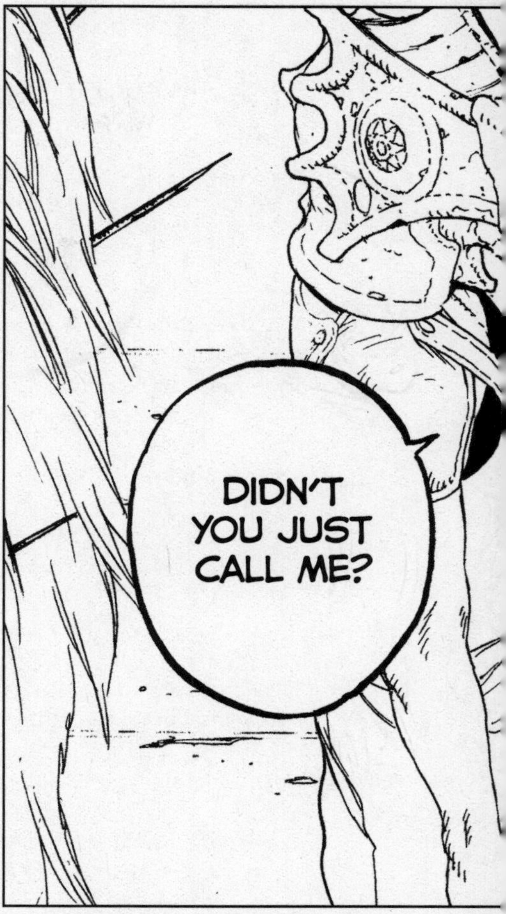
DIDN'T YOU JUST CALL ME?

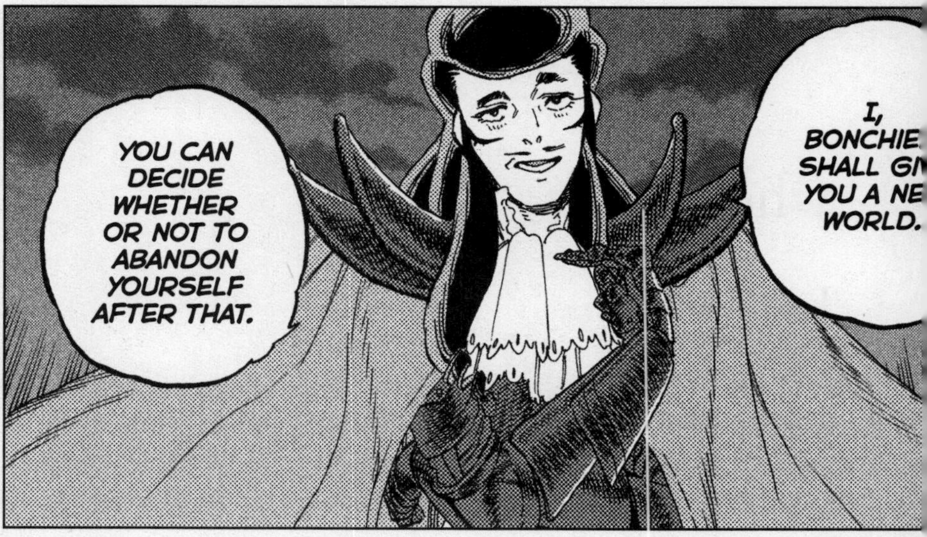
I, BONCHIE SHALL GI YOU A NE WORLD.
YOU CAN DECIDE WHETHER OR NOT TO ABANDON YOURSELF AFTER THAT.

A Kodansha Comics Trade Paperback Original.

To Your Eternity volume 7 copyright © 2018 Yoshitoki Oima
English translation copyright © 2018 Yoshitoki Oima

Published in the United States by Kodansha Comics,
an imprint of Kodansha USA Publishing, LLC, New York.

Publication rights for this English edition arranged through Kodansha Ltd., Tokyo.

First published in Japan in 2018 by Kodansha Ltd., Tokyo,
as *Fumetsu no Anata e* volume 7.

Cover Design: Tadashi Hisamochi (hive&co., Ltd.)
Title Logo Design: Shinobu Ohashi

ISBN 978-1-63236-683-2

Printed in Mexico.

www.kodansha.us

9 8 7 6 5 4 3

Translation: Steven LeCroy
Lettering: Darren Smith
Editing: Haruko Hashimoto, Alexandra Swanson
Editorial Assistance: YKS Services LLC/SKY Japan, INC.
Kodansha Comics Edition Cover Design: Phil Balsman